The Praeger Handbook on Stress and Coping

The Praeger Handbook on Stress and Coping

Volume 2

EDITED BY ALAN MONAT, RICHARD S. LAZARUS, AND GRETCHEN REEVY

Foreword by Yochi Cohen-Charash

Westport, Connecticut
London

Library of Congress Cataloging-in-Publication Data

The Praeger handbook on stress and coping / edited by Alan Monat,
Richard S. Lazarus, and Gretchen Reevy; foreword by Yochi Cohen-
Charash
    p. cm.
  Includes bibliographical references and index.
  ISBN-13: 978-0-275-99197-5 (set : alk. paper)
  ISBN-10: 0-275-99197-0 (set : alk. paper)
  ISBN-13: 978-0-275-99198-2 (v. 1 : alk. paper)
  ISBN-10: 0-275-99198-9 (v. 1 : alk. paper)
  [etc.]
1. Stress (Psychology) 2. Adjustment (Psychology) I. Monat, Alan, 1945-
II. Lazarus, Richard S. III. Reevy, Gretchen. IV. Title: Handbook on stress
and coping.
  BF575.S75P73 2007
  155.9′042—dc22   2006100437

British Library Cataloguing in Publication Data is available.

Library of Congress Catalog Card Number: 2006100437
ISBN-10: 0-275-99197-0 (set)
        0-275-99198-9 (vol. 1)
        0-275-99199-7 (vol. 2)

ISBN-13: 978-0-275-99197-5 (set)
        978-0-275-99198-2 (vol. 1)
        978-0-275-99199-9 (vol. 2)

First published in 2007

Praeger Publishers, 88 Post Road West, Westport, CT 06881
An imprint of Greenwood Publishing Group, Inc.
www.praeger.com

Printed in the United States of America

The paper used in this book complies with the
Permanent Paper Standard issued by the National
Information Standards Organization (Z39.48-1984).

10 9 8 7 6 5 4 3 2 1

Contents

Part II: Stress and Illness

Part III: Posttraumatic Stress

Part IV: The Coping Concept

Illustrations

BOXES

Abbreviations

AA	Alcoholics Anonymous
ABC	*Activating events, beliefs, emotional consequences* (model) (Albert Ellis)
ACTH	Adreno-corticotropic hormone
AD	Alzheimer's disease
ADHD	Attention deficit hyperactivity disorder
AIDS	Acquired Immune Deficiency Syndrome
ANS	Autonomic nervous system
AVLT	Auditory-Verbal Learning Test
BDI	Beck Depression Inventory
CBT	Cognitive-behavioral therapy
CHD	Coronary heart disease
CNS	Central nervous system
COPE	Coping Orientations to Problems Experienced (scale)
CPT	Continuous Performance Test
CRF	Corticotropin-releasing factor
CRP	C-reactive protein
CVD	Cardiovascular disease
CVLT	California Verbal Learning Test
dB	Decibels
DIS	Diagnostic Interview Schedule
DNA	Deoxyribonucleic acid

DSM	*Diagnostic and Statistical Manual of Mental Disorders* (American Psychiatric Association)
EDRF	Endothelium-derived relaxation factor
EEG	Electroencephalogram
EMG	Electromyography
ENMG	Electroneuromyography
FSIQ	Full-scale intelligence quotient
GAS	General Adaptation Syndrome
GHQ	General Health Questionnaire
HIV	Human immunodeficiency virus
HPA	Hypothalamic-pituitary-adrenal (axis)
H-reflex	Hoffman reflex
HRSD	Hamilton Rating Scale for Depression
IDDM	Insulin-dependent diabetes mellitus
IQ	Intelligence quotient
ISSB	Inventory of Socially Supportive Behaviors
JAS	Jenkins Activity Survey
LEDS	Life Events and Difficulties Schedule
LES	Life Experiences Survey
MBSR	Mindfulness-based stress reduction
MDD	Major depressive disorder
MMSE	Mini-mental state exam
MRI	Magnetic resonance imaging
MSD	Musculoskeletal disorder
NA	Narcotics Anonymous
NDRI	National Development and Research Institutes
NIDA	National Institute on Drug Abuse
NIMH-DIS	National Institute of Mental Health—Diagnostic Interview Schedule
NIOSH	National Institute for Occupational Safety and Health
NK	Natural killer (cells)
NPY	Neuropeptide-Y
OR	Odds ratio
OSHA	Occupational Safety and Health Administration
PET	Positron Emission Tomography
PNS	Peripheral nervous system
POW	Prisoner of war
PRP	Penn Resiliency Program

PSS-Fa	Perceived Social Support from Family (scale)
PSS-Fr	Perceived Social Support from Friends (scale)
PTSD	Posttraumatic stress disorder
RET	Rational Emotive Therapy
SBS	Sick building syndrome
SD	Standard deviation
SHAM TENS	Transcutaneous electrical nerve stimulation without current
SI	Structured interview
SIT	Stress inoculation training
SMILE	Standard Medical Intervention and Long-term Exercise (study)
S-O-R	Stimulus-organism-response (model)
SOS	Secular Organization for Sobriety
S-R	Stimulus-response (model)
SRRS	Social Readjustment Rating Scale
SRT	Selective Reminding Test
TABP	Type A behavior pattern
TENS	Transcutaneous electrical nerve stimulation
TFA	Trans fatty acid
12SG	12-step groups
UCB	University of California, Berkeley
USDA	U.S. Department of Agriculture
VAS	Visual analog scale
WAIS-R	Wechsler Adult Intelligence Scale–Revised
WFS	Women for Sobriety
WHO-CIDI	World Health Organization—Composite International Diagnostic Interview
WMS	Wechsler Memory Scale

Part IV

The Coping Concept

Introduction to "The Coping Concept"

This fourth part of our book and the first part of Volume 2 is an introduction to the concept of coping. The first chapter provides an introduction to coping in general, and those that follow focus on several specific coping behaviors or attitudes: optimism, personality hardiness, Type A behavior pattern, and utilizing social support. We do not intend to discuss all known coping techniques in depth. Rather, the reader will gain an understanding of what it means to cope, of ways that psychologists and other professionals have attempted to apply their coping knowledge to specific populations, and of the current state of knowledge about and research issues surrounding specific coping behaviors and attitudes. Several other texts provide a good introduction to the wide variety of coping responses that have been studied (e.g., Kleinke, 2002; Seaward, 2006), including discussion of some techniques not covered in our book, such as utilizing a sense of humor, journal writing, and prayer and faith.

Chapter 16, from Kleinke's book *Coping with Life Challenges* (2002), introduces the coping concept. As Kleinke describes, *coping* refers to one's attempts to manage situations and does not necessarily imply that the outcome of the coping behavior or attitude is positive. Thus, for example, using drugs or alcohol is a type of coping behavior. Kleinke describes many common coping responses, examines research about these responses, and presents and discusses the more common scales that are used to measure coping in research. Lazarus's "appraisal" concept appears again in this chapter (like it appears throughout our book), since one's evaluation of situations has a considerable impact on one's choice of coping responses. Kleinke closes with a consideration of some types of responses that appear to be self-handicapping and makes some comparisons between relatively successful and relatively unsuccessful coping responses. An update is required regarding information presented in Kleinke's chapter: the COPE scale that Kleinke describes (Carver, Scheier, & Weintraub, 1989) now includes a fifteenth coping style: humor.

The second chapter in this part, "Cultivating Optimism in Childhood and Adolescence" (Gillham & Reivich, 2004), is a review of the literature on optimism and related concepts and a description of the authors' program for cultivating optimism in young people. Gillham and Reivich begin by discussing optimism and comparing and contrasting it with a number of related concepts. They describe some benefits of optimism, including its protective effect against depression, and some negative outcomes associated with pessimism. The authors then discuss the Penn Resiliency Program, their method for teaching optimism. The Penn Resiliency Program includes many elements of cognitive-behavioral therapy, which is also discussed in other chapters in this book, such as Everly and Lating's chapter in Part VI and Kennedy's chapter in Part II. Gillham and Reivich conclude by discussing some of the current issues in the theorizing and research regarding optimism. For example, can an individual be too optimistic? The authors' position is a qualified yes—optimism must be tempered with realism.

Research on optimism is part of the "positive psychology" paradigm that has been influential in psychology in the past ten or fifteen years. Gillham and Reivich reference important works in positive psychology, including articles written by preeminent psychologists Martin Seligman and Christopher Peterson. The reader with an interest in positive psychology should refer to Seligman and Csikszentmihalyi (2000) and Snyder and Lopez (2002) for an introduction.

The third chapter, "The Story of Hardiness: Twenty Years of Theorizing, Research, and Practice" (Maddi, 2002), provides a history of an important concept in coping research: personality hardiness. Maddi describes how he and his colleagues, in their early research with Illinois Bell Telephone, found that high hardiness in managers was protective against both physical and psychological symptoms of stress. Maddi argues that all components of hardiness—commitment, control, and challenge—exert the protective effect, but it is his perception that American psychologists are enamored with the control component and, relatively speaking, neglect the other variables in research and theorizing. Next, Maddi, much like Gillham and Reivich in the prior chapter, explains his program for developing hardiness. He briefly describes research on hardiness and positive outcomes, including that hardiness is protective against depression and posttraumatic stress disorder. He closes with further discussion of the program and its applications, for use both by individuals and within organizations. The programs described by Maddi and by Gillham and Reivich, although far from identical, bear some similarities. Both optimism and hardiness are attitudes, and attitudes can be taught. Both training programs involve reinterpreting situations, or reappraisal, and attitudes that are encouraged by the programs include realism, with a positive bias, and a sense of commitment.

Chapter 19, "Racing against Your Heart," is Hock's (2005) highly comprehensible summary and discussion of the classic study by Friedman and Rosenman (1959) that established Type A behavior pattern as a risk factor for coronary heart disease. In this study, Friedman and Rosenman compared people with Type A and Type B personalities, and they found that people with Type A attributes suffered higher risks for a variety of vascular problems or symptoms, such as high serum cholesterol and rapid blood-clotting time. The reader may wonder why this personality type, negative from a health point of view, would appear in a book about coping and stress management, but recall from the Kleinke reading that coping does not imply positive outcomes. Coping is singularly an attempt to deal with the threats and challenges of life. Type A behavior pattern is an example of a coping strategy that tends to produce positive outcomes in one arena of life—occupational success—but wreaks havoc with health. To close, Hock discusses Friedman and Rosenman's later research on Type A behavior pattern and the broader significance of their work, which was instrumental in providing a theoretical and research-based rationale for establishing a new subfield in psychology: health psychology.

The final chapter in this part, "Sex-Related Differences in the Social Support–Stress Relationship," discusses another important coping technique—the use of social support. Reevy presents previously unpublished data supporting the notions that social support, stress, and the relationship between the two may be understood from the point of view of gender. The stress concepts she utilizes are ones described elsewhere in our book: life events stress (major life events) and daily hassles. For a more thorough discussion of these concepts, refer especially to the Cooper and Dewe's chapter in Part I.

Some comments about research methods and statistics may be necessary to understand Reevy's study. First, to test some of her hypotheses, she utilized a "t-test." The t-test is a statistic that is used to determine whether two arithmetic means differ from one another in a way that is not due to chance. In order to draw the conclusion that two means are different and that this difference is not due to chance, the reader observes both the t statistic and the associated p statistic, both reported either in the text of an empirical study or in a table. A larger value for t generally means a larger difference between means, but it is the p statistic (p is short for probability) that provides the information about probability that the two means are the same (that any apparent difference in means is not due to chance.)

In Table 20.1 in Reevy's chapter, an *, **, or *** appears next to some t statistics. As indicated in the table, * indicates that p is less than .05, ** corresponds to $p < .01$, and *** to $p < .001$. If p is less than .05, this means that the probability that this difference between means really does not exist—that the finding was due to chance and is not truly representative—is less than 5 percent. If p is less than .01, this means that the probability that the finding is due to chance is less than 1 percent, and so on. If a t statistic is *not* marked with one or more asterisks, then there is a relatively higher probability that there is really no difference between the means that were tested.

For example, the first means that were tested in Table 20.1 were 14.04 (the mean of Perceived Social Support from Friends for men) and 15.89 (the mean for women). The t statistic that is testing for a difference between these means is "flagged" with two asterisks. Therefore, we can be quite confident that these means are truly different—the probability that this finding was due to chance is less than 1 percent (hence, "$p < .01$")

—and men and women most likely *do* differ in the amount of perceived social support from friends, as they reported. Other information is necessary for a complete understanding of *t*-tests. The interested reader should refer to an excellent introductory statistics text such as *Comprehending Behavioral Statistics* by Russell Hurlburt (2006).

To test other hypotheses, Reevy used a *correlation coefficient*. A correlation coefficient (abbreviated *r*) is a statistic that describes the degree of linear relationship between two variables. The correlation coefficient ranges from −1.0 to +1.0. The direction of the correlation is indicated by the "−" and "+" signs: A positive correlation means that as one variable increases, the other also increases. For example, in Reevy's study, for men, the measure of enacted social support correlated positively with the measure of positive (but potentially stressful) life events—that is, as enacted social support increased, positive life events tended to increase. Put another way, the more supportive behaviors an individual received from others, the more positive (but potentially stressful) life events he experienced, in general. A negative correlation means that as one variable increases, the other tends to decrease. The correlation described above would have been negative if Reevy had simply measured one of the variables inversely. So, for example, if the social support variable had been measured inversely, so that higher scores on the variable meant a greater social support *deficit*, the correlation between enacted social support and positive life events would have been negative—As social support deficit increases, positive life events tend to decrease.

The *magnitude* of the correlation is the absolute value of the correlation coefficient. The higher the absolute value of the correlation coefficient, the greater the relationship. A correlation coefficient of 1.0 (either − or +) means that each variable can be perfectly predicted from the other. A correlation of 0 means that two variables are completely unrelated to one another—the value of one tells us nothing about the value of the other. In Reevy's study, the correlation between enacted social support and positive life events for men is +0.38. This indicates a moderate correlation. There is some ability to predict one variable from the other.

Two more statistics require some explanation. They appear in the tables in Reevy's article. First, *n* means "number of participants." Second, *SD* means "standard deviation." The *standard deviation* is a measure of spread or dispersion of a list of scores. A large standard deviation indicates a greater spread. A zero standard deviation means no spread (all scores are identical). Reevy followed conventions in psychology regarding the reporting of research findings. Thus, this discussion about the reporting of the *t*-test, correlation coefficient, the statistics *p* and *n*, and the standard deviation apply to empirical studies in psychology in general.

TERMS

The chapters in Part IV include a number of technical terms. Can you define these terms? Definitions are included in the glossary in the back of the book.

General Stress and General Psychology Terms

- Affect (affectivity)
- Appraisal
- Attribution
- Behaviorism
- Cognitive-behavioral therapy
- Ellis's ABC Model of Emotional Reaction
- Emotion-focused coping
- Enacted support (received support)
- Existential psychology
- Explanatory style
- Gender role theory
- Hardiness (including commitment, control, and challenge)
- Hassles (also called "daily hassles" or "minor hassles")
- Life events stress (also called "major life events stress" or "life events")
- Minnesota Multiphasic Personality Inventory (MMPI)
- Perceived support
- Posttraumatic stress disorder (PTSD)
- Primary appraisal
- Problem-focused coping
- Psychoanalysis
- Repressive coping style
- Secondary appraisal
- Self-derogation
- Self-disputing
- Self-efficacy
- Stress prevention model
- Support deterioration model

Physiological Terms

- Arcus senilis
- Coronary heart disease (CHD)

Statistical or Research Methods Terms

- Correlation coefficient
- Longitudinal study
- Mediation
- Moderation
- Operationalization
- Prospective study
- Retrospective study
- Standard deviation
- t-test

Stress Researchers and Theorists

- Albert Ellis
- Richard Lazarus
- Salvatore Maddi

REFERENCES

Carver, C. S., Scheier, M. F., & Weintraub, J. K. (1989). Assessing coping strategies: A theoretically based approach. *Journal of Personality and Social Psychology, 56,* 267–283.

Friedman, M., & Rosenman, R. H. (1959). Association of specific overt behavior pattern with blood and cardiovascular findings: Blood cholesterol level, blood clotting time, incidence of arcus senilis, and clinical coronary artery disease. *Journal of the American Medical Association, 169,* 1286–1296.

Gillham, J., & Reivich, K. (2004). Cultivating optimism in childhood and adolescence. *Annals of the American Academy of Political and Social Science, 591,* 146–163.

Hock, R. (2005). *Forty studies that changed psychology: Explorations into the history of psychological research.* Upper Saddle River, NJ: Pearson/Prentice Hall.

Hurlburt, R. T. (2006). *Comprehending behavioral statistics.* Belmont, CA: Thomson Wadsworth.

Kleinke, C. (2002). *Coping with life challenges.* Prospect Heights, IL: Waveland Press.

Maddi, S. R. (2002). The story of hardiness: Twenty years of theorizing, research, and practice. *Consulting Psychology Journal: Practice and Research, 54*(3), 173–185.

Seaward, B. L. (2006). Managing stress: Principles and strategies for health and well-being (5th ed.). Sudbury, MA: Jones and Bartlett.

Seligman, M. E. P., & Csikszentmihalyi, M. (2000). Positive psychology: An introduction. *American Psychologist, 55*(1), 5–14.

Snyder, C. R., & Lopez, S. J. (Eds.). (2002). *Handbook of positive psychology.* New York: Oxford University Press.

CHAPTER 16

What Does It Mean to Cope?

Chris L. Kleinke

This chapter is about dealing with the challenges, traumas, and hassles in our lives. It is about "keeping the faith," "hanging in," and managing our fears, hostilities, doubts, frustrations, and sadness. It is a tribute to people's adaptability and capacity to overcome adversity. My goal in writing this chapter is to teach you a number of useful coping skills that you can rely on when confronted with life challenges. I also want to communicate a philosophy—a coping skills attitude toward life—that no matter how tough things seem, you can make a plan and survive. If you apply a coping attitude in your life, you will enhance your own potential for personal growth. You can make your life more interesting by mastering new skills and taking on meaningful challenges.

I will begin with a definition of coping and a description of how the coping process works. A good place to start is with the process of *appraisal*. R. S. Lazarus and S. Folkman (1984) define two kinds of appraisal: *primary appraisal* and *secondary appraisal*. When humans are faced with a potential challenge or stress, we first determine whether we are in jeopardy or danger. We ask ourselves whether this is something worth getting upset about. This is primary appraisal. Primary appraisal is concerned with our physical as well as our psychological well-being. If we determine that we *are* in jeopardy or danger, we ask ourselves whether there is something we can do about it and, if so, what? This is secondary appraisal.

PRIMARY APPRAISAL

Let's say that a company executive, in a harsh tone of voice, tells three of her assistants that she wants to see them in her office "first thing next morning." What sorts of primary appraisals might the assistants make?

One, Tim, might think: "This means trouble. That harsh tone can only mean I did something wrong and that I'm in hot water. There's nothing I can do now. I probably won't sleep all night, and I'll be really tired and anxious tomorrow."

Another, Lisa, might think: "Sometimes when the boss uses that harsh tone it doesn't mean anything, and sometimes it does. I won't know until tomorrow if there is any trouble, but it will be in my best interest to be up on my facts and figures. And, just in case, I'll dress extra professionally tomorrow."

The third, Ed, might think: "If the boss sounds harsh, that's her problem. Her problems don't concern me, so I'll just pretend nothing happened and come in tomorrow just as I always do."

Note the different impact as well as the subjectivity of primary appraisals. Tim has appraised the director's harsh tone as a definite threat. Lisa has appraised it as a possible threat. Ed has appraised it as posing no threat. At this point, we don't know whose appraisal is correct, but you would probably agree that Lisa's is most prudent. Tim is being a "catastrophizer," and by assuming the worst he will suffer a good deal of stress. Ed is being a "denier"; he is not under any stress right now, but he may pay a price in the future. Lisa is taking the issue seriously but is managing her stress by making concrete plans.

SECONDARY APPRAISAL

If our primary appraisal tells us we are in jeopardy, we need to ask what we can do about it. This process is referred to as the secondary appraisal. In the example, each of the three employees decided on a different response. Tim's secondary appraisal tells him he is facing a threat that is beyond his control. Lisa concludes there is a possible threat, and she draws up a "battle plan." Because Ed assumes there is no threat, he feels no need for a secondary appraisal.

Primary and secondary appraisals have an impact on how you respond to a challenge or a threat. It is in your best interest to make a realistic primary appraisal. You don't want to fly off the handle and panic, but you don't want to ignore real problems either. If your primary appraisal indicates reason for concern, you want to make a secondary appraisal that is adaptive. Here is an example of this appraisal process: "This is a genuine problem. Things look tough. I've got to come up with some good plans. Let me dig into my bag of coping strategies and make plan A and plan B, and possibly plan C."

Most of the time, your secondary appraisal will suggest some steps you can take to manage the situation. On other occasions, however, you may determine that the situation is beyond your control and that the best plan is to "exert control" by not fighting a battle you can't win. Sometimes it is better to be flexible and roll with the punches.

A DEFINITION OF COPING

Rose Kennedy was once asked about her adjustment to the many tragedies that have befallen her family. She replied, "I cope." *Coping* can be defined as *the efforts we take to manage situations we have appraised as being potentially harmful or stressful.* This definition, which is adapted from Lazarus and Folkman (1984), has three key features:

1. It implies that coping involves a certain amount of effort and planning.
2. It does not assume that the outcome of a coping response will always be positive.
3. It emphasizes coping as a process taking place over time.

These features are important in defining coping because they allow us to study different styles and strategies of coping and to evaluate which ones work best in different situations. The goal of researchers has been to find out whether specific personality traits, beliefs, or ways of viewing the world are more or less adaptive in various situations. Once you have looked at what has been learned about these questions, you will be able to distinguish effective coping strategies you can use in your life.

TWO GENERAL COPING STRATEGIES

Lazarus and Folkman (1984) identify two general forms of coping: *problem-focused* coping and *emotion-focused* coping. Problem-focused coping strategies can be outer directed or inner directed. Outer-directed strategies are oriented toward altering the situation or the behaviors of others; inner-directed ones include efforts we make to reconsider our own attitudes and needs and to develop new skills and responses. Emotion-focused coping is geared toward managing emotional distress. Emotion-focused coping strategies include physical exercise, meditation, expressing feelings, and seeking support.

You are more likely to engage in problem-focused coping when you feel there is something you can do about a problem or a challenge. When a problem or challenge appears to be beyond your control, you are more likely to rely on emotion-focused coping (Folkman & Lazarus, 1980; Vitaliano, DeWolfe, Maiuro, Russo, & Katon, 1990). In most situations, we probably benefit most by combining these coping strategies. For example, you can prepare for a job interview by practicing your responses to questions and choosing appropriate attire (problem-focused) and by being relaxed and maintaining a nondefensive attitude (emotion-focused). When you must face a difficult confrontation, you may cope by keeping your cool (emotion-focused) and using effective negotiation skills (problem-focused).

The distinction between problem-focused and emotion-focused coping provides a broad framework for understanding the concept of coping. More specific coping responses are discussed next.

RESEARCH ON COPING RESPONSES

Take a few minutes to think about the most stressful event that has happened to you during the past month. With this event in mind, check how often you did each of the things in Table 16.1. These nine coping responses were studied in a community survey (Billings & Moos, 1981;

Table 16.1. Checklist of Coping Responses

	Never	Sometimes	Often
1. Tried to see the positive side			
2. Took things one step at a time			
3. Stepped back to be more objective			
4. Took some positive action			
5. Exercised more			
6. Talked with friends			
7. Kept my feelings to myself			
8. Ate more, smoked cigarettes, or used drugs			
9. Refused to acknowledge the problem			

Holahan & Moos, 1987). You may have noticed that responses 1, 5, 7, 8, and 9 are emotion focused, and responses 2, 4, and 6 are problem focused. Another way to categorize these coping responses is according to whether they represent an *active-cognitive* method (1, 2, 3), an *active-behavioral* method (4, 5, 6), or *avoidance* (7, 8, 9). Results of the survey indicated that women used active-behavioral methods and avoidance more often than men. Men and women did not differ in their use of active-cognitive methods. People who used active-cognitive and active-behavioral coping responses tended to be easygoing and less anxious. They also had relatively high self-confidence. People who were avoiders tended to be more depressed and anxious, and they suffered greater physical stress. Avoiders also had fewer educational and financial resources and less family support.

In another survey of how people cope, married couples were questioned about their responses to four sources of stress: marriage, parenting, household finances, and work (Pearlin & Schooler, 1978). A number of coping responses were employed by people who suffered comparatively low levels of emotional stress. These included taking an active, self-reliant, problem-solving approach. Greater amounts of emotional distress were experienced by people who felt helpless, blamed themselves, and engaged in denial and avoidance.

A third group of researchers surveyed people on their experiences with various coping responses when faced with losses, threats, and challenges (McCrae & Costa, 1986). The most effective coping responses included seeking help, communicating feelings, taking rational action, drawing strength from adversity, using humor, and maintaining faith, self-confidence, and feelings of control. The least effective coping responses included hostility, indecisiveness, self-blame, and attempting to escape or withdraw from the situation.

A fourth example of effective and ineffective coping responses comes from a community survey in which people reported how they coped with a recent stressful experience, such as a loss of self-esteem, concern for a loved one, interpersonal conflict, financial strain, health problems, or lack of success at work (Folkman, Lazarus, Dunkel-Schetter, DeLongis, & Gruen, 1986). People who reported satisfactory resolution of their stressful experience tended to cope by maintaining their composure and working out a plan and by using the stressful experience as an opportunity for personal growth. Those who did not successfully resolve their problem responded by being impulsive, aggressive, or angry, or by ignoring the problem and downplaying its importance.

In yet another study investigating the relationship between coping and emotions (Folkman & Lazarus, 1988), participants reported how often they used the following types of coping responses for a recent stressful event:

- *Confrontive coping:* "I stood my ground and fought for what I wanted."
- *Distancing:* "I went on as if nothing had happened."
- *Self-control:* "I tried to keep my feelings to myself."
- *Seeking social support:* "I talked to someone who could do something concrete about the problem."
- *Accepting responsibility:* "I criticized or lectured myself."
- *Escape-avoidance:* "I wished that the situation would go away or somehow be over with."
- *Planful problem solving:* "I knew what had to be done, so I doubled my efforts to make things work."
- *Positive reappraisal:* "I changed or grew as a person in a good way."

The respondents also reported which emotions they experienced as a result of their response to the stressful situation, choosing from *worried/fearful, disgusted/angry, confident,* or *pleased/happy.*

After analyzing the correlation between the respondents' coping responses and their resulting emotions, the researchers reached the following conclusions: Planful problem solving appeared to be the most effective coping response because it was associated with the most positive emotions. Confrontive coping and distancing turned out to be the least effective coping responses because they were associated with the most negative emotions. Positive reappraisal was more effective for the types of problems faced by adults in their 30s and 40s. Seeking social support was more effective for adults who were 60 and older. Results for the remaining coping responses did not show a strong pattern, but there was no evidence that they were particularly effective.

COPING SCALES

Researchers have classified coping responses that are effective and not so effective for dealing with life problems by creating various kinds of coping scales. I have already described some coping strategies that are measured on such scales. In this section, I will give you a closer look at three coping scales that were constructed to assess people's strategies for responding to life challenges. On all of these, respondents are asked to state how often they rely on various coping responses in stressful situations, using numerical scales ranging from *not at all* to *very much.*

It stands to reason that the coping strategies people choose will depend on the situation. However, people also develop certain styles in the kinds of coping strategies they prefer (Terry, 1994). Coping scales give a general idea of how people cope with stressful situations and whether or not these preferred coping strategies are in their best interest.

The Coping Strategy Indicator

The Coping Strategy Indicator measures people's preferences for three coping strategies that have been identified in the research literature: problem solving, seeking support, and avoidance (Amirkhan, 1990b, 1994).

Problem solving is assessed by items such as "I formed a plan of action in my mind," "I tried to solve the problem," "I tried to carefully plan a course of action rather than acting on impulse," or "I weighed my options carefully." The advantage of problem solving as a coping strategy is that it provides a feeling of control over our life.

Seeking support is assessed by such items as "I let my feelings out to a friend," "I accepted help from a friend or relative," "I told people about the situation," or "I went to a friend to help me feel better about the problem." Seeking support can be a useful coping strategy if other people can help you take active steps to solve your problems.

Avoidance is assessed by "I daydreamed about better times," "I watched TV more than usual," "I avoided being with people," "I fantasized about how things could be different," and the like. Avoidance is often not a good coping strategy, because it is associated with passivity and an attitude of being stuck.

The Coping Inventory for Stressful Situations

The Coping Inventory for Stressful Situations was designed to measure three of the most commonly discussed coping strategies in the research literature: task coping, emotion coping, and avoidance coping (Endler & Parker, 1990, 1994).

Task coping is assessed by items such as "I schedule my time better," "I focus on the problem and see how I can solve it," "I think about how I have solved similar problems," "I work to understand the situation," or "I come up with several different solutions to the problem." Task coping is similar to the *problem solving* measure on the Coping Strategy Indicator.

Emotion coping is assessed by statements like "I blame myself for not knowing what to do," "I become preoccupied with aches and pains," "I become very tense," "I focus on my general inadequacies," or "I take it out on other people." Emotion coping is a somewhat broader coping strategy than the *social support* measure on the Coping Strategy Indicator. Emotion coping reflects a general style of reacting to a stressful event, which may or may not involve relying on other people.

Avoidance coping is assessed by such items as "I phone or visit a friend," "I go to a movie or watch TV," "I go out for a snack or meal,"

"I take time off and get away from the situation," or "I buy myself something." Avoidance coping is comparable to the measure of *avoidance* on the Coping Strategy Indicator.

Researchers have determined that task coping is the most adaptive coping strategy (Endler & Parker, 1990, 1994). People who use task coping tend to be satisfied with how they handle stressful events, and they are less anxious and depressed. Emotion coping and avoidance coping result in a less satisfactory adjustment to stressful events, and people who use these coping strategies tend to be anxious and depressed.

The COPE Scale

The Coping Orientations to Problems Experienced (COPE) Scale was developed in an attempt to include a greater variety of coping styles than those assessed on other scales (Carver, Scheier, & Weintraub, 1989; adapted with permission). The fourteen coping styles measured on the COPE Scale are based on conclusions from personality theories about how people handle stressful events. The fourteen coping styles assessed on the COPE Scale, along with representative questions and the personality factors correlated with a preference for each of these coping styles, are:

- **Active coping** (*personal correlates: optimism, confidence, self-esteem, low anxiety*): "I take additional action to try to get rid of the problem." "I concentrate my efforts on doing something about it." "I do what has to be done, one step at a time."
- **Planning** (*personal correlates: optimism, confidence, self-esteem*): "I try to come up with a strategy about what to do." "I make a plan of action." "I think hard about what steps to take."
- **Suppression of competing activities** (*personal correlates: none*): "I put aside other activities so I can concentrate on this." "I focus on dealing with this problem and, if necessary, let other things slide a little." "I keep myself from getting distracted by other thoughts or activities."
- **Restraint coping** (*personal correlates: optimism, low anxiety*): "I force myself to wait for the right time to do something." "I hold off doing anything about it until the situation permits." "I make sure not to make matters worse by acting too soon."
- **Seeking social support for instrumental reasons** (*personal correlates: optimism*): "I ask people who have had similar experiences what they did." "I try to get advice from someone about what to do." "I talk to someone to find out more about the situation."
- **Seeking social support for emotional reasons** (*personal correlates: none*): "I talk to someone about how I feel." "I try to get emotional support from friends or relatives." "I discuss my feelings with someone."
- **Positive reinterpretation and growth** (*personal correlates: optimism, confidence, self-esteem, low anxiety*): "I look for something good in what is happening." "I try to see it in a different light, to make it seem more positive." "I learn something from the experience."

- **Acceptance** *(personal correlates: optimism):* "I learn to live with it." "I accept that this has happened and that it can't be changed." "I get used to the idea that it happened."
- **Turning to religion** *(personal correlates: optimism):* "I seek God's help." "I put my trust in God." "I try to find comfort in my religion."
- **Focus on and venting of emotions** *(personal correlates: low confidence, anxiety):* "I get upset and let my emotions out." "I let my feelings out." "I feel a lot of emotional distress, and I find myself expressing those feelings a lot."
- **Denial** *(personal correlates: pessimism, low confidence, low self-esteem, anxiety):* "I refuse to believe that it has happened." "I pretend that it hasn't really happened." "I act as though it hasn't happened."
- **Behavioral disengagement** *(personal correlates: pessimism, low confidence, low self-esteem, anxiety):* "I give up the attempt to get what I want." "I just give up trying to reach my goal." "I admit to myself that I can't deal with it and quit trying."
- **Mental disengagement** *(personal correlates: pessimism, low confidence, anxiety):* "I turn to work or other substitute activities to take my mind off things." "I go to movies or watch TV so that I think about it less." "I daydream about things other than this."
- **Alcohol and/or other drugs** *(personal correlates: pessimism):* "I use alcohol or drugs to make myself feel better." "I try to lose myself for a while by drinking alcohol or taking drugs." "I use alcohol or drugs to help me get through it."

What We Can Learn from Coping Scales

Research on coping scales leads to the conclusion that it is most adaptive to cope with life challenges by taking an active, self-reliant approach that includes planning and problem solving. It is advantageous to develop a reasonable amount of outgoingness and extroversion (Amirkhan, Risinger, & Swickert, 1995; Cooper, Okamura, & McNeil, 1995). This will help when you need to respond actively to life challenges and when it is appropriate to seek assistance from others. It is least adaptive to cope by avoiding and denying the challenge or by responding in an impulsive manner.

Coping scales prompt us to consider our strategies for coping with stressful events and to ask ourselves if our coping responses are working in our best interest. Assessing your coping strategies helps in two ways. First, you want to be flexible enough to choose the coping response that will work best in a given situation. A second benefit of assessing your coping strategies is that this process will go a long way toward reinforcing your feelings of self-confidence and control. The goal is not so much to choose the "correct" coping response as it is to maintain a "coping attitude" characterized by thoughtfulness, problem solving, and self-confidence (Amirkhan, 1990a; Carver & Scheier, 1994).

UNDERSTANDING ADAPTIVE PERSONALITY STYLES

To cope successfully with life challenges, it is helpful to be aware of your own personality style. Because personality styles are intimately related to how a person perceives the world and reacts to stressful events, it is understandable that some personality styles are more flexible than others. People who have the most trouble coping with life challenges are those whose personality styles are not flexible and who are therefore unable to adapt their responses to fit the demands of a specific situation.

The study of personality styles is as old as the field of psychology. Countless theories of personality have been proposed, and it would require a large volume to catalog all the models of personality that have been developed. One model of personality that has been around in one form or another for more than a hundred years, and that has been widely recognized for its effectiveness in predicting adaptive and maladaptive behaviors, identifies five distinct personality styles: neuroticism, extroversion, openness, agreeableness, and conscientiousness (Costa & McCrae, 1992; Goldberg, 1993; McCrae & John, 1992). Conclusions from research studies on these five personality styles are summarized below (Costa & McCrae, 1990, 1992; Marshall, Wortman, Vickers, Kusulas, & Hervig, 1994; McCrae, 1991; McCrae & Costa, 1991; Trull, 1992).

Neuroticism

The worldview of people with a neurotic personality style is characterized by these kinds of statements:

- "I often feel helpless and want someone else to tell me what to do."
- "I often worry and feel anxious."
- "I don't match up to other people."
- "I get angry at others because they don't respect me."
- "When things go wrong, I get depressed and give up."

Neuroticism is rarely, if ever, an adaptive personality style. It is associated with depression, anxiety, self-deprecation, poor mental health, difficulty getting along with others, pessimism, hopelessness, low self-esteem, unresolved anger, and lack of satisfaction with life. People with a neurotic personality style have a tendency to rely on maladaptive coping styles, such as wishful thinking and self-blame (Bolger, 1990).

Extroversion

The worldview of people with an extroverted personality style is characterized by these kinds of statements:

- "I like to be around people."
- "I like to laugh and joke with others."
- "I am cheerful, talkative, and energetic."

- "I am very active."
- "I spend most of my time with others."

Extroversion is an adaptive personality style, unless it becomes extreme. In moderation, extroversion is associated with low levels of depression and anxiety and with a positive self-image, good mental health, good interpersonal relationships, optimism, hope, high self-esteem, and satisfaction with life. If extroversion becomes too rigid or extreme, however, it can be correlated with impulsivity, antisocial behavior, aggression, narcissism, and manic behavior.

Openness

The worldview of people with an open personality style is characterized by these kinds of statements:

- "I am excited by literature, poetry, and the arts."
- "I love playing with theories and abstract ideas."
- "I am a curious person."
- "I enjoy being exposed to new ideas."
- "I experiment with new ways of solving problems."

Openness is a fairly neutral personality style. It is associated with positive self-image, optimism, and curiosity. If openness becomes too rigid or extreme, it can be correlated with impulsivity and manic behavior.

Agreeableness

The worldview of people with an agreeable personality style is characterized by these kinds of statements:

- "I try to be courteous with everyone."
- "I hardly ever get into arguments."
- "I generally trust other people."
- "I get along with others."
- "I am seen by others as being fair and honest."

Agreeableness is associated with good interpersonal relationships, closeness with others, good mental health, optimism, good self-control, and satisfaction with life. If agreeableness becomes extreme, it can be associated with lack of individuality.

Conscientiousness

The worldview of people with a conscientious personality style is characterized by these kinds of statements:

- "I take good care of things that belong to me."
- "I am very reliable."

- "I am well organized."
- "I set high standards for myself."
- "I take a lot of pride in my work."

Conscientiousness is associated with low levels of depression and anxiety, positive self-image, good self-control, good mental health, optimism, and satisfaction with life. If conscientiousness becomes too rigid or extreme, however, it can cause a person to become too dependent on the approval of others.

The Repressive Coping Style

In addition to the five personality styles described above, another personality style that is not very adaptive is repressive coping style (Weinberger & Davidson, 1994; Weinberger & Schwartz, 1990). This style can be understood by appreciating how children learn to deal with their emotions. On the one hand, children are taught to control their feelings and to refrain from acting out and throwing temper tantrums. On the other hand, children need to learn to communicate with others about how they are feeling. They want to be open, alive, and spontaneous. When people become rigid about communicating any negative feelings, they can become so repressed that they don't even admit their negative feelings to themselves. People who use a repressive coping style say these kinds of things to themselves:

- "I am always courteous, even to people who are disagreeable."
- "I don't get upset or angry when people are rude to me."
- "I'm surprised when people ask me if I get anxious before an exam, because I don't."
- "When I'm under stress, I just stay calm and rational."

People with a repressive coping style have learned to look at the world, and at themselves, in a very biased way. They have repressed their "unacceptable" feelings for so long that they hardly know they have them anymore.

A repressive coping style has two major disadvantages. First, although people can deny on the outside that stress bothers them, living under too much stress without engaging in adaptive coping responses will take its toll. A second disadvantage of a repressive coping style is that it is very isolating. It is difficult to have meaningful relationships with others if you suppress your spontaneity and always act like you have everything under control.

The Costs of Interpersonal Dependency

Developing a good support system is a useful skill to add to your coping arsenal. It is advantageous to be able to form close relationships with others so you can lean on them during times of stress. It must be remembered, however, that having a good support system means giving as well as receiving support. It is not adaptive to let yourself become so dependent on others that you lose touch with your sense of internal control.

The lives of people who are overly dependent on others are compromised in the following ways (Bornstein, 1993):

- *Motivational:* It is difficult for dependent people to motivate themselves because they can't function without guidance, support, and approval from others.
- *Cognitive:* Dependent people perceive themselves as being powerless and ineffectual because they assume that others have control over what happens to them.
- *Affective:* Dependent people become anxious and fearful when they are required to take care of themselves.
- *Behavioral:* Dependent people interact with others in a needy and helpless manner.

Because dependent people rely so much on other people, they suffer a considerable amount of stress. For one thing, dependent people have little confidence in their own ability to cope with life challenges because they have come to count on help from others. Compounding this problem is the fact that the interpersonal style of dependent people is often annoying and causes others to avoid or reject them. It is no wonder that dependent people are at higher risk for the physical and psychological detriments of stress (Bornstein, 1995).

The Possibility for Personal Growth

An individual's personality style is relatively stable and enduring (McCrae, 1993). However, this does not mean that you can't change. It is possible to become aware of your personality style so you can modify the perceptions and responses to challenging life events that are not in your best interest.

DISTINGUISHING BETWEEN SELF-BLAME AND SELF-RESPONSIBILITY

It is not helpful to cope with life challenges by engaging in *self-blame.* People who blame themselves when faced with threats and trauma tend to be less happy, less well adjusted, and more depressed than those who don't employ this self-defeating coping style (Kleinke, 1988; Revenson & Felton, 1989; Vitaliano, Katon, Maiuro, & Russo, 1989). Compared with self-blame, *self-responsibility* is a very different kind of coping style. Self-responsibility is *not* blaming or derogating ourselves for negative and unhappy events in our lives. Self-responsibility means developing our sense of mastery and internal control and making the effort to learn and practice coping skills. Self-responsibility requires that we honestly determine when we are responsible (and not responsible) for the causes and solutions of our problems.

THE PROS AND CONS OF AVOIDANCE

We are all tempted at times to respond to life challenges with avoidance. Here are some examples (Schmidt, 1994):

- *Social isolation:* "I avoid getting close to others."
- *Avoidance of intimacy:* "I avoid becoming involved in close, intimate relationships."
- *Avoidance of expressing negative emotions:* "I avoid situations where I might have to express negative feelings."
- *Procrastination:* "I avoid working on tasks that are dull and boring."
- *Avoidance of conflict through subjugation:* "I avoid situations where I have to give in to the demands of others."
- *Avoidance of evaluation and competition:* "I avoid situations where my performance will be evaluated and made public."
- *Emotional distancing:* "I avoid situations where I would need to depend on others."
- *Avoidance of work and financial matters:* "I avoid turning in my work." "I avoid dealing with financial matters."

Avoidance means not putting out the effort to cope when we should. Instead of heading off problems at their source, we ignore them and hope they will go away. Unfortunately, most challenges in life don't automatically disappear. Although avoidance may reduce immediate anxiety, it often results in greater stress in the long run because we never know when problems will catch up with us.

Avoidance is a useful strategy for coping with problems that don't have long-term consequences. It is often more adaptive to let brief irritations pass rather than to get upset about them. There is no point in suffering stress from problems that will resolve themselves. But avoidance is not a good strategy for coping with life challenges requiring involvement. Under these circumstances, you need to control your stress by taking a coping attitude and using coping skills (Suls & Fletcher, 1985).

A major disadvantage of avoidance as a coping strategy is that it prevents the constructive use of personal feedback (Bednar, Wells, & Peterson, 1989). It is inevitable that you will receive both positive and negative reactions from other people. People who avoid negative feedback are not able to use this information (much of which is accurate) to make effective changes in their ways of thinking and acting. Avoiders also miss out on the benefits of positive feedback. Because they are so used to putting up a false front, they can't distinguish when another person's compliments are believable. In this sense, avoidance is a form of denial that hinders the use of feedback from others for one's personal growth.

Monitoring and Blunting

The pros and cons of avoidance can be further appreciated by considering the concepts of monitoring and blunting (Miller, 1987). *Monitoring* concerns the importance we attach to being alert, vigilant, and prepared for potential threats. People who are monitors exert a lot of effort to gain information about threatening events. High monitors read warning labels and safety information and collect facts about illness and health. They expend high amounts of energy trying to anticipate what is going to happen to them. Low monitors live their lives without paying much attention to potential dangers. They wait until threats happen before reacting to them.

Blunting refers to our tendency to distract ourselves from feelings and emotions associated with danger and threat. Blunters are people who shield themselves from the emotional impact of negative experiences. They don't focus on what's happening inside their bodies. Nonblunters are sensitive to their emotions when faced with threat. They are in touch with their feelings during challenging situations.

Research studies have found that it is best to seek information (high monitoring) and be emotionally sensitive (nonblunting) when we are confronted with threats we can overcome (Miller, 1987; Miller & Birnbaum, 1988; Miller, Brody, & Summerton, 1988). When a potential danger is surmountable, it is advantageous to be vigilant and energized by heightened emotions. When faced with threats beyond our control, on the other hand, it is more adaptive to cope by allowing life to take its course. It is stressful to try to monitor every threat that might potentially affect us. People who do this are at risk of being hypertensive (Miller, Leinbach, & Brody, 1989). We need to direct our information-seeking and emotional energies toward challenges where we believe we can be most effective.

Self-Escape

Another kind of avoidance is *self-escape* (Baumeister, 1991). Self-escape can be harmful or beneficial, depending on the circumstances. Harmful self-escape occurs when the demands people place on themselves become so extreme that they find it intolerable to face their shortcomings. This kind of self-escape results in an evasion of self-responsibility through behaviors that are passive, rigid, or impulsive. The desire to avoid looking at oneself can become so intense that people will resort to self-harm, substance abuse, and binge eating. Beneficial self-escape occurs when people put aside their self-focus and allow themselves to be creative and achieve pleasurable experiences. To use self-escape beneficially, it is advisable to practice the following skills:

- Set realistic goals for yourself so that you can achieve success without a chronic fear of failure.
- Don't avoid problems that require your immediate attention, but take a break when you need one—don't burn yourself out.
- Learn how to take a "time-out" from your problems by using your imagination and engaging in creative activities.

HOW PEOPLE DEFEAT THEMSELVES

People can defeat themselves by *primary self-destruction, trade-offs, counterproductive strategies,* and *self-derogation* (Baumeister & Scher, 1988). Understanding these self-destructive tendencies can help you to avoid them.

Primary Self-Destruction

The most common primary self-defeating behaviors are outlined in Table 16.2. See how much you agree or disagree with the statements in the table. These statements come from the Chronic Self-Destructiveness Scale (Kelley et al., 1985). People tend to be more self-destructive if they agree with statements 1, 2, 3, 5, 6, 8, and 10, and disagree with statements 4, 7, and 9. People with high scores on self-destructiveness do not take responsibility for their own well-being. They have low feelings of internal control and often do things that are not in their best interest, such as cheating, driving unsafely, and ignoring their health.

Examples of primary self-destruction include masochism, eating disorders, drug abuse, recklessness, and suicide. People usually know they are in emotional pain when they engage in these harmful behaviors; unfortunately, they are not always ready or able to change.

Trade-offs

Trade-offs result in self-defeating behaviors when people choose immediate pleasure or relief despite the long-term costs of health risk or anxiety. Some examples of trade-offs include smoking, drinking, failing to wear seat belts, engaging in unsafe sex, avoiding exercise, eating poorly, neglecting health care, and using recreational drugs. Trade-offs also occur when people choose safe but nonchallenging goals and when they allow excuses

Table 16.2. Checklist of Self-Defeating Behaviors

	Strongly agree	Agree	Disagree	Strongly disagree
1. I have done dangerous things just for the thrill of it.				
2. Sometimes I don't seem to care what happens to me.				
3. Often I don't take very good care of myself.				
4. I usually call a doctor when I'm sure I'm becoming ill.				
5. I seem to keep making the same mistakes.				
6. I am frequently late for important meetings.				
7. I do not believe in gambling.				
8. I smoke more than a pack of cigarettes a day.				
9. I usually eat breakfast.				
10. I frequently fall in love with the wrong person.				

to stand in the way of achieving gratifications they could enjoy from more effortful accomplishments. People often make poor trade-offs when they have not learned how to cope with failure.

Counterproductive Strategies

Counterproductive strategies result from poor insight and lack of good judgment. These strategies are often not very effective and can be recognized by their rigidity. For example, when trying to solve a difficult problem or negotiate a sensitive issue, people sometimes hinder themselves by not considering all their options. They get stuck on one track and forget alternative solutions. Or they make demands from which they can't retreat. A successful solution or fruitful negotiation requires flexibility. In some situations, it may be best to be firm. At other times, more may be gained by compromising or even allowing others to have their way. People who avoid counterproductive strategies know how to use a problem-solving approach.

Self-Derogation

Look at Table 16.3 and decide whether you agree or disagree with the statements listed. These statements come from the Self-Derogation Scale (Kaplan, 1970). People with a strong tendency to derogate themselves agree with statements 1, 3, 4, 6, and 7 and disagree with statements 2 and 5. People who derogate themselves are less well adjusted. They are anxious and depressed and have a hard time adapting to life challenges. They are also more likely to experience physical and psychological stress, to become suicidal, and to engage in drug abuse or violent behavior (Kaplan, 1970; Kaplan & Peck, 1992; Kaplan & Pokorny, 1969, 1976a, 1976b).

Self-derogation results from the experience of growing up in a family or social group where it is difficult to get credit for engaging in appropriate behaviors. People with a history of rejection and nonacceptance often feel like underdogs and identify themselves as members of outgroups. Because they have failed to gain self-esteem and recognition by following societal norms, they sometimes become antisocial. Over time, this antisocial

Table 16.3. Checklist of Self-Derogatory Statements

	True	False
1. I wish I could have more respect for myself.		
2. On the whole, I am satisfied with myself.		
3. I feel I do not have much to be proud of.		
4. I'm inclined to think I'm a failure.		
5. I take a positive attitude toward myself.		
6. At times, I think I'm no good at all.		
7. I certainly feel useless at times.		

orientation can become the only way for them to maintain identity and self-esteem (Kaplan, Johnson, & Bailey, 1986; Kaplan, Martin, & Johnson, 1986).

It is understandable that people with a history of rejection would have a harder time learning adaptive coping responses than those who had good role models as they were growing up. It is difficult to have a coping attitude toward life when positive rewards seem beyond your control. However, our own thoughts, feelings, attitudes, and behaviors are ours to manage in the best way we can. The coping skills discussed in this chapter are meant to increase your power over yourself. By increasing your personal sense of competence and effectiveness, you stand a chance of gaining more positive reactions from others.

SOME CONCLUSIONS ABOUT SUCCESSFUL COPING STRATEGIES

Research studies on coping allow us to reach a number of useful conclusions. People who cope most successfully are those who are equipped with a battery of coping strategies and who are flexible in adapting their responses to the situation. Good copers have developed the following three skills (Antonovsky, 1979):

1. *Flexibility:* being able to create and consider alternative plans
2. *Farsightedness:* anticipating long-range effects of coping responses
3. *Rationality:* making accurate appraisals

In this chapter, we looked at a number of research studies analyzing the effectiveness of people's coping responses. Although these studies used somewhat different terms for their coping measures, they all agreed with these conclusions:

- *Successful copers* respond to life challenges by taking responsibility for finding a solution to their problems. They approach problems with a sense of competence and mastery. Their goal is to assess the situation, get advice and support from others, and work out a plan that will be in their best interest. Successful copers use life challenges as an opportunity for personal growth, and they attempt to face these challenges with hope, patience, and a sense of humor.
- *Unsuccessful copers* respond to life challenges with denial and avoidance. They either withdraw from problems or react impulsively without taking the time and effort to seek the best solution. Unsuccessful copers are angry and aggressive or depressed and passive. They blame themselves or others for their problems and don't appreciate the value of approaching life challenges with a sense of hope, mastery, and personal control.

We live in a society where people want easy answers to their problems—a pill, a quick fix, or a guaranteed solution that doesn't require much cost or effort. Successful coping is not the result of discovering a single, fail-proof response. It is an attitude and a life philosophy. Successful copers teach themselves to use primary and secondary appraisal to derive coping responses best suited to the particular life event they are facing.

SUGGESTIONS FOR FURTHER READING

Antonovsky, Aaron. *Health, stress, and coping.* San Francisco: Jossey-Bass, 1979.
Baumeister, Roy F. *Escaping the self: Alcoholism, spirituality, masochism, and other flights from the burden of selfhood.* New York: Basic Books, 1991.
Goleman, Daniel. *Vital lies, simple truths: The psychology of self-deception.* New York: Simon & Schuster, 1985.
Lazarus, Richard S., and Susan Folkman. *Stress, appraisal, and coping.* New York: Springer, 1984.
Menninger, Karl A. *Man against himself.* New York: Harcourt, Brace, 1938. Reprint, San Diego: Harcourt Brace Jovanovich, 1966.
Teger, Allan I., with Mark Cary, Aaron Katcher, and Jay Hillis. *Too much invested to quit.* New York: Pergamon, 1980.

REFERENCES

Amirkhan, J. H. (1990a). Applying attribution theory to the study of stress and coping. In S. Graham & V. S. Folkes (Eds.), *Attribution theory: Applications to achievement, mental health, and interpersonal conflict* (pp. 79–102). Hillsdale, NJ: Erlbaum.
Amirkhan, J. H. (1990b). A factor analytically derived measure of coping: The Coping Strategy Indicator. *Journal of Personality and Social Psychology, 59*(5), 1066–1074.
Amirkhan, J. H. (1994). Criterion validity of a coping measure. *Journal of Personality Assessment, 62*(2), 242–261.
Amirkhan, J. H., Risinger, R. T., & Swickert, R. J. (1995). Extraversion: A "hidden" personality factor in coping? *Journal of Personality, 63*(2), 189–212.
Antonovsky, A. (1979). *Health, stress, and coping.* San Francisco: Jossey-Bass.
Baumeister, R. F. (1991). *Escaping the self: Alcoholism, spirituality, masochism, and other flights from the burden of selfhood.* New York: Basic Books.
Baumeister, R. F., & Scher, S. J. (1988). Self-defeating behavior patterns among normal individuals: Review and analysis of common self-destructive tendencies. *Psychological Bulletin, 104*(1), 3–22.
Bednar, R. L., Wells, M. G., & Peterson, S. R. (1989). *Self-esteem: Paradoxes and innovations in clinical theory and practice.* Washington, DC: American Psychological Association.
Billings, A. G., & Moos, R. H. (1981). The role of coping responses and social resources in attenuating the stress of life events. *Journal of Behavioral Medicine, 4*(2), 139–157.
Bolger, N. (1990). Coping as a personality process: A prospective study. *Journal of Personality and Social Psychology, 59*(3), 525–537.
Bornstein, R. F. (1993). *The dependent personality.* New York: Guilford Press.
Bornstein, R. F. (1995). Interpersonal dependency and physical illness: The mediating roles of stress and social support. *Journal of Social and Clinical Psychology, 14*, 225–243.
Carver, C. S., & Scheier, M. F. (1994). Situational coping and coping dispositions in a stressful transaction. *Journal of Personality and Social Psychology, 66*, 184–195.

Carver, C. S., Scheier, M. F., & Weintraub, J. K. (1989). Assessing coping strategies: A theoretically based approach. *Journal of Personality and Social Psychology, 56,* 267–283.

Cooper, H., Okamura, L., & McNeil, P. (1995). Situation and personality correlates of psychological well-being: Social activity and personal control. *Journal of Research in Personality, 29*(4), 395–417.

Costa, P. T., & McCrae, R. R. (1990). Personality disorders and the five-factor model of personality. *Journal of Personality Disorders, 4*(4), 362–371.

Costa, P. T., & McCrae, R. R. (1992). Normal personality assessment in clinical practice: The NEO Personality Inventory. *Psychological Assessment, 4,* 5–13.

Endler, N. S., & Parker, J. D. (1990). Multidimensional assessment of coping: A critical evaluation. *Journal of Personality and Social Psychology, 58*(5), 844–854.

Endler, N. S., & Parker, J. D. A. (1994). Assessment of multidimensional coping: Task, emotion, and avoidance strategies. *Psychological Assessment, 6,* 50–60.

Folkman, S., & Lazarus, R. S. (1980). An analysis of coping in a middle-aged community sample. *Journal of Health and Social Behavior, 21*(3), 219–239.

Folkman S., & Lazarus, R. S. (1988). Coping as a mediator of emotion. *Journal of Personality and Social Psychology, 54*(3), 466–475.

Folkman, S., Lazarus, R. S., Dunkel-Schetter, C., DeLongis, A., & Gruen, R. J. (1986). Dynamics of a stressful encounter: Cognitive appraisal, coping, and encounter outcomes. *Journal of Personality and Social Psychology, 50*(5), 992–1003.

Goldberg, L. R. (1993). The structure of phenotypic personality traits. *American Psychologist, 48*(1), 26–34.

Holahan, C. J., & Moos, R. H. (1987). Personal and contextual determinants of coping strategies. *Journal of Personality and Social Psychology, 52*(5), 946–955.

Kaplan, H. B. (1970). Self-derogation and adjustment to recent life experiences. *Archives of General Psychiatry, 22,* 324–331.

Kaplan, H. B., Johnson, R. J., & Bailey, C. A. (1986). Self-rejection and the explanation of deviance: Refinement and elaboration of a latent structure. *Social Psychology Quarterly, 49*(2), 110–128.

Kaplan, H. B., Martin, S. S., & Johnson, R. J. (1986). Self-rejection and the explanation of deviance: Specification of the structure among latent constructs. *American Journal of Sociology, 92*(2), 384–411.

Kaplan, H. B., & Peck, B. M. (1992). Self-rejection, coping style, and mode of deviant response. *Social Science Quarterly, 73*(4), 903–919.

Kaplan, H. B., & Pokorny, A. D. (1969). Self-derogation and psychosocial adjustment. *Journal of Nervous and Mental Disease, 149*(5), 421–434.

Kaplan, H. B., & Pokorny, A. D. (1976a). Self-derogation and suicide: I. Self-derogation as an antecedent of suicidal responses. *Social Science & Medicine, 10*(2), 113–118.

Kaplan, H. B., & Pokorny, A. D. (1976b). Self-derogation and suicide: II. Suicidal responses, self-derogation, and accidents. *Social Science & Medicine, 10*(2), 119–121.

Kelley, K., Byrne, D., Przbyla, D. P. J., Eberly, C., Eberly, B., Greendlinger, V., et al. (1985). Chronic self-destructiveness: Conceptualization, measurement, and initial validation of the construct. *Motivation and Emotion, 9*(2), 135–151.

Kleinke, C. L. (1988). The Depression Coping Questionnaire. *Journal of Clinical Psychology, 44*(4), 516–526.

Lazarus, R. S., and Folkman, S. (1984). *Stress, appraisal, and coping.* New York: Springer.

Marshall, G. N., Wortman, C. B., Vickers, R. R., Jr., Kusulas, J. W., & Hervig, L. K. (1994). The five-factor model of personality as a framework for personality-health research. *Journal of Personality and Social Psychology, 67*(2), 278–286.

McCrae, R. R. (1991). The five-factor model and its assessment in clinical settings. *Journal of Personality Assessment, 57*(3), 399–414.

McCrae, R. R. (1993). Moderated analyses of longitudinal personality stability. *Journal of Personality and Social Psychology, 65*(3), 577–585.

McCrae, R. R., & Costa, P. T. (1986). Personality, coping, and coping effectiveness in an adult sample. *Journal of Personality, 54*(2), 385–405.

McCrae, R. R., & Costa, P. T. (1991). Adding Liebe und Arbeit: The full five-factor model and well-being. *Personality and Social Psychology Bulletin, 17*, 227–232.

McCrae, R. R., & John, O. P. (1992). An introduction to the five-factor model and its applications. *Journal of Personality, 60*(2), 175–215.

Miller, S. M. (1987). Monitoring and blunting: Validation of a questionnaire to assess styles of information seeking under threat. *Journal of Personality and Social Psychology, 52*(2), 345–353.

Miller, S. M., & Birnbaum, A. (1988). Putting the life back into "life events": Toward a cognitive social learning analysis of the coping process. In S. Fisher & J. Reason (Eds.), *Handbook of life stress, cognition and health* (pp. 499–511). New York: John Wiley & Sons.

Miller, S. M., Brody, D. S., & Summerton, J. (1988). Styles of coping with threat: Implications for health. *Journal of Personality and Social Psychology, 54*, 142–148.

Miller, S. M., Leinbach, A., & Brody, D. S. (1989). Coping style in hypertensive patients: Nature and consequences. *Journal of Consulting and Clinical Psychology, 57*(3), 333–337.

Pearlin, L. I., & Schooler, C. (1978). The structure of coping. *Journal of Health and Social Behavior, 19*, 2–21.

Revenson, T. A., & Felton, B. J. (1989). Disability and coping as predictors of psychological adjustment to rheumatoid arthritis. *Journal of Consulting and Clinical Psychology, 57*(3), 344–348.

Schmidt, N. B. (1994). The Schema Questionnaire and the Schema Avoidance Questionnaire. *Behavior Therapist, 17*, 90–92.

Suls, J., & Fletcher, B. (1985). The relative efficacy of avoidant and nonavoidant coping strategies: A meta-analysis. *Health Psychology, 4*(3), 249–288.

Terry, D. J. (1994). Determinants of coping: The role of stable and situational factors. *Journal of Personality and Social Psychology, 66*(5), 895–910.

Trull, T. J. (1992). *DSM-III-R* personality disorders and the five-factor model of personality: An empirical comparison. *Journal of Abnormal Psychology, 101*(3), 553–560.

Vitaliano, P. P., DeWolfe, D. J., Maiuro, R. D., Russo, J., & Katon, W. (1990). Appraised changeability of a stressor as a modifier of the relationship between coping and depression: A test of the hypothesis of fit. *Journal of Personality and Social Psychology, 59*(3), 582–592.

Vitaliano, P. P., Katon, W., Maiuro, R. D., & Russo, J. (1989). Coping in chest pain patients with and without psychiatric disorders. *Journal of Consulting and Clinical Psychology, 57*(3), 338–343.

Weinberger, D. A., & Davidson, M. N. (1994). Style of inhibiting emotional expression: Distinguishing repressive coping from impression management. *Journal of Personality, 62*(4), 587–613.

Weinberger D. A., & Schwartz, G. E. (1990). Distress and restraint as superordinate dimensions of self-reported adjustment: A typological perspective. *Journal of Personality, 58*(2), 381–417.

CHAPTER 17

Cultivating Optimism in Childhood and Adolescence

Jane Gillham and Karen Reivich

> Hope is both the earliest and the most indispensable virtue inherent in the
> state of being alive. If life is to be sustained, hope must remain, even where
> confidence is wounded, trust impaired.
>
> —Erik H. Erikson

Hope and optimism are valued as strengths by most cultures. Yet in
our own culture, there has been a dramatic rise in psychological difficulties
that signal hopelessness. This rise has been particularly steep in young people. For example, as many as 20 percent of youth may experience clinical
depression by the time they graduate high school (Lewinsohn, Hops,
Roberts, Seeley, & Andrews, 1993). Similar increases have been reported
for anxiety and suicide rates among youth (Twenge, 2000; Centers for
Disease Control, 1991). These statistics suggest the importance of interventions that promote optimism and hope in young people.

This chapter explores the development of hope and optimism in youth.
We begin with a brief summary of the different definitions and aspects of
hope and the benefits of hope that have been documented in the research
literature. We then turn to the origins of hope and interventions that
appear to be successful in promoting hope and optimism in young people.
We close with a discussion of the relationship of hope to other psychological strengths and recommendations for interventions that may promote
sustainable hope in youth.

DEFINITIONS OF HOPE AND OPTIMISM

Hope is often defined as a wish for something with some expectation
that it will happen, while *optimism* is typically defined as a tendency or disposition to expect the best. Thus, hope typically refers to expectations in a

specific situation, while optimism refers to general expectations. In the psychological literature, however, this distinction is usually blurred. Researchers study general levels of optimism and hopefulness, as well as optimistic and hopeful expectations for specific situations.

A detailed analysis of hope versus optimism is beyond the scope of this article, and we will use these terms interchangeably in this chapter. We recognize, however, that others have argued that hope and optimism may be different—but overlapping—constructs (Snyder, 2000d).

Recent reviews discuss several overlapping models and constructs related to optimism (Peterson, 2000; Snyder, 2000d). The construct *dispositional optimism* most closely matches intuitive notions (and dictionary definitions) of optimism. Dispositional optimism refers to a general tendency to expect positive outcomes. In part, these positive expectations may result from the individual's belief that he or she can control good outcomes. But positive expectations may also result from a general belief that good things will befall us.

Positive expectations closely relate to the concept of *self-efficacy*, which refers to an expectation that one's behavior will be effective (Bandura, 1997). Traditionally, self-efficacy has focused on situation-specific expectations, although more-general models and measures of self-efficacy have been proposed (Sherer et al., 1982). People who score high on self-efficacy tend to be optimistic because they believe that they can solve problems, overcome adversity, and take control of the events that occur in their lives. Self-efficacy and optimism are both important elements in *resilience*, and resilience, in turn, bolsters hope (Reivich & Shatté, 2002).

The Reformulated Learned-Helplessness and Hopelessness models of depression emphasize the explanations people give for the events that occur in their lives (Abramson, Metalsky, & Alloy, 1989; Abramson, Seligman, & Teasdale, 1978). Individuals who routinely make stable and global (and often internal) attributions for negative events (e.g., "I got in trouble at school because I'm a bad person") are considered to have a pessimistic explanatory style. According to the Reformulated Learned-Helplessness and Hopelessness models, causal attributions are important because they produce expectations about the future. When adversity is attributed to stable and global causes, hopeless and helpless expectations typically ensue. That is, individuals expect that things will continue to go badly in the future and that they will not be able to control or create positive outcomes.

Hope theory emphasizes the importance of goals, agency, and pathways (Snyder, 2000d). *Agency* includes motivation, willpower, or a sense an individual has that he or she can meet goals. *Pathways* include the routes to the goals—specific plans, strategies, or solutions. As Snyder suggests, agency reflects the willpower component of hope, and pathways reflect the "way-power."

Taken together, these models suggest that hopeful people make more optimistic attributions, expect good things to happen, and believe that they will be able to control events in their lives. Hopeful people also have goals and the motivation and plans to meet goals. These models also suggest that skills and the ability to think flexibly about alternate routes to goals are important for building hope.

BENEFITS OF OPTIMISM

Optimism is the faith that leads to achievement. Nothing can be done without hope and confidence.

—Helen Keller

Optimism and hope are associated with a variety of positive outcomes and are important to nourish for this reason. Optimistic individuals have greater success in school, on the job, and on the playing field (Rettew & Reivich, 1995; Schulman, 1995). They report less depression and anxiety (Gladstone & Kaslow, 1995; Joiner & Wagner, 1995; Robins & Hayes, 1995; Scheier & Carver, 1992, 1993), and they enjoy greater marital satisfaction, have better physical health, and live longer than pessimists (Buchanan, 1995; Fincham & Bradbury, 1987; Peterson & Bossio, 1991; Peterson, Seligman, & Vaillant, 1988; Scheier & Carver, 1992).

Although there is some debate about whether pessimism predicts negative outcomes or simply results from them, there is some evidence that it is a risk factor and may even play a causal role. For example, Abramson et al. (2000) found that young adults with pessimistic cognitive styles were more likely than their optimistic peers to develop clinical depression and clinical anxiety over a two-and-a-half-year follow-up period. Similarly, in a five-year longitudinal study, Nolen-Hoeksema, Girgus, and Seligman (1992) found that children with pessimistic explanatory styles were more likely than their peers to develop high levels of depressive symptoms (cf. Hammen, Adrian, & Hiroto, 1988). Cognitive-behavioral therapy, an effective therapy for depression, targets pessimistic interpretive styles and promotes more flexible and optimistic thinking (Beck, Rush, Shaw, & Emery, 1979).

Many have interpreted these results as support for the "power of positive thinking"—that by thinking positive thoughts, good things will happen. Although optimism certainly enhances one's mood, optimism also leads to changes in behaviors that may drive the changes in mood, productivity, performance, and health. For example, optimists are more persistent, particularly when tasks become difficult or when they encounter obstacles (Dweck, 1975), and greater persistence increases the likelihood that a solution will be found. Optimists may take better care of themselves; they are more likely than pessimists to participate in preventive health care and to attend regular checkups (Buchanan, Gardenswartz, & Seligman, 1999). Although somewhat counterintuitive, they are also more likely to seek out information about potential health risks, particularly if these might be avoidable (Aspinwall & Brunhart, 2000), and then to change their behavior to lower their risk levels.

DEVELOPMENT OF OPTIMISM

There is relatively little empirical research on the origins of optimism. Fortunately, this is starting to change. Recent research suggests a combination of genetic and environmental factors that together predispose a person to think optimistically.

Genetics

Twin studies suggest that dispositional optimism has a heritable component. Schulman, Keith, and Seligman (1993) found that explanatory style
was significantly correlated in monozygotic twins but was not significantly
correlated in dizygotic twins. Plomin et al. (1992) estimated that about
25 percent of the variability in optimism is due to genetic factors. These
findings, however, do not necessarily imply that optimism is transmitted
genetically. Much of the variance in optimism may reflect genetically predisposed differences in positive and negative affectivity (Davidson, 1998,
1999). People who feel happier may think more optimistically (Watson &
Clark, 1984).

Negative Events

Negative life events, particularly chronic or traumatic events, increase pessimism. For example, children who have been abused or exposed to high
levels of parental conflict are more likely to have a pessimistic explanatory
style (Gibb et al., 2001; Gold, 1986; Kaufman, 1991; Nolen-Hoeksema,
Girgus, & Seligman, 1986). In addition, people who have survived trauma
often catastrophize nontraumatic events, which fuels continued anxiety and
depression (Peterson & Moon, 1999).

Parenting

Parenting appears to play a strong role in the development of hope.
Adolescents and adults who report that their parents were caring and
affectionate report higher levels of hope. Many clinical and developmental
psychologists have suggested that parental affection and care are essential
for the development of a basic trust in the world. The sense that one's
parents are a secure base and the world is a good place allows young children to explore, to take risks, and to develop competence and optimism
(Bowlby, 1969; Cicchetti & Toth, 1998; Erikson, 1963; Snyder, 2000a).
It is also likely that modeling plays a role in the development of hope
(Garber & Flynn, 1998; Seligman, Reivich, Jaycox, & Gillham, 1995;
Snyder, 2000a). Parents' responses to adversities in their own lives often
convey optimism or pessimism. Caregivers who routinely voice negative
explanations or predictions for events in their lives may instill pessimism in
their children. Research on the relationship between optimism in parents
and children has yielded conflicting findings. For example, several studies
have found that parents with pessimistic explanatory styles are more likely
to have children with pessimistic styles. However, other studies have found
that optimism is not significantly related in parents and children (Joiner &
Wagner, 1996).
Parents may also influence their children's optimism through the
explanations and expectations they voice about events in their children's

lives. Children may be especially sensitive to the feedback they receive. A child who is continually criticized as difficult or lazy or who repeatedly hears "that won't work" may be especially vulnerable to pessimism. Garber and Flynn (2001) found that children's explanatory style was more closely related to parents' explanations for child events than parents' explanations for parent events.

The development of skills, particularly coping skills, is also important for hope. Although repeated negative events and failures may instill hopelessness, a life without difficulty (i.e., in which the child is shielded from adversity and failure) is unlikely to promote optimism (Snyder, 2000a). Children need to face challenges to build skills and to develop the belief that they can surmount the challenges that will confront them in the future. Of course, it is important that the challenges are appropriate for the child. When challenges are too high, children become overwhelmed and helpless. When challenges are too low, children may fail to develop skills or a sense of mastery. Parenting and teaching often involve paying careful attention to the child's individual level of competence and creating challenges near or just above this level (Bruner, 1986; Vygotsky, 1978). Knowledge about the relationship between competence and challenge helps caregivers to decide when it is best to jump in and solve things for a child, to "coach," or to let the child struggle on his or her own. Thus, parenting that promotes hope requires careful attention to the development of children's cognitive, linguistic, emotional, and other competencies.

Teachers, Peers, and Other Influences

Children may also learn optimistic or pessimistic thinking styles from teachers, peers, and other community members. For example, Dweck, Davidson, Nelson, and Enna (1978) propose that children internalize attributions made by their teachers regarding their failures and successes. These researchers found that girls gave more pessimistic explanations for failure than boys and that this difference was consistent with sex differences in teachers' feedback.

There is much less research on the role that peers may have in the development of optimism in youth. Teachers and parents are often concerned about a culture of negativity, cynicism, and low hope that can develop and become popular among groups of adolescents. Close friendships can also be healing (Sullivan, 1953) and may provide a foundation for hope in the face of difficult family or environmental circumstances.

On a societal level, children likely internalize optimism or pessimism that is conveyed by the institutions and communities with which they interact. Stories, movies, television, and other media provide messages about hope that may provide models or be internalized by children (Snyder, 2000a).

LOW HOPE AND DEPRESSION

It is hopelessness rather than pain that crushes the soul.

—William Styron

Childhood and Adolescent Depression

Low hope is a core symptom of clinical depression. Recent research reveals that psychological disorders characterized by low hope are quite common in this country, particularly in young people. One in five adolescents may experience an episode of clinical depression by the end of high school. Fourteen percent may experience clinical depression by the end of middle school (Garrison, Schluchter, Schoenbach, & Kaplan, 1989). High (but subclinical) levels of depression and anxiety are also quite common, with some studies finding that as many as 25 percent of adolescents experience high levels of these symptoms at any point in time (Angold, 1988).

Over the past century, depression and anxiety have increased dramatically (Cross-National Collaborative Group, 1992; Murphy, Laird, Monson, Sobol, & Leighton, 2000). Adolescents today may be at ten times the risk for depression as adolescents at the turn of the last century (Klerman et al., 1985). Self-reported anxiety symptoms, which correlate strongly with depression, have increased by about one standard deviation in the last fifty years alone. Average anxiety scores obtained in research with children today were in the clinical range a few decades ago (Twenge, 2000).

The high prevalence of depression is concerning for many reasons. Depression is associated with enormous suffering. Adolescents with depression are more likely than their peers to experience social rejection and isolation (Klein, Lewinsohn, & Seeley, 1997) and academic difficulties (Nolen-Hoeksema et al., 1992). They are more likely to smoke cigarettes, to abuse substances, and to become pregnant (Blechman & Culhane, 1993; Covey, Glassman, & Stetner, 1998; Rohde, Lewinsohn, & Seeley, 1991). In the worst cases, depression includes a profound sense of hopelessness that can lead to suicide. Each year, approximately 13 of every 100,000 American adolescents commit suicide (Centers for Disease Control, 1991; Lewinsohn, Rohde, & Seeley 1996).

Depression is often a recurrent disorder. Most individuals who suffer depression will suffer subsequent episodes. Thus, in adulthood, these individuals are at increased risk for suffering from depression and for transmitting depression to their own children.

Therapy for Depression and Low Hope

Therapies that build hope and promote optimism are effective in treating depression. According to the cognitive-behavioral model, depression and anxiety often result from overly negative or pessimistic thinking styles. Cognitive-behavioral therapy (CBT) attempts to change these thinking patterns by teaching clients to identify negative beliefs, to evaluate these beliefs, and to generate alternative interpretations that are more realistic and more hopeful. In this way, CBT directly targets pessimistic explanations and expectations. Cognitive-behavioral therapists also teach active coping skills such as relaxation training and assertiveness.

CBT is a very effective treatment for adult depression (Elkin et al., 1989; Evans et al., 1992), and recent research suggests that it is also effective in treating depression in adolescents (Harrington, Whittaker, & Shoebridge, 1998; Kaslow & Thompson, 1998). Improvement during CBT is linked to decreases in pessimism (DeRubeis & Hollon, 1995; Seligman et al., 1988).

It is important to note that several other therapies appear to be effective in treating depression, as well. In fact, a common and intriguing finding in psychotherapy outcome research is that different kinds of therapy are often equally effective. It is possible that effective therapies work for different reasons, but it is also possible that effective therapies share common ingredients. One important common ingredient may be the fostering of hope (Snyder & Taylor, 2000).

Preventing Depression and Promoting Hope

Several studies suggest that patients treated with CBT are less likely to experience a recurrence of depression than those treated with medication (Evans et al., 1992). This finding is encouraging, because it implies that the CBT teaches skills that can be used to ward off depression long after therapy has ended. With these findings in mind, several research groups have attempted to use cognitive-behavioral interventions to prevent depression from occurring in the first place. Results of these studies have been promising (Compas, Connor, & Wadsworth, 1997; Gillham, Shatté, & Freres, 2000; Muñoz, 1993).

Some of the strongest evidence for prevention has been produced by Clarke and colleagues (1995, 2001). This research group has conducted several studies of a group cognitive-behavioral intervention that focuses on interpersonal, problem-solving, and cognitive skills, including identifying and challenging negative thoughts. This intervention has had a significant and dramatic effect in preventing depressive disorders. For example, in an early study of adolescents with high but subclinical levels of symptoms, nearly 26 percent of the control group experienced major depression or dysthymia over the twelve-month follow-up period. In contrast, only 14.5 percent of prevention-program participants were diagnosed with depressive disorders during this time (Clarke et al., 1995). In a recent extension of this work, Clarke et al. (2001) evaluated the intervention with adolescents who had high levels of depressive symptoms and whose parents suffered from clinical depression. The intervention significantly prevented major depressive episodes over a fifteen-month follow-up period. Nearly 29 percent of participants in a usual care control group experienced major depression or dysthymia, compared with only 7 percent of the prevention group.

The Penn Resiliency Program

Our research has focused on the prevention of depressive symptoms in early adolescence (eleven- to fourteen-year-olds). We have conducted several studies evaluating a cognitive-behavioral intervention called the Penn Resiliency Program (PRP), which can be delivered by teachers and counselors in the school setting. Research on PRP has been promising. In an early study, for example, we found that PRP significantly improved explanatory style and other thinking styles associated with depression. PRP halved the rates of moderate to severe depressive symptoms over a two-year follow-up (Gillham, Reivich, Jaycox, & Seligman, 1995). Our research suggests that PRP is effective for children with high and low levels of initial symptoms. That is, PRP reduces and prevents future depressive symptoms in children who have high levels of initial symptoms, and it also appears to prevent depressive symptoms from developing in many children (Gillham et al., 1995).

Our recent work suggests that PRP may have even more dramatic effects on anxiety. In our first study to assess anxiety, 25 percent of controls reported moderate to severe levels of anxiety during a twelve-month follow-up, as compared with only 5 percent of PRP participants (Gillham, Reivich, Freres, Shatté, & Seligman, 2003). These findings suggest that cognitive-behavioral interventions such as PRP could be used on a wide scale to promote optimism and prevent depression and anxiety in young people.

Cognitive-Behavioral Techniques That Promote Hope

In this section, we describe several techniques included in the Penn Resiliency Program that may be especially important for building and promoting hope. These techniques have been adapted from adult CBT (Beck, 1976; Beck et al., 1979; Ellis, 1962) and are used in many other intervention programs.

The foundation of PRP is the ABC model developed by Albert Ellis (1962). Ellis and his colleagues based their premise on the observation that different people feel and respond differently in the wake of the same event, and thus the activating event (A) cannot be directly and proximally causal of the consequences (Cs, emotions and behaviors). According to Ellis, our thoughts and beliefs about the event (our Bs) are important mediators of the effect of events on our behavior and feelings.

By identifying the link between their thoughts and feelings or behaviors, adolescents discover that they do not have a direct read on reality—that their information about the world is screened through their belief systems and therefore may not be accurate. This discovery is particularly important for children and adolescents who are struggling with helplessness and hopelessness, because it serves as the first step toward changing the beliefs that are fueling their anxiety and despair. PRP participants learn the ABC model through the use of three-panel cartoons, in which they are presented with an adversity and the emotional consequences, and they must fill in a thought bubble with a belief that fits the logic of ABC. For example, in one cartoon, the first frame depicts a student being handed back a test that shows many incorrect items. The third frame shows that he is feeling extremely sad. The adolescents are asked to identify what the boy might be saying to himself that is causing him to feel extremely sad (e.g., "I'm stupid" or "I'll never do well in this class"). After working through a series of these cartoons, the students practice identifying their own self-talk in situations from their lives and then identifying the emotions and behaviors that their self-talk generates.

The ABC skill represents a snapshot in time—a specific automatic thought in response to a specific activating event. However, it is well documented that our automatic thoughts are not random. We develop styles of processing information that to some degree predetermine our responses to stimuli. One example is explanatory style, our habitual and reflexive way of explaining the events in our lives (Abramson et al., 1978). Any causal attribution can be coded along three dimensions:

- *Internal versus external:* Is the cause something about the individual or other people/circumstances?
- *Stable versus unstable:* Is the cause likely to be present for a long time or is it relatively temporary?
- *Global versus specific:* Is the cause operating in few or many life domains?

There is a tendency for people to develop explanatory styles for negative events that are either stable and global (pessimists) or unstable and specific (optimists). For example, a child who attributes her math-test failure to "I'm stupid" is making a pessimistic attribution—the failure is due to some characteristic of hers that is permanent and affects not just math performance but most areas of functioning. Alternatively, a child who believes her poor performance on a math test is because "I didn't study hard enough" is offering a more optimistic explanation, because she can change her study habits for the next test.

Once adolescents are familiar with the ABC model, we teach them to identify their explanatory style (using the terms *me* versus *not me, always* versus *not always, everything* versus *not everything*) and, most important, to challenge the accuracy of their beliefs. Although pessimistic explanations tend to lead to helplessness and hopelessness, our goal is not merely to replace pessimistic beliefs with optimistic ones, but to teach the students how to think accurately about the causes and implications of the problems they face. We call this process of generating more accurate beliefs *self-disputing.*

Students are taught to use the three dimensions of explanatory style as guidelines for generating other ways of understanding the event. For example, if they tend to be overly internal, they are encouraged to derive plausible explanations about others or circumstances. If their explanations are overly characterological or stable, they are rewarded for generating explanations that focus on more changeable and temporary causal factors. Therefore, the student who says he got a low grade because he is stupid (internal, stable, global) is encouraged to generate an alternative belief that is different on at least one of the explanatory style dimensions. For example, the belief "I didn't spend enough time on my homework" is still internal, but it is less stable and less global.

After the students have generated alternative beliefs, they are taught how to use evidence to determine which beliefs are most accurate. We have found that self-disputing is a powerful tool for overcoming the negative beliefs that often fuel hopelessness and depression.

The focus of self-disputing is on teaching students how to identify the most accurate causes of the problems they face, so that they are in a better position to focus on beliefs about the implications of problems, or what we call *what-next beliefs*. Thus, the attention shifts from beliefs about the past (causal explanations for past events) to beliefs about the future.

Children and adolescents at risk for depression are also at heightened risk for anxiety, which, as ABC predicts, is often the consequence of catastrophic beliefs about the future. Small problems are seen as insurmountable, and dire outcomes are feared. Putting it in perspective teaches adolescents how to identify and list their worst-case thoughts about the implications of adversity. These thoughts tend to come in chains of conditional probabilities; for example, "If my parents argue, they'll get divorced. If they get divorced, I'll never see my father again, and my mother will never be happy. If that happens, I'll run away from home, and kids who run away from home end up in foster care or prison." The causal link between parents' arguing and foster care or prison is extremely tenuous, but the connection from link to link is more plausible. We guide children out of the chain by teaching them to estimate the probability of each link, given only that the initial adversity (parents arguing) has occurred. Participants are then taught to generate equally improbable best-case scenarios and then to use worst-case and best-case scenarios as anchors to arrive at most-likely outcomes. Once the most-likely outcomes have been identified, the adolescents are taught to develop a plan for dealing with them. The skill of putting it in perspective not only reduces adolescents' anxiety but also helps them to develop strategies for dealing with the real-world outcomes of the problems they face—and thus lowers their hopelessness about their future and their own abilities to cope with adversity.

Goal setting is a critical component of hopefulness. Hopeless adolescents often feel that it is useless to set goals for the future because they expect their future to be bleak, and even when they do have goals, they often lack the motivation and confidence to develop a clear plan for achieving their goals and then for following the plans they develop. In PRP, we target this deficit by teaching realistic goal setting and the one-step-at-a-time technique for breaking large projects or goals into manageable steps. The one-step-at-a-time technique is important because adolescents often feel overwhelmed by projects—such as writing reports or studying for exams (even cleaning their rooms)—and their hopelessness causes them to give up at the earliest sign of difficulty. By breaking projects into small components, the adolescents find it much easier to get started on the project—and once started, it is easier for them to continue.

We also teach students to construct a reward system so that they receive ongoing reinforcement for their efforts. This also serves to improve their mood and decrease their negativity, and once in a better mood, they find it easier to continue with the task at hand.

PRP also includes assertiveness and negotiation training. We have found that these skills, particularly assertiveness, help adolescents to feel more hopeful about approaching others with their concerns, needs, or requests. Because hopeless adolescents underestimate the likelihood that a situation can be improved, they tend to respond to interpersonal problems with passivity. In PRP, we first apply the skills of self-disputing and of putting it in perspective to beliefs that fuel passivity such as "She'll never take me seriously" or "There's no point in asking—people never change." After the adolescents have challenged the beliefs that fuel passivity, we teach them a four-step approach to assertiveness. This skill is particularly challenging for adolescents—especially those feeling hopeless—so we include assertiveness practice in many of the sessions. We have found that many adolescents are initially reluctant to practice assertiveness, but that with practice, they find assertiveness to be one of the most useful and potent skills they have learned in the program. Given their initial reluctance, it is important to continue to identify their beliefs about trying the skill and to help them to use the basic cognitive skills of the program to challenge these pessimistic beliefs.

Hope therapy, developed by Snyder, McDermott, Cook, and Rapoff (1997), uses many of these techniques but also includes more specific focus on narrative (Lopez, Floyd, Ulven, & Snyder, 2000). Clients are encouraged to examine the level of hope expressed in their personal narratives and to generate more hopeful narratives, when appropriate. With children, therapists may use storytelling as a way to model optimism and striving toward goals (McDermott & Hastings, 2000; Snyder et al., 1997). CBT for depression and the prevention programs developed by Clarke et al. (1995) also use many of the same skills, including the ABC model, self-disputing, assertiveness, and negotiation techniques.

THE LIMITS AND THE FUTURE OF HOPE

In this section, we explore some of the current controversies about optimism, the limits of current research, and the future directions for interventions that promote optimism in young people.

Is More Optimism Always Better?

One question that is currently being debated in the literature has to do with the importance of optimism versus accuracy. Cognitive-behavioral therapists are often struck by the degree of inaccuracy in the interpretations their clinically depressed clients make for events in their lives. These therapists help their clients to develop less pessimistic and more realistic thinking styles. Many of these same therapists would strive for greater pessimism (and accuracy) with other clients, for example, clients who are in a manic phase of bipolar disorder. Thus, accuracy is an important goal in CBT.

Contrasting with this view is empirical literature suggesting that an optimistic bias is adaptive (e.g., Taylor & Brown, 1988). This literature suggests that nondepressed individuals typically display unrealistic optimism. They underestimate the likelihood that bad events (cancer, car accidents, etc.) will befall them and overestimate the likelihood of positive events. An optimistic bias, it is argued, is essential for happiness and well-being.

In running our PRP intervention, our experience has been that accuracy is important for doing well in the world. Adolescents who do not take responsibility for their problems or who minimize problems often score high on measures of optimism and hope, but this does not necessarily imply that they are better able to solve problems or handle adversity. And we have found that people who are extreme and unrealistic optimists often have interpersonal difficulties because they do not take responsibility for problems and may minimize the meaning and importance of the interpersonal conflict. In addition, extreme optimists sometimes have an "it can't happen to me" attitude and then, when bad things do happen, are left unprepared to cope with the situation. In our PRP sessions, we attempt to teach accuracy, even when this means attributing a problem to internal and fairly stable factors. Our hope for these children is that they will encounter fewer difficulties (and hence greater realistic optimism) in the future if they can analyze problems accurately, generate solutions, and feel confident in the skills they have developed to cope with adversity.

Research has documented that individuals who engage in dangerous health-related behaviors (e.g., smoking) underestimate the degree of risk involved (Weinstein & Lyon, 1999). In addition, students who are extremely optimistic may actually perform lower than peers who are more moderate in their optimism (Satterfield, Monahan, & Seligman, 1997). These findings suggest that optimism is associated with both positive and negative outcomes and that a happy medium—an optimism that is closely tied to the strength of wisdom—is most adaptive.

Optimism and Meaning

Goals are central to hope therapy and are implicit in other models of optimism and hope. Yet they are often neglected in psychological research on optimism and hope. We may have confidence in achieving relatively simple goals (e.g., finding a good dinner wine, buying a new car), and this can be important, particularly for an individual struggling with depression. But it is the larger goals that give us a sense of meaning or purpose in life. And hopefulness about these larger goals seems essential for well-being.

Programs that attempt to increase optimism, including our PRP, help individuals to set their own goals and to develop strategies for reaching them. But these programs are often neutral about the goals that individuals choose, so long as these goals appear to be realistic. It is likely that many of the goals discussed are individualistic goals.

Working toward collective goals (e.g., a safer community, a cleaner environment, a more peaceful world) increases hope and meaning by allowing us to strive for goals that are much larger than we could accomplish individually or within our individual lifetimes (Snyder, 2000c, 2000d). Collective goals allow us to strive for things we may not even have thought of on our own. Yet social connectedness and attention to collective goals declined dramatically over the past century (Myers, 2000; Putnam, 2000; Seligman et al., 1995). It is likely that these changes have contributed to the parallel rises in anxiety, depression, and suicide (Myers, 2000; Seligman et al., 1995). Thus, as Seligman wrote, optimism by itself

> cannot provide meaning. Optimism is a tool to help the individual achieve the goals he has set for himself. It is in the choice of the goals themselves that meaning—or emptiness—resides. When learned optimism is coupled with a renewed commitment to the commons, our epidemic of depression and meaningless may end. (1990, p. 291)

These findings and speculations suggest that if we are to build high optimism and hope in youth, we must also help young people to focus on the ways in which they are connected to others and to larger group and community goals. We will need interventions that nurture friendships and family relationships and that encourage teamwork and community involvement.

Specificity

The cognitive-behavioral treatment and prevention programs discussed specifically target optimism and hope, but they also promote other strengths. In addition to optimism, CBT techniques likely promote courage, interpersonal skills, insight, rationality, and perspective. The most competent therapists and group leaders also probably encourage honesty and guide participants to finding purpose or meaning (Shatté, Seligman, Gillham, & Reivich, 2002). These observations raise questions about intervention specificity. Which skills and strengths are required to prevent depression, for example? Although this is an interesting theoretical question, we believe that optimism is closely connected to many of these other strengths and that unrealistic optimism on its own may even be harmful. Thus, in practice, positive youth development will be best achieved when families, schools, and communities promote a wide variety of strengths in addition to optimism.

CONCLUSION

Epidemiological studies indicate that young people are experiencing hopelessness and its consequences—depression, anxiety, and suicide—at alarming levels. Fortunately, research has begun to identify the pathways by which high hope and optimism develop. Our own research focuses on structured school-based interventions that promote optimism and resilience. We believe, however, that structured interventions reflect only one of many possible pathways for increasing hope. Optimism may also be increased through interventions that affect parenting behaviors, teaching styles, and messages that are conveyed to children through the mass media, for example. Structured interventions are inadequate unless they are embedded in an environment that includes families, schools, communities, and institutions that encourage the development of hope and other psychological strengths in young people.

REFERENCES

Abramson, L. Y., Alloy, L. B., Hankin, B. L., Clements, C. M., Zhu, L., Hogan, M. E., et al. (2000). Optimistic cognitive styles and invulnerability to depression. In J. E. Gillham (Ed.), *The science of optimism and hope: Research essays in honor of Martin E. P. Seligman* (pp. 75–98). Radnor, PA: Templeton Foundation Press.

Abramson, L. Y., Metalsky, G. I., & Alloy, L. B. (1989). Hopelessness depression: A theory-based subtype of depression. *Psychological Review, 96*, 358–372.

Abramson, L. Y., Seligman, M. E., & Teasdale, J. D. (1978). Learned helplessness in humans: Critique and reformulation. *Journal of Abnormal Psychology, 87*, 49–74.

Angold, A. (1988). Childhood and adolescent depression. I. Epidemiological and aetiological aspects. *British Journal of Psychiatry, 152*, 601–617.

Aspinwall, L. G., & Brunhart, S. M. (2000). What I do know won't hurt me: Optimism, attention to negative information, coping, and health. In J. E. Gillham (Ed.), *The science of optimism and hope: Research essays in honor of Martin E. P. Seligman* (pp. 163–200). Radnor, PA: Templeton Foundation Press.

Bandura, A. (1997). *Self-efficacy: The exercise of control*. New York: Freeman.

Beck, A. T. (1976). *Cognitive therapy and the emotional disorders*. New York: International Universities Press.

Beck, A. T., Rush, A. J., Shaw, B. F., & Emery, G. (1979). *Cognitive therapy of depression*. New York: Guilford Press.

Blechman, E. A., & Culhane, S. E. (1993). Aggressive, depressive, and prosocial coping with affective challenges in early adolescence. *Journal of Early Adolescence, 13*, 361–382.

Bowlby, J. (1969). *Attachment and loss*. New York: Basic Books.

Bruner, J. (1986). *Actual minds, possible worlds*. Cambridge, MA: Harvard University Press.

Buchanan, G. M. (1995). Explanatory style and coronary heart disease. In Buchanan & Seligman 1995 (pp. 225–232).

Buchanan, G. M., Gardenswartz, C. A. R., & Seligman, M. E. P. (1999). Physical health following a cognitive behavioral-intervention. *Prevention & Treatment, 2*(1).

Buchanan, G. M., & Seligman, M. E. P. (Eds.). (1995). *Explanatory style*. Hillsdale, NJ: Erlbaum.

Centers for Disease Control. (1991). Attempted suicide among high school students—United States, 1990. *Morbidity and Mortality Weekly Report, 40*, 633–635.

Cicchetti, D., & Toth, S. L. (1998). The development of depression in children and adolescents. *American Psychologist, 53*(2), 221–241.

Clarke, G. N., Hawkins, W., Murphy, M., Sheeber, L. B., Lewinsohn, P. M., & Seeley, J. R. (1995). Targeted prevention of unipolar depressive disorder in an at-risk sample of high school adolescents: A randomized trial of a group cognitive intervention. *Journal of the American Academy of Child and Adolescent Psychiatry, 34*, 312–321.

Clarke, G. N., Hornbrook, M., Lynch, F., Polen, M., Gale, J., Beardslee, W., et al. (2001). A randomized trial of a group cognitive intervention for preventing depression in adolescent offspring of depressed parents. *Archives of General Psychiatry, 58*, 1127–1134.

Compas, B. E., Connor, J., & Wadsworth, M. (1997). Prevention of depression. In R. P. Weissberg, T. P. Gullotta, R. L. Hampton, B. A. Ryan, & G. R. Adams (Eds.), *Enhancing children's wellness* (pp. 129–174). Thousand Oaks, CA: Sage.

Covey, L. S., Glassman, A. H., & Stetner, F. (1998). Cigarette smoking and major depression. *Journal of Addictive Diseases, 17*, 35–46.

Cross-National Collaborative Group (1992). The changing rate of major depression: Cross-national comparisons. *Journal of the American Medical Association, 268*, 3098–3105.

Davidson, R. J. (1998). Affective style and affective disorders: Perspectives from affective neuroscience. *Cognition & Emotion, 12*, 307–330.

Davidson, R. J. (1999). Neuropsychological perspectives on affective styles and their cognitive consequences. In T. Dalgleish & M. Power (Eds.), *Handbook of cognition and emotion* (pp. 103–124). New York: John Wiley & Sons.

DeRubeis, R. J., & Hollon, S. D. (1995). Explanatory style in the treatment of depression. In Buchanan & Seligman 1995 (pp. 99–111).

Dweck, C. S. (1975). The role of expectations and attributions in the alleviation of learned helplessness. *Journal of Personality and Social Psychology, 31*, 674–685.

Dweck, C. S., Davidson, W., Nelson, S., & Enna, B. (1978). Sex differences in learned helplessness. II. The contingencies of evaluative feedback in the classroom. III. An experimental analysis. *Developmental Psychology, 14*, 268–276.

Elkin, I., Shea, M. T., Watkins, J. T., Imber, S. D., Sotsky, S. M., Collins, J. F., et al. (1989). National Institute of Mental Health Treatment of Depression Collaborative Research Program: General effectiveness of treatments. *Archives of General Psychiatry, 46*, 971–982.

Ellis, A. (1962). *Reason and emotion in psychotherapy.* New York: Lyle Stuart.

Erikson, E. H. (1963). *Childhood and society.* New York: Norton.

Evans, M. D., Hollon, S. D., DeRubeis, R. J., Piasecki, J. M., Grove, W. M., Garvey, M. J., et al. (1992). Differential relapse following cognitive therapy and pharmacotherapy for depression. *Archives of General Psychiatry, 49*, 802–808.

Fincham, F. D., & Bradbury, T. N. (1987). The impact of attributions in marriage: A longitudinal analysis. *Journal of Personality and Social Psychology, 53*, 510–517.

Garber, J., & Flynn, C. (1998). Origins of the depressive cognitive style. In D. K. Routh & R. J. DeRubeis (Eds.), *The science of clinical psychology: Accomplishments and future directions* (pp. 53–93). Washington, DC: American Psychological Association.

Garber, J., & Flynn, C. (2001). Predictors of depressive cognitions in young adolescents. *Cognitive Therapy and Research, 25*, 353–376.

Garrison, C. Z., Schluchter, M. D., Schoenbach, V. J., & Kaplan, B. K. (1989). Epidemiology of depressive symptoms in young adolescents. *Journal of the American Academy of Child and Adolescent Psychiatry, 28*, 343–351.

Gibb, B. E., Alloy, L. B., Abramson, L. Y., Rose, D. T., Whitehouse, W. G., Donovan, P., et al. (2001). History of childhood maltreatment, negative cognitive styles, and episodes of depression in adulthood. *Cognitive Therapy and Research, 25,* 425–446.

Gillham, J. E., Reivich, K. J., Freres, D. R., Shatté, A. J., & Seligman, M. E. P. (2003). School-based prevention of depression and anxiety symptoms: Pilot of a parent component to the Penn Resiliency Program. University of Pennsylvania.

Gillham, J. E., Reivich, K. J., Jaycox, L. H., & Seligman, M. E. P. (1995). Preventing depressive symptoms in schoolchildren: Two-year follow-up. *Psychological Science, 6,* 343–351.

Gillham, J. E., Shatté, A. J., & Freres, D. R. (2000). Depression prevention: A review of cognitive-behavioral and family interventions. *Applied & Preventive Psychology, 9,* 63–88.

Gladstone, T. R., & Kaslow, N. J. (1995). Depression and attributions in children and adolescents: A meta-analytic review. *Journal of Abnormal Child Psychology, 23,* 597–606.

Gold, E. R. (1986). Long-term effects of sexual victimization in childhood: An attributional approach. *Journal of Consulting and Clinical Psychology, 54,* 471–475.

Hammen, C., Adrian, C., & Hiroto, D. (1988). A longitudinal test of the attributional vulnerability model in children at risk for depression. *British Journal of Clinical Psychology, 27*(Pt. 1), 37–46.

Harrington, R., Whittaker, J., & Shoebridge, P. (1998). Psychological treatment of depression in children and adolescents: A review of treatment research. *British Journal of Psychiatry, 173,* 291–298.

Joiner, T. E., & Wagner, K. D. (1995). Attributional style and depression in children and adolescents: A meta-analytic review. *Clinical Psychology Review, 15,* 777–798.

Joiner, T. E., & Wagner, K. D. (1996). Parental, child-centered attributions and outcome: A meta-analytic review with conceptual and methodological implications. *Journal of Abnormal Child Psychology, 24,* 37–52.

Kaslow, N. J., & Thompson, M. P. (1998). Applying the criteria for empirically supported treatments to studies of psychosocial interventions for child and adolescent depression. *Journal of Clinical Child Psychology, 27,* 146–155.

Kaufman, J. (1991). Depressive disorders in maltreated children. *Journal of the American Academy of Child and Adolescent Psychiatry, 30,* 257–265.

Klein, D. N., Lewinsohn, P. M., & Seeley, J. R. (1997). Psychosocial characteristics of adolescents with a past history of dysthymic disorder: Comparison with adolescents with past histories of major depressive and non-affective disorders, and never mentally ill controls. *Journal of Affective Disorders, 42,* 127–135.

Klerman, G. L., Lavori, P. W., Rice, J., Reich, T., Endicott, J., Andreasen, N. C., et al. (1985). Birth-cohort trends in rates of major depressive disorder among relatives of patients with affective disorder. *Archives of General Psychiatry, 42,* 689–693.

Lewinsohn, P. M., Hops, H., Roberts, R. E., Seeley, J. R., & Andrews, J. A. (1993). Adolescent psychopathology. I. Prevalence and incidence of depression and other *DSM-III-R* disorders in high school students. *Journal of Abnormal Psychology, 102,* 133–144.

Lewinsohn, P. M., Rohde, P., & Seeley, J. R. (1996). Adolescent suicidal ideation and attempts: Prevalence, risk factors, and clinical implications. *Clinical Psychology: Science and Practice, 3,* 25–46.

Lopez, S. J., Floyd, R. K., Ulven, J. C., & Snyder, C. R. (2000). Hope therapy: Helping clients build a house of hope. In Snyder 2000b (pp. 123–150).

McDermott, D., & Hastings, S. (2000). Children: Raising future hopes. In Snyder 2000b (pp. 185–199).

Muñoz, R. F. (1993). The prevention of depression: Current research and practice. *Applied & Preventive Psychology, 2*, 21–33.

Murphy, J. M., Laird, N. M., Monson, R. R., Sobol, A. M., & Leighton, A. H. (2000). A 40-year perspective on the prevalence of depression: The Stirling County study. *Archives of General Psychiatry, 57*, 209–215.

Myers, D. G. (2000). *The American paradox: Spiritual hunger in an age of plenty.* New Haven, CT: Yale University Press.

Nolen-Hoeksema, S., Girgus, J. S., & Seligman, M. E. P. (1986). Depression in children of families in turmoil. University of Pennsylvania.

Nolen-Hoeksema, S., Girgus, J. S., & Seligman, M. E. P. (1992). Predictors and consequences of childhood depressive symptoms: A 5-year longitudinal study. *Journal of Abnormal Psychology, 101*, 405–422.

Peterson, C. (2000). The future of optimism. *American Psychologist, 55*(1), 44–55.

Peterson, C., & Bossio, L. M. (1991). *Health and optimism.* New York: Free Press.

Peterson, C., & Moon, C. H. (1999). Avoiding catastrophic thinking. In C. R. Snyder (Ed.), *Coping: The psychology of what works* (pp. 252–278). New York: Oxford University Press.

Peterson, C., Seligman, M. E. P., & Vaillant, G. E. (1988). Pessimistic explanatory style is a risk factor for physical illness: A thirty-five-year longitudinal study. *Journal of Personality and Social Psychology, 55*, 23–27.

Plomin, R., Scheier, M. F., Bergeman, C. S., Pederson, N. L., Nesselroade, J. R., & McClearn, G. E. (1992). Optimism, pessimism and mental health: A twin/adoption analysis. *Personality and Individual Differences, 13*, 921–930.

Putnam, R. D. (2000). *Bowling alone: The collapse and revival of American community.* Cambridge, MA: Harvard University Press.

Reivich, K., & Shatté, A. J. (2002). *The resilience factor: Seven essential skills for overcoming life's inevitable obstacles.* New York: Broadway Books.

Rettew, D., & Reivich, K. (1995). Sports and explanatory style. In Buchanan & Seligman 1995 pp. 173–186.

Robins, C. J., & Hayes, A. M. (1995). The role of causal attributions in the prediction of depression. In Buchanan & Seligman 1995 (pp. 71–98).

Rohde, P., Lewinsohn, P. M., & Seeley, J. R. (1991). Comorbidity of unipolar depression. II. Comorbidity with other mental disorders in adolescents and adults. *Journal of Abnormal Psychology, 100*, 214–222.

Satterfield, J. M., Monahan, J., & Seligman, M. E. P. (1997). Law school performance predicted by explanatory style. *Behavioral Sciences & the Law, 15*, 95–105.

Scheier, M. F., & Carver, C. S. (1992). Effects of optimism on psychological and physical well-being: Theoretical overview and empirical update. *Cognitive Therapy and Research, 16*, 201–228.

Scheier, M. F., & Carver, C. S. (1993). On the power of positive thinking: The benefits of being optimistic. *Current Directions in Psychological Science, 2*, 26–30.

Schulman, P. (1995). Explanatory style and achievement in school and work. In Buchanan & Seligman 1995 (pp. 159–172).

Schulman, P., Keith, D., & Seligman, M. E. (1993). Is optimism heritable? A study of twins. *Behaviour Research and Therapy, 31*, 569–574.

Seligman, M. E. P. (1990). *Learned optimism.* New York: Knopf.

Seligman, M. E. P., Castellon, C., Cacciola, J., Schulman, P., Luborsky, L., Ollove, M., et al. (1988). Explanatory style change during cognitive therapy for unipolar depression. *Journal of Abnormal Psychology, 97*, 13–18.

Seligman, M. E. P., Reivich, K. J., Jaycox, L., & Gillham, J. (1995). *The optimistic child.* Boston: Houghton Mifflin.

Shatté, A. J., Seligman, M. E. P., Gillham, J. E., & Reivich, K. (2002). The role of positive psychology in child, adolescent, and family development. In R. M. Lerner, F. Jacobs, & D. Wertlieb (Eds.), *Promoting positive child, adolescent, and family development through research, policies, and programs* (pp. 207–226). Thousand Oaks, CA: Sage.

Sherer, M., Maddux, J. E., Mercandante, B., Prentice-Dunn, S., Jacobs, B., & Rogers, R. W. (1982). The self-efficacy scale: Construction and validation. *Psychological Reports, 51,* 663–671.

Snyder, C. R. (2000a). Genesis: The birth and growth of hope. In Snyder 2000b (pp. 25–38).

Snyder, C. R. (Ed.). (2000b). *Handbook of hope: Theory, measures, and applications.* San Diego: Academic Press.

Snyder, C. R. (2000c). Hope for the many: An empowering social agenda. In Snyder 2000b (pp. 389–412).

Snyder, C. R. (2000d). Hypothesis: There is hope. In Snyder 2000b (pp. 3–21).

Snyder, C. R., McDermott, D., Cook, W., & Rapoff, M. A. (1997). *Hope for the journey: Helping children through good times and bad.* Boulder, CO: Westview Press.

Snyder, C. R., & Taylor, J. D. (2000). Hope as a common factor across psychotherapy approaches: A lesson from the dodo's verdict. In Snyder 2000b (pp. 89–108).

Sullivan, H. S. (1953). *The interpersonal theory of psychiatry.* New York: Norton.

Taylor, S. E., & Brown, J. D. (1988). Illusion and well-being: A social psychological perspective on mental health. *Psychological Bulletin, 103,* 193–210.

Twenge, J. M. (2000). The age of anxiety? Birth-cohort change in anxiety and neuroticism, 1952–1993. *Journal of Personality and Social Psychology, 79,* 1007–1021.

Vygotsky, L. S. (1978). *Mind in society: The development of higher psychological processes.* Cambridge, MA: Harvard University Press.

Watson, D., & Clark, L. A. (1984). Negative affectivity: The disposition to experience aversive emotional states. *Psychological Bulletin, 96,* 465–490.

Weinstein, N. D., & Lyon, J. E. (1999). Mindset, optimistic bias about personal risk and health-protective behaviour. *British Journal of Health Psychology, 4,* 289–300.

CHAPTER 18

The Story of Hardiness: Twenty Years of Theorizing, Research, and Practice

Salvatore R. Maddi

Twenty years have gone by since the introduction of the notion of hardiness. In the ensuing years, the hardiness approach has been considerably elaborated and is now an established aspect of psychology. Important in this development has been an active interplay between theorizing, research, and practice that is certainly informative and possibly instructive as to how ideas take hold in psychology. What follows is a summarization of this cross-fertilization that has taken place in hardiness theorizing, research, and practice efforts.

HOW HARDINESS STARTED

The seeds of hardiness were planted in 1974 when a graduate student of mine at the University of Chicago brought me an article she had found in *Family Circle* magazine about how it is best to avoid stress, lest it kill you. I was at the time so preoccupied with my work on creativity that I had not become aware of the trend in research and practice concerning the debilitating effects of disruptive changes on which the magazine article was based. As I quickly discovered, this trend presented a challenge to my contention that creative people actively search for changes, finding them more stimulating than debilitating.

The disagreement between the two positions seemed to highlight an issue of individual differences to me: Although stressful changes may be debilitating for some people, perhaps they are developmentally provocative for others. My research team and I at the University of Chicago discussed this issue, and before long we decided to collect some relevant research data.

THE ILLINOIS BELL TELEPHONE
RESEARCH PROJECT

In looking around for a sample of highly stressed people, we hit upon Illinois Bell Telephone (IBT), a company that had used me from time to time as a creativity consultant. Decision makers at IBT were delighted at our interest in researching stress reactions in their managers, as its parent company, AT&T, was facing federal deregulation and mandated divestiture of its subsidiaries. In 1975, we began our twelve-year longitudinal research program in which managers in the sample were tested psychologically and medically every year. In 1981, the cataclysmic deregulation and divestiture took place and is still regarded as the greatest upheaval in corporate history. In barely a year, IBT decreased its workforce by almost half. One manager told me that he had had ten different supervisors in one year, and that neither they nor he knew what they were supposed to do.

Several studies at IBT demonstrated that hardiness moderates the stress–illness relationship. In her dissertation, Kobasa (1979) found through a retrospective design that among managers, all of whom were high in stresses, those who showed certain attitudes experienced fewer mental and physical illness symptoms. Subsequent IBT studies (Kobasa, Maddi, & Courington, 1981; Kobasa, Maddi, & Kahn, 1982; Kobasa, Maddi, & Puccetti, 1982) used prospective designs to show that these attitudes, along with social support and physical exercise, did indeed provide causative protection against stress-related illnesses, despite the fact that inherited vulnerabilities increase the risk of such illnesses.

Measured by a number of existing scales, the attitudes that emerged as stress buffers seemed to be well conceptualized as commitment, control, and challenge. What we called *commitment* was a predisposition to be involved with people, things, and contexts rather than be detached, isolated, or alienated. *Control* involved struggling to have an influence on outcomes going on around oneself, rather than sinking into passivity and powerlessness. *Challenge* signified wanting to learn continually from one's experience, whether positive or negative, rather than playing it safe by avoiding uncertainties and potential threats. Before long, we were calling these interrelated attitudes the "three Cs" of hardiness.

As we tried to learn more about stress management at IBT, two additional studies stimulated thought on the larger picture of hardiness. In one study (Kobasa, Maddi, Puccetti, & Zola, 1985), hardiness, social support, and physical exercise were compared in their stress-management effectiveness. Among managers who were all above the sample median in stresses, hardiness was roughly twice as effective in decreasing the subsequent risk of illness than were social support and physical exercise. Of particular interest was the synergistic beneficial effect of these three stress-buffering variables: Managers with two stress buffers did somewhat better than those with only one, but those with all three stress buffers did remarkably better than those with only two.

The other study was Khoshaba's dissertation (Khoshaba, 1990; Khoshaba & Maddi, 1999a), which concerned the early development of hardiness.

THE STORY OF HARDINESS: THEORIZING, RESEARCH, AND PRACTICE

A subsample of managers selected to be either very high or very low in hardiness were interviewed blind concerning their early life experiences. Content analyses of their statements showed that, by comparison with the others, the managers high in hardiness remembered not only a disruptive, stressful early family life but also that they were selected by their parents to be successful nonetheless, accepted that role, and worked hard to justify being the family's hope.

THEORIZING ABOUT THE PLACE OF HARDINESS IN A LIFE

There was, of course, specific theorizing involved in coming up with the three hardy attitudes as descriptive of what was going on in the findings. That there were individual differences in these attitudes led to the more comprehensive theoretical questions that arose in the late 1970s and early 1980s of the overall difference hardiness makes in a life. By that time, I was using existential psychology to good effect in my clinical practice, and it seemed a more natural context for hardiness than other viewpoints, such as behaviorism or psychoanalysis. According to existential psychology (Frankl, 1965; Kierkegaard, 1954; Maddi, 1970; May, 1958), meaning is not *given* but rather is *created* through the decisions people make and implement. Virtually everything we do or fail to do constitutes a decision, whether we recognize this or not. Needless to say, some decisions are big and others are small. As specific decisions accumulate, more pervasive meaning systems and general directions emerge. Once established, meaning systems and directions can be changed only by sharpened awareness and a concerted effort.

Whatever their specific content, decisions by their nature require that we choose the future—that is, the path that is relatively unfamiliar—or the past—the path that is relatively familiar (Maddi, 1988, 1998). A simple example is being confronted with a decision either to take a different job in another industry that may require new learning or to remain in our present job, which is certainly adequate, if by now routine. According to existential psychology, consistently choosing the future leads to continued personal development and fulfillment and is therefore the most desirable stance. But what often deters people from future-oriented decisions is that they arouse ontological anxiety, because we cannot predict in advance what the outcome will be. After all, taking that new job may severely shake our foundation of security, perhaps even leading to failure. Resting on our laurels by staying in the present job may seem wisest. To be sure, turning down the new job will bring a bit of ontological guilt over missed opportunity, but this may well seem like less of a problem for us than the anxiety of uncertainty.

What is needed for us to be provoked regularly toward the developmentally more valuable choices for the future is existential courage. For the theologian Kierkegaard (1954), this courage was the faith that, in choosing the future, one was drawing oneself closer to God, who is, after all, the prototypical future-chooser. Although also a theologian, Tillich (1952) more recently defined existential courage secularly as self-confidence and life acceptance.

It is my view that the combined hardy attitudes of commitment, control, and challenge constitute the best available operationalization of existential courage (Maddi, 1988). The hardy attitudes structure how you think about your interaction with the world around you and provide motivation to do difficult things. When they occur together, the three Cs of hardy attitudes facilitate awareness that you formulate life's meaning for yourself by the decisions you make and that choosing the future regularly, despite the anxiety of uncertainty, leads to the most vibrant life.

Why Is It Important to Have All Three Hardy Attitudes?

It is important to recognize that to truly express existential courage, a person must possess all three Cs—commitment, control, and challenge. American psychology is currently preoccupied with the importance of the control attitude, and I have encountered the opinion from others that it is this attitude that fully defines hardiness. But imagine people high in control and simultaneously low in commitment and challenge. Such people would want to determine outcomes, but would not want to waste time and effort learning from experience or feeling involved with people, things, and events. In that these people would be riddled with impatience, irritability, isolation, and bitter suffering whenever control efforts fail, we see something close to the Type A behavior pattern, with all of its physical, mental, and social vulnerabilities. Such people would also be egotistical and would be vulnerable to seeing themselves as better than the others and as having nothing more to learn. There is surprisingly little to call hardiness in this orientation.

Now imagine people high in commitment and simultaneously low in control and challenge. Such people would be completely enmeshed with the people, things, and events around them, never thinking to have an influence through, or to reflect on their experience of, their interactions. They would have little or no individuality, and their sense of meaning would be completely given by the social institutions in which they would lose themselves. Such people would be extremely vulnerable whenever any but the most trivial changes were imposed on them. There is certainly little to call hardiness here, either.

Finally, imagine people who, though high in challenge, are simultaneously low in control and commitment. Such people would be preoccupied with novelty, caring little for the others, things, and events around them and not imagining they could have an influence on anything. They might appear to be learning constantly, but this would be trivial by comparison with their investment in the thrill of novelty per se. They would resemble adventurers (Maddi, 1970) and could be expected to engage in games of chance and risky activities for the excitement that they bring. Once again, there is little of hardiness in this.

I could continue by showing you how any two of the three Cs, without the third, is still shy of hardiness. However, I hope that this is not

necessary and that the point is clear that it is the combination of all three
Cs that truly constitutes hardiness.

Where Does Hardiness Come From?

Existential courage is presumably not inborn, to judge from Nietzsche's
exclamation, "Whatever doesn't kill me makes me stronger" (1968,
p. 254). But existential psychology has little else to say about the conditions
leading to the development of courage. Fortunately, one of the studies
mentioned before (Khoshaba & Maddi, 1999a) provides an empirical basis
for assuming that hardiness develops in people who are encouraged by those
around them to believe that they can turn adversity into opportunity and
who observe themselves actually making this happen. Over time, the feedback one obtains from this pattern of reaction to stresses should build the
hardy attitudes of commitment, control, and challenge that constitute existential courage.

FURTHER DEVELOPMENT OF THE HARDINESS
APPROACH THROUGH PRACTICE

Soon after the cataclysmic deregulation and divestiture, IBT asked us if
we could use the research findings we had accumulated to help them
weather the storm. We took on the challenge and incorporated the Hardiness Institute as a consulting firm. What emerged for IBT was the early
version of hardiness training.

The Training Approach

The approach involved fifteen weekly sessions in which small groups of
managers were taught and encouraged to cope with their major stressors
by the use of four hardy coping techniques and to use the feedback from
their efforts to deepen their hardy attitudes (Maddi, 1987; Maddi, Kahn, &
Maddi, 1998). These managers were sorely stressed, and the trainers not
only helped them to believe that they could solve the problems for their
own and the company's good but also taught them the techniques
through which they could actually turn disruptions into opportunities. We
tried to make this training program incorporate the factors that in the
early history study (Khoshaba & Maddi, 1999a) led to the development of
hardiness by forming an analogy between the disrupted family and the disrupted company and between the parents who encouraged and assisted
their offspring and the trainers who did the same for their trainees.

As to the specifics of the approach, trainees try to turn a stressor into
an opportunity by starting with situational reconstruction (Maddi, 1987),
an imaginative task designed to suggest alternative ways of thinking about
the stressor that may provoke a broadened perspective and a deepened
understanding. Success positions them to go on to the action plan technique, carry out the plan developed, and use the ensuing feedback to

deepen their hardy attitudes. But if their efforts with situational reconstruction are unsuccessful, they go on to *focusing* (Gendlin, 1978), a way
of checking whether insufficiently recognized emotional reactions are
interfering with their imagination. If emotionally based insights from this
technique free up their imagination, then they are ready to go on to the
action plan technique in hopes of resolving the stressor and deepening
their hardy attitudes. However, if they still remain stuck despite efforts
with situational reconstruction and focusing, then the stressor is regarded
as a given, something they cannot fix. At that point, they need to protect
their hardiness by avoiding bitterness and self-pity through the compensa-
tory self-improvement technique (Maddi, 1987). In this technique, they
work on a related stressor that *can* be resolved so as not to be undermined
by the given.

Training Effectiveness

In a waiting-list control study (Maddi, 1987), this early version of hardiness training increased not only hardiness levels but also job satisfaction
and social support, while simultaneously decreasing both self-report and
objective indices of strain. The beneficial results lasted for the six-month
follow-up period. For more precise control purposes, a subsequent study
(Maddi et al., 1998) compared hardiness with two other forms of training,
namely, relaxation-meditation (a common stress management approach)
and passive listening (a placebo and social support control). The passive
listening condition tended to help a bit, the relaxation-meditation condition helped even more, but the hardiness training condition was clearly
the most effective approach.

CONCEPTUALIZING THE HARDINESS MODEL

Although the mechanisms through which hardiness influences health
and performance in the face of stressful circumstances had been an
ongoing theoretical concern, the current hardiness model emerged only
when the more abstract initial conceptual and research knowledge was supplemented by practice applications in the form of hardiness training.

Figure 18.1 shows the hardiness model of the vulnerability and resistance factors influencing well-being. The bad news is that as acute and
chronic stresses mount, organismic strain may become so intense and prolonged as to deplete bodily resources, thereby increasing the risk of breakdowns in the form of physical illnesses, mental disorders, or behavioral
failures. Furthermore, the breakdowns are most likely to occur along the
lines of inherited vulnerabilities. The good news in Figure 18.1 is that
there is a breakdown-prevention system, in which hardy attitudes motivate
people to react to stresses with effective coping, social support interactions, and lifestyle patterns. That the arrows linking components of the
breakdown-prevention system run both ways signifies the transactional
nature of the components. Not only do hardy attitudes motivate hardy

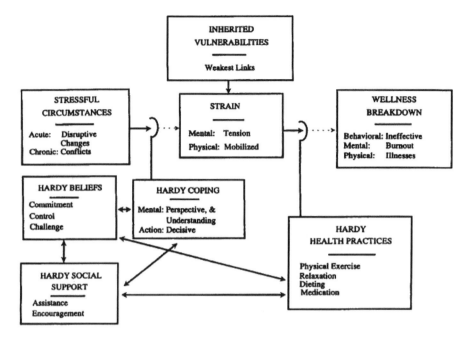

Figure 18.1. The Hardiness Model
Source: Copyright © 1993 by the Hardiness Institute, Inc. Reprinted by
permission.

coping, social support, and lifestyle skills, but practice of these hardy skills
(such as in training programs), properly reflected on, can also deepen the
hardy attitudes that will help to keep the whole process going.

MORE RESEARCH ON THE BEHAVIORAL
AND HEALTH IMPLICATIONS OF HARDINESS

Literature searches show close to a thousand hardiness references over
the last twenty years. Also, our hardy attitudes test has been translated into
ten Asian and European languages, to say nothing of the numerous countries that use it in English. There is by now so much hardiness research
around the world that summarizing it all here is not feasible. Fortunately,
there have been some recent reviews of this body of work (e.g., Funk,
1992; Maddi, 1990; Orr & Westman, 1990; Ouellette, 1993). What I will
concentrate on here is research done by my present and former students
and myself aimed at determining the validity of the hardiness model and
addressing issues that have arisen.

Health, Performance, and Conduct Studies

Similar results to those obtained at IBT have been reported for people
working in other occupations, such as bus drivers (Bartone, 1989), lawyers

(Kobasa, 1982), and nurses (Keane, Ducette, & Adler, 1985). Further-more, Bartone (1999) has been studying military personnel in various stressful circumstances, such as peacekeeping and combat missions. Using various dependent variables and prospective designs, he has found consid-erable evidence that the lower hardy attitudes are, the greater the likeli-hood is that the life-threatening stresses and the culture shock of military engagement abroad will lead to such mental breakdowns as depression and posttraumatic stress disorder. Similar results have been found in the con-text of non–life-threatening culture shock for American employees on work missions abroad (Atella, 1989) and for immigrants to the United States (Kuo & Tsai, 1986).

The studies mentioned thus far tended to use self-report measures not only of hardiness but also of stress-related illness symptoms. This led to the criticism that perhaps all the results show is the pervasive effect of neg-ative affectivity or neuroticism (e.g., Funk & Houston, 1987; Hull, Van Treuren, & Virnelli, 1987). That the findings cannot be explained away like this is indicated by a study in which hardy attitudes and an accepted measure of negative affectivity were entered into regression analyses as independent variables in the attempt to predict the clinical scales of the Minnesota Multiphasic Personality Inventory (MMPI) as dependent variables (Maddi & Khoshaba, 1994). With the effects of negative affectivity con-trolled, hardiness was still a pervasive negative predictor of MMPI clinical scale scores. Further undermining the criticism is a study that used an objec-tive measure of strain, showing hardiness to be higher among employees whose blood pressure was in the normal range than it was among those with high blood pressure (Maddi, 1999).

The negative affectivity criticism is also undermined by the studies to be discussed now, which used some objective measures of performance and conduct. As to performance, Maddi and Hess (1992) measured hardi-ness levels of male high school varsity basketball players in the summer and obtained the objective statistics accumulated on them by their coaches throughout the ensuing season. Hardiness predicted six out of seven indi-ces of performance in the expected direction, showing that even among players good enough to be on the varsity team, hardiness predicted per-formance excellence. The only index not predicted was free throw percent-age, which, of course, reflects what happens in the only period of relative calm in an otherwise tumultuous game. Similarly relevant to performance, Bartone and Snook (1999) found that hardiness, assessed at the arrival of a cohort of U.S. Military Academy cadets at West Point, was the strongest predictor of leadership behavior over the four years of their schooling.

As to conduct, Maddi, Wadhwa, and Haier (1996) studied the rela-tionship of hardiness to alcohol and drug use among high school gradu-ates about to register in college. Whereas a family risk factor index was positively correlated with self-report of whether alcohol and drugs were tried, hardiness was negatively correlated with self-report of the frequency with which alcohol and drugs were used. For a more objective measure-ment, drug use assessed through urine screens correlated negatively with hardiness.

Although the relevant studies are not numerous enough for a finished conclusion, it appears that hardiness protects against not only illness, but performance and conduct breakdown as well.

The Growing Practical Need for Hardiness Assessment, Training, and Consulting

The days when the upheavals at IBT were unusual are behind us. The rising rate of change these days truly amounts to turbulence or even chaos (Peters, 1988). Megatrends (Naisbitt, 1982) beyond anyone's control abound. There is the breathtakingly fast transition we are making from an industrial to an information society, with everyone scurrying to keep up with the continual, dramatic advances in computer and Internet technology and the changes they introduce into everyday life. There is the worldwide increase in competition and redistribution of wealth that has been taking place as U.S. post–World War II supremacy has waned. There is the collapse of the Soviet Union and the U.S. defense industry along with it. There is the technology-fueled transition from parochialism to globalization. There are the shock waves produced by the very justifiable, inexorable pressures toward equal opportunity for minorities and women. Trying desperately to adapt to the pressures of change, companies are continually restructuring—sometimes decentralizing and other times merging, sometimes decreasing and other times increasing management levels, sometimes downsizing and other times upsizing.

The trickle-down effect of these and other megatrends has been a powerful disruption of the relatively stable living patterns we had over many years come to regard as natural. In all this, our individual existences have been greatly stressed, as shown in increasing levels of physical and mental illnesses, decreased job performance and morale, and increased substance abuse and violence. The disruptive changes and their debilitating effects on our functioning have also sorely taxed, if not disconfirmed, our tradition-based patterns of the meaning of life. This has brought many of us to the brink of spiritual bankruptcy.

Hardiness, or existential courage, is needed now more than ever. The solution to destructive or deteriorated behaviors and spiritual bankruptcy will come when we not only accept change as normal but also see the developmental value in it and use our imagination and energy to discern and pursue the future directions it provides. It is this hardy approach that will turn change into opportunity.

Perhaps this is why hardiness assessment, training, and consulting have increased in demand so much in recent years. In response to this demand, we have elaborated the services available through the Hardiness Institute. In the attempt to respond more effectively to the mounting stress problems of individuals and organizations, we now advocate a more comprehensive expression of the hardiness model shown in Figure 18.1. Deborah M. Khoshaba, director of program development and training at the institute, has taken the lead in these new developments.

HardiSurvey Assessment

Specifically, assessment now involves the HardiSurvey III-R, a sixty-five-item questionnaire that measures the vulnerability factors of stress, strain, and regressive coping and the resistance factors of hardy attitudes, hardy coping, and hardy social support. The vulnerability and resistance factors are compared with each other in a wellness ratio. This test can be supplemented by the HardiSurvey IV, which adds information about the resistance factors of hardy relaxation and hardy physical activity. Accumulating reliability and validity data augur well for these two tests. Available on the Internet or in hard copy, the questionnaires generate customized individual reports. Individual questionnaires can also be aggregated into organizational or group reports.

HardiTraining

The emphasis of our current approach is to train both hardy skills and hardy attitudes (Khoshaba & Maddi, 1999b; Maddi, 1994). The hardy skills of coping, social support, relaxation, nutrition, and physical activity are what we call the "five fingers of the hand." In the training process, feedback obtained from exercise of the hardy skills is used to build the hardy attitudes of commitment, control, and challenge, which we call the "palm of the hand." In other words, there is a synergistic articulation between the motivation constituted by hardy attitudes and the actions involved in hardy skills.

Central to the HardiTraining program are workbooks (Khoshaba & Maddi, 1999b) covering all components of the hardy skills and attitudes. These workbooks contain narrative, examples, exercises, and checkpoints. Trainees go through the workbooks until they encounter the checkpoints, which are placed at regular intervals. These checkpoints are the occasion of small-group or one-on-one interactions between trainees and trainers.

The HardiTraining program is designed to be flexible. Any combination or all of the hardy skills may be included, as long as there remains emphasis on the feedback from efforts that builds the hardy attitudes. We are often guided as to the composition of the program by the results of the pretraining HardiSurveys. Whenever possible, we also administer the HardiSurvey posttraining in order to provide some evaluation of the effects of the program.

Individual Applications

To be sure, hardiness assessment and training are important in tertiary prevention, that is, for people whose health or performance is already compromised, so that they will not be further undermined and will have a greater likelihood of improving. Those who can be helped in this way are patients already suffering from degenerative disorders (e.g., heart disease, cancer) and lawbreakers who need rehabilitation. We have taken one step in this direction by working with several health maintenance organizations.

The hardiness approach is similarly important in secondary prevention, where people are at risk of but have not yet undergone health or performance decrements. This includes people in especially risky and stressful professions (e.g., military personnel on combat or peacekeeping missions, police officers) or people whose work or private lives are especially disrupted (because of such things as divorces or deaths in the family or company divestitures or mergers). Most of our work with adults falls into this category of secondary prevention.

In our tumultuous times, however, it is essential that hardiness also be applied in primary prevention, where the people involved have not yet encountered the level of stresses that threaten to undermine them. Youngsters in school need hardiness assessment and training in order that they be adequately prepared in adulthood to turn the rising tide of disruptive changes into opportunities rather than let them be disasters. Currently, there are several two- and four-year colleges offering hardiness assessment and training as regular credit courses. This is a step in the direction of primary prevention, but it would be even better to expose elementary and high school students to hardiness assessment and training. We are currently taking steps in this needed direction.

Organizational Applications

The distressed status of companies we encounter these days has led us into organizational consulting. In expanding the hardiness approach from individuals to organizations (Maddi, Khoshaba, & Pammenter, 1999), we have asserted that resiliency and effectiveness are what organizations, too, need if they are to be successful in our changing times. HardiOrganizations have a characteristic culture, climate, structure, and workforce.

The values forming the culture of HardiOrganizations are isomorphic with the hardy attitudes at the individual level. Specifically, the attitudes of commitment, control, and challenge framing individual hardiness correspond at the organizational level to the hardy values of cooperation, credibility, and creativity. When HardiIndividuals interact in a group, translation occurs—of their attitude of commitment into valuing collaboration with each other, of their attitude of control into valuing the credibility that signifies taking responsibility for actions, and of their attitude of challenge into valuing creativity as the search for innovative problem solutions.

At the level of climate, people in a HardiOrganization will not just pay lip service to its values but, rather, will exemplify them in their day-to-day, moment-to-moment interactions with each other. This will form a healthy learning environment in which people will work together in solving problems through a coping process that involves searching for perspective and understanding and using what is learned thereby to take decisive actions. In interacting with each other, they will both want for themselves and extend to others assistance and encouragement, thereby really functioning as a team. And when a HardiOrganization member exhibits the various behaviors mentioned here, the others will applaud that and use it as a model for their own advancement.

The structure of a HardiOrganization will facilitate the values and climate already identified. In most instances, a matrix management approach will be used in which teams devoted to change-oriented projects will have a significant decision-making role in the directions and emphases of the organization.

As to personnel makeup, the HardiOrganization will, over time, include an increasingly higher proportion of HardiIndividuals. This is ensured because the usual functions of promotions, hiring and firing, gain sharing, member benefits, and job training will reflect the ongoing culture, climate, and structure of the HardiOrganization. Despite the continually changing work environment, HardiIndividuals will not wish to leave employment at HardiOrganizations that understand and value them. But, if they are forced to leave by company reorganization, these HardiIndividuals will not go away mad but will instead continue their proactive, innovative ways in other jobs.

CLOSING REMARKS

What has been attempted here is a comprehensive picture of hardiness and its development over the last twenty years. From the beginning, we have been involved in conceptual, research, and practice efforts. It has been conceptual effort that highlighted what made sense and nonsense, how things fit together, and the role of hardiness in a broader life view. It has been research effort that clarified strengths and weaknesses, improved assessment and training approaches, and lent credibility to the enterprise. It has been practice effort that underscored individual and organizational requirements and the need to respond to them directly and effectively. But without the continual interplay of the conceptual, research, and practice efforts and the heightened provocation that ensued, the hardiness approach would not have developed as it has.

As the twenty-first century unfolds, our world seems embroiled in an ever-increasing rate of change. Perhaps it is hardiness that will help us turn this turbulence into meaningful and fulfilling directions, rather than succumbing to behavioral, conduct, and health breakdowns.

REFERENCES

Atella, M. (1989). Crossing boundaries: Effectiveness and health among Western managers living in China. Dissertation, University of Chicago.

Bartone, P. T. (1989). Predictors of stress-related illness in city bus drivers. *Journal of Occupational Medicine, 31*, 657–663.

Bartone, P. T. (1999). Hardiness protects against war-related stress in Army Reserve forces. *Consulting Psychology Journal, 51*, 72–82.

Bartone, P. T., & Snook, S. A. (1999). Cognitive and personality factors predict leader development in U.S. Army cadets. Paper presented at 35th International Applied Military Psychology Symposium (IAMPS), Florence, Italy, May.

Frankl, V. E. (1965). *The doctor and the soul: From psychotherapy to logotherapy.* New York: Knopf.

Funk, S. C. (1992). Hardiness: A review of theory and research. *Health Psychology, 11*, 335–345.

Funk, S. C., & Houston, B. K. (1987). A critical analysis of the Hardiness Scale's validity and utility. *Journal of Personality and Social Psychology, 53*, 572–578.

Gendlin, E. T. (1978). *Focusing* (2nd ed.). New York: Everest House.

Hull, J. G., Van Treuren, R. R., & Virnelli, S. (1987). Hardiness and health: A critique and alternative approach. *Journal of Personality and Social Psychology, 53*, 518–530.

Keane, A., Ducette, J., & Adler, D. C. (1985). Stress in ICU and non-ICU nurses. *Nursing Research, 34*, 231–236.

Khoshaba, D. M. (1990). Early antecedents of hardiness. Dissertation, Illinois School of Professional Psychology.

Khoshaba, D. M., & Maddi, S. R. (1999a). Early experiences in hardiness development. *Consulting Psychology Journal: Practice and Research, 51*, 106–116.

Khoshaba, D. M., & Maddi, S. R. (1999b). *HardiTraining* (2 vols.; 2nd ed., rev.). Newport Beach, CA: Hardiness Institute.

Kierkegaard, S. (1954). *The sickness unto death*. New York: Doubleday.

Kobasa, S. C. (1979). Stressful life events, personality, and health: An inquiry into hardiness. *Journal of Personality and Social Psychology, 37*, 1–11.

Kobasa, S. C. (1982). Commitment and coping in stress resistance among lawyers. *Journal of Personality and Social Psychology, 42*, 707–717.

Kobasa, S. C., Maddi, S. R., & Courington, S. (1981). Personality and constitution as mediators of the stress–illness relationship. *Journal of Health and Social behavior, 22*, 368–378.

Kobasa, S. C., Maddi, S. R., & Kahn, S. (1982). Hardiness and health: A prospective study. *Journal of Personality and Social Psychology, 42*, 168–177.

Kobasa, S. C., Maddi, S. R., & Puccetti, M. C. (1982). Personality and exercise as buffers in the stress–illness relationship. *Journal of Behavioral Medicine, 4*, 391–404.

Kobasa, S. C., Maddi, S. R., Puccetti, M. C., & Zola, M. A. (1985). Effectiveness of hardiness, exercise, and social support as resources against illness. *Journal of Psychosomatic Research, 29*, 525–533.

Kuo, W. H., & Tsai, Y. (1986). Social networking, hardiness, and immigrant's mental health. *Journal of Health and Social Behavior, 27*, 133–149.

Maddi, S. R. (1970). The search for meaning. In A. Williams & M. Page (Eds.), *The Nebraska symposium on motivation* (pp. 137–183). Lincoln: University of Nebraska Press.

Maddi, S. R. (1987). Hardiness training at Illinois Bell Telephone. In J. P. Opatz (Ed.), *Health promotion evaluation* (pp. 101–115). Stevens Point, WI: National Wellness Institute.

Maddi, S. R. (1988). On the problem of accepting facticity and pursuing possibility. In S. B. Messer, L. A. Sass, & R. L. Woolfolk (Eds.), *Hermeneutics and psychological theory: Interpretive perspectives on personality, psychotherapy, and psychopathology*. New Brunswick, NJ: Rutgers University Press.

Maddi, S. R. (1990). Issues and interventions in stress mastery. In H. S. Friedman (Ed.), *Personality and disease* (pp. 121–154). New York: John Wiley & Sons.

Maddi, S. R. (1994). The Hardiness Enhancing Lifestyle Program (HELP) for improving physical, mental, and social wellness. In C. Hopper (Ed.), *Wellness lecture series* (pp. 1–16). Oakland: University of California/HealthNet.

Maddi, S. R. (1998). Hardiness in health and effectiveness. In H. S. Friedman (Ed.), *Encyclopedia of mental health* (pp. 323–335). San Diego: Academic Press.

Maddi, S. R. (1999). The personality construct of hardiness. I. Effects on experiencing, coping, and strain. *Consulting Psychology Journal, 51,* 83–94.

Maddi, S. R., & Hess, M. (1992). Hardiness and success in basketball. *International Journal of Sport Psychology, 23,* 360–368.

Maddi, S. R., Kahn, S., & Maddi, K. L. (1998). The effectiveness of hardiness training. *Consulting Psychology Journal, 50,* 78–86.

Maddi, S. R., & Khoshaba, D. M. (1994). Hardiness and mental health. *Journal of Personality Assessment, 63,* 265–274.

Maddi, S. R., Khoshaba, D. M., & Pammenter, A. (1999). The hardy organization: Success by turning change to advantage. *Consulting Psychology Journal, 51,* 117–124.

Maddi, S. R., Wadhwa, P., & Haier, R. J. (1996). Relationship of hardiness to alcohol and drug use in adolescents. *American Journal of Drug and Alcohol Abuse, 22,* 247–257.

May, R. (1958). Contributions of existential psychotherapy. In R. May, E. Angel, & H. F. Ellenberger (Eds.), *Existence: A new dimension of psychiatry and psychology.* New York: Basic Books.

Naisbitt, J. (1982). *Megatrends: Ten new directions transforming our lives.* New York: Warner Books.

Nietzsche, F. (1968). *The will to power* (W. Kaufmann, ed.). New York: Vintage.

Orr, E., & Westman, M. (1990). Hardiness as a stress moderator: A review. In M. Rosenbaum (Ed.), *Learned resourcefulness: On coping skills, self-control, and adaptive behavior* (pp. 64–94). New York: Springer-Verlag.

Ouellette, S. C. (1993). Inquiries into hardiness. In L. Goldberger & S. Bresnitz (Eds.), *Handbook of stress: Theoretical and clinical aspects* (2nd ed., pp. 77–100). New York: Free Press.

Peters, T. (1988). *Thriving on chaos: Handbook for a management revolution.* New York: Knopf.

Tillich, P. (1952). *The courage to be.* New Haven, CT: Yale University Press.

CHAPTER 19

Racing against Your Heart

Roger R. Hock

Who are you? If someone were to ask you that question, you would probably respond by describing some of your more obvious or dominant characteristics. Such characteristics, often referred to as *traits*, are important in making you the unique person that you are. Traits are assumed to be consistent across situations and over time. Psychologists who have supported the trait theory of personality (and not all have) have proposed that personality consists of various groups of traits that exist in all of us, but in varying amounts. Most interesting to psychologists (and everyone, really) is the ability of a person's traits to predict their behavior in given situations and over time. In other words, trait theorists believe that insight into your unique profile of traits will allow us to predict various behavioral outcomes for you now and in the future. Therefore, it is easy to imagine how dramatically this interest would increase if certain personality characteristics were found to predict how healthy you will be or even predict your chances of dying from a heart attack.

You are probably aware of one group of personality characteristics related to health, popularly known as the "Type A personality." To be precise, *Type A* refers to a specific *pattern of behaviors* rather than the overall personality of an individual. This behavior pattern was first reported in the late 1950s by two cardiologists, Meyer Friedman and Ray Rosenman. Their theory and findings have exerted a huge influence in linking psychology and health and in our understanding of the role of personality in the development and prevention of illness.

THEORETICAL PROPOSITIONS

The story about how these doctors first realized the idea for their research demonstrates how careful observation of small, seemingly unimportant details can lead to major scientific breakthroughs. Dr. Friedman was having the furniture in his office waiting room reupholstered. The upholsterer pointed out how the material on the couches and chairs had worn out in an odd way. The front edges of the seat cushions had worn away faster than the rest. It was as if Dr. Friedman's cardiac patients were literally "sitting on the edge of their seats." This observation prompted Friedman to wonder if his patients (people with heart disease) were different in some important characteristic, compared to those of doctors in other specialties.

Through surveys of executives and physicians, Friedman and Rosenman found a common belief that people exposed over long periods of time to chronic stress stemming from excessive drive, pressure to meet deadlines, competitive situations, and economic frustration are more likely to develop heart disease. They decided to put these ideas to a scientific test.

METHOD

Using their earlier research and clinical observations, the two cardiologists developed a *model*, or set of characteristics, for a specific overt (observable) behavior pattern that they believed was related to increased levels of cholesterol and consequently to coronary heart disease (CHD). This pattern, labeled *pattern A*, consisted of the following characteristics (Friedman & Rosenman, 1959, p. 1286):

1. An intense, sustained drive to achieve one's personal goals
2. A profound tendency and eagerness to compete in all situations
3. A persistent desire for recognition and advancement
4. Continuous involvement in multiple activities that are constantly subject to deadlines
5. Habitual tendency to rush to finish activities
6. Extraordinary mental and physical alertness

The researchers then developed a second set of overt behaviors, labeled *pattern B*. Pattern B was described as essentially the opposite of pattern A and was characterized by a relative absence of drive, ambition, sense of time urgency, desire to compete, and involvement in deadlines.

Friedman and Rosenman next needed to find subjects for their research who fit the descriptions of patterns A and B. To do this they contacted managers and supervisors of various large companies and corporations. They explained the behavior patterns and asked the managers to select from among their associates those who most closely fit the particular patterns. The groups that were finally selected consisted of various levels of executives and nonexecutives, all males. There were eighty-three men in each group, with an average age in group A of 45 and in group B, 43. All subjects were given several tests relating to the goals of the study.

First, the researchers designed interviews to assess the history of CHD in the subjects' parents; the subjects' own history of heart trouble; their number of hours of work, sleep, and exercise each week; and their smoking, alcohol, and dietary habits. Also during these interviews, the researchers determined if a subject had a fully or only partially developed behavior pattern in his group (either A or B), based on body movements, tone of conversation, teeth clenching, gesturing, general air of impatience, and the subjects' own admission of drive, competitiveness, and time urgency. It was determined that sixty-nine of the eighty-three men in group A exhibited this fully developed pattern, while fifty-eight of the eighty-three subjects in group B were judged to be of the fully developed Type B.

Second, all subjects were asked to keep a diary of everything they ate or drank over one week's time. Code numbers were assigned to the subjects so that they would not feel reluctant to report alcohol consumption honestly. The diets of the subjects were then broken down and analyzed by a hospital dietitian who was not aware of the subjects' identities or to which group they belonged.

Third, research assistants took blood samples from all subjects to measure cholesterol levels and clotting time. Instances of CHD were determined through careful questioning of the subjects about past coronary health and through standard electrocardiogram readings. Rosenman and a cardiologist not involved in the study interpreted these findings independently (to avoid bias). With one exception, their interpretations agreed for all subjects.

Finally, the researchers determined the number of subjects with *arcus senilis*, through illuminated inspection of the subjects' eyes. *Arcus senilis* refers to the formation of an opaque ring around the cornea of the eye caused by the breakdown of fatty deposits in the bloodstream.

RESULTS

Boiling down Friedman and Rosenman's data, the interviews indicated that the men chosen for each group fit the profiles developed by the researchers. Group A subjects were found to be chronically harassed by commitments, ambitions, and drives. Also, they were clearly eager to compete in all of their activities, both professional and recreational. In addition, they also admitted a strong desire to win. The men in group B were found to be strikingly different from those in group A, especially their lack of the sense of time urgency. The men in group B appeared to be satisfied with their present positions in life and avoided pursuing multiple goals and competitive situations. They were much less concerned about advancement and typically spent more time with their families and in noncompetitive recreational activities.

Table 19.1 is a summary of the most relevant comparisons for the two groups on the characteristics from the tests and surveys. Table 19.2 summarizes the outcome measurements relating to blood levels and illnesses.

As can be seen in Table 19.1, the two groups were similar on nearly all of the measured characteristics. Although the men in group A tended to be a little higher on most of the measurements, the only differences that

Table 19.1. Comparison of Characteristics for Group A and Group B

	Group A	Group B
Average weight	176	172
Average work hours/week	51	45
Average exercise hours/week	10	7
Number of smokers	67%	56%
Average no. of cigarettes/day	23	15
Average alcohol calories/day	194	149
Average total daily calories	2,049	2,134
Average daily fat calories	944	978
Parents with CHD	36%	27%

Source: Compiled from data in Friedman & Rosenman, 1959, pp. 1289–1293.

were statistically significant were the number of cigarettes smoked each day and the percentage of men whose parents had a history of coronary heart disease.

However, if you take a look at the cholesterol and illness levels in Table 19.2, some very convincing differences emerge. First, though, considering the overall results in the table, it appears that no meaningful difference in blood clotting time was found for the two groups. The speed at which your blood coagulates relates to your potential for heart disease and other vascular illness. The slower your clotting time, the less your risk. In order to examine this statistic more closely, Friedman and Rosenman compared the clotting times for those subjects who exhibited a *fully developed* Type A pattern (6.8 minutes) with those judged as *fully developed* Type B's (7.2 minutes). This difference in clotting time was statistically significant.

The other findings in Table 19.2 are unambiguous. Cholesterol levels were clearly and significantly higher for group A subjects. This difference was even greater if the subjects with the fully developed patterns were compared. The incidence of arcus senilis was three times greater for group A and five times greater in the fully developed comparison groups.

Finally, the key finding of the entire study, and the one that secured its place in history, was the striking difference in the incidence of clinical coronary heart disease found in the two groups. In group A, twenty-three of

Table 19.2. Comparisons of Blood and Illness for Group A and Group B

	Group A	Group B
Average clotting time (minutes)	6.9	7.0
Average serum cholesterol	253	215
Arcus senilis	38%	11%
Coronary heart disease	28%	4%

Source: Compiled from data in Friedman & Rosenman, 1959, p. 1293.

the subjects (28%) exhibited clear evidence of CHD, compared with three men (4%) in group B. When the researchers examined these findings in terms of the fully developed subgroups, the evidence became even stronger. All twenty-three of the CHD cases in group A came from those men with the fully developed Type A pattern. For group B, all three of the cases were from those subjects exhibiting the *incomplete* Type B pattern.

DISCUSSION OF FINDINGS

The conclusion implied by the authors was that the Type A behavior pattern was a major cause of CHD and related blood abnormalities. However, if you carefully examine the data in the tables, you will notice a couple of possible alternative explanations for those results. One was that group A men reported a greater incidence of CHD in their parents. Therefore, maybe something *genetic*, rather than the behavior pattern, accounted for the differences found. The other rather glaring difference was the greater number of cigarettes smoked per day by group A subjects. Today we *know* that smoking contributes to CHD. So, perhaps it was not the Type A behavior pattern that produced the results, but rather the heavier smoking.

Friedman and Rosenman responded to both of those potential criticisms in their discussion of the findings. First, they found that, within group A, an equal number of light smokers (ten cigarettes or fewer per day) had CHD as did heavy smokers (more than ten cigarettes per day). Second, in group B there were forty-six men who smoked heavily, yet only two exhibited CHD. These findings led the authors to suggest that cigarette smoking may have been a characteristic of the Type A behavior pattern, but not a direct cause of the CHD that was found. It is important to remember that this study was done more than thirty years ago, before the link between smoking and CHD was as firmly established as it is today.

As for the possibility of parental history creating the differences:

> The data also revealed that of the 30 group A men having a positive parental history, only eight (27%) had heart disease and of 53 men without a parental history, 15 (28%) had heart disease. None of the 23 group B men with a positive parental history exhibited clinical heart disease. (Friedman & Rosenman, 1959, p. 1293)

Again, more recent research that controlled carefully for this factor has demonstrated a family link in CHD. However, it is not clear whether it is a tendency toward heart disease or toward a certain behavior pattern (such as Type A) that is inherited.

SIGNIFICANCE OF THE RESEARCH
AND SUBSEQUENT FINDINGS

This study by Friedman and Rosenman was of crucial importance to the history of psychological research for three basic reasons. First, it was one of the earliest systematic studies to establish clearly that specific behavior patterns characteristic of some individuals can contribute in dramatic ways to serious illness. This sent a message to physicians that to consider only the physiological aspects of illnesses may be wholly inadequate for successful diagnosis, treatment, intervention, and prevention.

Second, this study began a new line of scientific inquiry into the relationship between behavior and CHD that has produced scores of research articles. The concept of the *Type A personality* and its connection to CHD has been refined to the point that it may be possible to prevent heart attacks in high-risk individuals before the first one occurs.

The third long-range outcome of Friedman and Rosenman's research is that it has played an important role in the creation and growth of a relatively new branch of the behavioral sciences called *health psychology*. Health psychologists study all aspects of health and medicine in terms of the psychological influences that exist in health promotion and maintenance, the prevention and treatment of illness, the causes of illness, and the health care system.

One subsequent study is especially important to report here. In 1976, Rosenman and Friedman published the results of a major eight-year study of more than three thousand men who were diagnosed at the beginning of the study as being free of heart disease and who fit the Type A behavior pattern. Compared with the subjects with Type B behavior pattern, these men were twice as likely to develop CHD, suffered significantly more fatal heart attacks, and reported five times more coronary problems. What was perhaps even more important, however, was that the Type A pattern predicted who would develop CHD independently of other predictors such as age, cholesterol level, blood pressure, or smoking habits (Rosenman, Brand, Sholtz, & Friedman, 1976).

One question you might be asking yourself by now is, Why? What is it about this Type A pattern that causes CHD? The most widely accepted theory answers that Type A's respond to stressful events by becoming more intensely physiologically aroused than non–Type A's. This extreme arousal causes the body to produce more hormones such as adrenaline and also increases heart rate and blood pressure. Over time, these exaggerated reactions to stress damage the arteries, which, in turn, leads to heart disease (Matthews, 1982).

RECENT APPLICATIONS

Both Friedman and Rosenman, together and separately, have continued in their role as leading researchers in the field of personality and behavioral variables in CHD. Their research, along with many others', has spawned a new research niche referred to as *cardiopsychology*, which focuses on the psychological factors involved in the development, course, rehabilitation, and coping mechanisms of CHD (Jordan, Barde, & Zeiher, 2001). Their original article discussed here, as well as more recent research, is cited in a broad range of studies published in many countries. The Type A concept has been refined, strengthened, and applied to numerous research areas, some of which follow quite logically, while others might surprise you.

For example, one study examined the relationship between Type A behavior and driving (Perry & Baldwin, 2000). The results left little doubt that "friends should not let Type A friends drive!" The study found a clear association between Type A personality and an increase in driving-related incidents: more traffic accidents, more tickets, greater impatience on the road, more displays of road rage, and overall riskier driving behaviors. You might want to respond to the Type A assessment items below before you get behind the wheel next time.

A study from the field of health psychology applied the Type A concept in exploring the link between stress and burnout to CHD in working women (Hallman, Thomsson, Burell, Lissers, & Setterlind, 2003). As you are probably aware, as women have entered the professional workforce in increasing numbers over the past forty years, they have also become more prone to many stress-related health problems previously found mainly in men. This study confirms that women with CHD did indeed report higher levels of burnout and lesser coping abilities. The authors suggest that "in order to optimize the outcome of rehabilitation and prevention, we need more research on women, of women, and especially from women's point of view" (p. 433).

Finally, Friedman and Rosenman's 1959 article was incorporated into a study of the relationships between parents and their adolescent children (Forgays, 1996). In this study, Type A characteristics and family environments of more than nine hundred subjects were analyzed. Results indicated that teenage children of Type A parents tend to be Type A's themselves—not surprising, but, once again, this brings up the nature–nurture question: Do kids inherit a genetic tendency toward Type A behavior, or do they learn it from being raised by Type A parents? Forgays addressed this in his study: "Further analyses indicated an *independent* contribution of perceived family environment to the development of TABP [Type A Behavior Pattern] in adolescents" (p. 841, emphasis added). However, it would not be particularly surprising, in light of recent research trends, if adoption and twin studies reveal a significant inherited, genetic influence on the Type A and Type B personality dimension.

CONCLUSION

Do you have a Type A personality? How would you know? As with your level of introversion or extroversion, your "Type A-ness" versus your "Type B-ness" is a part of who you are. Tests have been developed to assess people's Type A or Type B behavior patterns. You can get a rough idea by examining the list of Type A characteristics below to see how many apply to you:

1. Frequently doing more than one thing at a time.
2. Urging others to hurry up and finish what they are saying.
3. Becoming very irritated when traffic is blocked or when you are waiting in line.
4. Gesturing a lot while talking.

5. Having a hard time sitting with nothing to do.
6. Speaking explosively and using obscenities often.
7. Playing to win all the time, even in games with children.
8. Becoming impatient when watching others carry out a task.

If you suspect that you are a Type A, you may want to consider a more careful evaluation by a trained physician or a psychologist. Several successful programs to intervene in the connection between Type A behavior and serious illness have been developed, largely in response to the work of Friedman and Rosenman (e.g., George, Prasadaro, Kumaraiah, & Yavagal, 1998).

REFERENCES

Forgays, D. K. (1996). The relationship between Type-A parenting and adolescent perceptions of family environment. *Adolescence, 31*(124), 841–862.

Friedman, M., & Rosenman, R. H. (1959). Association of specific overt behavior pattern with blood and cardiovascular findings: Blood cholesterol level, blood clotting time, incidence of arcus senilis, and clinical coronary artery disease. *Journal of the American Medical Association, 169,* 1286–1296.

George, I., Prasadaro, P., Kumaraiah, V., & Yavagal, S. (1998). Modification of Type A behavior pattern in coronary heart disease: A cognitive-behavioral intervention program. *NIMHANS Journal, 16*(1), 29–35.

Hallman, T., Thomsson, H., Burell, G., Lissers, J., & Setterlind, S. (2003). Stress, burnout, and coping: Differences between women with coronary heart disease and healthy matched women. *Journal of Health Psychology, 8,* 433–445.

Jordan, J., Barde, B., & Zeiher, A. M. (2001). Cardiopsychology today. *Herz, 26,* 335–344.

Matthews, K. A. (1982). Psychological perspectives on the Type A behavior pattern. *Psychological Bulletin, 91,* 293–323.

Perry, A. R., & Baldwin, D. A. (2000). Further evidence of associations of Type A personality scores and driving-related attitudes and behaviors. *Perceptual and Motor Skills, 91*(1), 147–154.

Rosenman, R. H., Brand, R. J., Sholtz, R. I., & Friedman, M. (1976). Multivariate prediction of coronary heart disease during 8.5 year follow-up in the Western Collaborative Group Study. *American Journal of Cardiology, 37,* 903–910.

CHAPTER 20

Sex-Related Differences in the Social Support– Stress Relationship

Gretchen Reevy

A good relationship with a friend, family member, or significant other can be a primary source of pleasure. One of the benefits provided by a relationship is social support, through which people feel experiences of belonging and of being cared for. Social support comes in several different forms, including emotional, tangible, and informational (Cutrona & Russell, 1990). It can be provided by different sources: a spouse or partner, relatives, friends, coworkers, work supervisors, therapists, even pets.

Social support is important because it has been associated with better health, both physical and psychological, and even longer life (e.g., Berkman and Syme, 1979; House, Robbins, & Metzner, 1982; Stroebe & Stroebe, 1996). It may also protect individuals from the uncomfortable feeling of stress (Wills, 1984).

Social support can be viewed and measured in different ways. One way to measure it is to ask the recipient about particular supportive acts that have occurred. This is called *enacted* or *received support* (Barrera, Sandler, & Ramsay, 1981). A second way support is measured is to ask people about their perceived availability of support, should they need it, and their satisfaction with their support. This is called *perceived support* (e.g., Cohen, 1988; House, 1981). These two types of support are distinct and are most often not highly correlated (Barrera, 1986). The study discussed in this chapter includes both types of social support concepts.

As described in other chapters in this book, stress may also be defined or conceived of in many different ways. One way stress is conceptualized is as "life events stress" (Holmes & Rahe, 1967)—relatively major events that may occur and cause stress, such as death of a spouse, being fired at work, or experiencing a jail term. This stress concept has been criticized because it fails to consider individual differences in appraisal or assessment of stressfulness of events (Schroeder & Costa, 1984). For example, being fired from a job could be extremely stressful for one individual but only a minor setback for another. Partly for this reason, Lazarus, Kanner, and Folkman (1980) developed a new stress concept: "daily hassles," or simply, "hassles stress," which includes events such as getting stuck in traffic, losing things, or not getting enough sleep. These hassles potentially occur on a daily basis and are strongly influenced by appraisal; some people experience great upset from the occurrence of such events, while others recover quickly from their occurrence. Both life events stress and hassles stress have been correlated with psychological and physical symptoms. The correlation between hassles and symptoms is stronger than the correlation between life events and symptoms (Lazarus, 1997).

SOCIAL SUPPORT IS DIFFERENT FOR WOMEN AND MEN

Social support is different for women and men. Women clearly receive more support from friends than do men, whereas men receive more support from their spouses. Regarding other sources of support, such as family and work sources, research findings are mixed (see Reevy & Maslach, 2001, for a review). However, evidence indicates that, overall, women report receiving more support (Cohen, McGowan, Fooskas, & Rose, 1984).

The above results apply to perceived support and some other social support concepts, but very little research has explored potential sex differences in terms of enacted support. In a recent literature review, I found that only two studies have reported sex comparisons in enacted support. In these studies, results indicated that total enacted support did not differ between the sexes, but some differences existed in regard to specific *types* of support, especially that women reported receiving more emotional support than did men (Piko, 1998; Stokes & Wilson, 1984). However, theories regarding gender role—*gender role theories*—which emphasize that women and men have different roles in a particular culture, face different demands, and experience different socialization practices, would predict sex differences for both perceived and received support.

According to gender role theories, women are better prepared for relationships than men; they are socialized for connectivity and for comfort with disclosure and some degree of vulnerability in relationships (Deaux & LaFrance, 1998), whereas men are socialized to be more competitive (Bakan, 1966; Brannon, 1976). Based on these ideas, men should hesitate to be vulnerable. Thus, women should not only have the *perception* of greater support than men have (perceived support) but should also *receive* more supportive acts than do men (enacted support). Given the small number of studies on sex differences in enacted support, this research question deserves further investigation.

STRESS IS DIFFERENT FOR WOMEN AND MEN

According to gender role theories, stress should also be different for women and men. A general argument is that adult women experience more stress in the workplace, partly because they are stepping outside of their gender role by working. Research findings lend support to this argument. For example, women still make less money than men for comparable work (e.g., Cohn, 2000; Robinson, 2001; Roos & Gatta, 1999), women are more likely than men to receive a negative evaluation in the workplace (e.g., Gerber, 2001; Heilman, 2001), and sexual harassment is still prevalent (e.g., Frank, Brogan, & Schiffman, 1998; Yoder, 2001). Women may also experience more stress domestically and socially. For example, when women are married, they perform more household work than do their male partners, even if both partners have jobs (e.g., Coltrane & Adams, 2001; Perkins & DeMeis, 1996). Furthermore, women are more often care providers than are men, even of people other than children, such as aging parents and friends (Kessler, McLeod, & Wethington, 1985). In a research review, Greenglass and Noguchi (2000) concluded that women experience more stressful life events than do men.

Relative to adult, often working, women, college-age women have been neglected in theorizing and research regarding sex comparisons in stress levels. However, results of a few studies indicate that sex differences in stressful life events occur by college age. For example, sexual harassment is common in college (Rabinowitz, 1996; Sandler & Shoop, 1997), and women have adopted their caretaker role by college age (Belansky & Boggiano, 1994). Additionally, in one study on undergraduates, the researchers found that women reported more stressful life events than did men (Wohlgemuth & Betz, 1991).

According to gender role theories and past research, women should report more stress than men when stress is conceived as either life events or hassles; past research has detected greater stress for women in both major events, such as negative evaluation at work, and minor events (hassles), such as amount of housework performed. Furthermore, since the experience of hassles has a greater subjective component, one would expect a greater sex difference in reporting of hassles than in reporting of life events stress. This result would be expected in light of women's greater reporting of both physical and psychological symptoms (Greenglass & Noguchi, 2000).

THE SOCIAL SUPPORT–STRESS RELATIONSHIP AND WHY IT SHOULD BE DIFFERENT FOR WOMEN AND MEN

Because social support has been found to be generally helpful to people, social support and stress should be negatively correlated. That is, higher social support should be associated with less stress, and lower social support should be associated with more stress. Overall, research indicates that this pattern exists for most social support and stress concepts that have been studied in conjunction (Barrera, 1986). However, enacted support and stress are often positively correlated—more enacted support is associated with more stress and less enacted support is associated with less stress. Barrera (1986) has explained this finding. Measures of enacted support assess specific supportive behaviors that have been received and do not highly correlate with one's perception that support is available or that one is cared for (perceived support). The neediness that one experiences when one is under stress may be communicated to others, either directly or indirectly. Then these supportive behaviors occur with greater frequency when one is under stress.

Although very little research has been devoted to sex differences in the relationship between social support and stress, numerous studies have investigated sex differences in social support and distress relationships, with distress conceptualized as, for example, depression or anxiety (Flaherty & Richman, 1989), physical symptoms (Wohlgemuth & Betz, 1991), or psychological distress (Miller & Ingham, 1976). In each of these studies, the relationship between social support and distress was stronger for women than for men. Furthermore, social support benefits both women and men in terms of life expectancy, but this effect is stronger for women than for men (Berkman & Syme, 1979). Because women appear to benefit more from social support in general than do men, one might expect that the correlation between social support and stress would be stronger for women than for men. This should apply to both types of stress and to both types of support.

Based on gender role theories and on previous research results, the following predictions were developed:

- Hypothesis 1: Women will report more social support than men, for both social support concepts (perceived support and enacted support).
- Hypothesis 2: Women will report more stress than men, for both stress concepts (life events stress and hassles).
- Hypothesis 3: The correlation between social support and stress, when social support is conceived as perceived support and stress as hassles, will be negative and stronger for women than for men.
- Hypothesis 4: The correlation between social support and stress, when social support is conceived as perceived support and stress as life events, will be negative and stronger for women than for men.
- Hypothesis 5: The correlation between social support and stress, when social support is conceived as enacted support and stress as hassles, will be positive and stronger for women than for men.
- Hypothesis 6: The correlation between social support and stress, when social support is conceived as enacted support and stress as life events, will be positive and stronger for women than for men.

METHOD

Participants/Procedures

The participants in this study were 154 undergraduates (65 women, 89 men) enrolled in introductory psychology classes at the University of California, Berkeley (UCB), during the summer or fall of 1989. The sample was 32.0 percent Asian, 25.3 percent Caucasian, 8.4 percent African American, 5.2 percent Filipino, 4.5 percent Hispanic, and 2.7 percent other ethnicities; 22 percent of participants did not report an ethnicity. Ages ranged from 16 to 51, with a mean age of 19.9 years. Participants were tested in classrooms at UCB, in groups ranging from one to twenty-five persons. Participation consisted of completing questionnaires which took a total of forty-five minutes to two hours to fill out.

Measures

Social Support

Perceived social support was measured by the Perceived Social Support (PSS) from Friends and from Family scales (Procidano & Heller, 1983). Each of these two scales (i.e., the "Friends" scale and "Family" scale) consists of twenty statements, which respondents mark yes, no, or "don't know." The items assess perceived availability of and satisfaction with social support. Examples are: "My friends are sensitive to my personal needs" and "My family enjoys hearing about what I think." Scores on each of the two scales range from 0 (no support) to 20 (highest support).

Enacted support was measured by the Inventory of Socially Supportive Behaviors (ISSB) (Barrera et al., 1981), which consists of forty items measuring supportive behaviors. Examples of items are: "Told you what she/he did in a situation that was similar to yours" and "Provided you with a place to stay." Respondents indicate how frequently each of the behaviors occurred in the past month. Each item is scored on a five-point scale, from 0 (not at all) to 4 (about every day). Total scores thus range from 0 to 160. Average frequency (the mean of all forty responses) can be obtained, ranging from 0 to 4.

Stress

Daily hassles stress was measured by the Daily Hassles Scale (Lazarus & Folkman, 1989), which consists of 117 items such as "Misplacing or losing things," "Too many interruptions," and "Not seeing enough people." Each item is endorsed by the respondent if she experienced the event in the past month and the event produced some degree of stress. Additionally, respondents rate each item in terms of the severity of the stress produced, ranging from 1 (least severe) to 3 (most severe). Two hassles scores can be obtained: a hassles frequency score, ranging from 0 to 117, and an average hassles severity score, ranging from 1 to 3.

Major life events stress was measured by the Life Experiences Survey (LES) (Sarason, Johnson, & Siegel, 1978). It consists of sixty items, representing relatively major, potentially stressful life events, such as "detention in jail or comparable institution," "marriage," and "serious illness or injury of close family member." Each respondent endorses each item that he has experienced in the past twelve months. Each item is rated on seven-point scale, ranging from -3 to $+3$. An event is rated negatively if the respondent experienced the stress as negative, with the severity of the negative event ranging from -1 (least negative) to -3 (most negative). An event is rated positively, from $+1$ (least positive) to $+3$ (most positive), if the respondent experienced the stress as positive. If the event occurred but the respondent experienced no impact, it is rated as 0. Thus for any given event, such as marriage, the respondent could rate it as a positive event, a negative event, or an event of no impact. Total scores can be obtained for both negative life events stress (total severity of all events that were rated as negative) and positive life events stress (total severity of all events that were rated as positive), each ranging from 0 to 180.

RESULTS

The results of the study revealed significant sex differences in perceived social support from friends and in enacted support, with women reporting more support in both cases, but no sex difference was found in perceived social support from family. Thus, hypothesis 1, predicting sex differences in all types of social support, was partially supported. Regarding measures of stress, there was a significant sex difference in hassles severity, with women reporting greater severity, but not in hassles frequency nor in life events stress. Thus, hypothesis 2, predicting sex differences in all measures of stress, was partially supported (see Table 20.1).

Correlations between social support and stress were computed, separately for women and men (refer to Table 20.2 for these statistics). Perceived social support from friends was negatively and significantly correlated with hassles frequency, hassles severity, and negative life events stress for women but not for men. Thus, for women, higher support from friends tended to be associated with lower stress. Perceived social support from family was negatively and significantly correlated with hassles frequency and negative life events stress for women but not for men. Hypotheses 3 and 4, predicting negative correlations between perceived support and both types of stress (hassles and life events) for women but not for men, were therefore almost completely supported.

Enacted support was not correlated with hassles frequency, hassles severity, or negative life events stress for either women or for men. Thus, hypotheses 5 and 6, predicting a positive relationship between enacted support and both types of stress for women but not for men, were not supported. However, enacted support was correlated positively with positive life events stress for men, but not for women, indicating that higher enacted support tended to be associated with a higher level of positive life events stress for men.

DISCUSSION

The results of this study support the idea that social support experiences, stress experiences (to some extent), and the relationship between social support and stress may be better understood in light of gender role

Table 20.1. Means and Standard Deviations on All Social Support and Stress Measures, for Women, for Men, and for the Total Sample

Variable	Range	Mean Total	SD Total	Mean Women	SD Women	Mean Men	SD Men	t
PSS-Fr	2–20	14.83	4.22	15.89	4.09	14.04	4.16	2.72**
PSS-Fa	0–20	13.43	5.45	14.02	5.77	12.99	5.19	1.14
ISSB	1.15–4.28	2.39	0.55	2.50	0.56	2.32	0.53	1.96*
Hassles-freq	5–99	41.35	17.28	43.73	17.69	39.61	16.88	1.43
Hassles-sev	1–2.86	1.45	0.33	1.55	0.40	1.38	0.24	3.36***
LES-neg	0–79	9.59	10.08	10.78	12.08	8.69	8.21	1.26
LES-pos	0–34	8.22	6.89	9.25	7.49	7.44	6.33	1.60

$^{*}p < .05$, $^{**}p < .01$, $^{***}p < .001$

Abbreviations:

PSS-Fr	perceived social support from friends
PSS-Fa	perceived social support from family
ISSB	enacted support (inventory of socially supportive behaviors)
Hassles-freq	hassles frequency
Hassles-sev	hassles severity
LES-neg	negative life events stress
LES-pos	positive life events stress
SD	standard deviation

Table 20.2. Correlations between Social Support and Stress for Women and Men

	PSS-Fr	PSS-Fa	ISSB	Hass-freq	Hass-sev	LES-neg	LES-pos
PSS-Fr	1.0	.48***	.12	-.39**	-.30*	-.36**	.16
PSS-Fa	.17	1.0	.24*	-.44***	-.20	-.30*	.20
ISSB	.35***	.15	1.0	.05	.19	.03	.21
Hass-freq	.03	-.12	.09	1.0	.55***	.53***	-.30*
Hass-sev	-.02	-.01	-.05	.21	1.0	.61***	-.06
LES-neg	-.00	-.17	.17	.50***	.30**	1.0	.04
LES-pos	.15	-.00	.36***	.27*	.02	.28**	1.0

*$p < .05$, **$p < .01$, ***$p < .001$

Note: Correlations above the diagonal are for women ($n = 65$); correlations below the diagonal are for men ($n = 89$). Three pairs of correlations between social support and stress for women and for men were significantly different from one another, determined by transforming the correlations to Fisher Z's and testing the Z's for significant differences: PSS-Fr and Hassles frequency ($r = -.39$ for women and $r = .03$ for men, $p < .01$); PSS-Fr and LES-neg ($r = -.36$ for women and $r = .00$ for men, $p < .05$); and PSS-Fa and Hassles frequency ($r = -.44$ for women and $r = -.12$ for men, $p < .05$).

Abbreviations:

PSS-Fr	perceived social support from friends
PSS-Fa	perceived social support from family
ISSB	enacted support (inventory of socially supportive behaviors)
Hassles-freq	hassles frequency
Hassles-sev	hassles severity
LES-neg	negative life events stress
LES-pos	positive life events stress

theories. As has been demonstrated in many studies, women have a general advantage over men in seeking and receiving social support, attributable in part to the socialization for relationships that girls undergo beginning in early childhood. The results of this research suggest that the social support advantage of women may extend beyond perceived support to actual supportive acts (enacted support).

Lessons Men May Learn from Women Regarding Social Support

Particular features or aspects of social support are especially beneficial. Uno et al. (2002) have discussed the importance of peer support. They found a relationship between quality of friendships and cardiovascular health. Given that both past research and the current study results indicate that women receive more support from friends than do men, this may be an area of support to target for men. Other researchers (e.g., Blazina & Marks, 2001) discuss the importance of peer support and suggest that men who have been socialized to be "tough" may have the potential to change this hypermasculine attitude through a behavioral method—recurrent exposure to social interactions that are emotional and characterized by disclosure, such as may occur in peer support groups.

Most social support and most stress measures were negatively correlated for women but not for men. A negative correlation between social support and stress can be interpreted in at least two ways. One possible interpretation is the *stress prevention model* (Barrera, 1986): Social support either prevents the occurrence of stressful conditions or reduces the perceived stressfulness of events. A second interpretation is the *support deterioration model* (Barrera, 1986): Stress deteriorates the perceived availability or the perceived effectiveness of social support. Studies that have followed peoples' experiences with social support and stress have supported both models; the Albany Area Health Survey is consistent with a support deterioration interpretation (Dean & Ensel, 1982; Lin & Dean, 1984; Lin, Dean, & Ensel, 1986; Lin & Ensel, 1984), and Lin's (1986) epidemiological study supported a stress prevention interpretation. Other interpretations that do not involve a direct causal relationship between social support and stress are also possible.

In the current study, it is not possible to determine the direction of the causal relationship between social support and stress nor to exclude the possibility that there is no direct causal relationship between support and stress. However, the negative correlation between social support and stress for women but not for men is robust in the current study; it exists for both types of stress and for both family and friend support. This finding is consistent with the general research results that women benefit more from social support than do men (a variant of the stress prevention model). It is possible that men are not as attuned to or sensitive to their social support resources and thus do not allow themselves to find comfort in these resources when they are under stress.

In a Stress and Coping class I teach, one coping technique I recommend to students, as suggested by Girdano, Dusek, and Everly (2005), is to "list your resources." Students are encouraged to take a few minutes to think about all of the resources they have in life: material, personal (one's positive personality characteristics), and sources of social support. Such an introspective exercise may be helpful for both women and men—especially men. Again, men may learn a lesson from women: appreciate those people who support you, and seek solace from them in bad times.

The Benefit of Enacted Support for Men

The positive correlation between enacted support and positive events for men was unpredicted but is thought-provoking. It suggests that a support network is present for men, providing supportive acts, during "good times" such as marriage, outstanding personal achievement, or a new job. Sharing in and assisting in one's good fortune are important functions of good relationships, a function that is somewhat neglected in the social support literature. Men may not be hesitant to seek support in general, but rather only when they are vulnerable; this interpretation is consistent with gender role theories. The current research results fail to support the idea that women utilize social support for positive events (although the results do not exclude this possibility). Future research could determine if these general and differential results for women and men repeat in other samples and, if they do, explore such findings more thoroughly.

Suggestions for Future Directions

A sex difference in reported stress emerged for women and men, as predicted by gender role theories and consistent with past research. That the only significant difference was in the most subjective report of stress (hassles severity) suggests that if stronger sex differences exist in adult women and men, they may not yet exist in college-age women. These young women have yet to experience the stress of a career, adult responsibilities with children and romantic relationships, and other adult stressors, which may be where sex differences in stress emerge more fully. Studying the developmental aspects of experiences of stress and ways they differ for males and females should prove to be a fruitful area of exploration.

A stress prevention interpretation of the negative correlation between social support and stress for women is consistent with gender role theories; women, in their focus on relationships, may be especially able to utilize relationship resources in order to cope with stress. However, as mentioned above, the direction of the causal relationship between social support and stress, if a direct causal relationship exists, has not been proven by the methodology used in the current study. Thus, future research could focus on further exploring the meaning of this negative correlation for women. For example, researchers could ask participants (especially women) about insights regarding the relationship between social support and stress for women, and the general lack of relationship between social support and stress for men. Since people may not be aware of why and how this relationship exists, however, other studies could employ a longitudinal design, examining whether, for women, social support tends to increase before stress decreases (support for the stress prevention model) or stress tends to increase before social support decreases (support for the stress deterioration model).

CONCLUSION

Gender role theories provide a helpful framework for understanding sex differences in social support and stress experiences. According to these theories, sex differences are determined largely by differences in socialization rather than by biological sex per se. Some recent social support research has supported this idea. Reevy and Maslach (2001) and Reevy and Malamud Ozer (2006) have found that gender-related personality variables, such as femininity, masculinity, nurturance, and self-confidence, are more predictive of social support than is being male or female. This research provides a hopeful message: anatomy is not destiny; presumably, the personality variables that predict social support can be learned.

REFERENCES

Bakan, D. (1966). *The duality of human existence.* Chicago: Rand McNally.

Barrera, M. (1986). Distinctions between social support concepts, measures, and models. *American Journal of Community Psychology, 14,* 413–445.

Barrera, M., Sandler, I. N., & Ramsay, T. B. (1981). Preliminary development of a scale of social support: Studies on college students. *American Journal of Community Psychology, 9,* 435–447.

Belansky, E. S., & Boggiano, A. K. (1994). Predicting helping behaviors: The role of gender and instrumental/expressive self-schemata. *Sex Roles, 30,* 647–661.

Berkman, L. F., & Syme, S. L. (1979). Social networks, host resistance, and mortality: A nine-year follow-up study of Alameda County residents. *American Journal of Epidemiology, 109,* 186–204.

Blazina, C., & Marks, L. I. (2001). College men's affective reactions to individual therapy, psychoeducational workshops, and men's support group brochures: The influence of gender-role conflict and power dynamics upon help-seeking attitudes. *Psychotherapy: Theory/Research/Practice/Training, 38*(3), 297–305.

Brannon, R. (1976). The male sex role: Our culture's blueprint for manhood and what it's done for us lately. In D. S. David & R. Brannon (Eds.), *The forty-nine percent majority: The male sex role* (pp. 1–45). Reading, MA: Addison-Wesley.

Cohen, L. H., McGowan, J., Fooskas, S., & Rose, S. (1984). Positive life events and social support and the relationship between life stress and psychological disorder. *American Journal of Community Psychology, 12,* 567–587.

Cohen, S. (1988). Psychosocial models of the role of social support in the etiology of physical disease. *Health Psychology, 7,* 269–297.

Cohn, S. (2000). *Race and gender discrimination at work.* Boulder, CO: Westview Press.

Coltrane, S., & Adams, M. (2001). Men, women, and housework. In D. Vannoy (Ed.), *Gender mosaics: Social perspectives* (pp. 145–154). New York: Roxbury.

Cutrona, C., & Russell, D. (1990). Type of social support and specific stress: Toward a theory of optimal matching. In B. R. Sarason, I. G. Sarason, & G. R. Pierce (Eds.), *Social support: An interactional view* (pp. 319–366). New York: John Wiley & Sons.

Dean, A., & Ensel, W. M. (1982). Modeling social support, life events, competence, and depression in the context of age and sex. *Journal of Community Psychology, 10,* 392–408.

Deaux, K., & LaFrance, M. (1998). Gender. In D. T. Gilbert, S. T. Fiske, & G. Lindzey (Eds.), *The handbook of social psychology* (4th ed., vol. 1, pp. 788–827). Boston: McGraw-Hill.

Flaherty, J., & Richman, J. (1989). Gender differences in the perception and utilization of social support: Theoretical perspectives and an empirical test. *Social Science & Medicine, 28,* 1221–1228.

Frank, E., Brogan, D., & Schiffman, M. (1998). Prevalence and correlates of harassment among US women physicians. *Archives of Internal Medicine, 158,* 352–358.

Gerber, G. L. (2001). *Women and men police officers: Status, gender, and personality.* Westport, CT: Praeger.

Girdano, D. A., Dusek, D. E., & Everly, G. S., Jr. (2005). *Controlling stress and tension* (7th ed.). San Francisco: Pearson/Benjamin Cummings.

Greenglass, E., & Noguchi, K. (2000). Longevity, gender, and health: A psychocultural perspective. In Y. Haruki (Ed.), *Proceedings of the First Asian Congress of Health Psychology, Tokyo, August 28–29, 2000.*

Heilman, M. E. (2001). Description and prescription: How gender stereotypes prevent women's ascent up the organizational ladder. *Journal of Social Issues, 57,* 657–674.

Holmes, T. H., & Rahe, R. H. (1967). The Social Readjustment Rating Scale. *Journal of Psychosomatic Research, 11,* 213–218.

House, J. S. (1981). *Work stress and social support.* Menlo Park, CA: Addison-Wesley.

House, J. S., Robbins, C., & Metzner, H. L. (1982). The association of social relationships and activities with mortality: Prospective evidence from the Tecumseh Community Health Study. *American Journal of Epidemiology, 116,* 123–140.

Kessler, R. C., McLeod, J. D., & Wethington, E. (1985). The costs of caring: A perspective on the relationship between sex and psychological distress. In I. G. Sarason & B. R. Sarason (Eds.), *Social support: Theory, research, and applications* (pp. 491–506). Dordrecht, The Netherlands: Martinus Nijhoff.

Lazarus, R. S. (1997). *Fifty years of the research and history of R. S. Lazarus: An analysis of historical and perennial issues.* Hillsdale, NJ: Erlbaum.

Lazarus, R. S., & Folkman, S. (1989). *Manual for the Hassles and Uplifts Scales.* Palo Alto, CA: Consulting Psychologists Press.

Lazarus, R. S., Kanner, A. D., & Folkman, S. (1980). Emotions: A cognitive-phenomenological analysis. In R. Plutchik & H. Hellerman (Eds.), *Theories of emotion* (pp. 189–217). New York: Academic Press.

Lin, N. (1986). Modeling the effects of social support. In Lin, Dean, & Ensel 1986, pp. 173–209.

Lin, N., & Dean, A. (1984). Social support and depression: A panel study. *Social Psychiatry, 19,* 83–91.

Lin, N., Dean, A., & Ensel, W. M. (1986). *Social support, life events, and depression.* Orlando, FL: Academic Press.

Lin, N., & Ensel, W. M. (1984). Depression-mobility and its social etiology: The role of life events and social support. *Journal of Health and Social Behavior, 25,* 176–188.

Miller, P., & Ingham, J. G. (1976). Friends, confidants, and symptoms. *Social Psychiatry, 11,* 51–58.

Perkins, H. W., & DeMeis, D. K. (1996). Gender and family effects on the "second-shift" domestic activity of college-educated young adults. *Gender & Society, 10,* 78–93.

Piko, B. (1998). Social support and health in adolescence: A factor analytic study. *British Journal of Health Psychology, 3,* 333–344.

Procidano, M. E., & Heller, K. (1983). Measures of perceived social support from friends and from family: Three validation studies. *American Journal of Community Psychology, 11,* 1–24.

Rabinowitz, V. C. (1996). Coping with sexual harassment. In M. A. Paludi (Ed.), *Sexual harassment on college campuses: Abusing the ivory power* (pp. 199–213). Albany: State University of New York Press.

Reevy, G., & Malamud Ozer, Y. (2006). How power dynamics and gender-related personality influence social support. Poster session presented at the annual convention of the American Psychological Association, New Orleans, August.

Reevy, G. M., & Maslach, C. (2001). Use of social support: Gender and personality differences. *Sex Roles, 44*(7/8), 437–459.

Robinson, D. (2001). Differences in occupational earnings by sex. In M. F. Loutfi (Ed.), *Women, gender & work* (pp. 140–149). Boston: Allyn & Bacon.

Roos, P. A., & Gatta, M. L. (1999). The gender gap in earnings: Trends, explanations, and prospects. In G. N. Powell (Ed.), *Handbook of gender and work* (pp. 95–123). Thousand Oaks, CA: Sage.

Sandler, B. R., & Shoop, R. J. (1997). What is sexual harassment? In B. R. Sandler & R. J. Shoop (Eds.), *Sexual harassment on campus: A guide for administrators, faculty, and students* (pp. 1–21). Boston: Allyn & Bacon.

Sarason, I. G., Johnson, J. H., & Siegel, J. M. (1978). Assessing the impact of life changes: Development of the Life Experiences Survey. *Journal of Consulting and Clinical Psychology, 46,* 932–946.

Schroeder, D. H., & Costa, P. T., Jr. (1984). Influence of life events stress on physical illness: Substantive effects or methodological flaws? *Journal of Personality and Social Psychology, 46,* 853–863.

Stokes, J. P., & Wilson, D. G. (1984). The inventory of socially supportive behaviors: Dimensionality, prediction, and gender differences. *American Journal of Community Psychology, 12*(1), 53–69.

Stroebe, W., & Stroebe, M. (1996). The social psychology of social support. In E. T. Higgins & A. W. Kruglanski (Eds.), *Social psychology: Handbook of basic principles* (pp. 597–621). New York: Guilford Press.

Uno, D., Uchino, B. N., & Smith, T. W. (2002). Relationship quality moderates the effect of social support given by close friends on cardiovascular reactivity in women. *International Journal of Behavioral Medicine, 9*(3), 243–262.

Wills, T. A. (1984). Supportive functions of interpersonal relationships. In S. Cohen & S. L. Syme (Eds.), *Social support and health* (pp. 61–82). New York: Academic Press.

Wohlgemuth, E., & Betz, N. E. (1991). Gender as a moderator of the relationships of stress and social support to physical health in college students. *Journal of Counseling Psychology, 38,* 367–374.

Yoder, J. D. (2001). Military women. In J. Worell (Ed.), *Encyclopedia of women and gender: Sex similarities and differences and the impact of society on gender* (pp. 771–782). San Diego: Academic Press.

Part V

Examples of Coping

Introduction to "Examples of Coping"

This fifth part of our book is a presentation of examples of coping. We have chosen descriptions of individuals coping with cancer, early-stage Alzheimer's disease, exam stress, and racism. The first three chapters illustrate a main point presented in the introduction to our book: when stressors are long-lasting, coping is a transactional process in which coping responses are reactive to the stress context. All four chapters well illustrate some of the principles of coping we have already discussed.

In Chapter 21, an excerpt from *It's Not about the Bike: My Journey Back to Life* (2001), international star cyclist Lance Armstrong openly and candidly describes his experience with testicular cancer, which spread to his lungs, his brain, and other parts of his body. He used many of the coping strategies discussed in Part IV. Throughout his experience, Armstrong enlisted both emotional and instrumental social support. He engaged in many forms of problem-focused coping, including proactively following the treatment advice of his doctors, seeking out information about cancer on the Internet and in libraries, and soliciting second opinions about his medical conditions. He exercised daily when he could. Shortly after diagnosis, Armstrong introspected about his value system and deeply held beliefs. He made a decision to be optimistic: to have faith in himself, his doctors, and his treatments. From that point on, as he describes it, the majority of his experience was filled with hope. He describes his use of humor during his hospital stay following brain surgery. In Armstrong's account, his approach to coping was both flexible and prolific. There is much to learn, and appreciate, about these and other ways that Armstrong managed his cancer.

The second chapter of this part, "Experiences in Early-Stage Alzheimer's Disease: Understanding the Paradox of Acceptance and Denial" (MacQuarrie, 2005), describes some of the psychological experiences, including coping processes, of early stage Alzheimer's disease patients. MacQuarrie's research participants presented an awareness of some aspects of the disease in themselves, accompanied by minimization and other forms of denial. The patients expressed frustration at losing some of their autonomy and general competencies. MacQuarrie explains that these apparently contradictory coping mechanisms utilized by the patients (acceptance and denial) have some purpose. The patients accept reality to a degree, but resist knowing in order to hold onto a sense of agency. These themes remained fairly consistent over the two times that MacQuarrie interviewed the patients, six months apart. This study represents a unique description of the experiences of early Alzheimer's disease patients.

The study of coping with illness has a long history, and coping processes for many common diseases and conditions have been subject to study. For example, before complex models about coping had been developed, Janis (1958) researched how patients cope with surgery. More than two decades later, Cohen (1980) produced a research review on the same topic. As other examples, Dunkel-Schetter, Feinstein, Taylor, and Falk (1992) have researched coping processes among people with cancer; Macrodimitris and Endler (2001) studied coping with diabetes; and Fleishman and Fogel (1994) researched coping with AIDS. Recently, Lazarus and Lazarus (2006) in their book *Coping with Aging*, have discussed theory and research on coping with a number of diseases or conditions associated with aging; the text also includes a number of case studies of individuals coping with various aspects of aging.

Zeidner reviews the research on test anxiety in the third chapter, an excerpt from his book *Test Anxiety: The State of the Art* (1998). As Zeidner discusses, coping responses and emotions have been studied both before and after exams, and to a lesser extent, during exams. The results indicate that both coping responses and emotions differ, depending upon whether the individual is in the anticipatory stage, the confrontation stage, the waiting stage, or the outcome stage of the exam. Zeidner also reviews research on the relationship between personality traits and coping with exams, and the relationship between coping and various outcomes, including anxiety and examination performance. He makes some tentative conclusions about coping with examinations. For example, coping with exams requires flexibility and a variety of coping strategies. Additionally, the effectiveness of any particular coping mechanism is dependent upon context.

In Chapter 24, "*The Black Scholar* Interviews Maya Angelou" (Chrisman, 1977), Angelou and Chrisman are engaged in a free-flowing dialogue that touches upon issues of race, work, and value systems. Angelou describes her perception of challenges faced by African Americans in the United States in the 1970s. Much of what she discusses remains relevant today. For example, she describes her feeling that, if she was rejected or slighted during daily experiences, she may have attributed these insults to her race. Her defensiveness in this regard was so habitual that she continued to experience slights as racially based even while living in Africa among Africans, where, as she states, she was probably not experiencing racial prejudice. Angelou talks about the value of commitments in her life, exemplifying the "commitment" aspect of hardiness. She is committed to her work, her marriage, and her son, and she speaks of these commitments with reverence and passion.

TERMS

The chapters in Part V include a number of technical terms. Can you define these terms? Definitions are included in the glossary in the back of the book.

General Stress and General Psychology Terms

- Affect
- Alzheimer's disease
- Appraisal
- Behavioral disengagement
- Emotion-focused coping
- Hardiness (including commitment, control, and challenge)
- Mental disengagement
- Problem-focused coping
- Self-efficacy
- Social support
- State anxiety
- Trait anxiety

Statistical or Research Methods Terms

- Dependent variable
- Factor analysis
- Independent variable
- Longitudinal study
- Moderation
- Path analysis
- Prospective study
- Regression
- Standard deviation

REFERENCES

Armstrong, L. (2000). *It's not about the bike: My journey back to life*. New York: G. P. Putnam's Sons.

Chrisman, R. (1977). *The Black Scholar* interviews Maya Angelou. *Black Scholar*, January/February, 52–67.

Cohen, F. (1980). Coping with surgery: Information, psychological preparation, and recovery. In L. W. Poon (Ed.), *Aging in the 1980s: Psychological issues* (pp. 375–382). Washington, DC: American Psychological Association.

Dunkel-Schetter, C., Feinstein, L. G., Taylor, S. E., & Falke, R. L. (1992). Patterns of coping with cancer. *Health Psychology, 11*, 79–87.

Fleishman, J. A., & Fogel, B. (1994). Coping and depressive symptoms among people with AIDS. *Health Psychology, 13*, 156–169.

Janis, I. L. (1958). *Psychological stress: Psychoanalytic and behavioral studies of surgical patients*. New York: John Wiley & Sons.

Lazarus, R. S., & Lazarus, B. N. (2006). *Coping with aging*. New York: Oxford University Press.

MacQuarrie, C. R. (2005). Experiences in early stage Alzheimer's disease: Understanding the paradox of acceptance and denial. *Aging & Mental Health, 9*(5), 430–441.

Macrodimitris, S. D., & Endler, N. S. (2001). Coping, control, and adjustment in Type 2 diabetes. *Health Psychology, 20*, 208–216.

Zeidner, M. (1998). *Test anxiety: The state of the art*. New York: Plenum Press.

CHAPTER 21

It's Not about the Bike: My Journey Back to Life

Lance Armstrong, with Sally Jenkins

I thought I knew what fear was, until I heard the words *you have cancer*. Real fear came with an unmistakable sensation: it was as though all my blood started flowing in the wrong direction. My previous fears, fear of not being liked, fear of being laughed at, fear of losing my money, suddenly seemed like small cowardices. Everything now stacked up differently: the anxieties of life—a flat tire, losing my career, a traffic jam—were reprioritized into need versus want, real problem as opposed to minor scare. A bumpy plane ride was just a bumpy plane ride, it wasn't cancer.

One definition of "human" is as follows: *characteristic of people as opposed to God or animals or machines, especially susceptible to weakness, and therefore showing the qualities of man*. Athletes don't tend to think of themselves in these terms; they're too busy cultivating the aura of invincibility to admit to being fearful, weak, defenseless, vulnerable, or fallible, and for that reason neither are they especially kind, considerate, merciful, benign, lenient, or forgiving, to themselves or anyone around them. But as I sat in my house alone that first night, it was humbling to be so scared. More than that, it was humanizing.

I wasn't strong enough to break it to my mother that I was sick. Not long after I arrived home from Dr. Reeves's office, Rick Parker came over because he didn't think I should be alone. I told Rick that I simply couldn't bear to call my mother with the news. "I don't want to tell her," I said. Rick offered to do it for me, and I accepted.

There was no gentle way to say it. She had just gotten home from work and was sitting outside in her garden, reading the paper, when the call came. Rick said, "Linda, Lance is going to need to talk to you about this himself, but I just want to let you know what's going on. He's been diagnosed with testicular cancer, and he's having surgery tomorrow at 7 A.M."

My mother said, "No. How can this be?"

Rick said, "I'm sorry, but I think you need to come down here tonight."

My mother began to cry, and Rick tried to comfort her, but he also wanted her to get on a shuttle to Austin as quickly as possible. My mother changed gears. "Okay," she said. "Okay, I'll be right there." She hung up without even speaking with me, and immediately threw whatever she could think of into a small bag and raced to the airport.

After Rick hung up from talking with my mother, I broke down again. Rick calmly talked me through it. "It's natural for you to cry," he said. "It's even good for you. Lance, this is curable. It's a speed bump. We need to get on with whipping this thing."

Shored up, I went into my study and I began to make calls to the other people I felt I needed to tell immediately. I called my friend and Motorola teammate Kevin Livingston, who was in Europe racing. Kevin was like a younger brother to me; we were so close that we had plans to get an apartment together in Europe the following season, and I had persuaded him to move to Austin to train with me. When I reached him in Italy, I still felt spaced out. "I have something to tell you—something bad has happened."

"What? Did something go wrong with a race?"

"I have cancer."

I wanted to tell Kevin how I felt and how urgently I wanted to see him, but he was in an apartment with three other members of the U.S. national team, and I didn't want them to know. So we had to talk in code.

"You know," I said.

He replied, "Yeah. I know."

And that was it. We got off the phone. The very next day, he was on a plane for home.

Next, I reached Bart Knaggs, perhaps my oldest and best friend in Austin, a former cyclist who was working for a start-up computer technology company. I found him at his office, where he was working late, like always. "Bart, I have testicular cancer," I said. Bart stammered, not sure what to say, and then he said, "Lance, they do wonders with cancer now, and I think if you have to get it, that's a good one to have."

I said, "I don't know. I'm sitting here alone in my house, man, and I'm really scared."

Bart, typically, entered a search command into his computer and called up everything there was to know about the disease. He sat there until late, researching testicular cancer, and printed out what he found until he had a pile a foot high. He called up clinical trials, studies, and treatment options, and downloaded it all. Then he gathered it up and drove over to my house. He had to go to Orlando early the following morning with his fiancée, Barbara, but he came by to tell me he loved me, and gave me all of the cancer material.

One by one, my friends and family began to arrive. Lisa came, after I paged her; she had been studying in the library and she was glassy-eyed with shock at the news. Next, Bill Stapleton arrived with his wife, Laura. Bill was a young attorney for a firm in Austin, and I had chosen him to represent me because he exuded loyalty. He was an ambling sort out-wardly, but he was a competitor, too, a former Olympic swimmer from the University of Texas who still had the look of an athlete. When he came in, I fixated on what I was sure was the loss of my career.

"I'm done racing," I said. "I won't need an agent anymore."

"Lance, we just need to deal with this one step at a time," Bill said. "You have no idea what this means, or what's going to happen."

"You don't understand, Bill. I'm not going to have an agent anymore. I'm not going to have any contracts."

"Well, I'm not here as an agent, I'm here as your friend. How can I help?"

It was one of those moments when everything shifted. I was obsessing over the fact that I was going to lose my career, when there were more important things to attend to.

"You can pick up my mother at the airport," I said.

Bill and Laura immediately got up from the sofa and drove to the air-port to get my mother. I was just as glad not to meet her flight, because as soon as she saw Bill, she broke down in tears again. "This is my baby," she told Bill and Laura. "How could this happen? What are we going to do?" But during the drive to my house, my mother collected herself. She was born without an ounce of self-pity, and by the time she reached my driveway she was strong again. As soon as she walked in the house, I met her in the center of the living room and gave her a bear hug.

"We're going to be okay," my mother said into my ear. "This isn't going to get us. We've had too many things to deal with. This is one thing that won't happen. Don't even try this with me."

We both cried a little then, but not for very long, because there was too much to discuss. I sat down with my friends and my mother and explained to them what the diagnosis from Dr. Reeves was. There were some issues to go over and some decisions to be made, and we didn't have much time, because I was scheduled for surgery at 7 A.M. I pulled out the X-ray that I'd brought home from Dr. Reeves and showed it to everybody. You could see the tumors, like white golf balls, floating in my lungs.

I was concerned about keeping the illness quiet until I'd had time to tell my sponsors and teammates. While I continued to talk to my mother, Bill called the hospital and asked that my diagnosis be kept confidential and that I be checked in under an assumed name. Also, we had to tell my sponsors, Nike, Giro, Oakley, and Milton-Bradley, as well as the Cofidis organization, and it would be necessary to hold a press conference. But first and foremost, I had to tell the people who were closest to me, friends like Och, and Chris, and my teammates, and most of them were scattered overseas and difficult to reach.

Everyone reacted differently to the news; some people stuttered, and some tried to reassure me, but what all of my friends had in common was their urge to come to Austin as quickly as possible. Och was at home in Wisconsin having dinner when I reached him, and his reaction was, in ret-rospect, pure him.

"Are you sitting down?" I asked.

"What's going on?"

"I've got cancer."

"Okay. What does that mean?"

"It means I've got testicular cancer and I'm having surgery tomorrow."

"All right, let me think about this," Och said, calmly. "I'll see you tomorrow."

Finally, it was time to go to bed. The funny thing was, I slept deeply that night. I went into a state of absolutely perfect rest, as if I was getting ready for a big competition. If I had a tough race in front of me, I always made sure to get the optimum amount of sleep, and this was no different, I suppose. On some unconscious level, I wanted to be in absolutely peak form for what I would be faced with in the coming days.

The next morning, I reported to the hospital at five o'clock. I drove myself there, with my mother in the passenger seat, and I walked through the entrance in a baggy sweat suit to begin life as a cancer patient. First came a series of basic tests, things like MRIs and blood work. I had a faint hope that the doctors would do all their tests and tell me they had been wrong, that my illness wasn't that serious. But those words didn't come.

I had never stayed overnight in a hospital, and I didn't know about things like registration, so I hadn't even brought my wallet. I guess I was always too busy throwing away my crutches and taking out my own stitches. I looked at my mother—and she immediately volunteered to take care of the paperwork. While I was having blood tests done, she filled out the stack of forms the hospital required.

I was in surgery and recovery for about three hours. It seemed like an eternity to my mother, who sat in my hospital room with Bill Stapleton and waited for me to come back. Dr. Reeves came by and told her that it had gone well; they had removed the tumor with no problem. Then Och arrived. True to his word, he had gotten on an early-morning plane for Austin. While I was still in surgery, my mom filled Och in on what was happening. She said she was determined that I was going to be okay, as if the sheer force of her will could make things all right.

Finally, they wheeled me back to my room. I was still foggy from the anesthesia, but I was alert enough to talk to Och as he leaned over my bed. "I'm going to beat this thing, whatever it is," I said.

The hospital kept me overnight, and my mother stayed with me, sleeping on a small sofa. Neither of us rested well. The aftermath of the surgery was very painful—the incision was long and deep and in a tender place, and every time my mother heard my sheets rustle, she would jump up and come to my bedside to make sure I was all right. I was hooked up to an IV, and when I had to go to the bathroom she helped me out of bed and wheeled the pole for me while I limped across the room, and then she helped me back to bed. The hospital bed had a plastic cover over the mattress, and it made me sweat; I woke up every couple of hours to find the sheets under my back were soaking wet, but she would dry me off.

The next morning, Dr. Youman came in to give me the initial results of the pathology reports and blood work. I was still clinging to my notion that somehow the cancer might not be as bad as we'd thought, until Dr. Youman began to tick off the numbers. He said it appeared from the biopsy and the blood tests that the cancer was spreading rapidly. It was typical of testicular cancer to move up the blood line into the lymph glands, and they had discovered some in my abdomen.

In the twenty-four hours since I'd first been diagnosed, I'd done as much homework as I could. I knew oncologists broke testicular cancer down into three stages: in stage one, the cancer was confined to the testicles and patients had excellent prognoses; in stage two, the cancer had moved into the abdominal lymph nodes; and in stage three, it had spread to vital organs, such as the lungs. The tests showed that I was stage three, with three different cancers in my body, the most malignant of which was choriocarcinoma, a very aggressive, blood-borne type that was difficult to arrest.

My chemo treatments would begin in a week, via a Grosjean catheter implanted in my chest, and they would last for three months. I would require so many blood tests and intravenous drugs that it was impractical to use standard individual IV needles, so the Grosjean catheter was unavoidable. It was frightening to look at, bulging under my skin, and the opening in my chest seemed unnatural, almost like a gill.

There was another piece of business to discuss: I would be at least temporarily sterile. My first round of chemotherapy was scheduled for the following week, and Youman advised me to bank as much sperm as possible before then. It was the first time the subject of sterility had come up, and I was taken aback. Youman explained that some chemotherapy patients recovered their virility, and some did not; studies showed about a 50 percent return to normalcy after a year. There was a sperm bank two hours away in San Antonio, and Youman recommended I go there.

That night, before we came home from the hospital, my mother went by the oncology unit and picked up all the supplies for my catheter, and my prescriptions for antinausea medications, and more literature on testicular cancer. If you've never been to an oncology unit, let me tell you—it can be unsettling. She saw people wrapped in blankets, with no hair, hooked up every which way to IVs, looking pale and deathly sick. My mother gazed around the unit as she waited for the supplies. When they came, she piled it all into a large canvas bag that became our traveling cancer kit and made her way back to my room. She said, "Son, I just want to let you know that when you go for your treatment, it's not a pleasant sight. But I want you to keep one thing in mind. They're all there for the same reason you are: to get well."

And then she took me home.

* * *

That afternoon, I walked into yet another nondescript brown brick medical building for my first chemotherapy treatment. I was taken aback by how informal it was: a simple waiting room with some recliners and La-Z-Boys and assorted chairs, a coffee table, and a TV. It looked like somebody's living room full of guests. It might have been a party, except for the giveaway—everybody was attached to his or her very own IV drip.

Dr. Youman explained that the standard treatment protocol for testicular cancer was called BEP, a cocktail of three different drugs, bleomycin, etoposide, and cisplatin, and they were so toxic that the nurses wore radioactive protection when handling them. The most important ingredient of the three was cisplatin, which is actually platinum, and its use against testicular cancer had been pioneered by a man named Dr. Lawrence Einhorn, who practiced at the Indiana University medical center in Indianapolis. Prior to Einhorn's discovery, testicular cancer was almost always fatal—twenty-five years earlier it had killed a Chicago Bears football star named Brian Piccolo, among many others. But the first man who Einhorn had treated with platinum, an Indianapolis schoolteacher, was still alive.

Had I lived twenty years ago, I would have been dead in six months, Youman explained. Most people think Piccolo died of lung cancer, but it started as testicular cancer, and they couldn't save him. He died in 1970 at the age of 26. Since then, cisplatin has become the magic bullet for testicular cancer, and Einhorn's first patient, the Indianapolis teacher, has been cancer-free for over two decades—on his anniversaries they have a big party at his house, and Dr. Einhorn and all his former nurses come to visit him.

I thought, *bring it on, give me platinum*. But Youman warned that the treatment could make me feel very sick. The three different anticancer toxins would be leaked into my system for five hours at a time, over five straight days. They would have a cumulative effect. Anti-emetics would be given to me along with the toxins, to prevent me from suffering severe nausea, but they couldn't curb it entirely.

Chemo is so potent that you can't take it every day. Instead it's administered in three-week cycles; I would take the treatment for one week, and then have two weeks off to allow my body to recover and produce new red blood cells.

Dr. Youman explained everything carefully, preparing us for what we were about to face. When he finished, I had just one question. It was a question I would ask repeatedly over the next several weeks. "What's the cure rate for this?" I asked. "What are my chances?"

Dr. Youman said, "Sixty to sixty-five percent."

My first chemo treatment was strangely undramatic. For one thing, I didn't feel sick. I walked in and chose a chair in the corner, the last one along a wall in a row of six or seven people. My mother kissed me and went off to do some errands, and left me with my fellow patients. I took my place among them.

She had prepared me to be disturbed by my first encounter with other cancer patients, but I wasn't. Instead, I felt a sense of belonging. I was relieved to be able to talk to other people who shared the illness and compare experiences. By the time my mother got back, I was chatting cheerfully with the guy next to me. He was about my grandfather's age, but we hit it off, and we were jabbering away when my mother walked in. "Hey, Mom," I said brightly. "This is Paul, and he's got prostate cancer."

I had to keep moving, I told myself. Every morning during that first week of chemo, I rose early, put on a pair of sweats and my headphones, and walked. I would stride up the road for an hour or more, breathing and working up a sweat. Every evening, I rode my bike.

Bart Knaggs returned from Orlando with a Mickey Mouse hat he had picked up at Disney World. He handed it to me and told me he knew I would need something to wear when I lost my hair.

We would go riding together, and Kevin Livingston often joined us. Bart made huge maps for us, as large as six feet in diameter. He would get maps of counties from the Department of Highways and cut and paste them together, and we would stand over them choosing new routes for ourselves, long winding rides out in the middle of nowhere. The deal was to always find a new road, someplace we hadn't been before, instead of the same old out-and-back. I couldn't stand to ride the same road twice. The training can be so monotonous that you need newness, even if half the time you end up on a bad piece of road or get lost. It's okay to get lost sometimes.

Why did I ride when I had cancer? Cycling is so hard, the suffering is so intense, that it's absolutely cleansing. You can go out there with the weight of the world on your shoulders, and after a six-hour ride at a high pain threshold, you feel at peace. The pain is so deep and strong that a curtain descends over your brain. At least for a while you have a kind of hall pass and don't have to brood on your problems; you can shut everything else out, because the effort and subsequent fatigue are absolute.

There is an unthinking simplicity in something so hard, which is why there's probably some truth to the idea that all world-class athletes are actually running away from something. Once, someone asked me what pleasure I took in riding for so long. "Pleasure?" I said. "I don't understand the question." I didn't do it for pleasure. I did it for pain.

Before the cancer, I had never examined the psychology of jumping on a bicycle and riding for six hours. The reasons weren't especially tangible to me; a lot of what we do doesn't make sense to us while we're doing it. I didn't want to dissect it, because that might let the genie out of the bottle.

But now I knew exactly why I was riding: if I could continue to pedal a bike, somehow I wouldn't be so sick.

The physical pain of cancer didn't bother me so much, because I was used to it. In fact, if I didn't suffer, I'd feel cheated. The more I thought about it, the more cancer began to seem like a race to me. Only the destination had changed. They shared grueling physical aspects, as well as a dependence on time, and progress reports every interval, with checkpoints and a slavish reliance on numbers and blood tests. The only difference was that I had to focus better and harder than I ever did on the bike. With this illness, I couldn't afford impatience or a lapse in concentration; I had to think about living, just making it through, every single moment. The idea was oddly restorative: winning my life back would be the biggest victory.

I was so focused on getting better that during that first round of chemotherapy, I didn't feel anything. Nothing. I even said to Dr. Youman, "Maybe you need to give me more." I didn't realize that I was extremely lucky in how my body tolerated the chemo. Before it was over, I would meet other patients who had uncontrollable vomiting after the first cycle, and by the end of my own treatments I would experience a nausea that no drug could get a grip on.

The only thing that suffered at first was my appetite. When you undergo chemotherapy, things taste different because of the chemicals in your body. My mother would fix me a plate of food, and she'd say, "Son, if you're not hungry and you don't want to eat this, it won't hurt my feelings." But I tried to eat. When I woke up from a nap, she would put a plate of sliced fruit and a large bottle of water in front of me. I needed to eat so I could keep moving.

Move, I told myself. I would get up, throw on my warm-up clothes, put my Walkman on, and walk. I don't even know how far. I'd walk up the steep hill and out of the front gates, and trudge on up the road.

As long as I could move, I was healthy.

* * *

I became a student of cancer. I went to the biggest bookstore in Austin and bought everything there on the subject. I came home with ten different volumes: diet books, books on coping emotionally, meditation guides. I was willing to consider any option, no matter how goofy. I read about flaxseed oil, which was supposed to be a "true aid" against arthritis, heart infarction, cancer, and other diseases. I read about soy powder, a "proven anticancer fighter." I read *Yoga Journal* and became deeply, if only momentarily, interested in something called The Raj, "an invitation to perfect health." I tore out pages of *Discover* magazine and collected newspaper stories on far-off clinics and far-fetched cures. I perused a pamphlet about the Clinic of the Americas in the Dominican Republic, describing an "absolutely certain cure for cancer."

I devoured what Bart had given me, and every time he called, I said, "What else you got?" I had never been a devoted reader, but now I became voracious. Bart went to Amazon.com and cleaned them out on the subject. "Look, do you want me to feed you what I find?" he asked.

"Yeah, I want everything. Everything, everything."

Here I was, a high school graduate who'd received an eclectic education in Europe, and now I was reading medical journals. I had always liked to study financial magazines and architectural-design magazines, but I didn't care much for books; I had an impossibly short attention span and I couldn't sit still for that long. Now all of a sudden I had to tackle blood counts and basic oncology. It was a second education, and there were days that I thought, *well, I might as well go back to school and try to become a doctor, because I'm becoming so well-versed in this.*

I sat on the sofa flipping through books, talking on the phone, reading off numbers. I wanted to know exactly what my odds were, so I could figure out how to beat them. The more research I did, the better I felt my chances were—even though what I was reading suggested that they weren't very good. But knowledge was more reassuring than ignorance: at least I knew what I was dealing with, or thought I did anyway.

There was an odd commonality in the language of cancer and the language of cycling. They were both about blood. In cycling, one way of cheating is to take a drug that boosts your red blood cell count. In fighting cancer, if my hemoglobin fell below a certain level, the doctors would give me the very same drug, Epogen. There was a baseline of numbers I had to meet in my blood tests, and the doctors measured my blood for the very same thing they measured in cycling: my threshold for physiological stress.

I mastered a whole new language, terms like *ifosfamide* (a chemotherapy drug), *seminoma* (a kind of tumor), and *lactate dehydrogenase* (LDH, another blood marker). I began to throw around phrases like "treatment protocol." I wanted to know it all. I wanted second, third, and fourth opinions.

I began to receive mountains of mail, get-well cards, best wishes, and off-the-wall suggestions for cures, and I read them all. Reading the mail was a way to keep from brooding, so in the evenings Lisa and my mother and I would sort through the letters and answer as many as possible.

One evening, I opened a letter with an embossed letterhead from Vanderbilt University's medical center. The writer was a man named Dr. Steven Wolff, the head of the bone marrow transplant department. In the letter, Dr. Wolff explained that he was a professor of medicine and an oncologist, as well as an ardent cycling fan, and he wanted to help in any way he could. He urged me to explore all the various treatment options and offered to be available for any advice or support. Two things about the letter drew my attention; the first was Wolff's obvious cycling knowledge, and the other was a paragraph that urged me in strong terms to get a second opinion from Dr. Larry Einhorn himself at Indiana University because he was the foremost expert on the disease. Wolff added, "You should note that there are equally effective chemotherapy treatments that could minimize possible side effects to not compromise your racing capabilities."

I picked up the phone and dialed Wolff. "Hi, this is Lance Armstrong," I said. Wolff was taken aback, but he recovered quickly, and after we exchanged a few pleasantries, he began a hesitant inquiry about my treatment. Wolff explained that he was reluctant to encroach on the authority of my doctors in Austin, but he wanted to help. I told him that I was on the standard treatment protocol for testicular cancer with lung metastasis, BEP.

"My prognosis isn't good," I said.

From that moment on, my treatment became a medical collaboration. Previously, I thought of medicine as something practiced by individual doctors on individual patients. The doctor was all-knowing and all-powerful, the patient was helpless. But it was beginning to dawn on me that there was nothing wrong with seeking a cure from a combination of people and sources, and that the patient was as important as the doctor. Dr. Reeves was my urologist, Dr. Youman my oncologist, and now Dr. Wolff became my friend and treatment advocate, a third medical eye and someone to whom I could turn to ask questions. Each doctor involved played a crucial role. No one person could take sole responsibility for the state of my health, and most important, I began to share the responsibility with them.

"What's your HCG level?" Wolff asked me.

HCG is the endocrine protein that stimulates women's ovaries, I had learned, and it was a telling blood marker because it should not be present in healthy males. I shuffled through the papers, looking at the various figures. "It says a hundred and nine," I said.

"Well, that's high," Wolff said. "But not extraordinary."

As I stared at the page, I saw another notation after the number.

"Uh, what's this 'K' mean?" I asked.

He was silent for a moment, and so was I.

"It means it's a hundred and nine thousand," Wolff said.

If a count of 109 was high, then what was *109,000?* Wolff began to ask me about my other marker levels, AFB and LDH. I shot questions back at him. "What does this mean?" I asked bluntly.

Wolff explained that there was too much HCG in my body, even with the lung tumors. Where was it coming from? He gently suggested that perhaps I should explore other therapies, more aggressive treatment. Then he let me have it: the HCG level automatically put me in the worst prognosis category.

Something else bothered Wolff. Bleomycin was extremely toxic on the liver and lungs, he explained. In his view, treatment was very personal; what might be right for one patient wasn't necessarily right for another, and for my case, bleomycin might be the wrong choice. A cyclist needs his lung capacity the way he needs his legs, and prolonged exposure to bleomycin would almost certainly end my career. There were other drugs, Wolff suggested. I had choices.

"There are some guys who are the world's best at treating this," Wolff said. He told me he was a friend of Einhorn and the other oncologists at the Indiana University medical center in Indianapolis. He also recommended two other cancer centers—one in Houston and one in New York. Moreover, he offered to arrange consultations for me. Immensely relieved, I accepted.

Once again, my mother leaped into action. By the next morning, she had gathered all of my medical records and faxed them to Houston and Indianapolis for the consults. I was out riding my bike at about 10 A.M. when a reply came from the Houston facility. Two doctors were on a conference call, both oncologists. My mother listened to two disembodied voices as they discussed my case with her.

"We've reviewed the information," one said. "Why haven't you had an MRI done on the brain?"

"Well, why would we need that?" my mother asked.

"His numbers are so high that we believe he has it in his brain, too," he said.

"You gotta be kidding me," my mother said.

"Normally when we see numbers like that, it's because it's in the brain. We feel he needs more aggressive treatment."

Stunned, my mother said, "But he just started chemotherapy."

"Look," one of them said, "we don't think your son is going to make it at this rate."

"Don't do this, okay?" she said. "I have fought for this child my entire life."

"We feel you should come down here immediately, and start treatments with us."

"Lance will be back in a little while," my mother said, shakily. "I'll talk to him, and we'll call you back."

A few minutes later, I walked in the door, and my mother said, "Son, I've got to talk to you." I could see that she was a wreck, and I had that familiar sinking sensation in my stomach. As my mother tremulously summarized what the doctors had said, I didn't respond, I just sat there silently—it seemed like the more serious matters grew, the quieter I became. After a minute, I calmly told her that I wanted to talk to the doctors myself and hear what they had to say.

I called them back, and I listened as they reiterated what they had already told my mother. Wearily, I told them that I wanted to go to Houston and see them as soon as possible. After I got off the phone, I paged Dr. Youman. I gave him a brief encapsulation of my conversation with the Houston doctors. "Dr. Youman, they think I have it in my brain. They say I should have a brain MRI."

"Well, I was going to have you in for one tomorrow," Youman said. "You're actually already scheduled for noon."

Dr. Youman told me that he had scheduled the MRI because he had been thinking along the same lines, that it had probably moved into my brain.

I called Steve Wolff and told him about the conversation. I said that I intended to go to Houston the next day. Steve agreed that I should go, but he again recommended that I also talk to the people at Indiana University, because it was the epicenter for dealing with testicular cancer. Everyone took their treatments from the protocols established by Einhorn, so why didn't I go straight to the source? Steve told me that Einhorn was traveling in Australia, but he offered to refer me to Einhorn's chief associate, Dr. Craig Nichols. I agreed, and he called Nichols to ask for a consultation on my behalf.

The next morning, I reported to the hospital for the MRI. For moral support, Lisa, my mother, and Bill Stapleton all came with me, and my grandmother flew in from Dallas as well. As soon as I saw Dr. Youman, I said fatalistically, "I fully expect that I have it in my brain. I already know that's what you're going to tell me."

A brain MRI is a claustrophobic procedure in which you are passed through a tunnel so tight that it practically touches your nose and forehead and makes you feel that you might suffocate. I hated it.

The results of the scan came back almost immediately. My mother and grandmother and Bill waited in the lobby, but I wanted Lisa with me in Dr. Youman's office. I gripped her hand. Dr. Youman took one look at the image and said, reluctantly, "You have two spots on your brain."

Lisa covered her eyes. I was braced for it, but she wasn't. Neither was my mother, who sat in the lobby waiting for me. I walked outside, and I simply said, "We need to go to Houston." That was all I had to say; she knew the rest.

Dr. Youman said, "Okay, why don't you go to talk to the Houston people. That's a very good idea." I already knew he was an excellent doctor, but now I appreciated his lack of ego. He would remain my local oncologist, and I would see him for countless more blood tests and checkups, but thanks to his generous spirit and willingness to collaborate with others in my treatment, he also became my friend.

Lisa and my mother could not keep from crying; they sat in the lobby with tears running from their eyes. But I was oddly unemotional. It had been a busy week, I thought to myself. I was diagnosed on a Wednesday, had surgery Thursday, was released Friday night, banked sperm on Saturday, had a press conference announcing to the world that I had testicular cancer on Monday morning, started chemo on Monday afternoon. Now it was Thursday, and it was in my brain. This opponent was turning out to be much tougher than I'd thought. I couldn't seem to get any *good* news: *It's in your lungs, it's stage three, you have no insurance, now it's in your brain.*

We drove home, and my mother composed herself and sat at the fax machine feeding more papers into it for the doctors in Houston. Lisa sat in the living room, seeming lost. I called Bart and told him about my plans. Bart asked if I wanted company on the trip, and I said yes. We would leave at 6 A.M. the next day.

But believe it or not, there was a certain relief in hearing the worst news yet—because I felt like that was the end of it all. No doctor could tell me anything more; now I knew every terrible thing in the world.

Each time I was more fully diagnosed, I asked my doctors hard questions. *What are my chances?* I wanted to know the numbers. My percentage was shrinking daily. Dr. Reeves told me 50 percent, "but really I was thinking 20," he admitted to me later. If he was perfectly honest, he would have told me that he nearly wept when he examined me, because he thought he was looking at a terminally ill twenty-five-year-old, and he couldn't help but think of his own son, who was my age. If Bart Knaggs had been totally candid, he would have told me that when his prospective father-in-law, who was a doctor, had heard that the cancer had moved into my lungs, he said to Bart, "Well, your friend is dead."

What are my chances? It was a question I would repeat over and over. But it was irrelevant, wasn't it? It didn't matter, because the medical odds don't take into account the unfathomable. There is no proper way to estimate somebody's chances, and we shouldn't try, because we can never be entirely right, and it deprives people of hope. Hope that is the only antidote to fear.

Those questions, *Why me? What are my chances?* were unknowable, and I would even come to feel that they were too self-absorbed. For most of my life, I had operated under a simple schematic of winning and losing, but cancer was teaching me a tolerance for ambiguities. I was coming to understand that the disease doesn't discriminate or listen to the odds—it will decimate a strong person with a wonderful attitude, while it somehow miraculously spares the weaker person who is resigned to failure. I had always assumed that if I won bike races, it made me a stronger and more worthy person. Not so.

Why me? Why anybody? I was no more or less valuable than the man sitting next to me in the chemo center. It was not a question of worthiness.

What is stronger, fear or hope? It's an interesting question, and perhaps even an important one. Initially, I was very fearful and without much hope, but as I sat there and absorbed the full extent of my illness, I refused to let the fear completely blot out my optimism. Something told me that fear should never fully rule the heart, and I decided not to be afraid.

I wanted to live, but whether I would or not was a mystery, and in the midst of confronting that fact, even at that moment, I was beginning to sense that to stare into the heart of such a fearful mystery wasn't a bad thing. To be afraid is a priceless education. Once you have been that scared, you know more about your frailty than most people, and I think that changes a man. I was brought low, and there was nothing to take refuge in but the philosophical: this disease would force me to ask more of myself as person than I ever had before, and to seek out a different ethic.

* * *

How do you confront your own death? Sometimes I think the blood–brain barrier is more than just physical, it's emotional, too. Maybe there's a protective mechanism in our psyche that prevents us from accepting our mortality unless we absolutely have to.

The night before brain surgery, I thought about death. I searched out my larger values, and I asked myself, if I was going to die, did I want to do it fighting and clawing or in peaceful surrender? What sort of character did I hope to show? Was I content with myself and what I had done with my life so far? I decided that I was essentially a good person, although I could have been better—but at the same time I understood that the cancer didn't care.

I asked myself what I believed. I had never prayed a lot. I hoped hard, I wished hard, but I didn't pray. I had developed a certain distrust of organized religion growing up, but I felt I had the capacity to be a spiritual person and to hold some fervent beliefs. Quite simply, I believed I had a responsibility to be a good person, and that meant fair, honest, hardworking, and honorable. If I did that, if I was good to my family, true to my friends, if I gave back to my community or to some cause, if I wasn't a liar, a cheat, or a thief, then I believed that should be enough. At the end of the day, if there was indeed some Body or presence standing there to judge me, I hoped I would be judged on whether I had lived a true life, not on whether I believed in a certain book or whether I'd been baptized. If there was indeed a God at the end of my days, I hoped he didn't say, "But you were never a Christian, so you're going the other way from heaven." If so, I was going to reply, "You know what? You're right. Fine."

I believed, too, in the doctors and the medicine and the surgeries—I believed in that. I believed in them. A person like Dr. Einhorn, that's someone to believe in, I thought, a person with the mind to develop an experimental treatment twenty years ago that now could save my life. I believed in the hard currency of his intelligence and his research.

Beyond that, I had no idea where to draw the line between spiritual belief and science. But I knew this much: I believed in belief, for its own shining sake. To believe in the face of utter hopelessness, every article of evidence to the contrary, to ignore apparent catastrophe—what other choice was there? We do it every day, I realized. We are so much stronger than we imagine, and belief is one of the most valiant and long-lived human characteristics. To believe, when all along we humans know that nothing can cure the briefness of this life, that there is no remedy for our basic mortality, that is a form of bravery.

To continue believing in yourself, believing in the doctors, believing in the treatment, believing in whatever I chose to believe in—that was the most important thing, I decided. It had to be.

Without belief, we would be left with nothing but an overwhelming doom, every single day. And it will beat you. I didn't fully see, until the cancer, how we fight every day against the creeping negatives of the world, how we struggle daily against the slow lapping of cynicism. Dispiritedness and disappointment, these were the real perils of life, not some sudden illness or cataclysmic millennium doomsday. I knew now why people fear cancer: because it is a slow and inevitable death, it *is* the very definition of cynicism and loss of spirit.

So, I believed.

* * *

When LaTrice came in to give me the chemo, no matter how sick I was, I would sit up and be as attentive as I could.

"What are you putting in me?" I'd ask. "What's the mix?"

By now I could read a chest X-ray as well as any doctor could, and I knew all the terms and antinausea dosages. I quizzed LaTrice on them and told her what felt better or worse from the standpoint of nausea. I'd say, "Try a little less of this," or, "Give me a little more of that."

I was not a compliant cancer patient. I was salty, aggressive, and pestering. I personalized the disease. "The Bastard," I called it. I made it my enemy, my challenge. When LaTrice said, "Drink five glasses of water in a day," I drank fifteen, draining them one after the other until the water ran down my chin.

Chemo threatened to deprive me of my independence and self-determination, and that was galling. I was tied to an IV pole for twenty-four hours a day, and it was a hard thing for me to cede control to my nurses and doctors. I insisted on behaving as if I was a full participant in the cure. I followed the blood work and the X-rays closely, and badgered LaTrice as if I were the Grand Inquisitor.

"Who are my nurses today, LaTrice?"

"What's that drug called, LaTrice?"

"What does that one do, LaTrice?"

I questioned her constantly, as if somehow I was the one in charge. LaTrice coordinated the chemo with the nurses on the unit: she made out my schedule and the anti-emetic regime and managed the symptoms. I kept track of everything, I knew exactly what I was supposed to get, and when, and I noticed every slight variation in the routine.

LaTrice adopted an air of exaggerated patience with me. This was a typical day for her:

"What dose am I getting, LaTrice?" I'd ask.

"What's that based on?"

"Am I getting the same thing as yesterday?"

"Why am I getting a different one?"

"What time do we start, LaTrice?"

"When do I finish, LaTrice?"

I made a game out of timing the completion of treatments. I would look at my wristwatch and stare at the IV bags as they emptied into my body by droplets. I tried to calculate the rate of drip and time the end of the treatment down to the last second.

"When, exactly, is my last drop, LaTrice?"

As the time went on, LaTrice and I developed a kidding relationship. I accused her of withholding anti-emetics out of cruelty. They were all that kept me from cringing with illness from the chemo. But I could only have a dose every four hours, so I'd hassle LaTrice for more.

"I can't give you more," she'd say. "You got it three hours ago, you've just got an hour left."

"Come on, LaTrice. You run the show around here. You know you can do it. You just don't want to."

Every once in a while, I'd give in to the retching and vomit so hard I thought I might pass out. "I feel much better now," I'd tell LaTrice, sarcastically, once I was through.

Sometimes food triggered me, especially breakfast food. Finally, I stopped them from bringing the tray at all. One morning I stared balefully at a plateful of eggs that seemed hopelessly gooey and toast that looked like plasterboard, and I exploded.

"What is this shit?" I said. "LaTrice, would *you* eat this? Look at this. You *feed* this to people? Can someone please get me something to *eat?*"

"Lance, you can have whatever you want," LaTrice said serenely.

LaTrice gave as good as she got. She would tease me back, even when I was too ill to laugh.

"Is it me, Lance?" LaTrice would ask with exaggerated sympathy. "Am I what's making you sick?"

I would just grin, soundlessly, and retch again. We were becoming friends, comrades in chemo. Between cycles, I went home to Austin for two-week rest periods to regain my strength, and LaTrice always called to check up on me and make sure I was drinking my fluids. The chemo could damage my urinary tract, so she was always after me to hydrate. One night she called when I was fooling around in my carport with a present from Oakley. It was a small remote-control car made out of titanium that could do up to 70 miles per hour.

"What's that loud buzzing noise?" she said.

"I'm in my garage," I said.

"What are you doing?" she said.
"I'm playing with my toy car," I said.
"Of course you are," she said.

* * *

On December 13, 1996, I took my last chemo treatment. It was almost time to go home.

Shortly before I received the final dose, Craig Nichols came by to see me. He wanted to talk with me about the larger implications of cancer. He wanted to talk about "the obligation of the cured."

It was a subject I had become deeply immersed in. I had said to Nichols and to LaTrice many times over the last three months, "People need to know about this." As I went through therapy, I felt increasing companionship with my fellow patients. Often I was too sick for much socializing, but one afternoon LaTrice asked me to go to the children's ward to talk to a young boy who was about to start his first cycle. He was scared and self-conscious, just like me. I visited with him for a while, and I told him, "I've been so sick. But I'm getting better." Then I showed him my driver's license.

In the midst of chemo, my license had expired. I could have put off renewing it until I felt better and had grown some hair back, but I decided not to. I pulled on some sweatclothes and hauled myself down to the Department of Motor Vehicles and stood in front of the camera. I was completely bald, with no eyelashes or eyebrows, and my skin was the color of a pigeon's underbelly. But I looked into the lens, and I smiled.

"I wanted this picture so that when I got better, I would never forget how sick I've been," I said. "You *have* to fight."

After that, LaTrice asked me to speak with other patients more and more often. It seemed to help them to know that an athlete was fighting the fight alongside them. One afternoon, LaTrice pointed out that I was still asking her questions, but the nature of them had changed. At first, the questions I had asked were strictly about myself, my own treatments, my doses, my particular problems. Now I asked about other people. I was startled to read that eight million Americans were living with some form of cancer; how could I possibly feel like mine was an isolated problem? "Can you believe how many people have this?" I asked LaTrice.

"You've changed," she said, approvingly. "You're going global."

Dr. Nichols told me that there was every sign now that I was going to be among the lucky ones who cheated the disease. He said that as my health improved, I might feel that I had a larger purpose than just myself. Cancer could be an opportunity as well as a responsibility. Dr. Nichols had seen all kinds of cancer patients become dedicated activists against the disease, and he hoped I would be one of them.

I hoped so, too. I was beginning to see cancer as something that I was given for the good of others. I wanted to launch a foundation, and I asked Dr. Nichols for some suggestions about what it might accomplish. I wasn't yet clear on what the exact purpose of the organization would be; all I knew was that I felt I had a mission to serve others that I'd never had before, and I took it more seriously than anything in the world.

I had a new sense of purpose, and it had nothing to do with my recognition and exploits on a bike. Some people won't understand this, but I no longer felt that it was my role in life to be a cyclist. Maybe my role was to be a cancer survivor. My strongest connections and feelings were with people who were fighting cancer and asking the same question I was: "Am I going to die?"

I had talked to Steve Wolff about what I was feeling, and he said, "I think you were fated to get this type of illness. One, because maybe you could overcome it, and two, because your potential as a human was so much greater than just being a cyclist."

At the end of my third cycle of chemo, I had called Bill Stapleton and said, "Can you research what it takes to start a charitable foundation?" Bill and Bart and another close friend and amateur cyclist, John Korioth, met with me one afternoon at an Austin restaurant to kick around some ideas. We had no idea how to go about launching a foundation or how to raise money, but by the end of the lunch we came up with the idea of staging a charity bicycle race around Austin. We would call it the Ride for the Roses. I asked if anyone would have time to oversee the project, and Korioth raised his hand. Korioth was a bartender at a nightspot where I had hung out some in my former life, and I would even take a turn as a guest bartender occasionally. He said his schedule would allow him to put some real time into it. It was the perfect solution: we didn't want a lot of overhead, and whatever we raised, we wanted to give straight back to the cause.

But I still wasn't clear on the basic purpose of the foundation. I knew that because my case was such a cause célèbre, people would listen, but I didn't want the foundation as a pulpit for me personally. I didn't think I was special—and I would never know how much a part of my own cure I was. On the meaning of it, I wasn't really clear. All I wanted to do was tell people, "Fight like hell, just like I did."

As I talked to Dr. Nichols about how I could help, I decided that I wanted the foundation to involve research. I was so indebted to Dr. Einhorn and Dr. Nichols for their erudition, I wanted to try to pay them back in some small way for all of the energy and caring that they and their staff had put into my well-being. I envisioned a scientific advisory board that would review requests for funding, decide which ones were the best and most worthy, and dole the money out accordingly.

But there were so many fronts to the cancer fight that I couldn't focus solely on one. I had a host of new friends who were involved in the fight, directly and indirectly—patients, doctors, nurses, families, and scientists—and I was beginning to feel closer to them than to some cyclists I knew. The foundation could keep me tied very closely to all of them.

I wanted the foundation to manifest all of the issues I had dealt with in the past few months: coping with fear, the importance of alternate opinions, thorough knowledge of the disease, the patient's role in cure, and above all, the idea that cancer did not have to be a death sentence. It could be a route to a second life, an inner life, a better life.

After the final chemo treatment, I stayed in the hospital for a couple more days, recovering my strength and tying up loose ends. One of the loose ends was my catheter. The day that it was removed was a momentous occasion for me, because I had been living with it for nearly four months. I said to Nichols, "Hey, can we take this thing out?"

He said, "Sure."

I felt a surge of relief—if he agreed to take it out, he must have been confident I wouldn't need it again. No more chemo, hopefully.

The next day an intern came to my room and removed that ugly, torturous device from my chest. But there were complications; the thing had been buried in me for so long that it had grown into my skin. The intern dug around, but couldn't get it out. He had to call in a more experienced doctor, who practically ripped it out of my chest. It was agony. I even imagined I heard a tearing noise as it came out. Next, the gash it left became infected, and they had to go back in and perform a day surgery to clean out the wound and sew me up again. It was awful, maybe the worst experience of the whole four months, and I was so mad when it was finally over that I demanded the catheter. I wanted to keep it, and I still have it, in a little Ziploc bag, a memento.

There was one more detail to discuss: Nichols gave me a final analysis of my health. I would have to go through a period of uncertainty. Quite often the final chemo treatment did not erase every trace of cancer, and I would need monthly blood tests and checkups to ensure that the disease was in full retreat. He warned me that my blood markers were not quite normal and my chest X-ray still showed signs of scar tissue from the tumors.

I was concerned. Nichols said, reassuringly, "We see it a lot. These are minor abnormalities, and we're highly confident they will go away." If I was cured, the scar tissue and markers should resolve themselves in time. But there was no guarantee; the first year was key. If the disease was going to come back, that's when we would see it.

I wanted to be cured, and cured now. I didn't want to wait a year to find out.

I went back home and tried to piece my life back together. I took it easy at first, just played a little golf and worked on plans for the foundation. As my system cleaned out, my body didn't seem broken by the chemo, I realized with relief. But I still felt like a cancer patient, and the feelings I'd held at bay for the last three months began to surface.

One afternoon I agreed to play a little golf with Bill Stapleton and another friend of ours named Dru Dunworth, who was a lymphoma survivor, at a club called Onion Creek. My hair hadn't grown back yet, and I wasn't supposed to get a lot of sun, so I put on one of those goofy caps that you pull down over your ears. I went into the pro shop to buy some balls. There was a young guy working behind the counter. He looked at me, smirking, and said, "Are you going to wear that hat?"

"Yeah," I said shortly.

"Don't you think it's warm out there?" he said.

I ripped the hat off so he could see that I was bald and scarred, and leaped across the counter.

"You see these fucking scars?" I snarled.

The guy backed away.

"That's why I'm going to wear that hat," I said. "Because I have cancer."

I pulled the cap on and I stalked out of the shop, so angry I was trembling.

I was tense, admittedly. I still spent a lot of time at the doctors' offices. I had blood drawn each week by Dr. Youman so the doctors in Indianapolis could keep track of me. I was constantly monitored. With an illness like cancer, monitoring is critical, and you live by the results, the blood work, CT scans, MRIs. You live by knowing your progress. In my case, I'd had a fast-growing cancer that had gone away quickly—but it could come back just as quickly.

One day after I had been back in Austin for a few weeks, LaTrice called Dr. Youman for the numbers. After she wrote them down, she took them to Dr. Nichols. He looked at the sheet of paper she had handed him, and he smiled and gave it back to her. "Why don't you call him this time," he said.

LaTrice dialed my home phone. Like I say, the numbers were all-important for me, and I would wait nervously by the phone for every result. I picked up right away.

"We got the blood counts back," LaTrice said.

"Yeah?" I said, nervously.

"Lance, they're normal," she said.

I held the thought up in my mind and looked at it: I was no longer sick. I might not stay that way; I still had a long year ahead of me, and if the illness returned it would probably happen in the next twelve months. But for this moment, at least for this brief and priceless moment, there wasn't a physical trace of cancer left in my body.

I didn't know what to say. I was afraid if I opened my mouth, nothing would come out but one long, inarticulate shout of relief.

"I'm so glad I can bring you good news," LaTrice said.

I sighed.

CHAPTER 22

Experiences in Early-Stage Alzheimer's Disease: Understanding the Paradox of Acceptance and Denial

Colleen R. MacQuarrie

How do people in the early stages of Alzheimer's disease (AD) experience their illness? The processes of awareness and coping are an enigma in much of the scientific literature surrounding AD. This is so even though dementia of the Alzheimer's type is the most prevalent dementia among people over the age of 65. A wealth of information about the biomedical aspects of the disease stands in counterpoint to the lack of systematic inquiry around the lived experiences of people with AD (Aggarwal et al., 2003; Stocker, 2002). The research described in this chapter contributes to knowledge about AD by focusing on the experiences of people who have recently been clinically diagnosed with possible or probable AD.

As the biomedical understanding of AD has become more detailed and technologically sophisticated, there has been a deterministic tendency to attribute the experience of people with AD exclusively to a disease process. There remains much individual variation in the outward symptoms of AD that a strictly biomedical model cannot explain. Explanatory value can be added if disease symptoms are understood to reflect not only a neurogenic but also psychological and sociohistorical processes (Cotrell, 1997; Cotrell & Schulz, 1993; Lebert, Pasquier, Souliez, & Petit, 1998; Lyman, 1989; Vittoria, 1998).

The cornerstone for this research, methodological hermeneutics, is an inductive approach to understanding and interpreting experiences of people with AD based on two semistructured interviews over a six-month period. Hermeneutics (Gadamer, 1975; Gergen, 1989; Heidegger, 1927; Packer & Addison, 1989; Ricoeur, 1979) as a qualitative interpretive methodology lends itself well to the research purpose of understanding the phenomenon of early-stage AD.

METHOD

Participants

Thirteen people (four women and nine men) recently diagnosed as early-stage AD patients, along with their spouses, participated in this six-month longitudinal study.[1] Participants lived within a six-hour radius of the study center. Criteria for inclusion of a dyad included:

1. Diagnosis within the last six months of possible/probable AD (Crockett, Tuokko, Koch, & Parks, 1989), communicated to the participant
2. Absence of fluent aphasia and ability to communicate in English
3. Minimum age of 50
4. Spouse as a primary caregiver
5. Spouse not diagnosed with a dementia

Rather than a specific cutoff score on a cognitive measure, a qualitative clinical assessment of cognitive impairment was used to determine eligibility. Twelve of the participants were recruited through the Clinic for Alzheimer Disease and Related Disorders. One was recruited through an advertisement in a newsletter for the Alzheimer's Society.

The clinic was the primary source for participants. Over a two-year period, 321 files were examined, thirty-nine (12%) of which fit the inclusion criteria. Of these thirty-nine, fourteen (36%) agreed to participate (two were pilot participants and did not go on to longitudinal analyses for this paper); thirteen (33%) refused; eight (21%) could not be contacted or were traveling; and four (10%) had been placed in extended care. Examining the thirteen refusals, caregivers' reasons for refusing to participate ranged from disinterest in the project to concern about the implications of participating.

Of the 321 files examined at the clinic, 282 (88%) were excluded because the diagnosis was not AD ($n = 120$, 43%), the AD person was too impaired ($n = 110$, 39%), there was no spousal caregiver ($n = 35$, 12%), or other reasons ($n = 17$, 6%) such as language.

Measures

A semistructured Transition Interview for Persons with Alzheimer's Disease (TIPAD) was developed to systematically gather information on a series of issues ranging across personal, social, and existential concerns. Personal questions examined self-image, adaptation, resilience, and coping. Social questions focused around relationships (spouse, family, friends) and examined conceptions of care and dependence. Existential questions looked at the meaning of the disease and the future in terms of hopes and fears. Topics were covered in a conversational format and, if not addressed specifically during the course of conversation, were returned to at the end of the interview (Mathieson, 1999).

Procedure

Interview

Following the family conference with the clinic's geriatrician, eligible clinic participants were mailed a contact letter and, within two weeks, follow-up phone calls to caregivers answered any questions about the research before inviting the couple to participate. Interested community participants responding to advertisements phoned on their own initiative. All interviews were in participants' homes at their convenience. After the informed-consent process, the caregiver spouse moved to a separate room while the AD person participated in a sixty-minute interview. For the six-month follow-up, the process was repeated.

Data Analysis

The researcher transcribed interviews using a two-step process. The first step, a verbatim record, was followed with an iteration to produce contextually enriched transcriptions (MacQuarrie, 2001). A constant comparative methodology (Burnard, 1991; Patton, 2002; Pieranunzi, 1997) was used to develop an organizing structure across the narratives. Open coding (Emerson, Fretz, & Shaw, 1995) of the transcriptions provided an overview of emergent topics and processes. Based on the open codings, participants' narratives were condensed into a set of thematic codes from which the constitutive organizing structure was developed (Pieranunzi, 1997). Theme definitions were written, and the original unmarked transcripts were recoded for key exemplars of the definitions.

Narrative Editing and Respect

Transcribed conversation will not flow as well-written prose. Therefore, to enhance the readability of the paper and to portray AD participants in the most respectful manner (Jones, 1997), the passages included here are edited. Unedited excerpts are available from the author. Editing involved removal of material superfluous to the central point of the passage, such as repetitive phrases. To facilitate the readability of quotations, information in brackets was added for sentence structure or clarification. All names have been changed to preserve anonymity.

RESULTS

Participants

Longitudinal study participants were four women and nine men diagnosed as possible or probable AD within the previous six months. The average age was 76.5 (*SD* [standard deviation] = 8.26; range, 60 to 89 years). Clinic records at diagnosis included a measure of cognitive functioning, the Mini-Mental State Exam (MMSE; Folstein, Folstein, & McHugh, 1975), that showed this to be a highly functioning group of AD participants with a mean MMSE of 22.4 (*SD* = 2.99; range, 17 to 26). Participants represented a range of occupations, with women in the study speaking about their work as secretaries, office clerks, homemakers, mothers, and grandmothers, and men describing their work as soldiers, laborers, engineers, financial consultants, fathers, and grandfathers.

Constitutive Theme: Dialectical Tension between Agency and Objectification

The narratives revealed a pervasive tension between remaining an independent agent even while processes were under way that objectified and undermined one's sense of personal competence. Table 22.1 shows the constitutive theme structure, Dialectical Tension between Agency and Objectification, that organized the narratives. This constitutive theme was composed of two second-order themes—Aspects of Acknowledgment, and Aspects of Resistance—each of which was constructed from subthemes of acknowledgment (Knowing, Feeling, and Doing) and resistance (Resist Knowing, Recontextualized Knowing, and Constructing the Agentic Self in the Face of Loss).

At the most abstract level, all narratives enacted an oppositional and dynamic tension that included both an agentic and an objectified self. Portrayals of an agentic self embraced aspects of autonomy reflective of the individual in charge of her or his own life. Conversely, depiction of an objectified self reflected a disempowerment process, where the person became redefined as a patient. The abstract dichotomy between agency and objectification was articulated throughout the narratives. Both acknowledgment and resistance themes captured how AD participants' patterns of understanding drew from positions of agency and objectification and gave rise to the paradox of speaking from standpoints of both

Table 22.1. Constitutive Theme Structure of Narratives: Agency–Objectification Dialectic

Constitutive Theme: Agency versus Objectification	
Second-Order Theme: Aspects of Acknowledgment	Second-Order Theme: Aspects of Resistance
Subtheme: Knowing	Subtheme: Resist Knowing
Subtheme: Feeling	Subtheme: Recontextualized Knowing
	• Minimization
	• Normalization
Subtheme: Doing	Subtheme: Constructing the Agentic Self in the Face of Loss
• In the Moment	
• Movement Away	• All That I Am: Pride & Enjoyment
• Movement Toward	• All That I Was: Pride & Enjoyment

acceptance and denial. Examination of interviews across time showed all participants illustrated both agency and objectification coexisting in the same narrative at both interviews.

Exemplars of the Dialectical Tension between Agency and Objectification

The tension between agency and objectification arises for people with AD because their autonomy has been threatened:

> So the kids got together and they decided that this [AD] is what it was. From there on, I wasn't going to go [for a diagnosis], I was going to fight it and say, "No way was there anything wrong with me!" but that's not the way it turned out to be. I have not yet [decided that it really is AD], and I'm not going to give in because, well, if it does, I have a good husband. He's come to all the times over at the AD clinic. But as it was the kids that dragged me into this, I don't know whether they're sorry about it now or not!
> *Q: Are you sorry about it?*
> No, I'm not sorry I went into it. That was your question, wasn't it?
> *Q: Yeah.*
> That I had gone ahead with it?
> *Q: Yeah.*
> [My husband] Isaac bullied me into that one, sort of, you know.

References to feeling bullied illustrated the tension around the diagnostic process in which this participant felt her autonomy was compromised. At the same time, fighting the process represented agency.

The disequilibria between the autonomous and the objectified selves were evident when participants with AD reflected upon the discrepancy of what they held to be true about themselves and what their family or friends held to be true. Participants were aware of a disjuncture between their and others' perceptions:

> But aside from that, I don't really have too much problem. At least, I don't. Maybe other people do. You know, maybe, the wife and my kids, they probably find a big change or something.

Shifts in the spectrum of control over one's life came with a redefinition of the spousal relationship that reflected compromised mutuality. This shift in mutuality played itself out in ways that were subtle yet profound: "A tough thing to live with is the overly protective." The burden on autonomy was not lessened by the fact that the AD spouse understood the vigilance: "[The] annoying thing is she keeps me under observation. Probably a lot to do with household survival."

Feeling objectified did not limit itself to the spousal relationship. It was also present in the services that participants utilized: "So, I'd like to be asked by the Handi Dart drivers how well am I on my feet (rather than) have this 200-pounder pick me up like a bag of potatoes and help me in! That's not help!" Some acts of care, no matter how well meaning, were interpreted by the recipients of care as a diminishment of their personhood. These acts worked to shift the balance toward objectification of the people the services were designed to benefit and were not perceived as helpful. This contributed to the tension between agency and objectification.

The issue for people with AD was one of control over their lives and of being full participants in matters concerning them:

> *Q: You're no longer driving?*
> No! No! That irked, that irked me! Oh, I was furious! It wasn't the idea of what they did. It was not to have talked to me, too! You know, like, say to me, "We think this is the best for you, and we will look after you."
>
> Like, if you need to go someplace, okay. And they've done that. But I didn't like the idea that they could just take those license and say, "Ha, ha, ha!" as my dear spouse [did]. [I don't know] whether they [the family] talked it over together or [what]. But it is not the fact of them taking the license, it was how it was done. So there's been a couple of little things like that that are really bad. But, I will say that they have been quite good about picking me up and taking me someplace. But that kind of aggravates you, too! 'Cause you can't spend all those years driving and not feel lost without it. My spouse is quite okay with that [driving places], but it's a real jolt. All of a sudden, it's like being locked up!

Thus, the struggle was not only with another loss of a sense of freedom but also with how the family was dealing with the challenges of ensuring safety in the face of the progression of the disease.

Participants with AD worked to assert control over areas of their life where their independence had been taken away:

> Initially they didn't want to compromise. Just stay in there and stay in the room. Basically they just keep an eye on me. And they didn't realize how quick I could slip a latch with a Swiss Army knife or a nail file or whatever.... Yeah, I said, if they can't bring the fireplace here, I'll have to go there (quiet laughter).

Assertions of independence in the face of restrictions illustrated the tension between agency and objectification:

> *Q: So you've noticed changes in your personality, then? I'd like to know about those.*
> I stand up for myself more. Like when [my spouse] says something about "We'll do it another time. We don't need them right now." Well, I mean, I might just say, "Well, I'm going out for a walk." And I'd end up down at the store buying what I want anyway. I mean that's my way of standing up for myself. Whether that's important or not, I don't know.
> *Q: Do you think it is?*
> Yes, because is keeps my independence. It makes me independent. Rather than have somebody say, "Well we will pick them up next week." That annoys me. 'Cause if I want them, I want them now.

In conclusion, the overarching theme that organized narratives was the tension between being an agent and being objectified. Agency meant independence and control over one's life. Objectification meant dependence upon others for care and losing autonomy over areas of life where one had previously been in control. This central organizing dialectical tension was expressed through second-order themes: Aspects of Acknowledgment and Aspects of Resistance. Acknowledgment and resistance worked together in the narratives in a complex interplay that reflected the person's struggles to cope with the disease as a paradox of understanding. In the following sections, these secondary themes will be highlighted.

Aspects of Acknowledgment

Acknowledgment was woven throughout the interviews as an understanding of the limitations of AD. All participants' narratives held forms of acknowledgment at both time points. Aspects of Acknowledgment were a series of interconnected subthemes that corresponded to Knowing, Feeling, and Doing.

Knowing

The Knowing subtheme was comprised of specific references to AD or its symptoms. It reflected an understanding that the participant is not what he or she used to be, that there were changes taking place, and that something was amiss.

Participants acknowledged their struggles with AD in a variety of ways. Narratives began with the diagnostic process, and the storied reactions to the diagnosis are reported elsewhere as ranging from relief to resistance (MacQuarrie, 2001). Participants talked about the impact that AD has had and continued to have in their lives. However, AD was not a central focus for most participants. Indeed, for some participants, part of acknowledging they had the disease was to see it as just a part of life now. "It's now I feel it's the natural thing for me to have that Alzheimer's." However, symptoms could challenge participants' sense of worth, "Well, I think that I'm stupid."

Participants spoke about the daily annoyances and hassles that came with memory loss.

> I can look up somebody's name, go to the phone book, once I've got the number, I've forgotten whose name I'm looking for. And you get into a cycle like this, about four or five steps long, a closed loop. The mind does funny things to you. In this situation, your memory, you feel that somebody or something is pulling strings and gaming with you. And I remember things back in the Second World War, Korean War, all of them avidly. Read, I've worked in electronics all my life, and this is largely a memory game. And the last sixty seconds are a real problem. Remembering what was going on, I mean, I can lose a phrase or lose a word in the middle of a phrase. And oh, it'll turn up perhaps nine or ten o'clock tonight (quiet laugh). So in that respect, it's a bit chaotic.

Participants confided the limitations that come with disorientation to one's surroundings.

> It's more than a little turned around. It's pretty serious. But it happens. As I say, I always find them. But people think, "Well, what are you wasting so much time for? How come you've been away for ten minutes?" Or something like that. But they don't know that I been just mixed up.

Relationships with others were also affected. Some participants spoke about their facades when dealing with others: "Oh. No, it's not easy. No. This is a false face. A lot of it is false. Here this laughing or anything like that, a lot of it is false." Some participants acknowledged their relationship with their spouse had been changed as a result of their limitations:

> Yeah I probably deserved it anyway if she did say something.
> *Q: I'm just trying to get a sense of what you're going through memory-wise and whether it's had any impact on your relationship.*
> Oh, I imagine it would because I'm not adhering to everything that I should be paying attention to or something like that. It's going out of me.

In addition to the daily lived impact of the disease, participants spoke about the future impact of the disease: "The House of False Lies! Well, I think the worst is yet to come (sniffs)."

Thus participants explicitly acknowledged they knew they had the disease or problems associated with it in a myriad of ways. Some used the term *Alzheimer's*, while others preferred to communicate from the standpoint of symptoms.

Feeling

The Feeling subtheme reflected an emotional awareness that something was wrong. Candor in emotional acknowledgment was notable, so coding for feeling used participants' words or explanations of feelings.

In coping with their disease, all participants expressed a range of emotions. Annoyance, anger, hurt, shock, sadness, and exasperation were common sentiments: "I can't even think! That's disgusting to me." Participants spoke about frustration when they cannot remember how to do things they had done for years and about feeling limited by their disease: "I'm really trapped as far as I feel."

Many participants expressed fears and feelings of dread: "And the thing that's so bad is, when I'm laying there, I can't think of anything. See, if I look at this or this (picks up a piece of paper), you know? Yeah. It's kinda scary to me, yeah. Oh, yeah, and I know I'm nearing something. And I'll hate going out or anything." Fears about disorientation in public were expressed: "Well, that part is a little bit frightening, when all of a sudden you find yourself, you know, what do I do? Like, where am I? Or what?" Feelings of humiliation in front of others were part of their experiences: "This is the worst part, when I lose my train of thoughts and stand there like an idiot!" and "It gets a little bit embarrassing." Participants spoke about feelings of resentment at the changes, "Really, it cheeses me off. [I feel] resentful sometimes."

Doing

The Doing subtheme illustrated how all participants showed aspects of acknowledgment in how they dealt with their losses and challenges. These strategies were actions that acknowledged changes or symptoms and ways to cope with them. Strategies were of three forms: In the Moment, Movement Away, and Movement Toward.

In the Moment

In-the-Moment communication strategies were described or illustrated by participants in the interview. Often participants used several strategies in one passage, which is predictable given their desire to communicate their thoughts to me and my interest in understanding their perspectives. The strategies included two categories: self and others.

Self-strategies described the process for word finding:[2] "Just dig. (Exhales.) Dig till you find a word if you get ahmm ... (two-second pause) ... if ah ... (two seconds) ... a word, a word path to it isn't going, isn't going anywhere, then do a long dogleg." Pausing to try to recollect words, stretching out verbalizations, and reflecting on their struggles were common occurrences:

> And we just turn loose with ahhhh ... (4 seconds) ... I was going to tell you her name ... it'll come ... (9 seconds) ... ohhhh it's ... (6 seconds) ... oh, I'll tell it to you when it comes back.
> *Q: That's okay.*
> Anne! (said with finality and confidence).

Sometimes participants used an open methodical approach to self-question and answer: "He's got two ah ... he's got a girl and a boy ... over there ... he's ... is that all there is? Yeah, I think there's just ah ... there's Shannon ... no Shannon's Pat ... (laughs) Shannon's my daughter over here (laughs). ..."

Participants monitored their words to ensure they were communicating what they intended: "But I know that's not the (laughs through words) proper word but (inhales) ... but ahh we've got a flock of great-grandchildren. A flock doesn't sound right (laughs through words) but we've got quite a number."

In addition to the self-strategies described above, participants used strategies that involved others. A common one was appealing to another for recall assistance—"I believe ... three years ... three ... (three seconds) what's in between? (laughs)"—or enlisting the help of their spouse: "I'll have to ask her the name. Go, go, give a shout and ask her what it, what it is."

Participants used others to help structure their communications: "(inhales) ... umm ... (six seconds) ... Now what else? ... (four seconds) ... I'm trying to think (laughs through words) of what else. I have to have somebody ask me the question, okay? You ask them. 'Cause then it's easier for me to say." Encouraging others to give them a structure was a strategy used by participants to keep their interactions going.

During the interview, participants were resourceful in their communications. They used household communication props such as family photos, mementos, and collections as reminders. Some participants were quite theatrical in reenacting and illustrating points with body movements and gestures in addition to words.

Movement Away

Participants described Movement Away coping strategies of delimiting their involvement based on an awareness of limitations. Participants spoke about how easily they could be upset and how they coped: "Well I've gotta walk away! Get away!" In removing themselves, some confided: "I probably am making excuses myself by shunning people, you know, too many people away, stepping away from them. I'm shunning them." Withdrawal was attributed to a reduction in confidence:

> Yeah, another bad thing is I find now that I don't want to speak to anybody in here [the housing complex]. Because I can't talk to them soon as they talk.
> Q: 'Cause you're not recognizing who they are or ...?
> No, I know everybody. But their names are all gone.

Other aspects of Movement Away were witnessed in participants' decisions to relinquish activities, as in this response to a question about driving:

> No, I gave that up as soon as I knew what my problem was. I stopped right then, because that's when I'm phasing everything out that could hurt anybody on my behalf.

An important aspect of relinquishing activities centered around participant's agentic assertions that they made the decision:

> Q: So when you had to give up traveling with the Service Club ...
> Oh, I didn't have to. Nobody stopped me. I did it myself.
> Q: When you decided to do that, how did that affect how you felt about yourself?
> Well, I felt relieved. I'll miss going up there. [But if I were working in the souvenir booth,] it would be, "Who gave me that ten-dollar bill?" You feel that you don't want that to happen.

To the extent it enables the perception that withdrawal was one's own decision and not imposed from others, Movement Away can promote feelings of agency and delimit objectification.

Movement Toward

Participants illustrated Movement Toward strategies by reaching out for help, assistance, and support with the disease. There were two different categories: informal and formal.

The informal genre involved communication about the disease with others. Participants' first level of communication occurred within their family, usually before diagnosis, and typically with a spouse: "Yeah, and she said to me, 'What's the matter?' I says, 'I don't know where I am!'" Communication then expanded to include children, other family members, and friends.

Beyond one's immediate familial circle, participants described how "eventually you just have to tell your friends, 'Sorry, I've been having some memory problems lately.'" This openness may have been a way to continue enjoyment of interactions with friends: "My best hope is to be able to live more to be able to continue with my friendships, I guess." A participant described her friend's persistent support when she was reluctant to return to their group following an embarrassing episode where she'd had a hallucination: "[She said to me,] 'Yes, you are coming back.' I mean, she knows how much I enjoy the mornings because they're just a super bunch of women that sit down and talk."

Participants acknowledged that their dependence on others was connected to security and was within the context of compromised mutuality: "So if we're going somewhere, I always make sure that, this situation that I'm in, that I want somebody to, if I get turned around or something, to come looking for me." Reliance upon one's spouse, often based on need, was common, as this participant affirmed: "I've got to."

Movement Toward strategies also involved reaching out to more formalized services for information and support, including wandering registry bracelets: "I ought to get one." For some participants, this included extensive reading on the topic of Alzheimer's etiology, research, and cure, "Yes! I read and tear out every little thing you can on the paper. And that helps, too, a lot of it! ... So, like to me, if somebody said, 'Hey something is on about Alzheimer's,' I'd drop everything and, of course, I want to see, too." In some cases, reading material was purchased for family members so they could become more comfortable discussing the disease: "A paperback, *When Someone You Love Has Alzheimer's.*"

Connected to the formalized aspect was the attendance or interest in support groups for people with AD.

> *Q: Have you received all the information that you wanted to about Alzheimer's?*
> Actually, I haven't. No, I don't think so.
> *Q: What kind of information would you like? Do you have questions that you want answers to?*
> Is there a place in town for people to congregate to discuss their own problem with somebody else that's got something similar?

Another aspect to the formalized Movement Toward form of acknowledgment involved thinking about leaving a legacy by donating one's body to science or participation in research: "I have volunteered myself to these particular things [drug and research trials] that may run out on me, but it may help somebody else someday."

In conclusion, all participants illustrated diverse ways of acknowledging the disease in their lives. The next section demonstrates how participants also spoke paradoxically from the standpoint of resistance as they balanced between agency and objectification.

Aspects of Resistance

Aspects of Resistance were characterized along three general subthemes: Resist Knowing, Recontextualized Knowing, and Constructing Agency in the Face of Loss. All participants' narratives illustrated forms of resistance at both time points.

Resist Knowing

Resistance to knowing was centered around disavowal of problems or limitations. In a most basic sense, these passages may be understood as variations on the theme of denial. Some participants did not construct AD as particularly relevant to their experiences: "No. I don't have any trouble with my memory. I don't have any trouble with my memory! People, other people might have trouble with my memory, but I don't have any trouble.... As far as I'm concerned, Alzheimer's is not bothering me at all!"

By our second interview, a participant's story of reactions provided some clarity around resistance:

First senses are no. No way. I don't have such a thing! You know? I mean, this is how your first reaction is. I'm just tired. I've had a bad day. Or something that really upset me very much about the same time when I started. I mean, it was just one of those things. No. I don't. That's not me. I didn't! I don't want that! You know, as if you could just go up and brush it aside. Because anybody that knows the word, I think they know what it is, but you deny it!

Some participants were willing to discuss current experiences with AD but resistance was apparent in discussions about decisions for the future: "I don't really worry too much about the [future], you know, I don't trouble trouble unless trouble troubles you. You know. I tried not to think about these things at all!"

In order to resist discussion, participants sometimes deferred the question to another member of their family. The deferral directed the conversation away from the topic of the impact of the disease: "No. I can't say that anything's changed with me. No. You'd have to ask my wife, ask my kids, ask my friends."

Recontextualized Knowing

Most participants used a form of resistance whereby limitations were noticed, but their implications were recontextualized using strategies of minimization and normalization.

Minimization

The most prevalent strategy to Recontextualized Knowing was to diminish the impact of the symptoms. Participants downplayed the impact by contextualizing the frequency or intrusiveness of symptoms: "I just forget things now and again, but it's not, it's more of a natural forgetting, you know. It's not a big upheaval or anything like that."
They dismissed lapses:

> I don't know. It's hard to say, because if you forget something, what is it they say? Forget, I forget, I forgot, I forget, I forget and don't give a damn, and it's a little bit like that for me!

Participants revalued the lost attribute: "But I've never had a good memory, so I won't cry over that one!" Or they revalued their needs: "I don't really have too much to remember." They tended to attribute a symptom to situations rendering the perceived impact more transient than chronic and perhaps less threatening: "The only time that I really forget or anything is if I'm challenged."

Normalization

Another way symptoms were recontextualized was through an attribution strategy of normalization of the effects of the disease. Describing AD, participants included friends as also having memory problems, but it was nothing out of the ordinary, "Everybody has problems with memory, nobody's perfect." Participants used age attribution as another normalization tactic: "And it wouldn't at all surprise me that I have some symptoms of what people call Alzheimer's. I mean, after all, I'm well into my 80s. When does it start? And you grow older obviously."

Constructing Agency in the Face of Loss

All participants used a self-affirming strategy of Constructing Agency in the Face of Loss so that resistance was enacted through a construction of the self as agentic even as autonomy was being undermined through losses. This theme held the dimension of time: present (All That I Am: Pride and Enjoyment) and past (All That I Was: Pride and Enjoyment). Countering the processes of objectification with the promotion of an agentic self was a key aspect of resistance. Pride in one's past or present competencies, accomplishments, and familial and community connections formed the cornerstone for these forms of resistance.

All That I Am: Pride and Enjoyment

This category embraced the diverse ways participants celebrated aspects of their current selves in the context of an interview about their experiences with AD. By talking about their abilities, participants with AD performed acts of resistance to the disease and pushed against an undermining of their agency in a disease process. This resistance to the disease through bolstering pride in one's present agentic status was especially prevalent with regard to issues of independence and self-determination:

> I mean, as far as I'm concerned, I'm in complete control of my own. Whatever I want, intend to do, I get it done, and if I don't want to do it, I don't do it, and so on. So, I don't have any sense of having lost control of my actions or my thoughts or anything like that, if that's what you do if you've got Alzheimer's. I—you must have some trait. What are the traits of Alzheimer's?

Participants elaborated a range of activities they pursued. There was no verification of whether participants could actually do the activities, as their pride with involvement was the important element: "I do all the cleaning of the house. That keeps me going." Another participant's account was reflective of mastery in using an official-sounding way to describe his role in doing the laundry, "I've also got a driver's license for a three-speed washer." Discussion of interests bolstered agency: "Well, I like books. I don't like these slack stories. I'm still interested even now in mechanics. But not mechanics as in car mechanic. I don't mean that. I've still got a lot of tools in here (gestures to head)."

Walking was a central aspect in many participants' lives:

> And the thing is, I've got to walk! People don't really understand that. But anyway, I definitely have to. And I'm honored I have good health. And I can buzz these hills with my two legs faster than anybody else can, and boy, I can go!

All That I Was: Pride and Enjoyment

This theme encompassed those aspects of reminiscence that worked in the interview to resist loss of an agentic self. Reminiscence took the function of avoiding present difficulties while bringing forward a focus that constructed the self as competent. Reflecting on a past vital self, self-status was enhanced by orienting discussion to areas where participants held considerable confidence and could claim authority in their memories. Therefore the discussion reflected both an enactment of resistance through demonstrated recall and a logic of the moment whereby past competence is held to demonstrate current competence. The reification of one's past to portray a present competent self included reminisced physical prowess as well as intellectual involvement, and most were in connection with a work identity. For example, in the context of a question about dependencies within the home, one participant used his work identity to describe how after "thirteen years in the armed forces, I know what it is to clean barracks!" The function in the interview was to ensure that I knew there was much more to the person in front of me than someone with AD. The reminiscence was an important part of how the person with AD was able to push against the loss of an agentic self.

DISCUSSION

Speaking about their experiences, participants in the early stages of Alzheimer's disease portrayed a system of understanding not previously articulated in the AD literature. This system of understanding was organized around a dialectical tension between agency and objectification. The tension was voiced according to themes of resistance and acknowledgment working together in a spoken paradox of understanding. The paradox of speaking about AD from opposing standpoints exists because of the AD person's assertion of agency in the face of a disease that systematically undermines abilities and status and pushes toward objectification.

Acknowledgment of the disease consisted of components reflective of agency as well as objectification. Participants described their knowing about the disease with stories of loss that undermined agency. Juxtaposed to the loss were participants' agentic affirming actions in the interview and their stories of the choices and the decisions they have made. These sub-themes of acknowledgment illustrated agentic forms of engagement and withdrawal, as both were important ways to explain how they dealt with their experiences.

Resistance also contained exemplars of this dialectical tension between objectification and agency. Resistance was often the push against processes and situations of objectification. Reframing the symptoms of the disease through minimization and normalization strategies presses against the objectifying process of being identified as a patient with a disease. However, resistance was also the movement of embracing and promoting moments of agency.

Several findings from this research are relevant to the AD literature. First, the way in which people understand and communicate about their disease in the postdiagnostic early stages of AD is more complex than previously indicated. The research can serve as a guide to theorists and community care networks alike around a paradox of understanding. The paradox was that people in the early stages of AD demonstrated a variety of ways they acknowledged their disease, even when they would not use the term *Alzheimer's* to categorize their experiences. However, they also simultaneously held tenaciously to aspects of resistance, which appeared to contradict their acknowledgment. Hence the paradox of simultaneously acknowledging and resisting the disease emerged as a key finding. The contradiction was a paradox that worked to illustrate the central challenge of the preservation of self as able to act in the world while simultaneously experiencing symptoms with implications for objectification.

Without understanding the dialectic underlying these narratives, the paradox of symbiotic acknowledgment and resistance might be dismissed as artifacts of the neurogenic disease process underlying AD. This would miss the opportunity to better understand how people deal with a disease where they continue to experience themselves as agentic throughout a neurological and social transition process that undermines agency.

While participants readily acknowledged limitations, they also simultaneously constructed them as arising in specific situations. Thus participants engaged in a conversation about their experience with symptoms and how they were coping and also described how they resisted the implications. The convergence of these oppositional tendencies is the paradox of understanding and illustrates how people with early-stage AD experience their disease.

This research suggests the paradox of understanding was not merely an artifact of a neurogenic block to awareness, but rather was part of a system for dealing with this disease. Although this requires further empirical work to test it, there are several reasons to speculate that the paradox is not an artifact. First, the mean MMSE (Folstein et al., 1975) score (22.5) indicated a highly functioning group of participants. Second, the hermeneutic analyses systematically examined the interviews, and this paradox emerged from that process. The interviews held an overall coherency of using acknowledgment and resistance in functional patterns. If it were merely a neurogenic block, then it is unlikely these functional ways of using acknowledgment and resistance would have emerged across the narratives and consistently across time. Finally, a neurogenic block based on neuronal plaques would suggest more permanency in the resistance than was the case in the narratives for this research. Regardless of whether the paradox is an artifact of the neurological deterioration or represents a common process for people dealing with a terminal disease, it nonetheless describes the way in which people in the early stages of the disease spoke about their illness.

This research builds upon previous work around denial. Other theorists had suggested that denial of memory problems and attempts to cover up mistakes were examples of coping behaviors in AD participants (Cotrell, 1997). The current research locates denial and other acts of resistance as part of a system of understanding which balances tensions between agency and objectification. In this system, resistance is not static, as participants' narratives also illustrated acknowledgment. This work suggests that grouping reactions into a category of acceptance or denial misses the way people deal with their disease. For example, a participant's description of how she did not yet accept the diagnosis but was actively engaged in finding out as much information as she could about her disease shows this point. It is not from static categories of acceptance or denial that people understand their disease but rather through positioning themselves as agents against objectification. In this dynamic system, because acknowledgment and resistance are both important positions that people use strategically to explain their experiences, they coalesce within the same time frame.

This research contributes to literature that suggests empirically derived measures of personality changes in early-stage AD likely include elements reflective of both neurogenic as well as psychosocial processes (Aggarwal et al., 2003; Cotrell, 1997; Vittoria, 1998). Thus some of the constructs that are studied as personality change in AD are likely an interaction of the person with the disease and her or his psychosocial environment. For example, voluntary withdrawal from activities was understood by some participants as a strategy for coping with the changes taking place. From the perspective of the participant, this was a strategic reaction to the neurogenic changes, not a sign of being controlled by the deterioration process.

This research also illustrates the importance of the perspective of the person with AD in the characterization of care. One strength in the research was hearing the AD person's account of what "caring behavior" means. Caregivers need to be attuned to the dynamics of how care is offered and to be cognizant of the dialectic between agency and objectification. Care that respects the dialectic tension between agency and objectification needs to provide a range of options, including the AD person in making decisions as appropriate.

Limitations

It is also important to highlight some of the limitations of the current research. The highly selective sample was comprised of people who were able to access a diagnostic testing clinic. Further, the selection criteria were stringent so that over a two-year period only 12 percent of the patients tested at the clinic were eligible for inclusion. Granted, almost 43 percent of these did not have a diagnosis of possible or probable AD. However, in 39 percent of files, the AD person's level of impairment excluded them from participating in the research, and another 12 percent were excluded because they did not have a spousal caregiver. Caregivers were the first point of contact for the research. Almost as many caregivers refused as agreed to participate (13 versus 14). This refusal rate is comparable to those within medical research, where recruitment of participants is an ongoing challenge for researchers (Trauth, Musa, Siminoff, Jewell, & Ricci, 2000).

The results of the current research reflect the high level of functioning of the AD participants, their interest in speaking about the disease, and their spousal caregiver's willingness to participate in research. Specifically, it may be that people who want to participate in research are also more likely to articulate aspects of acknowledgment, while those who refuse to participate in research may be less so. Also, the people who participated were able to communicate; people whose communication abilities were too low for an interview-based research study were systematically excluded. In order to conduct an experiential analysis with early-stage AD participants, you need a select sample who have received a diagnosis, who are high in their verbal functioning, and who are interviewed in a setting that enhances their communication strengths. All three issues represent a challenge to any research project in this area.

Future Research

This study has several implications for future research. To date, there has been little focus on the AD person's awareness of and experiences with their disease in the AD literature. However, the gradual deterioration over time with AD makes awareness of abilities in the early stages a relevant construct and a plausible central consideration for research on how people live with the disease. In addition, given the sociohistorical ambience surrounding memory and aging, personal vigilance is likely to be heightened in the early stages of the disease. This heightened vigilance makes insight into the disease process as experienced by people with AD an important phenomenon.

As the disease progresses and insight diminishes, awareness may become a less relevant construct. Therefore, the system of understanding described in this current research is unlikely to be a useful schema for individuals in the latter stages of AD, where insight is lost. Research into the system of understanding will become vital as researchers, the pharmaceutical industry, and health systems develop, promote, and distribute drugs that slow the progression of AD and maintain people in the early to mid-stages of the disease for prolonged periods. Along with clinical trials research to test drugs to slow the progression of the disease, corollary research should shed light on how the extended period of mild to moderate dementia is handled by people with the disease and their caregiving networks both during and after pharmaceutical interventions.

This study illustrates the importance of conducting qualitative exploratory research, especially where concepts may be less well defined. Until more is known about the complexity of experiences, operationalization of constructs for early-stage AD will likely be inadequate. Both the acknowledgment and resistance second-order themes illustrated the multifaceted aspects to acceptance and denial. Thus this research showed how a qualitative approach can contribute to better understanding the transition process for people in the early stages of AD.

Primary concerns for future research should be the care context, the impact of AD on the marital relationship, and how this is connected to the quality of care. Caregiving research is notable not only for its lamentation of the strains of providing care in general (Schulz, O'Brien, Brookwala, & Fleissner, 1995) but also for its endorsement of the personal growth opportunities inherent in the process of providing care (Farran, Graham, & Loukissa, 2000; Marks, Lambert, & Choi, 2002; Paun, 2003). Mixed into the complexity of outcomes of providing care is the complexity of receiving care, and little research has focused on this dynamic. A superordinate research question embedded in care research concerns the definitions of *caregiver* and *receiver* used to guide the research. How is the reciprocity of the spousal relationship altered so that one member is consistently perceived as the caregiver and the other is perceived as the care recipient, and does this dichotomy exist in natural environments or is it an artifact of how information is collected and categorized for research?

Of special concern is the spousal care context. One of the enduring findings from the literature is that compromised psychiatric health is a common outcome for caregivers of people with dementia (Schulz et al., 1995). No research has examined how a depressed caregiver spouse influences the mood and behaviors of their spouse with AD and the AD person's ability to cope with the disease. Gwyther (1990) illustrates the clinical utility of enabling a spouse to "responsibly finish" rather than separate from a marital bond in the context of AD. Research is needed to determine how the meaning-making system changes over time, how some spousal caregivers come to hold more tightly to the role of caregiver than do others, and what influence this has on the quality of care experienced by care recipients. The perspective of the person with AD is reported in only one study investigating perceptions of the marital relationship. Wright (1991) examined the impact of AD on the marital relationship by comparing couples in which there was no dementia to those in which dementia was present. Incongruence about the quality of their relationship was found between spouses in the AD group such that persons with AD held more positive views of the relationship than did their spouses. This incongruence was attributed to the fact that the AD spouse either was unable to perceive a problem or distorted the interactions. Since an integral component of the relationship is missing if the perspectives of care recipients are not included as part of the analysis, future work would be strengthened with the perspectives of both caregivers and receivers. Key questions remaining to be answered revolve around the impact a declining relationship may have on care recipients in the quality of care and how this differs among the various care contexts that exist.

In conclusion, the major contribution of this research was an understanding of why people with Alzheimer's disease speak about their experiences using positions of both acceptance and denial. Another contribution was the demonstration of the feasibility of longitudinal home-based interviews with people in the early stages of AD. These interviews formed the foundation for the analyses and enabled an understanding of the tensions underlying how people experience AD. Central to the narratives was the balance between maintaining an agentic self, even while processes were under way that undermined agency and promoted objectification. This is part of a body of work in dementia research that seeks to uncover some of the lived experiences of people with AD.

NOTES

1. Data collected from spouses will be reported in future publications on dyadic patterns of coping across time.

2. Full, unedited quotes are used in this section to illustrate the nonverbal aspects of these strategies and to fully portray the context of In-the-Moment strategies.

REFERENCES

Aggarwal, N., Vass, A. A., Minardi, H. A., Ward, R., Garfield, C., & Cybyk, B. (2003). People with dementia and their relatives: Personal experiences of Alzheimer's and of the provision of care. *Journal of Psychiatric and Mental Health Nursing, 10*, 187–197.

Burnard, P. (1991). A method of analysing interview transcripts in qualitative research. *Nurse Education Today, 11*, 461–466.

Cotrell, V. (1997). Awareness deficits in Alzheimer's disease: Issues in assessment and intervention. *Journal of Applied Gerontology, 16,* 71–90.

Cotrell, V., & Schulz, R. (1993). The perspective of the patient with Alzheimer's disease: A neglected dimension of dementia research. *Gerontologist, 33,* 203–211.

Crockett, D. J., Tuokko, H., Koch, W., & Parks, R. (1989). The assessment of everyday functioning using the Present Functioning Questionnaire and the Functional Rating Scale in elderly samples. *Clinical Gerontologist,* 8, 3–25.

Emerson, R. M., Fretz, R. I., & Shaw, L. L. (1995). *Writing ethnographic fieldnotes.* Chicago: University of Chicago Press.

Farran, C. J., Graham, K. L., & Loukissa, D. (2000). Finding meaning in caregivers of persons with Alzheimer's disease: African American and white caregivers' perspectives. In G. T. Reker & K. Chamberlain (Eds.), *Exploring existential meaning: Optimizing human development across the life span* (pp. 139–156). Thousand Oaks, CA: Sage.

Folstein, M. F., Folstein, S. E., & McHugh, P. R. (1975). "Mini-mental state." A practical method for grading the cognitive state of patients for the clinician. *Journal of Psychiatric Research, 12,* 189–198.

Gadamer, H. (1975). *Truth and method* (D. E. Linge, trans.). Berkeley: University of California Press.

Gergen, K. J. (1989). The possibility of psychological knowledge: A hermeneutic inquiry. In Packer & Addison 1989, pp. 239–258.

Gwyther, L. P. (1990). Letting go: Separation-individuation in a wife of an Alzheimer's patient. *Gerontologist, 30,* 698–702.

Heidegger, M. (1927). *Being and time.* Reprint (J. Macquarrie & E. Robinson, trans.), San Francisco: Harper, 1962.

Jones, S. J. (1997). Reflexivity and feminist practice: Ethical dilemmas in negotiating meaning. *Feminism & Psychology, 7,* 348–353.

Lebert, F., Pasquier, F., Souliez, L., & Petit, H. (1998). Frontotemporal behavioral scale. *Alzheimer Disease and Associated Disorders, 12,* 335–339.

Lyman, K. A. (1989). Bringing the social back in: A critique of the biomedicalization of dementia. *Gerontologist, 29,* 597–605.

MacQuarrie, C. (2001). Experiences in early-stage Alzheimer's disease. Dissertation, Simon Fraser University, Burnaby, BC.

Marks, N. F., Lambert, J. D., & Choi, H. (2002). Transitions to caregiving, gender, and psychological well-being: A prospective U.S. national study. *Journal of Marriage and Family, 64,* 657–667.

Mathieson, C. M. (1999). Interviewing the ill and the healthy: Paradigm or process? In M. Murray & K. Chamberlain (Eds.), *Qualitative health psychology: Theories and methods* (pp. 117–132). London: Sage.

Packer, M. J., & Addison, R. B. (1989). *Entering the circle: Hermeneutic investigation in psychology.* New York: State University of New York Press.

Patton, M. Q. (2002). *Qualitative research and evaluation methods* (3rd ed.). Thousand Oaks, CA: Sage.

Paun, O. (2003). Older women caring for spouses with Alzheimer's disease at home: Making sense of the situation. *Health Care for Women International, 24,* 292–312.

Pieranunzi, V. (1997). The lived experience of power and powerlessness in psychiatric nursing: A Heideggerian hermeneutical analysis. *Archives of Psychiatric Nursing, 11*(3), 155–162.

Ricoeur, P. (1979). The model of the text: Meaningful action considered as a text. In P. Rabinow & W. M. Sullivan (Eds.), *Interpretive social science: A reader* (pp. 73–101). Berkeley: University of California Press.

Schulz, R., O'Brien, A. T., Brookwala, J., & Fleissner, K. (1995). Psychiatric and physical morbidity effects of dementia caregiving: Prevalence, correlates, and causes. *Gerontologist, 35*, 771–791.

Stocker, K. (2002). The personal experiences of coping with brain disease: A neglected area of research. Diss. University of Massachusetts *Abstracts International Section A: Humanities & Social Sciences, 62*, 3892.

Trauth, J. M., Musa, D., Siminoff, L., Jewell, I. K., & Ricci, E. (2000). Public attitudes regarding willingness to participate in medical research studies. *Journal of Health & Social Policy, 12*, 23–43.

Vittoria, A. K. (1998). Preserving selves: Identity work and dementia. *Research on Aging, 20*, 91–136.

Wright, L. K. (1991). The impact of Alzheimer's disease on the marital relationship. *Gerontologist, 31*, 224–237.

Coping with Test Situations: Resources, Strategies, and Adaptational Outcomes

Moshe Zeidner

Over the past decade an increasing number of empirical studies have investigated the various ways students cope with stressful social evaluative situations and the impact of coping on adaptational outcomes. Several well-conceived and implemented studies have explored students' appraisals, coping behaviors, and emotions across various phases of a stressful examination encounter.

STAGES OF A STRESSFUL EVALUATIVE ENCOUNTER

Current research suggests that coping with an evaluative encounter is a complex process, with significant changes in the use of various coping strategies across the stages of the evaluative encounter (Folkman & Lazarus, 1985). How do appraisals and coping responses unfold across the various phases of the stressful encounter?

Research by Folkman and Lazarus (1985) suggests that during the *anticipatory stage*—the preparatory phase prior to the exam—an individual becomes aware of an upcoming exam. Examinees are typically concerned about how best to prepare for the upcoming exam and how to regulate feelings and aversive emotions associated with the exam, as well as with the prospects for success on the exam. Since ambiguity is expected to be at its height during the anticipatory stage—because examinees do not know exactly what will be on the exam or what the outcome will be like— the possibilities for both positive and negative outcomes can be seen. This means that examinees can experience both threat and challenge emotions at the early stages of an exam encounter. Problem-focused activities would be considered to be adaptive at this stage, since something still can be done to enhance the prospects for success, while at the same time, emotion-focused coping would be needed to help alleviate the tensions and anxieties surrounding performance.

At the *confrontation stage*, examinees actually confront the stressor, that is, take the exam. Very few studies have assessed objectively how students actually feel and think about the exam at this critical stage, under "in vivo" evaluative conditions. Examinees would be expected to employ a variety of coping strategies, including task-oriented and palliative coping techniques, to handle the stress evoked during the exam.

During the *waiting stage*, uncertainty about the specific nature and qualities of the test and test atmosphere has been resolved or meaningfully reduced, and feedback cues from the examination may help examinees predict their exam performance reasonably well. However, individuals may still feel apprehension about the outcome. A decrease in instrumental coping would be expected at this stage (as little can be done to improve one's chances of success on the exam), along with a concomitant increase in emotion-focused coping to release built-up tension.

During the *outcome stage*, after grades are posted, students finally learn how well they performed on the exam. Any uncertainty about the outcome is resolved at this stage, and the concerns of students turn to the significance of what has already happened and its implications (harm, benefit). The more an encounter unfolds over time, the more firmly the examinee should be making either a negative or positive appraisal of the outcome. Students who succeed on the exam would be expected to be happy and experience an uplift, no longer needing to cope with the exam. By contrast, those who do poorly would be expected to become increasingly anxious and moody and engage in increased coping.

APPRAISALS AND EMOTIONS IN AN EVALUATIVE ENCOUNTER

Coping theory predicts that as the person's appraisal of a stressful encounter changes, so, too, will the associated emotions (Lazarus & Folkman, 1984). Recently, a number of studies have corroborated these predictions, showing that anxiety is in flux during various phases of an examination. Bolger (1990) assessed anxiety and coping in a sample of 150 students surrounding an important medical admissions exam. Data were collected at four points in time: five weeks before the exam, ten days before the exam, two and a half weeks after the exam, and thirty-five days after the exam. Almost all students reported heightened anxiety in the last several days before the exam, though there were marked differences in exactly when anxiety peaked; for some, it was the same day as the exam, whereas for others, it was as many as four days beforehand. Similar results were obtained for high school students (Lay, Edwards, Parker, & Endler, 1989).

Table 23.1 depicts the type of emotions, both positive and negative, expected to be prominent prior to and following an exam. As shown, the

Table 23.1. Anticipatory and Outcome Emotions in an Evaluative Encounter

	Timing	
Emotional valence	Before exam	After exam
Positive	Challenge	Benefit
Negative	Threat	Harm

Source: After Lazarus & Folkman (1984).

anticipatory emotions *threat* and *challenge* are expected to be prominent prior to the exam, whereas the outcome emotions *harm* and *benefit* are expected to be prominent afterward. Folkman and Lazarus (1985) reported that the intensity of anticipatory emotions (threat and challenge) decreases significantly from the postexam to the postgrade stage in college students. By contrast, outcome emotions (harm and benefit) increased significantly from the anticipatory to the postexam stage—but did not change after that. Furthermore, practically all the students (94%) reported both threat and challenge emotions prior to the exam, implying that during conditions of maximum ambiguity (i.e., before taking the exam), both types of emotions are likely to be expressed.

These data were replicated, in part, by Carver and Scheier (1994) in their prospective study on coping with exams and adaptational outcomes. Data were gathered on situational coping in a student population, along with four classes of appraisal: *threat* ("worried," "fearful," "anxious"), *challenges* ("confident," "hopeful," "eager"), *harm* ("angry," "disappointed," "guilty"), and *benefit* ("pleased," "happy," "relieved"). Appraisals and coping were assessed at the anticipatory, waiting, and postexam stages. Figure 23.1 presents the mean level of appraisals found in this study for the three phases of the exam. It can be seen that threat and challenge emotions were relatively high during the anticipatory stage of the threatening encounter, but fell off after the exam—particularly after grades were posted. By contrast, harm and benefit emotions increased significantly from postexam to after posting of grades. While threats and challenges were found to concur during the anticipatory or preparation stage, reflecting the anticipation of divergent future outcomes, harm and benefit emotions were inversely related, fitting the idea that these emotions reflect a sense that one or the other outcome has come to pass.

Research conducted by Smith and Ellsworth (1987) on a sample of eighty-six Stanford University students sheds additional light on the blend of emotions experienced by examinees during various stages of a stressful examination encounter. Students described their cognitive appraisals and emotions just before taking a college midterm psychology exam and again after receiving grades on the exam. The majority of college students in their study experienced two or more emotions during both stages. A combination of the *anticipatory* emotions of hope, challenge, and fear was the most common blend experienced prior to the exam. After the exam, by

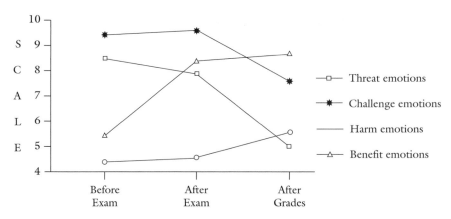

Figure 23.1. Emotions at Three Stages of the Test Situation
Source: Based on data presented in Carver & Scheier (1994).

contrast, the patterning was more varied: Anger, guilt, and fear combined in a variety of ways, with happiness co-occurring with hope and challenge. Subjects reported feeling considerably more hopeful, challenged, and fearful before taking the exam than they did after receiving their grades. Furthermore, subjects saw the exam as more difficult and important before they took it than they did after seeing their grades. Conversely, subjects reported higher levels of anger, happiness, and guilt after than before the exam. After receiving feedback about their performance (i.e., grades), subjects were more likely to evaluate their situation as both unfair and attributable to someone else. During the anticipatory stage, the experience of positive emotions did not preclude that of negative emotions. However, after posting of grades, positive emotions (e.g., happiness) were negatively correlated with negative emotions (i.e., ratings of fear, anger, and anxiety).

Research has evidenced a complex pattern of relations between appraisals and emotions in the test situation, as clearly demonstrated by the work of Carver and Scheier (1994) mentioned above. Appraisals and coping were assessed at the anticipatory, waiting, and postexam stage; data on coping styles were obtained at an earlier date. Students' appraisals were significantly related to their coping behaviors: students who perceived the test situation as a challenge used more problem-focused coping, whereas those who perceived the situation as a threat used less problem-focused coping. By contrast, harm, an outcome emotion, correlated with a number of palliative tactics. Thus students who felt they were harmed by the test tended to make greater use of alcohol, mental disengagement, and social support. Further, the grades students received on the exam correlated positively with benefit emotions and inversely with harm emotions. Carver and Scheier found that coping before an exam was a poor prospective predictor of emotions as assessed after the exam. The effects that did emerge reflected maladaptive coping (e.g., mental disengagement before the exam was associated with more threat afterward). Curiously, problem-focused coping predicted *high* levels of threat and challenge later on—possibly because task-focused coping promotes enthusiasm about confronting the next instance of a recurrent stressor (Bolger, 1990).

PERSONAL VARIABLES AND COPING

A number of studies have looked at the role of personal variables and resources in the coping process. In Bolger's (1990) study of students' anxiety and coping surrounding an important medical exam, students high on trait anxiety (anxiety as a personal characteristic) reported more escapist coping methods, and these styles were, in turn, related to state anxiety (temporary experience of anxiety) in the test situation. A path analysis (statistical procedure) showed that wishful thinking and self-blame are principal responses through which trait anxiety leads to higher anxiety. Overall, this study suggests that personality variables such as trait anxiety influence the coping strategies people select and that these strategies, in turn, may influence subsequent outcomes (trait anxiety → coping → state anxiety).

In 1995, I studied the relationship between coping resources, strategies, and outcomes in a sample of 241 Israeli undergraduates (Zeidner, 1995). First-order correlations showed that students with richer coping resources tend to use more problem-focused coping and less avoidance coping under test conditions. Regression analyses showed that when controlling for the effects of other resources, students with richer cognitive resources used *less* emotion-focused coping, whereas students with greater emotional and spiritual resources used *more* emotion-focused coping. However, coping resources were not predictive of problem-focused coping. Furthermore, students with higher cognitive, social, emotional, and physical resources evidenced lower test-anxiety levels in an evaluation situation.

Terry (1991) collected data on personality variables, situational appraisals of a stressful college exam situation, and coping strategies used by 138 college students surrounding an exam. Students characterized by low judgments of self-efficacy (perception of oneself as effective) also used more emotion-focused coping, and those prone to self-denial favored escapist strategies of coping. High levels of instrumental action (i.e., problem-oriented coping) predominated when the event was judged as important and when subjects reported high levels of stress.

SPECIFIC WAYS OF COPING WITH EXAMS

Folkman and Lazarus (1985) examined the particular coping strategies employed by a sample of 108 college students during the anticipatory, waiting, and outcome stages of a midterm exam. At every stage of the examination, students reported using combinations of most of the available forms of problem-focused and emotion-focused coping, rather than just one form or another. In fact, practically all the students used problem-focused coping and at least one form of emotion-focused coping during all three phases of the exam in order to cope with their anxieties. Problem-focused coping was at its height during the anticipatory stage, presumably in the service of studying for the exam. Similarly, two forms of emotion-focused coping—emphasizing the positive and seeking social support—were at their height at this stage, steadily decreasing thereafter. Distancing was the most frequently employed strategy during the waiting period, presumably because distancing is useful where there is little to do but wait. While there was a significant decrease in *informational* social support from the anticipatory to waiting period, there was a concomitant increase in *emotional* social support. Thus, subjects who sought informational support during the anticipatory stage, to help them prepare for the exam, shifted to emotional support during the waiting period to secure reassurance and comfort afterward. After grades were announced, coping responses were influenced mainly by individual differences in performance.

Carver and Scheier (1994) reported that problem-focused coping behaviors (i.e., "adaptive" responses) were reported to be employed more frequently throughout the exam than those characterized as potentially dysfunctional. Subjects reported relatively high levels of active coping, planning, suppression of competing activities, positive reframing, and acceptance in coping with exam situations. By contrast, subjects reported relatively low levels of denial, mental disengagement, behavioral disengagement, and use of alcohol. Further, coping responses were reported to change from one stage of the adaptational encounter to the other. Problem- or task-focused responses (e.g., active coping, planning, suppression, use of instrumental support, acceptance) were high during the period before the exam, but diminished afterward—remaining relatively stable thereafter. Certain palliative reactions (e.g., use of emotional social support and mental disengagement) declined significantly after exam scores were available. Curiously, only denial tended to increase across the transaction: Reports of denial were lowest before the exam, increased afterward, and continued to drift upward to the third measurement.

DIMENSIONS OF TEST COPING

What are the dimensions underlying students' coping responses in an evaluative situation? In my study of 241 college students mentioned above (Zeidner, 1995), I factor-analyzed a subset of items taken from the COPE scale (Carver, Scheier, & Weintraub, 1989) administered to the students prior to an important midterm exam (factor analysis is a statistical procedure designed to reduce redundant, overlapping information). The scale consisted of fifteen subscales (namely, active coping, planning, seeking instrumental social support, seeking emotional social support, suppression of competing activities, religion, positive reinterpretation, restraint coping, acceptance, ventilation of emotions, denial, mental disengagement, behavioral disengagement, alcohol/drug use, humor), with respondents indicating the degree to which they actually used each of the coping strategies when preparing for the final examination (0 = not at all, 3 = to a great extent). A principal factor analysis of the COPE scale intercorrelation matrix, followed by varimax rotations, revealed three orthogonal (unrelated) factors, each accounting for an equal percentage of the variance. These were:

1. Problem-focused coping (active coping, planning, suppression of competing activities)
2. Emotion-focused coping (emotional social support, instrumental social support, ventilation, positive reinterpretation, restraint, humor)
3. Avoidance coping (mental disengagement, behavioral disengagement, religion, denial, alcohol/drugs)

The dimensions uncovered in this study correspond to those identified by Endler and Parker (1990a; cf. Endler & Parker, 1990b) as being basic dimensions of coping behaviors and styles. These dimensions were found to be differentially predictive of affective outcomes: Whereas emotion-focused and avoidance coping were positively related to test anxiety, problem-focused coping was inversely related to it.

Another attempt to uncover the structure of coping responses in test situations was reported by Rost and Schermer (1989a, 1989b), who factor-analyzed the responses of 590 students to eighty-five coping inventory items pertaining to diverse cognitive, emotional, and behavioral aspects of coping with test anxiety. The following four components of coping with test anxiety were identified:

1. *Danger control* refers to attempts at controlling the impending threat (e.g., by improving learning and study strategies). Use of these strategies would be expected to increase one's subjectively estimated mastery of the subject matter and hence reduce the appraised harm and danger associated with the exam. Specific coping behaviors falling under this category would include "I prepare myself better," "I peruse the material before going to sleep," and "I go to bed early."
2. *Anxiety repression* refers to the palliative function of repressing the test-related aversive emotions. These strategies are intended to draw attention away from the dangerous environmental cues and divert attention to positive and pleasant cues and bring relief to the examinee—without modifying the cause of the underlying anxiety. Typical items would be "I stop thinking of the test" and "I say to myself that failure is not so serious."
3. *Anxiety control* refers to all strategies that result in continuous reduction of the cognitive, affective, and somatic anxiety symptoms (e.g., "I try to control breathing," "I try to calm down"), with the intent of relaxing and controlling arousal.
4. *Situational control* refers to the direct evasion or avoidance of the situational demands (e.g., "I report sick").

Additional research on the structure of coping in evaluative situations is clearly warranted.

COPING, ANXIETY, AND TEST PERFORMANCE

Coping and Anxiety

Research evidence suggests that emotion-focused coping is reliably associated with anxiety in a stressful evaluative situation and may therefore be indicative of poor adaptation to stress. In a study of coping and anxiety in an Israeli college student sample (Zeidner, 1994), I assessed 198 students under *daily-routine* versus *evaluative* test conditions. State anxiety scores obtained prior to an important college exam were regressed (a statistical procedure) on trait and situational coping scores, along with personality variables (depressive tendencies, trait anxiety) and academic hassles. Emotion-oriented coping responses, along with academic hassles, social evaluation trait anxiety, and depressive tendencies, were reported to be significant predictors of state anxiety in the regression analysis. It is also noteworthy that coping styles assessed during a neutral period were predictive of congruent coping responses in the evaluative situation (i.e., avoidance coping styles predicted avoidance behavior surrounding the exam, etc.).

Blankstein, Flett, and Watson (1992) reported that test anxiety, whether assessed as a trait or a state, was moderately correlated with both avoidance and emotion-focused coping strategies in a sample of college students. They reasoned that the elevated levels of tension and worry experienced by test-anxious students surrounding an evaluative situation would capture these students' attention and determine subsequent emotion-focused coping efforts. The authors further contended that since test-anxious students reported avoiding attempts to solve their academic problems, avoidance tendencies are due, in part, to perceived lack of ability and lack of control over outcomes.

Bolger (1990) reported that the more students engaged in direct or problem-solving behavior in preparing for a medical exam, the *higher* their anxiety prior to the exam was. This suggests that the activities surrounding preparation for an exam, including instrumental ones, may increase unavoidably one's awareness of the threatening event and consequently one's sense of anxiety (Bolger, 1990).

Coping and Examination Performance

Does coping help in improving exam performance? Reports on the nature of the association between coping behaviors and cognitive performance in an evaluative situation have been mixed, with the bulk of studies reporting unimpressive correlations between these two variables. Bolger (1990) reported a nonsignificant relationship between college students' coping responses assessed ten days prior to an exam and their performance on a medical admissions exam. Similarly, Carver and Scheier (1994) found that undergraduate students' coping responses before an exam did not generally predict their exam grades—save for mental disengagement, which related inversely to the grades obtained. Other studies have also reported nonsignificant predictive effects for coping in relation to exam performance (Abella & Heslin, 1989; Edelmann & Hardwick, 1986).

A number of modest correlations between coping before an exam and exam performance have been reported in the literature. In a study of a small sample *(n = 75)* of undergraduate psychology students, Edwards and Trimble (1992) reported that task-oriented and emotion-oriented *coping responses* are significant predictors of college test performance, even when background variables (sex, trait anxiety, and coping styles) were controlled for in a hierarchical regression analysis; *coping styles* did not have similar predictive effects on exam performance. Furthermore, correlational analysis indicated that whereas task-oriented coping behaviors were positively correlated with test scores, avoidance—whether measured as style or behavior—was inversely related to test performance. Similarly, Klinger (1984) found that instrumental coping behaviors (studying, reading, etc.) prior to the exam were related to test outcomes. These latter findings suggest that certain instrumental coping behaviors conducive to exam performance may enhance the examinee's prospects for doing well on the exam.

On the other hand, avoiding an important exam may result in negative cognitive outcomes, as students may not delegate adequate time for exam preparation and may be deficient in their mastery of the skills and information necessary to perform well on the exam. Endler, Kantor, and Parker (1994) reported that task-oriented coping related to exam grades, but only among male college students. They concluded that those who focus on the task in preparing for an exam receive better grades than those who do not.

COPING AND ADAPTATIONAL OUTCOMES

An understanding of the complex relations between coping processes and long-term adaptational outcomes has long been a major concern among stress researchers (Folkman, Lazarus, Dunkel-Schetter, DeLongis, & Gruen, 1986). Evidently, not all responses to a stressful evaluative encounter are adaptive. Some coping behaviors may help alleviate the problem and/or reduce the resulting distress, and therefore may be considered effective, but others may actually exacerbate the problem or become problems in themselves (e.g., alcohol consumption, disruptive anger, hopelessness).

About a decade or so ago, most researchers interested in stress and coping would probably not have seriously questioned the assumption that coping is an important determinant of people's emotional well-being during the various phases of a stressful transaction. Today, in contrast, researchers are asking more frequently whether coping helps (Aldwin & Revenson, 1987), whether it is epiphenomenal (McCrae, 1984), or whether it may even interfere with outcomes such as emotional adjustment (Aldwin & Revenson, 1987; Carver & Scheier, 1994).

A number of specific techniques have been typically judged by researchers as adaptive and others as maladaptive, whereas certain techniques present dilemmas to researchers (Carver et al., 1989). Theorists have frequently emphasized the positive effects of problem-focused coping and the negative effects of emotion-focused coping on psychological outcomes, especially when the threatening situation can be ameliorated by the subject's responses (Lazarus & Folkman, 1984). While emotion-focused coping or avoidance may help in maintaining emotional balance, an adaptive response to remediable situations still requires problem-solving activities to manage the threat. Active coping is preferred by most persons and is generally more effective in stress reduction (Gal & Lazarus, 1975). Active coping provides a sense of mastery over the stressor, diverts attention from the problem, and discharges energy following exposure to threat. Non–problem-solving strategies are increasingly used when the source of stress is unclear, when there is a lack of knowledge about stress modification, or when there is little one can do to eliminate stress (Pearlin & Schooler, 1978).

Thus, there is growing evidence that the use of certain strategies—including active coping, logical analysis, purposeful planning, positive reappraisal, suppression of competing activities, acceptance, and humor—may be adaptive in a variety of situations (Carver et al., 1989). On the other hand, behavioral or mental disengagement, ventilation of emotions, and tension-reduction strategies (e.g., use of alcohol and drugs) are generally candidates for dysfunctional coping tactics. While moderate use of some tactics in coping with exams (e.g., cigarette smoking, overeating) may serve as affect-regulation mechanisms and serve to reduce negative affect, if practiced in excess they may be injurious to health (Wills, 1986).

Researchers often face something of a dilemma in considering how to treat strategies that have multiple functions, such as avoidance behaviors, denial, and turning to prayer or religion (Carver et al., 1989). For example, a student might turn to religion in coping with exams as a source of emotional support, as a vehicle for positive reinforcement and growth, or even as a form of active coping. In the face of failure on an important exam, feelings of helplessness and depression may be moderated by the belief that one's fate is in the hands of God, much like in the case of loss or bereavement (see the review of the literature by Stone, Helder, & Schneider [1988]). Similarly, avoidance coping has both its adaptive and maladaptive aspects. On the one hand, there is a wealth of data to indicate that avoidance coping, reflecting a temporary disengagement from problem-focused coping, is positively tied to concurrent distress (Aldwin & Revenson, 1987; Billings & Moos, 1984; Holahan & Moos, 1985); this holds true for exam situations as well (Zeidner, 1995, 1996). On the other hand, avoidance has been argued to be a useful tactic at times, because it gives person a psychological breather and an opportunity to escape from the constant pressures of the stressful situation (Carver, Scheier, & Pozo, 1992).

It is commonly agreed that the major aim of coping with stress in an exam situation is to restore internal equilibrium by either resolving or alleviating the problem causing the stress or by channeling and controlling the emotional strain evoked by the exam. Clearly, deciding on whether particular coping strategies are adaptive or not in any context requires the joint consideration of situational factors (e.g., test difficulty level, test atmosphere) and personality factors (e.g., trait anxiety, beliefs about coping resources and their effectiveness). Further, the selection and efficacy of coping strategies must be viewed in relation to person–situation interactions, and a change in any element may affect the process and outcome.

SOME TENTATIVE GENERALIZATIONS ABOUT COPING AND COPING EFFECTIVENESS

In spite of recent advances in theory, research, and assessment, the issue of coping effectiveness in general, and in examination contexts in particular, is still open to debate. Deciding which coping behaviors are most effective, and for whom, poses a conceptual and empirical puzzle (Carver & Scheier, 1994). Although few unequivocal principles have been uncovered in coping research conducted in evaluative situations, a number of generalizations about adaptive coping garnered from the literature will now be put forward.

Adaptive coping in exam situations involves a flexible repertoire and combined use of alternative coping strategies. Stress is best managed when effective methods are used for removing the stressor (or its cause) and coping with affective reactions and emotions. Thus, stress reduction behaviors associated with a difficult university exam might include increased study time, peer assistance, or dropping the course until a later time. In the process, effective strategies for addressing the concurrent anxiety, worry, and depressed mood must be implemented. In instances where the stressor cannot be changed, personal management is critical in determining short- and long-term psychological adjustment to such stress.

The studies surveyed show that examinees use multiple forms of coping in adapting to exam situations, including a wide variety of problem-focused, emotion-focused, and avoidance strategies. Thus, the current research on coping with tests is consistent with research carried out in other settings showing that adults use multiple forms of coping in managing most stressful events (Zeidner & Endler, 1996). This would appear to be functional, for it allows for both regulation of emotion and management of the stressor (Lazarus & Folkman, 1984). One may want to try different strategies, in different combinations, to manage stress, rather than respond reflexively with the same limited response to varying stressors. A person must incorporate relevant problem-solving skills (e.g., study habits, planning) and/or emotion-focused skills (e.g., relaxation) to ensure personal coping efficacy.

Furthermore, the effects of various strategies are rather difficult to disentangle, with emotion-focused and problem-focused strategies impacting upon one another during various stages of a stressful encounter. Accordingly, emotion-focused coping before an important exam can facilitate problem-focused coping by removing some of the anxiety that can hamper problem-focused efforts in preparing for the exam. For example, a student who jogs, prays, drinks, and the like to cope with an upcoming exam may reduce her anxiety to the point where she can "hit the books" and prepare herself intensively for the exam. On the other hand, problem-focused coping can render the threat less forbidding and reduce distress emotions and the need for intensive emotion-focused coping. For example, the student who concentrates on studying for an upcoming exam may find that the exam material is not really that difficult, thus reducing the anxiety surrounding the exam.

It should be pointed out that research in other contexts suggests that while greater flexibility may relate to better emotional adjustment (Mattlin, Wethington, & Kessler, 1990), multiple coping reactions within a given period may reflect ineffective coping (Carver et al., 1989). This may hold true for exam situations as well. Further, each coping strategy has both its benefits and costs. For example, denying the seriousness of a failing score in a major course may reduce emotional distress, but it also negatively affects the amount of effort put into improving the course grade.

Coping with a stressful exam situation is a process; it is a transaction between a person and event that plays out across time and changing circumstances. The studies surveyed converge in painting a rather complex picture of the pattern of appraisals, emotions, and coping that unfold across stressful examination situations. Further, the relevance and effectiveness of a coping reaction appear to vary with the phase of the stressful transaction considered. Before an important exam, examinees' appraisals and emotions are generally reported to be homogeneous, and almost all examinees report strong feelings of challenge and fear combined. Thus, positive and negative anticipatory emotions tend to occur simultaneously in the early stages of the exam, but fall off once the uncertainty surrounding the outcome is resolved. As the outcome becomes clearer and less ambiguous, examinees who do well on the exam see the situation as pleasant, whereas those who do not do well see the situation in an aversive light. Inverse relations are observed between outcome emotions (i.e., benefit and harm) after the exam, reflecting the polarization of the subjects' emotions after seeing the grade.

With respect to coping, the studies surveyed tend to converge on the following picture of the coping process in an exam situation: During the anticipatory stages, the initial coping efforts focus on the upcoming exam, with active coping tactics predominating. Problem-focused coping responses at the preexam anticipatory stage are presumably prevalent because something can still be done to influence the outcome. By contrast, a decrease in active coping is evidenced following the exam, presumably because there is very little that can be done to change the results at this stage. Coping right after the exam appears to be an effort to deal with the negative emotions experienced preexam. For some, these efforts are channeled primarily into dysfunctional avoidance; for others, this means obtaining social support and emotion-focused coping. After grades are posted, the impetus behind coping now reflects responses to the grades received on the exam, with subjects who had done poorly now reporting higher levels of problem-focused coping than those who succeeded on the exam.

Coping strategies in exam situations are found to work with modest effects, with some people, and with some outcomes. Research in evaluative situations concurs that some kinds of coping responses to some kinds of test situations and exigencies do make a difference, mainly with respect to *affective* (emotional) outcomes. Specifically, palliative coping responses are positively related to students' test anxiety levels, whereas problem-focused coping responses tend to be inversely related to anxiety. Thus, in a manageable and controllable exam situation, the type of coping strategy employed may have significant consequences for the outcome. Active studying and planning would be especially important to success, whereas excessive avoidance behavior surrounding the final exam period can have potentially disastrous consequences. These conclusions are consistent with a large body of research suggesting that because problem-focused strategies actively confront the problem, they generally have a positive effect on well-being (Lazarus & Folkman, 1984). High levels of palliative coping are typically associated with poor adaptation to stress (Felton & Revenson, 1984).

Whereas emotion-focused and avoidance coping behaviors appear to be related concurrently to anxiety outcomes, the evidence for coping as a *prospective* predictor of either negative emotions or exam performance is sparse. The associations found in the literature are often concurrent, and thus equivocal about the direction of causal influence. As a result, it is not entirely clear whether coping influences outcomes, coping tactics merely co-vary with adjustment to exam situations, or coping and distress are mutually intertwined reflections of something else. The question of the utility of various coping strategies in evaluative situations is without firm answers, and more information will be needed before we can feel comfortable contending that coping has a causal influence on well-being.

With respect to *cognitive* outcomes, well-designed prospective studies concur that coping has little meaningful influence on exam performance. However, there is some evidence that students who use active coping strategies directly related to exam preparation or skill acquisition will do slightly better on the exam. Thus, students who devote time and energy to preparing for the exam and planning their work are often better equipped to master the exam, compared to those who use avoidance strategies. As pointed out by Carver et al. (1992) in a different context, active coping and continued effort are adaptive in any situation where such effort will produce the desired outcome. Avoidance behavior or giving up prematurely works against the person because by the criterion of successful goal attainment (i.e., maximization of test scores), disengaging in such a situation would be considered dysfunctional. The hypothesis that coping is a significant moderator of stress–outcome relations in an evaluative situation remains to be demonstrated.

Coping patterns should fit both the context and the individual. There is some research suggesting that a good fit between the perceived realities of the situation and coping methods is important, with coping effectiveness related to its appropriateness to the internal/external demands of the situation. This "matching" hypothesis suggests that adaptive coping requires a good fit between the person–environment transaction, the person's appraisal of the transaction, and the consequent coping behavior (Lazarus & Folkman, 1984; Lazarus, 1993).

The data surveyed in this chapter conform with the notion that the nature of the coping efforts used may vary, depending on the perceived controllability and manageability of the stressor. In a social-evaluative situation, where one can exert a substantial degree of objective control prior to the evaluative confrontation, students evidence more problem-focused than palliative coping responses. This conforms with prior research suggesting that problem-focused coping is more adaptive in situations viewed as changeable, whereas emotion-focused coping or avoidance behaviors are best used in unalterable situations (Lazarus & Folkman, 1984).

Coping strategies vary between and within individuals. Research attests to individual differences in reacting to an evaluative encounter. Coping is not a direct reflection of the objective evaluative situation; it stems in part from the frame of mind of the person experiencing the event. The sense of threat that triggers the anxiety in a test situation is partly attributable to personal vulnerabilities, which vary from one person to another. In the same way, what coping responses emerge is determined largely by students' knowledge of coping options and partly by their beliefs about the usefulness of these options. Both stress and coping, then, spring from the mental sets brought by the person to the event. Task-focused efforts (e.g., studying) may be activated by certain individuals, upon announcement of an exam. Others procrastinate or complain about the course or instructor, yet they may use adaptive coping methods to manage other stressors. Person–situation interactions may also occur; for example, one student might use problem-focused coping with little skill and be less successful than another who uses emotion-focused coping to alleviate anxiety. Coping strategies may change over time in order to manage both short- and long-term effects of a stressful examination. Yet it is also recognized that the other life stressors aside from examinations themselves may wear down the individual and lead to the use of less effective coping strategies under continued stress (Aldwin & Revenson, 1987; Zeidner, 1994).

Coping responses are not uniformly adaptive. Research has shown that specific coping strategies are more or less effective depending on the type of stress one encounters (Pearlin & Schooler, 1978), and applying the same coping strategies across all situations is not likely to be adaptive. Strategies often viewed as maladaptive (e.g., avoidance, distancing) in an exam situation may be adaptive under some circumstances (e.g., during the intermediary stages of a health crisis) and vice versa (Lazarus, 1993). The results of a given coping style are determined by the interaction of personal needs and preferences and the constraints of the specific situation under consideration.

Causal relationships among coping strategies and outcome indices are likely to be multidirectional rather than linear (Lazarus & Folkman, 1984). It appears that there is a mutually reinforcing causal cycle among stressful examination contexts, poor outcomes on the exam, and maladaptive coping strategies. Coping indices, often seen as dependent variables, might also serve as independent variables in a complex process of reciprocal and unfolding transactions over time.

SUMMARY

There is no consensus about which coping strategies are most effective and adaptive in promoting positive outcomes in exam situations. It is not entirely clear whether coping influences adjustment, coping tactics co-vary with adjustment, or coping and distress are mutually intertwined reflections of yet some other human condition or characteristic. Further research is needed to clarify how a coping strategy resolves problems, relieves emotional distress, and prevents future difficulties. Future research should shed light on what outcome measures should serve to validate coping as being adaptive or maladaptive in a test situation; how long a time lag there should be between assessment of coping and outcomes; how coping in test situations differs from coping in other situations; whether it makes sense to talk about coping when students are really responding to challenges as opposed to threats; and what the ordinary balance of helpful coping to harmful coping with exams is.

Furthermore, future research on the effectiveness of coping strategies in examination contexts would benefit from including more precise theoretical statements, continuous and longitudinal data collection, and the inclusion of situational and personal variables, including secondary stressors. Employing multiple assessment points, repeated measures of coping efforts, and various indices of outcomes at regular intervals over meaningful time spans would enhance the exploration of the complex pathways of effects. One may hope that future research will clarify the kind and extent of the effect of coping on adaptational outcomes.

REFERENCES

Abella, R., & Heslin, R. (1989). Appraisal processes, coping, and the regulation of stress-related emotions in a college examination. *Basic and Applied Social Psychology, 10,* 311–327.

Aldwin, C. M., & Revenson, T. A. (1987). Does coping help? A reexamination of the relation between coping and mental health. *Journal of Personality and Social Psychology, 53,* 337–348.

Billings, A. G., & Moos, R. H. (1984). Coping, stress, and social resources among adults with unipolar depression. *Journal of Personality and Social Psychology, 46,* 877–891.

Blankstein, K. R., Flett, G. L., & Watson, M. S. (1992). Coping and academic problem-solving ability in test anxiety. *Journal of Clinical Psychology, 48,* 37–46.

Bolger, N. (1990). Coping as a personality process: A prospective study. *Journal of Personality and Social Psychology, 59,* 525–537.

Carver, C. S., & Scheier, M. F. (1994). Situational coping and coping dispositions in a stressful transaction. *Journal of Personality and Social Psychology, 66,* 184–195.

Carver, C. S., Scheier, M. F., & Pozo, C. (1992). Conceptualizing the process of coping with health problems. In H. S. Friedman (Ed.), *Hostility, coping, and health* (pp. 167–199). Washington, DC: American Psychological Association.

Carver, C. S., Scheier, M. F., & Weintraub, J. K. (1989). Assessing coping strategies: A theoretically based approach. *Journal of Personality and Social Psychology, 56,* 267–283.

Edelmann, R. J., & Hardwick, S. (1986). Test anxiety, past performance and coping strategies. *Personality and Individual Differences, 7*, 255–257.

Edwards, J. M., & Trimble, K. (1992). Anxiety, coping, and academic performance. *Anxiety, Stress, and Coping, 5*, 337–350.

Endler, N. S., Kantor, L., & Parker, J. D. A. (1994). State-trait coping, state-trait anxiety and academic performance. *Personality and Individual Differences, 16*, 663–670.

Endler, N. S., & Parker, J. D. A. (1990a). *The Coping Inventory for Stressful Situations (CISS): Manual.* Toronto: Multi-Health Systems.

Endler, N. S., & Parker, J. D. A. (1990b). Multidimensional assessment of coping: A critical evaluation. *Journal of Personality and Social Psychology, 58*, 844–854.

Felton, B. J., & Revenson, T. A. (1984). Coping with chronic illness: A study of illness controllability and the influence of coping strategies on psychological adjustment. *Journal of Consulting and Clinical Psychology, 52*, 343–353.

Folkman, S., & Lazarus, R. S. (1985). If it changes, it must be a process: Study of emotion and coping during three stages of a college examination. *Journal of Personality and Social Psychology, 48*, 150–170.

Folkman, S., Lazarus, R. S., Dunkel-Schetter, C., DeLongis, A., & Gruen, R. (1986). Dynamics of a stressful encounter: Cognitive appraisal, coping, and encounter outcomes. *Journal of Personality and Social Psychology, 50*, 992–1003.

Gal, R., & Lazarus, R. (1975). The role of activity in anticipation and confronting stressful situations. *Journal of Human Stress, 1*, 4–20.

Holahan, C. J., & Moos, R. H. (1985). Life stress and health: Personality, coping, and family support in stress resistance. *Journal of Personality and Social Psychology, 49*, 739–747.

Klinger, E. (1984). A consciousness-sampling analysis of test anxiety and performance. *Journal of Personality and Social Psychology, 47*, 1376–1390.

Lay, C. H., Edwards, J. M., Parker, J. D. A., & Endler, N. S. (1989). An assessment of appraisal, anxiety, coping, and procrastination during an examination period. *European Journal of Personality, 3*, 195–208.

Lazarus, R. S. (1993). Coping theory and research: Past, present, and future. *Psychosomatic Medicine, 55*, 237–247.

Lazarus, R. S., & Folkman, S. (1984). *Stress, appraisal, and coping.* New York: Free Press.

Mattlin, J. A., Wethington, E., & Kessler, R. C. (1990). Situational determinants of coping and coping effectiveness. *Journal of Health and Social Behavior, 31*, 103–122.

McCrae, R. R. (1984). Situational determinants of coping responses: Loss, threat, and challenge. *Journal of Personality and Social Psychology, 46*, 919–928.

Pearlin, L. I., & Schooler, C. (1978). The structure of coping. *Journal of Health and Social Behavior, 19*, 2–21.

Rost, D. H., & Schermer, F. J. (1989a). The assessment of coping with test anxiety. In R. Schwarzer, H. M. van der Ploeg, & C. D. Spielberger (Eds.), *Advances in test anxiety research* (vol. 6, pp. 175–191). Lisse, The Netherlands: Swets & Zeitlinger.

Rost, D. H., & Schermer, F. J. (1989b). The various facets of test anxiety: A subcomponent model of test anxiety measurement. In R. Schwarzer, H. M. van der Ploeg, & C. D. Spielberger (Eds.), *Advances in test anxiety research* (vol. 6, pp. 37–52). Lisse, The Netherlands: Swets & Zeitlinger.

Smith, C. A., & Ellsworth, P. C. (1987). Patterns of appraisal and emotion related to taking an exam. *Journal of Personality and Social Psychology, 52*, 475–488.

Stone, A. A., Helder, L., & Schneider, M. M. (1988). Coping with stressful events: Coping dimensions and issues. In L. H. Cohen (Ed.), *Life events and psychological functioning: Theoretical and methodological issues* (pp. 182–210). Newbury Park, CA: Sage.

Terry, D. J. (1991). Coping resources and situational appraisals as predictors of coping behavior. *Personality and Individual Differences, 12,* 1031–1047.

Wills, T. A. (1986). Stress and coping in early adolescence: Relationships to substance use in urban school samples. *Health Psychology, 5,* 503–529.

Zeidner, M. (1994). Personal and contextual determinants of coping and anxiety in an evaluative situation: A prospective study. *Personality and Individual Differences, 16,* 899–918.

Zeidner, M. (1995). Coping with examination stress: Resources, strategies, and outcomes. *Anxiety, Stress, & Coping, 8,* 279–298.

Zeidner, M. (1996). How do high school and college students cope with test situations? *British Journal of Educational Psychology, 66,* 115–128.

Zeidner, M., & Endler, N. (Eds.). (1996). *Handbook of coping: Theory, research, applications.* New York: John Wiley & Sons.

CHAPTER 24

The Black Scholar Interviews Maya Angelou

Robert Chrisman

Maya Angelou, author of the best-selling *I Know Why the Caged Bird Sings* and *Gather Together in My Name*, has also written two collections of poetry, *Just Give Me a Cool Drink of Water 'Fore I Die* and *Oh Pray My Wings Are Gonna Fit Me Well*. In theater, she produced, directed, and starred in *Cabaret for Freedom* in collaboration with Godfrey Cambridge at New York's Village Gate, starred in Genet's *The Blacks* at the St. Mark's Playhouse, and adapted Sophocles' *Ajax*, which premiered at the Mark Taper Forum in Los Angeles in 1974. In film and television, Maya Angelou wrote the original screenplay and musical score for the film *Georgia, Georgia*, wrote and produced a ten-part TV series on African traditions in American life, and participated as a guest interviewer for the Public Broadcasting System program *Assignment America*. In the 1960s, at the request of the late Dr. Martin Luther King Jr., she became the northern coordinator for the Southern Christian Leadership Conference, and in 1975 Maya Angelou received the *Ladies' Home Journal* Woman of the Year Award in Communications. She has received honorary degrees from Smith, Mills, and Lawrence University. This interview was conducted by Robert Chrisman, publisher of *The Black Scholar*.

The Black Scholar:	*Maya, this fall* [1976] *you have produced your latest book,* Singin' and Swingin' and Gettin' Merry Like Christmas, *which is the third installment of your autobiography and the fifth of your published books.*
Maya Angelou:	Yes.
BS:	*Can you comment a bit on the importance of endurance in black writers?*

MA: Endurance is one thing. I think endurance with output, endurance
      with productivity is the issue. If one has the fortune, good or bad,
      to stay alive one endures, but to continue to write the books and
      get them out—that's the productivity and I think that is important
      to link with the endurance.

     I find myself taking issue with the term minor poet, minor writer
of the 18th century, minor writer of the 19th century; but I do
understand what people mean by that. Generally they mean that
the writer, the poet who only wrote one book of poetry or one
novel, or two, is considered a minor poet or minor writer because
of his or her output, its scarcity. I can't argue with that. I do
believe that it is important to get the work done, seen, read, published, and *given* to an audience. One has enjoyed oneself, one has
done what one has been put here to do, to write. Another thing is
that one has given a legacy of some quantity to generations to
come. Whether they like it or not, whether the writer values the
next generation, or values the work or not, at least there is something, there is a body of work to examine and to respond to, to
react to.

     I know a number of people who do work very slowly but I don't
believe, although I have close friends who write slowly, in taking
five years to write one book. Now I think they have psyched themselves into believing they cannot work more quickly, that hence
because they work slowly their work is of more value. They also
believe—they have bought that American baloney, the masterpiece
theory—everything you write must be a masterpiece, each painting
you paint must be a masterpiece.

BS: *I want to talk to you more about that. I think any artist in this soci-
      ety is inhibited in many ways because it is not an aesthetic society.*

MA: Materialistic.

BS: *I think the black writer has even more difficulty because his vision is
      antagonistic, it's a racist society, his whole stuff is different. Do you
      think that the masterpiece syndrome further inhibits the output of
      black writers?*

MA: To me that inhibits *all* artists. Every artist in this society is affected
      by it. I don't say he or she is inhibited, he or she might work
      against it and make that work for them, as I hope I do, but we are
      affected by it.

     It is in reaction to that dictate from a larger society that spurs my
output, makes me do all sorts of things, write movies and direct
them, write plays, write music, and write articles. That's because I
don't believe in the inhibition of my work; I am obliged, I am com-
pulsive, I will work against it. If necessary I will go to work on a dictionary, you understand, just to prove that that is a lot of bullshit.

     So every artist in the society has to deal with that dictate. Some
are crippled by it, others, I believe, are made more healthy. Because
they are made more strong, and become more ready to struggle
against it.

BS: *More vigilant.*

MA: Absolutely. But the black writer or black artist—I include every type, from graphics to entertainment—has generally further to come from than his or her white counterpart unless the artist is an entertainer. Often this black artist is the first in his family and possibly in his environment to strive to write a book, to strive to paint a painting, to sculpt, to make being an artist a life work. So the black writer, the black artist probably has to convince family and friends that what he or she is about is worthwhile.

Now that is damned difficult when one comes from a family, an environment, a neighborhood, or group of friends who have never met a writer, who have only heard of writers, maybe read some poetry in school.

But to try to explain to a middle-aged black that the life of art one wants to lead is a worthwhile one and can hopefully improve life, the quality of life for all people, that's already a chore.

Because, like most people anywhere, the middle-aged black American that comes from a poor background for the most part wants to see concrete evidence of success. So they want things. If you are really going to be a success go and become a nurse, be a doctor, be a mortician, but a *writer*? So there are obstacles to overcome, to be either done or else just given up on.

BS: *Or the relationships suspended?*

MA: Right. Then the work still has to be done on the artist's psyche, because he has to keep dealing with the issue that every artist, from the beginning of time, has had to deal with, and that is, "Am I an artist?" That public display of ego on the part of artists, 99 times out of 100 only tells of the doubt he has in private, especially when one has no precedent in one's personal family history. My grandfather Jason did not know anybody who was a painter, never met anybody who was an artist, or sculptor, or composer, certainly not a writer. I can talk to little white high school students and if they themselves have never met a writer in their school, Norman Mailer spoke in their school, or Eudora Welty, or James Dickey visited that auditorium. Well, there have not been that many black artists that visible for black youth. There was Langston Hughes, but he was the only one and that was thirty-five to forty years ago. And men of the Negro Renaissance were not given to get outside of Harlem, really.

BS: *That's true. And Langston Hughes had a very public philosophy of art.*

MA: That's right. He was one of the rare ones. So I am saying that all of the problems of artists in a mechanistic, materialistic society, all those problems are heightened, if not doubled, for the black American artist.

So as usual the black writer—I can only speak for the writer—the black writer in particular should throw out all of that propaganda and pressure, disbelieve everything one is told to believe and believe everything one is told *not* to believe. Start with a completely clean slate and decide, "I will put it out."

A great writer only writes one book every five years. Says who? Who made that rule? I don't believe it. Just because it is told to me I don't believe it; on general principle I don't believe it. And I look at a James Baldwin with those pieces of work out. If I want to read Ralph Ellison, I am obliged to reread and reread and reread *Invisible Man* or *Shadow and Art* and how many times can you reread it? You get the essence, then you get the details and there it is. But if I disagree with Baldwin in, say, *No Name in the Street*, I can pick up *Fire Next Time*, I can go to read *Blues for Mr. Charlie*—I just used a piece from *Blues for Mr. Charlie*—I can go to see *Amen Corner*, I can read a short story from *Going to Meet the Man*; I mean the work is there.

Whatever I say, I cannot ignore the fact that the man has put the work out there.

Now my problem I have is I love life, I love living life and I love the art of living, so I try to live my life as a poetic adventure, everything I do from the way I keep my house, cook, make my husband happy, or welcome my friends, raise my son; everything is a part of a large canvas I am creating, I am living beneath.

Now there is a very fine line between loving life and being greedy for it. And I refuse to be greedy, I want to walk away from it with as much flair and grace and humor as I have had living it. Okay, I am saying all this to say that when I write it would seem I am greedy to get the books done; I pray I am just this side of being greedy, on the safe side. But that determination and delight I have in working, in getting a piece done, in the achievement is delicious. I know I will have detractors who will think that I am greedy to do that—you know there will be.

BS: *They want you to write a book every five years rather than one book a year?*

MA: *Caged Bird* was published in 1970 and this is '76 and the fifth book is out. In the meantime I have written *Ajax*, another play, a movie, a television production, another movie script, a lot of stuff—you know I just haven't stopped—and a monthly article in *Playgirl*. I believe that life loves the liver of it.

BS: *That's for damned sure. And it loves the lover of it.*

MA: Yes, yes absolutely. Keeps you young and gay and courageous and spitting nails. It really does.

BS: *Well, that is one of the things I sensed in your autobiographies, is that you have a very definite point of view about work. In a lot of ways not only work as an artist, but in the general effort of life. Would you discuss that with me now?*

MA: I believe my feeling for work is something other than the puritan ethic of work.

I do believe that a person, a human being without his or her work is like a peapod where the peas have shriveled before they have come to full growth. I have very little to say to people who don't work. I don't know what to say, I mean not that I want to discuss sewing dresses with a seamstress but if she or he respects her or his work we have a jumping-off place because we at least separately know something about respect and respect for something outside our own selves. Something made greater by ourselves and in turn that makes us greater. And that's pretty fantastic, so that I honor the people who do what they do well, whatever it is. I feel that I am a part of that.

BS: *Black people are a working people and the sense of work pervades your autobiographies, your mother's rooming house, your own growth as a child, you were always around a working situation. One of your own primary motivations for work in autobiographies seems caring for your child.*

MA: Yes, that's right. Well I can't imagine what life would be like for me without having work that I cared about. I suspect that I have been a "liberated" woman in the sense that that term is now used most of my life. There may have been a couple of years in my life when I did not choose how I would live my life, who would pay my bills, who would raise my son, where we would live and so forth, but only for a few years.

I am so "liberated" that except on rare occasions my husband does not walk into the house without seeing his dinner prepared. He does not have to concern himself about a dirty house, I do that, for myself but also for my husband. I think it is important to make that very clear.

I think there is something gracious and graceful about serving. Now, unfortunately, or rather the truth is, our history in this country has been the history of the servers and because we were forced to serve and because dignity was absolutely drained from the servant, for anyone who serves in this country, black or white, is looked upon with such revilement, they are held in such contempt while that is not true in other parts of the world. In Africa it is a great honor to serve, to be allowed to serve somebody is a great honor. You can insult a person by not accepting something from him. In Europe from the great family traditions, work patterns are the patterns of the waiters and the maitre d's and the chefs and so forth. Generation after generation of servanthood. I don't mean to say that class issues are not at issue here too but there is something beyond that, when people have been made to serve or because of their economic circumstances, they have found within that some grace, some style, some marvelous flair.

Well, I refuse, simply because I happen to be born in this country, to take on the coloration of the larger society which says to serve, to take off your sister's shoes as she walks into the house, is really belittling yourself. I don't see that and ladies who travel with me, my friends, if we get into the car and it is only the two of us, I open the door for the ladies, and see them in and lock the door.

Most women are made uncomfortable when another woman serves them. It's unfortunate. I happen to be 6 foot tall, I can push a door stronger than somebody who is, say 5 foot 2, you know, and that is just the truth. And if somebody is helping me shop I'll carry the bag. I am physically stronger, if I were not I would certainly say, "Sister, would you take it," and feel no compunction at all.

So there is something about the way people look at work that I think is completely off. I believe I know why there are the negatives about work, especially in the black community, but I refuse to get out of one trick bag and get caught in another. Now that I know why it means that I don't have to fall into that.

BS: *Yes, there is that element, at the same time, of the disdain for work, there is the mystification of excellence so that people will talk about the inspired genius of John Coltrane while they forget he ran scales—*

MA: —for five hours a day.

BS: *Right. Hard work was at the base of Trane's revolutionary music— and the courage to be audacious.*

MA: Audacity is fine; it's splendid. I'd like to pursue that a bit. True revolution in music took place, as far as I can see it, took place only a few times, three times in this century. One was the revolution that took place aided and abetted if not instigated by Louis Armstrong. Louis Armstrong did something with the trumpet that had never been done. Things that have become so casual, so common to our ears now, Louis Armstrong introduced. One can say that for European music the innovation of Stravinsky was revolutionary because again, Stravinsky and that whole group of European composers who introduced African tone into European music. In "Afternoon of a Faun" and "The Rite of Spring" and all of that you can keep hearing, those notes, that pentatonic scale.

Then bebop was the third. Truly revolutionary; it did something to all of our ears and that has happened with those three, I believe. Now, of course, musicologists know more but I mean for me, I would say these were the three truly innovative times in modern music. Rhythm and blues or rock & roll, or blues, or spiritual or popular music, all that's been around; there's nothing new to that. Dizzy admittedly brought in Bossa Nova, but that was no real revolution whether it was Calypso or Bossa Nova, cha cha cha, no.

BS: *Sure. Bop changed the whole basic premises of the music.*

MA: And our ears. Amazing, when you think of the music as it was played until Louis Armstrong came up to Chicago, when he was down in Louisiana, New Orleans, he just put notes in that nobody had ever heard and he split notes and he did things that we think of as being there forever.

BS: *Yeah, improvisations in each of the major instruments.*

MA: Exactly, and eight bars or two verses, a bridge and a verse. That's like a stanza in AB, AB, ABC in poetry. Again we come back to your earlier question about work. When Louis Armstrong, according to a few of his biographies, came to Chicago he was wearing a suit, the pants of which were about three inches too short, his white socks showed, he had these brogans on and he wore a derby hat. He got up on the stage and all the musicians laughed until he started to play. When he finished playing, the next day all the musicians went out and bought some pants three inches too short, some white socks and some brogan shoes and a derby hat, you understand. Louis Armstrong was on J—and never got off his J—never, never stopped. I mean for all intents and purposes, died with his trumpet in his hand. So did Duke Ellington, all those people who inspire one, who inspire me. Duke was still going on the road right up till the last. Louis Armstrong still on the road till the very last.

    I appreciate that, I respect it and I am grateful for it. I am grateful, in the name of my grandson I am grateful.

BS: *Has the example of these men influenced your own development as a writer?*

MA: Well, certainly. I tell you one of the most aggravating things of all is to pick up a review of a work of mine and have a reviewer say, "She is a natural writer." That sometimes will make me so angry that I will cry, really, because my intent is to write so it seems to flow. I think it's Alexander Pope who says, "Easy writing is damn hard reading," and vice versa, easy reading is damn hard writing. Sometimes I will stay up in my room for a day trying to get two sentences that will flow, that will just seem as if they were always there. And many times I come home unable to get it so I go back the next day, 6:30 in the morning, every morning, 6:30 I go to work. I'm there by 7:00; I work till 2:00 alone in this tiny little room, 7 by 10 feet. I have had the room for two years and they have never changed the linen. I've never slept there. There is nothing in the room except a bed, a face basin, and that's it. I write in longhand. If it is going well I might go to 3:00 but then I pull myself out, come home, take a shower, start dinner, check my house, so that when Paul comes in at 5:30 I have had a little time out of that, although my heart and mind are there, I still try to live an honest life. Then when you go back it looks different to you. I think that a number of artists again, or people who have pretensions that in order to be an artist you must have the back of your hand glued to your forehead, you know, and walk around and be "terribly terribly ..." all the time, thinking great thoughts of pith and moment. That's bullshit. In order to get the work done and *finally that is all there is*, it's the *work!* all the posturing, all the lack of posturing, none of that matters, it is finally the work. You don't really get away from it but you try and I think that is very healthy. So it's good to take a swim and relax in some way.

BS: *You mentioned some of the attitudes toward life that one gets in this society. When you were abroad did you get a different perspective on being a black American?*

MA: Well I came to, if possible, regard my people, black Americans, even more affectionately. Once out from the daily pressure of oppression, hate and ridicule and all, the negatives that permeate this whole frigging air we breathe, just being out from under that, not having to use 30 to 40 percent of my energy just kicking that crap out of my doorway before I can even get out and go to work, it was amazing. First off I didn't know what to do with myself. I was so geared to struggle, when I was living in Ghana, for the first year, I had my fist balled up for nothing, it was like tilting at windmills. I was absolutely so highly sensitive as to be paranoid. Any time anything happened I would say, "Oh, yes, I see. I understand why you are saying this; you are saying it because I am black."

Well, of course, everybody around me was black, so for the first time in my life, my defenses not only did not work they were not necessary, not those particular ones. It took a year for my son to unball his fists.

Once I did relax and realize that if I was rejected from the job or whatever, it was not because I was black, now it may be because I was black *American*, which is another thing, but it wasn't because of the color of my skin.

Then I began to examine my people and I thought, my God! How did we survive this! Good Lord! It's like growing up with a terrible sound in your ears day and night. Terrible, a kind of sound that is unrelenting, that pulls your hairs up on your body. And then to be away from it. At first you miss it, naturally, but then when you get used to the *peace*, the quietude, the lack of pressure, then you begin to think, my God, how have my people survived that crap and still to survive it with some style, some passion, some humor; so living in Africa made me even more respectful of black Americans. That's one thing.

I suppose too my family directly and my people indirectly have given me the kind of strength that enables me to go anywhere. I can't think where I would be afraid, apprehensive about going in the world, on this planet. I have had some very rough times in my life ... so what else is new, you know. Many things that really are so gruesome I wouldn't even write about them, because writing about them just makes it melodramatic. There are places of course I would not like ... a Siberian salt mine or a Georgia chain gang, there are things I would rather not experience.

BS: *Going to another country allowed me to see what is permanent about human nature and what is imposed upon it.*

MA: I was very pleased actually to see so many Africanisms or to be in Africa and recognize what I thought were black American mores, but then to recognize them as Africanisms, to see them at their source. That was lovely because I grew up until I was thirteen in a small town in Arkansas and once I was married to a man who was an African and he came to the States doing a postdoctoral tour for UNICEF. He went down to Tuskegee and he told the professor down there he was looking for Africanisms still current in American lives. The professor told him, "Why don't you go to a small town in

Arkansas called Stamps," and I have no idea why that is, but my husband at that time, certainly I had never mentioned Stamps to him so he didn't recognize that, he didn't make that up. But that is the town I grew up in and I was back there about two months ago, first time in 30 years and it's true, absolutely. The town looks African Village, the people in it.

BS: *Well, some of the Africanisms are present in church services, dancing, and celebration.*

MA: Body language and black people anywhere from any place in the world can hold whole conversations without saying a word. Um um *um*. Um hum. Um hum. *Ummm* or take the words, auntie and uncle. That really boggles my mind because I knew that Aunt Jemima and Uncle Tom came from somewhere, but I didn't put it together. I thought white people had imposed those names. But in my town where I grew up, you had to call people Uncle or Auntie so and so, cousin; Tura, sister; bubba, brother, absolutely. For example, in raising my son Guy, or say, my grandson. He can say, "Hello, Mr. Chrisman," but it is too cold. On the other hand, he cannot call you Bob. That doesn't give him anything. If you are equal—he's seven and your equal—who the hell does he run to? So then properly as a friend of the family he is supposed to call you "Uncle Bob." That's the way I grew up, that's the way my son was raised, even though I raised him in the North so that Max, until Guy was 18, Max was Uncle Max and that was absolute, with all my friends, Uncle Jimmy. Until Guy became 17 or 18 and then they arranged, "Guy, call me Max," on an adult basis. If you encourage that particular distance, children can feel they have some shelters; each one of those aunties, uncles, sisters, all those people become shelters and when one lives in a threatening society, not only threatening but actively oppressive, you need as many shelters as possible. This is the way the African thinks and the way Southern blacks where I grew up think. So that's why it continues in the South. Well, seeing that in Ghana ... there are so many Africanisms ... that gave me another sense of continuity. I used to say on soap boxes in Harlem that slavery removed, stole our culture. But that's baloney. And I had to admit, I had to say, "Look, I was wrong."

BS: *In some respects it might even have reinforced it.*

MA: It might have. Certainly the prejudice, racism and Jim Crowism re-inforced it, kept us from moving into the mainstream as the American Indians have done in many, many cases. So many Americans that have more than one generation of their family in this country will say, "I am Cherokee and so and so, or Blackfoot and so and so." So many American Indians married into the white race and then, by the second generation, lost identity. We haven't done so.

BS: *I had marked one passage in* Singin' *and* Swingin' *in which you mention your dilemma. Let me read it here. "I hadn't asked them for help.... Nothing would bring me bowed to beg for aid from institutions which scorned me and a government that ignored me. It had*

seemed that I would be locked in the two jobs and the weekly baby sit-
ter terror until my life was done. Now with a good salary my son and
I could move back into my mother's house."

I am impressed throughout the autobiography with the dedication
to the rearing of your son. You said earlier that in a sense you were a
liberated woman but that, of course, obviously for you didn't mean
not raising your child.

MA: I think that one has to be liberated to do so. To bring up a person
healthily you have to be liberated. You have to be liberated from all
sorts of things, for one, from being in love with the child. A number of parents fall in love with their children and thereby want either vicarious or true existence through their children. And that's
baloney, that hampers, imprisons, and cripples the person, the small
person. He doesn't want all that weight on him; he's got his own
stuff to do. I had the good fortune of never being in love with my
son. That was one of my greatest blessings.

I really loved him, he amused me and tickled me and pleased me
and still does. But I have never been in love with him, so that
meant then that I could try to keep him as free as possible. And I
don't know how I knew that. I can't say, because I was very young
when he was born; I really don't know.

He was telling a story recently. We lived in Cleveland, he was
seven so I was 23. I rented a top floor in a private home. The
woman had a terribly rambunctious rooster, a few hens and a
rooster in her back yard which was the only place for Guy to play.
He went out to play and this rooster ran at him, so he came inside
and said he couldn't play. I took him back out and I gave him a
long stick and said, "Whenever the rooster comes, you run him
away." He played for some time and I came out and said, "Well,
the rooster hasn't bothered you yet so you can break the stick in
half." So he played and had the stick and broke it in half again,
until finally the stick was about four inches long. He said, "Do you
really think this will keep the rooster away?"

But how I knew how to do that, I don't know. But I do know
that I was concerned to see him stay healthy and balanced and it
was damn difficult because I knew too that I was 6 foot tall and
had a very heavy voice and for a small person, who is a foot and
half tall I must have looked like a mountain.

So I was aware of that and I managed to speak softly. He trained
me more than anyone else. I spoke softly and quietly and moved,
hopefully, not too fast so as not to frighten him. I remember hit-
ting him when he was seven and realizing that that just didn't do. I
felt so embarrassed, I felt, "Well, now that is the last time I will
ever do that," and that was the last time. But to raise a healthy
black boy without a father ... I was aware that he could end up
being a homosexual or a bully; somewhere between there was what
I wanted. I mean a bully in any kind of way, and that includes players, hustlers, pimps, and so on.

BS: *Well, in this respect the kinds of things that you talk about as a developing black woman don't always seem to be the same concerns as those the feminists have.*

MA: Yes, I know.

BS: *On the other hand, you are an egalitarian and an activist?*

MA: Absolutely. You see, there is one major difference between white American women and black American women. And it is this. White men have been able to say to white women and have said: "I don't need you. I can keep my factories running at top speed, I can send trains down silver tracks, and ships out to rolling seas. I can keep my institutes of higher education going without you, my banks going without you; I can run *wars* without you, I can go to the *moon* without you. I need you in the bedroom, the kitchen, and the nursery."

Now black men have never been able to say that to our women. There's a qualitative difference in our approach to our men and our approach to life and our approach to our children and our approach to ourselves. A total difference, because although white men and white women may say that to me in effect by the way they treat me, my own fathers and brothers and uncles do not say that.

But for a white woman to have her own brother, father, nephews, and uncles say that to her—"I don't really need you in the areas of my life of greatest importance, I don't need you"—has got to boggle the mind. I just *know* that this is what has happened and it is because of it that I support the women's liberation movement. Because I am for every person, or groups of people who intend to make it a better country for everybody, a better world for everybody. I mean I would be a liar if I said I thought I could enjoy my freedom without this white woman across the street enjoying hers. I cannot. She might be able to, or think she can—and obviously through slavery a number of people thought they could enjoy their freedom because I was enslaved. I don't make that mistake. So I am for it, but I see what the difference is between me and the average white woman.

BS: *So white male chauvinism willfully excludes women from all the important aspects of life.*

MA: Right. For example, let's say we're sitting with our gentlemen friends at a table or around a fire or something and I said, "It has occurred to me that I would like to talk to you about something that happened in China the other day. I really would like a clarification." If all my gentlemen friends, my brothers, said, "Oh yeah Maya, why don't you go and make some coffee?" If, historically, they did that to me, what would happen?

BS: *It would be impossible, you'd be alienated ... angry ...*

MA: No work ... the sense of having no work, no seriousness. Naturally then I would begin to use those things I could use, my sex, sexuality as such. Hysteria. You rarely see black women hysterical. Angry, yes, but that, no, and the way a black woman usually uses sex is in a way to enjoy it herself. I really have a lot of sympathy for white women. We don't have the same struggle.

BS: *That is a very complex thing—the moral, social, and political enforcement of slavery did not come from white males alone. The white female also had complicity.*

MA: Bea Richards has a poem; it's so great. It's called "Blackwoman Speaks to Whitewoman" and she says, You were brought here the same as I and if they praised my teeth they praised your thigh / they sold you to the highest bidder the same as I. But you snuggled down in your pink places and gave no reproach, accepted an added vote thinking that forgetting without realizing that the bracelet you accept in order to keep quiet about my house . . . and the necklace . . . and the man was your husband by law but mine at night and yet you stood there and watched him tell my son that what your husband did. Thinking that it's nothing just keep quiet and your slavery would be less. It's sad. It's sad.

Like most things it's the person who perpetuates the evil who is usually more crippled by it than the person upon whom the evil is perpetrated. There is something very healthy about struggling against evil. It's very positive, puts a little spring in your step.

BS: *In the theater and performing arts again, I think you are one of the few modern women today directing and producing television shows and theater. What kinds of problems do you encounter there?*

MA: The problems are the old-time ones of being the first black woman. In many cases the crews with which I am obliged to work are composed of middle-aged, middle-class white men who have never worked with a black *man*, for that matter; and I have been very fortunate. I have met some nice men, I try to give little pep talks, like saying, "Gentlemen, you have a chance to be really generous. I need to learn something and I work very hard and if you don't teach me I will learn anyway. It will cost me more, the project will be endangered, but I will learn." That is why I went to Sweden and took a course in cinematography, just so I would know something, I wouldn't have to be completely ignorant. But it gets results; all kinds of people will rise to heights greater than *their* expectations if you expect it of them. It's fantastic; the same people who would be very difficult if you said, "Gentlemen, I really need this and I know you can teach me and I will be very grateful, if you would, I expect you will." Many times they are made greater, they try to live up to other people's expectations. The same way people will live down to expectations.

BS: *I think that probably gets back to your philosophy of work concept, an honest effort or venture made stands a chance of success.*

MA: Exactly. And none can come if it's not tried.

BS: *Right. . . . Have you ever considered dramatizing parts of your autobiography?*

MA: Well, I hope to. I wrote out a screenplay to be done but I couldn't get the backing I wanted. The big companies wanted to buy it from me, *Caged Bird*, for an incredible amount of money but they wanted to provide their own directors and I said no. I wouldn't have it directed by anybody but me.

That's not really quite true, there are a couple of other directors I would consider, Gordon Parks Senior, Dick Williams, he's a brilliant actor/director, lives in New York. Those were the only two I would consider. My producer begs me to do it for the Broadway stage; I can't see it right now.

BS: *What are your plans for 1977?*

MA: Well, I will be writing and directing a musical drama, *And Still I Rise*, this January in New York. It is exciting to direct and I hope to be doing much more. This spring I hope to compile a kind of omnibus of plays, articles and short stories and poems of mine. The omnibus would contain, say, *Ajax*; the screenplay of *Georgia, Georgia*; and short stories, the scenario of a little short film called *All Day Long*, some articles from *Playgirl*, some of those, and some things I did for the *New York Times*. That would be the book for 1977.

BS: *Thank you, Maya Angelou.*

Part VI

Stress Management

Introduction to "Stress Management"

This last part of our book is an introduction to stress management. The first two chapters are literature reviews of important stress management techniques: massage and mindfulness-based stress reduction (MBSR, a type of meditation). The third, fourth, and fifth chapters discuss yoga, cognitive therapy, and nutrition, respectively. The final two are studies: one investigating exercise as a treatment for depression and the second researching 12-step programs for addictions. Brief "how-to's" are provided for some of the techniques—MBSR, cognitive therapy, and nutrition for stress reduction. For more thorough coverage about how to execute some of these and other techniques, several excellent books are available. See, for example, Davis, Eshelman, and McKay (2000); Girdano, Dusek, and Everly (2005); and Seaward (2006). These same texts also discuss stress management techniques not examined here, such as deep breathing, autogenics, and progressive muscle relaxation.

Chapter 25, "Massage Therapy Effects," is Field's (1998) review of research on the benefits of massage therapy. Research has been conducted with diverse populations, including infants, pregnant women, people suffering from a variety of physical or psychiatric conditions, and rats. The research reviewed investigated many potential positive effects of massage: growth, pain reduction; increased alertness; reduction of stress, anxiety, and depression; enhanced immune function; and others. Field concludes that, based on the evidence, massage may be a promising therapy for many conditions and many populations. She points out some of the weaknesses in the literature thus far. For example, research has mostly focused on clinical populations but not healthy ones. Some unanswered questions are: Does massage therapy have lasting effects? Are there contraindications for massage therapy? Would mechanical massage (delivered by a machine) work as well as massage provided by living humans (or rats)? Field is currently working to update some material covered in this chapter.

Field's chapter calls attention to an important issue regarding research methodology for studying treatments. That is, as much as possible, researchers should use controlled experiments to investigate the effectiveness of any treatment, including the stress management techniques that we are discussing in this part of our book. In her review, Field was careful to include studies with the best research methodologies—studies that possess many elements of the controlled experiment.

The controlled experiment is a type of study in which the researcher investigates two (or more) "variables" or "factors" (in this case, massage therapy as one variable and level of stress as another) in such a way that a cause–effect relationship can almost certainly be determined between them. At the conclusion of the experiment, we can determine with a high degree of certainty that massage therapy caused a decreased level of stress. The way that the researcher determines whether this cause–effect relationship truly exists is by creating "controls" in the study. Examples of controls will be described shortly.

The experiment is the only type of study in which the researcher manipulates one variable, called the *independent variable.* "Manipulation" means that the researcher assigns different levels of the variable to different groups of people. Thus, for example, when studying the effects of massage (the independent variable), the massage variable will be "manipulated" such that the people in one group receive massage and the people in the other group do not receive massage. In other words, there are two different "levels" of the massage variable: *massage* or *no massage.* Then the researcher measures the other variable of interest, a treatment effect variable, in the people in the study. The treatment effect variable is called the *dependent variable* and could be many things—for example, degree of pain, amount of the cortisol (a stress hormone), amount of depression, and so forth. In our example, the dependent variable is level of stress. If the study has been well designed, the researcher can conclude that the only difference between the groups—the massage group and the no-massage group—is whether or not they received massage. Thus, if, at the end of the study, the massage group has lower levels of stress than the no-massage group, the researchers can conclude that massage truly has an effect on stress level.

To be so confident that massage truly has an effect on stress, the researcher has to implement a number of *controls* in the study. The controls will ensure that the two groups (massage and no massage) will not differ in any way except that some people receive massage and some do not.

The first example of a good control is *random assignment of participants to treatment conditions.* That is, participants should be placed in the two groups in a random fashion. For example, the participants in the study could pick pieces of paper out of a hat—some papers saying "massage" and others "no massage." This random assignment generally (but not perfectly) ensures that participants in the massage and no-massage groups are not systematically different in any way other than which group they are in. So, with this procedure, it is unlikely that, for example, the massage group is populated with people whose health is superior to people in the no-massage group or vice versa, or that the massage group is composed of mostly women and the no-massage group of mostly men.

A second control is *standardized procedures*. That means that participants in both groups are treated in the same fashion so that, again, the only difference between the two groups is whether or not they receive massage. For example, the researchers will be equally polite to the two groups of participants, and the two groups will be exposed to the same temperature conditions, and so on.

A third control is *use of a control group*. A control group is a "no treatment" group, in this case the no-massage group. This is used because people's physical or psychological health may improve over time without any treatment. Field refers to this unassisted improvement as "spontaneous recovery." At the end of the study, the treatment group (massage) and control group (no massage) are compared in terms of their improvement on the dependent variable (stress level). Perhaps both groups report less stress at the end of the study (which, let's say, is ten massage treatments over five weeks) than at the beginning, due presumably to spontaneous recovery, but the decrease in stress in the massage group is greater than the decrease in the control group. This additional decrease would be a true treatment effect.

Another control that is useful in some studies is a *placebo group*. This is a group of people who receive a type of "sham" treatment that, to the subjects, is indistinguishable from the real treatment. The false treatment guards against the possibility that people may get better simply by receiving *any* treatment, not just the treatment of interest—a phenomenon called the *placebo effect*.

Other types of controls and control issues exist in experimental research. For a more thorough discussion, refer to Keppel and Wickens (2004). In sum, the controlled experiment, when done well, is a very powerful research methodology that can provide strong evidence about the true effectiveness of treatments.

The second chapter in this part, "What We Really Know about Mindfulness-Based Stress Reduction" (Bishop, 2002), is a review of research on MBSR in many populations. Broadly defined, *mindfulness* is the state of being aware of what is happening in the present moment. MBSR involves achieving this state of mindfulness as a means to relax and promote health. Bishop meticulously examines the research on MBSR over the past twenty years or so. In his review, he brings up the issue just described— that many studies have been lacking in controls. Thus, he concludes his literature review by stating that it is difficult, based on evidence, to recommend MBSR at this point. More research is needed. So far, the most promising effects have been in nonclinical populations and in patients with cancer (the latter finding based on only one study). Next, Bishop provides a brief, enlightening discussion about the meaning of mindfulness and some history of the concept and related concepts. Future research, Bishop states, should be well designed with appropriate controls, focus on identifying potential mechanisms of action of MBSR, and clearly operationalize the mindfulness concept. The reader who is interested in learning about a variety of meditative approaches (such as contemplation and transcendental meditation), with descriptions of each and a review of research on their effectiveness, and other issues regarding meditation should refer to Carrington (1993).

Chapter 27, "Yoga for Stress Reduction and Injury Prevention at Work" (Gura, 2002), focuses on reducing stress on the job. Gura reviews research on stress-related injuries or illnesses and their impact on work, then makes an argument that the workplace is an ideal setting for stress management training, yoga in particular. The type of yoga she emphasizes in her article is hatha yoga, which involves stretching movements, postures, and deep breathing. Gura summarizes research indicating the effectiveness of yoga in general. She presents data from two small studies in which participants rated themselves on pain and stress before and after yoga workshops; in both studies, the participants indicated improvement in both areas after the workshops. Gura's chapter highlights the paucity of research on yoga; more investigation is clearly needed about this technique that has been becoming more and more popular in the United States and other Western countries.

Chapter 28 is from Everly and Lating's book *A Clinical Guide to Treatment of the Human Stress Response* (2002) and focuses on cognitive psychotherapies. The authors first reintroduce the concept of appraisal, which has been discussed or referred to throughout our book, especially by Lazarus in Chapter 2 of Volume 1 and by Kleinke in Chapter 16 of this volume. Next, they discuss the idea of cognitive primacy, which means that the emotional reaction to an event (that includes a stress reaction; see Chapter 2) is caused more by one's interpretation of the event than by the event per se. In the remainder of their chapter, Everly and Lating describe three highly influential cognitive psychotherapy theories: Ellis's rational-emotive therapy, Beck's cognitive therapy model, and Meichenbaum's stress inoculation training. They close with a brief description of positive psychology.

The fifth chapter in this part is from Somer's book *Food and Mood* (1999). The chapter describes the relationships among stress, diet, and immunity—relationships that are all bidirectional (e.g., stress can affect diet, but diet can also affect stress, and so on). As examples of how stress can affect one's diet or nutrition, stress reduces the absorption of some nutrients and increases the body's requirements for some vitamins and minerals. Also, when under stress, people tend to eat badly. Somer identifies many ways to try to fight stress with nutrition. For example, since many foods—including sugar, many types of fat, and caffeine—contribute to increasing stress levels, reducing the intake of these foods while under stress can help to maintain physical and psychological health. Additionally, a number of nutrients are drained by stress, and thus, increased intake of these nutrients is recommended while under stress. Examples include magnesium, vitamins A and C, and the B vitamins. Somer is very specific in her dietary recommendations, and she includes lists of "stress-busting" foods and recipes.

Chapter 30, "Exercise Treatment for Major Depression: Maintenance of Therapeutic Benefit" (Babyak et al., 2000), is a report of a study that compared exercise, sertraline (the antidepressant Zoloft), and an exercise–sertraline combination as treatments for major depression. Based on the results, exercise is a promising form of therapy for depression. In these data, the effectiveness of exercise surpassed the effectiveness rates for the other two treatment groups at ten months. Exercise is also effective for reducing anxiety (Landers, 1999), and fitness level is associated with reduced levels of psychological distress (Brown, 1991).

Several statistical or methodological terms that appear in this study may require explanation. First, n means sample size (number of participants). Refer to the introduction to Part IV for a discussion of the standard deviation (SD) and the statistic p (an abbreviation for probability). Other, more advanced statistics and statistical terms are described in the article, such as chi-square (symbolized as χ^2), multiple logistic regression analysis, OR (an abbreviation for odds ratio), and covariate. When presenting these statistics, the authors also describe the findings represented by the statistics; thus, their results are comprehensible even without an understanding of the actual statistics. An explanation of these advanced statistics is beyond the scope of this book. For in-depth descriptions of many advanced statistics used in the social sciences, Sage Publications has a series of small books, each featuring description and applications of a particular statistical technique. The series is entitled "Quantitative Applications in the Social Sciences."

The final chapter of the book, "Attitudes and Beliefs about 12-Step Groups among Addiction Treatment Clients and Clinicians: Identifying Obstacles to Participation" (Laudet, 2003), addresses some issues about a type of coping technique that so often negatively impacts health, harms relationships, and may affect job performance: use of drugs and alcohol. The author introduces her topic by describing literature indicating that 12-step programs are helpful for people in recovery for substance use. She argues that, at present, 12-step groups (12SGs) have fairly high attrition rates. Additionally, many substance users never attend a 12-step meeting. Given that literature indicates the effectiveness of 12SGs, their wide availability, their cost-effectiveness (meetings are free), and the necessity for ongoing support for people in recovery, Laudet argues that 12SG participation should be incorporated as part of recovery treatment for many, perhaps most, people with substance use issues. The purpose of Laudet's study was to identify both clients' and clinicians' attitudes and beliefs about 12SGs in an attempt to determine how to encourage participation. Examples of obstacles to participation identified by clients included lack of motivation and lack of preparedness for change. Laudet discusses the clinical implications of her findings.

Laudet reports a number of statistical tests or procedures that require some explanation. She reports p values and standard deviations in the Results section, and t-tests in Table 31.2 and elsewhere in the Results section. Each of these statistics has already been described in the introduction to Part IV. In addition, she utilizes a type of *factor analysis* called "principle components analysis" (results are presented in Table 31.5).

Factor analysis is a statistical procedure that is used to summarize repetitive information. The procedure will usually be used when a researcher has a lot of information and expects that this information can be summarized as several "factors." The result of a factor analysis will therefore be at least one factor, most often more than one. The resultant factors are different from one another in meaning and can be viewed as "summaries" of the components of which they are made. For example, Laudet factor-analyzed her "negative aspects of 12-step groups" scale, which consists of twelve items, because she suspected that these items could be summarized in some meaningful way. The result was four factors. Each factor is composed of three items on the scale. (We have to note that the results of factor analyses are not always so "tidy"—in most cases, factors are *not* all composed of the same number of items.) One factor is called "Risks of Participation." The scale items that compose this factor are "Can get retraumatized or triggered in a 12SG," "12SGs can lead to pick-up or relapse," and "Can become dependent on 12SGs." These three items were correlated with one another and are poorly correlated with other items (hence they comprise a factor). A second factor, which is relatively unrelated to the first factor or its component items, is "Religion and Powerlessness." It is also composed of three items: "12SGs can be too intense for some people" and two others (see Table 31.5). The "factor loading" is a correlation between the item and the factor. For a thorough description of factor analysis, refer to Kline (1994).

TERMS

The chapters in Part VI include a number of technical terms and names of significant persons. Can you define these terms or identify these people? Definitions of terms are included in the glossary in the back of the book

General Stress and General Psychology Terms

- Absorption
- Affect (affectivity)
- Alcoholics Anonymous
- Appraisal
- Beck's cognitive therapy model
- Cognitive-behavioral therapy (CBT)
- Cognitive mediation
- Cognitive primacy perspective
- Cognitive therapy
- *Diagnostic and Statistical Manual of Mental Disorders (DSM)*
- Dissociative state
- Ellis's ABC Model of Emotional Reaction

- Hatha yoga
- Mindfulness
- Openness to experience
- Parasympathetic nervous system
- Positive psychology
- Posttraumatic stress disorder (PTSD)
- Primary appraisal
- Progressive muscle relaxation
- Psychoneuroimmunology
- Rational-emotive therapy (RET)
- Secondary appraisal
- Self-efficacy
- Sertraline (Zoloft)
- Social support

- Stress inoculation training
- Sympathetic nervous system
- Transactional model
- 12-step group (12SG)

Physiological Terms

- Adreno-corticotropic hormone (ACTH)
- Catecholamine
- Corticotropin-releasing factor (CRF)
- Cortisol
- Denditric arborization
- Dopamine
- Epinephrine
- Fibromyalgia
- Glucocorticoid
- Glucose
- Hippocampus
- Hypothalamus
- Insulin
- Lymphocyte
- Neurohormone
- Neuropeptide Y
- Neurotransmitter
- Norepinephrine
- Omega-3 fatty acid
- Polyunsaturated fat
- Saturated fat
- Serotonin
- Somatostatin
- Substance P
- Trans fatty acid (TFA)

Statistical or Research Methods Terms

- Confounding variable
- Construct validity
- Control group
- Correlation coefficient
- Dependent variable
- Double-blind study
- Factor analysis
- Independent variable
- Internal reliability
- Meta-analysis
- Operationalization
- Placebo effect
- Prospective study
- Random assignment to control group and experimental group
- Regression toward the mean
- Repeated measures design
- Social desirability effect
- Spontaneous recovery
- Standard deviation
- Standardized procedures
- *t*-test
- Within-subjects design

Stress Researchers and Theorists

- Aaron Beck
- Albert Ellis
- Richard Lazarus
- Donald Meichenbaum

REFERENCES

Babyak, M., Blumenthal, J. A., Herman, S., Khatri, P., Doraiswamy, M., Moore, K., et al. (2000). Exercise treatment for major depression: Maintenance of therapeutic benefit at 10 months. *Psychosomatic Medicine, 62,* 633–638.

Bishop, S. R. (2002). What do we really know about mindfulness-based stress reduction? *Psychosomatic Medicine, 64,* 71–83.

Brown, J. D. (1991). Staying fit and staying well: Physical fitness as a moderator of life stress. *Journal of Personality and Social Psychology, 60*(4), 555–561.

Carrington, P. (1993). Modern forms of meditation. In P. M. Lehrer & R. L. Woolfolk (Eds.), *Principles and practice of stress management* (pp. 139–168). New York: Guilford Press.

Davis, M., Eshelman, E. R., & McKay, M. (2000). *The relaxation and stress reduction workbook.* Oakland, CA: New Harbinger.

Everly, G. S., Jr., & Lating, J. M. (2002). *A clinical guide to the treatment of the human stress response.* New York: Kluwer Academic/Plenum Press.

Field, T. M. (1998). Massage therapy effects. *American Psychologist, 53*(12), 1270–1281.

Girdano, D. A., Dusek, D. E., & Everly, G. S., Jr. (2005). *Controlling stress and tension* (7th ed.). San Francisco: Pearson/Benjamin Cummings.

Gura, S. T. (2002). Yoga for stress reduction and injury prevention at work. *Work, 19,* 3–7.

Keppel, G., & Wickens, T. D. (2004). *Design and analysis: A researcher's handbook.* Upper Saddle River, NJ: Prentice Hall.

Kline, P. (1994). *An easy guide to factor analysis.* New York: Routledge.

Landers, D. M. (1999). The influence of exercise on mental health. In C. B. Corbin & R. P. Pangrazi (Eds.), *Toward a better understanding of physical fitness and activity.* Scottsdale, AZ: Holcomb Hathaway.

Laudet, A. B. (2003). Attitudes and beliefs about 12-step groups among addiction treatment clients and clinicians: Toward identifying obstacles to participation. *Substance Use & Misuse, 38*(14), 2017–2047.

Seaward, B. L. (2006). *Managing stress: Principles and strategies for health and well-being* (5th ed.). Sudbury, MA: Jones and Bartlett.

Somer, E. (1999). *Food and mood* (2nd ed.). New York: Henry Holt.

CHAPTER 25

Massage Therapy Effects

Tiffany M. Field

Massage therapy is one of the oldest forms of treatment in the world, having first been described in China during the second century B.C. and soon afterward in India and Egypt. Hippocrates, in 400 B.C., defined *medicine* as "the art of rubbing." Massage therapy disappeared from the American medical scene at approximately the time of the pharmaceutical revolution of the 1940s. Now considered an "alternative" therapy, massage is becoming popular again as part of the alternative medicine movement. At this time, it is commonly defined by massage therapists as the manipulation of soft tissue by trained therapists for therapeutic purposes.

Despite its long history and popularity, a Medline search yielded only about two hundred articles from the last thirty years regarding massage therapy. Much of this literature suffers from classic methodological problems. First, although the literature has focused on clinical conditions, very few studies are based on clinical trials. Typical sampling problems are the failure to include control groups and the lack of random assignment to treatment and control conditions. Often, the participants have served as their own controls, and the measures were simply collected at the beginning and the end of the treatment period. Although within-subject controls are important in controlling for individual differences, treatment individuals need to be compared with nontreatment or comparison-treatment individuals. Using a within-subjects design alone could result in effects that might be explained otherwise by spontaneous recovery, a placebo effect, and statistical regression. The control group would optimally be an attention control or a comparison-treatment control to avoid the possibility that the therapist's attention alone explained the effects.

A second problem is the very small sample sizes used in most of the studies, along with the fact that the treatment group often received more than one type of treatment. Another problem is the potential for initial-level effects, where the treatment may have differential effects depending on the initial level of the participants. This, in itself, could explain many of the mixed findings. Still another problem is the use of inappropriate statistics. Only two meta-analyses appear in the literature. This has occurred because there are not enough studies with comparable designs and standards, and too many different massage therapy techniques have been used across the studies. Very few replications and virtually no follow-up studies have been conducted. Although one might not expect massage therapy to have sustained effects, any more than temporary drugs, diet, or exercise, follow-ups are needed to assess that question. Finally, there would appear to be a publication bias, where positive results are inevitably published and negative results lay idle.

For the above reasons, I have conducted, along with colleagues at the Touch Research Institute, a number of massage therapy studies, focusing on a variety of different conditions that might benefit from massage therapy. In each of these studies, there was a theoretical reason to expect positive results. In addition, other studies from the literature were included in this review if they met the criteria of (1) adequate sample size determined by power analysis and (2) random assignment to a treatment group and a comparison-treatment or attention-control group.

The massage therapy technique used throughout all of these studies, unless otherwise specified, involved deep tissue manipulation with presumed stimulation of pressure receptors. Unless otherwise specified, adult studies involved eight sessions (two per week for four consecutive weeks) of thirty minutes' duration, and all child sessions were performed by parents on a nightly basis for thirty days for fifteen minutes' duration. The parameters for the adult sessions were based on practical considerations, namely, that most adults could not afford more than two half-hour sessions per week by a professional or a significant other. The parameters of the child sessions were based on the consideration that children with chronic illness may benefit from a "daily dose" and that their parents could also benefit from providing the massage at no monetary expense to themselves.

The studies are grouped thematically by the primary objective of treatment, for example, facilitating growth or reducing pain. They are organized in a sequence that may seem arbitrary but that seems to capture the longitudinal progression from primary agendas early in life to those later in life, for example, focusing on facilitating growth in premature infants for the early life agenda to enhancing immune function, a more primary agenda for later in life. An attempt was made throughout to address potential underlying mechanisms that are unique to the different conditions, as well as to discuss an overarching potential mechanism for massage therapy across conditions. Thus, the order selected is: facilitating growth; reducing pain; increasing alertness; diminishing stress, anxiety, and depression; and enhancing immune function.

ENHANCING GROWTH

Animal Models

Data from research on rat and monkey models support the use of touch as therapy. In a recent model developed by Schanberg and colleagues, rat pups were first removed from their mother to investigate touch deprivation (Schanberg, 1995). Then, the mother's behavior was simulated to restore the physiology and biochemistry of the rat pups to normal. In several studies, a decrease was noted in growth hormone (ornithine decarboxylase) when the pups were removed from their mother. This decrease was observed in all body organs, including the heart, liver, and brain (all parts of the brain, including the cerebrum, cerebellum, and brain stem). These values returned to normal when the pups were stimulated using techniques approximating the mother's behavior.

A graduate student observed rat mothers' nocturnal behavior and noted that they frequently tongue-lick, pinch, and carry the rat pups. When the researchers tried each of these maneuvers, only the tongue licking (simulated by a paintbrush dipped in water and briskly stroked all over the body of the rat pup) restored the growth hormone values to their normal level. Because thermo-regulation might also be a factor, the same study was conducted with an anesthetized mother rat (Schanberg, 1995). The pups could still suckle and maintain their body temperature by continuous contact with the mother rat but were not being tongue-licked. The pups experienced similar decreases in growth hormone. More recently, Schanberg and his colleagues discovered a near-immediate gene underlying protein synthesis that responds to tactile stimulation, suggesting genetic origins of this touch–growth relationship (Schanberg, 1995).

Related studies by Meaney et al. (1990) suggest a long-term impact of handling on the modulation of cortisol (stress hormone) production. Rats who were handled more as pups showed less corticosteroid production, more elaborate dendritic arborization in the hippocampal region, and better maze performance (memory function) in the aging rat. It is, of course, also possible that increased cortisol or increased stress could accelerate development, as in some animal models, and it is also possible that the enhanced hippocampal development may be mediated by some third element, for example, another neurotransmitter or neurohormone. For example, increased serotonin might account for both effects.

Preterm Infants

Parallels in the decreased cortisol–increased hippocampal development relationship have already been noted in human infants at the Hammersmith Hospital in London. Research by Modi and Glover (1995) provided similar documentation of lower cortisol levels in massaged preterm infants, and they currently are examining magnetic resonance imaging (MRI) data for examples of faster development of the hippocampal region in those infants. In a sample of very premature (29 weeks median gestational age) and very low birth weight (median = 980 g), neonates' cortisol concentrations decreased consistently after massage. Modi and Glover are using a computerized subtraction method to document hippocampal development across MRIs taken before and after the massage treatment period. The rat model developed by Meaney et al. for decreased cortisol leading to hippocampal development may have good parallels in the Modi and Glover preterm-infant model, just as the Schanberg (1995) rat model for stimulation-induced growth has been a good model for massage-induced weight gain in the preterm infant.

Greater weight gain has been reported in several studies on preterm infants, including those who are cocaine exposed and HIV exposed. In the preterm-infant studies, Swedish massage or heavy stroking (stroking with pressure) was used. Although infants, particularly premature infants, may seem to be fragile, some pressure is needed for the massage to be effective. A review of the infant massage literature suggests that those who used light stroking did not report weight gain, for example, whereas those who used stroking with pressure did (Scarfidi et al., 1986).

In a series of studies I recently reviewed (Field, 1998), preterm infants in the neonatal intensive care unit were given fifteen-minute massages three times a day for ten days while they were still in the incubator (massaged through the incubator portholes; Field et al., 1986; Scafidi et al., 1990). The treated infants, compared with control infants, gained 47 percent more weight and were hospitalized for six days less, at a hospital cost savings of $10,000 per infant. Norepinephrine and epinephrine levels increased in the massaged infants relative to the control infants (who did not receive massage therapy) across the treatment period. Because these neurotransmitters normally increase during the neonatal period, this finding was interpreted as massage therapy facilitating the normal developmental increase in these catecholamines in preterm infants during their newborn period (Kuhn et al., 1991). Finally, the treated infants performed better on the Brazelton Neonatal Behavior Assessment Scale (Brazelton, 1973).

At one year, the treated infants were still showing a weight advantage, and they also performed better on the Bayley Scales of Infant Development (Field, Scafidi, & Schanberg, 1987). Their scores averaged twelve points higher on the mental scale and thirteen points higher on the motor scale than the control group. The infants' more responsive behavior on the Brazelton Neonatal Behavior Assessment Scale apparently elicited more stimulation from their parents, which led to the later gains in growth and development.

Replication studies have been conducted in Israel (Goldstein-Ferber, 1998) and the Philippines (Jinon, 1996). In the Philippines study, which was an exact replication of the Field et al. (1986) methodology, the preterm infants who were massaged gained 45 percent more weight than the nonmassaged infants. In the Israeli study, which used mothers as therapists, 31 percent greater weight gain was reported for the massaged versus control preterm infants; in addition, the mothers who provided the massage experienced a decrease in depression. The Philippine and Israeli studies' weight gain data (45% and 31%, respectively) approximated that published a decade earlier by Field et al. (1986) and Scafidi et al. (1990) (47% and 31%, respectively). Finally, a more recent study by Dieter, Field, and Hernandez-Reif (1998) suggested that a 46 percent greater weight gain can be achieved in preterm infants following only one week of massage.

Cocaine-Exposed Infants

Similar weight gains were noted in a study on cocaine-exposed infants who were massaged versus those who were not (Wheeden et al., 1993). In addition, these infants showed superior motor behavior.

HIV-Exposed Infants

In a study on HIV-exposed infants, the mothers of the infants were used as the massage therapists. The mothers' treatment compliance rates were very high, perhaps because of the guilt they expressed for having exposed their infants to HIV and their own high anxiety levels (Scafidi & Field, 1996). Teaching parents to massage their infants often lowers their anxiety levels that are related to their feelings of helplessness about their infant's or child's condition. Helping with their children's treatment might be expected to decrease their anxiety levels and make them feel that they are contributing to the treatment. In addition, daily massages are economically feasible when the parents are used as therapists. In the study on HIV-exposed infants, the massaged infants' weight gain was significantly greater than the control group who did not receive massage therapy, and massaged infants showed significantly fewer stress behaviors. The parents' involvement and their own reduced stress can be thought of as a confounding or a contributing variable in all studies that use parents as the massage therapists.

Full-Term Infants

In a study of forty full-term one- to three-month-old infants born to adolescent mothers, infants were given fifteen minutes of either massage or rocking for twelve days over a six-week period. During the massage sessions, the massaged versus the rocked infants spent more time in active alert and active awake states; cried less; had lower salivary cortisol levels, suggesting lower stress levels; and spent less time in an active awake state after the massage session (as opposed to the rocking session), suggesting that massage may be more effective than rocking for inducing sleep (Field, Grizzle, Scafidi, Abrams, et al., 1996). Analyses of the longer-term effects suggested that by the end of the six-week treatment period, the massage group infants gained more weight; improved on emotionality, sociability, and soothability temperament dimensions; showed better face-to-face interaction behaviors;

had decreased urinary stress hormones (cortisol) and catecholamines (nor-epinephrine, epinephrine); and had increased serotonin levels.

Converging data may suggest a potential underlying mechanism for the massage therapy–weight gain relationship. Uvnas-Moberg, Widstrom, Marchini, and Winberg (1987) reported that stimulating the inside of the mouth of the newborn led to the increased release of gastrointestinal food absorption hormones, including gastrin and insulin. Field et al. (1982) reported that sucking on a pacifier during gavage feedings led to signifi-cantly greater weight gain in preterm infants. Stimulating the entire body, as in massage therapy, leads to increased vagal activity and insulin levels (Field, 1995) as well as increased weight gain (Field et al., 1986). The "vegetative" branch of the vagus is known to stimulate the release of food absorption hormones, including insulin and gastrin (Uvnas-Moberg et al., 1987). The massaged infants in the above studies did not eat more food and did not sleep more, so they were not simply consuming or conserving more calories. Rather, the weight gain seems to have been mediated by an increase in vagal activity, which in turn facilitated the release of food absorption hormones (at least insulin).

The superior habituation performance (an index of newborn memory) noted at the neonatal period and superior performance on the mental scale of the Bayley Scales for Infant Development at one year (also related to infant memory skills) may derive from enhanced hippocampal develop-ment. As noted earlier, Meaney et al. (1990) tracked a relationship in rats between increased glucocorticoids, decreased dendritic arborization in the hippocampal region, and inferior maze performance, suggesting impaired memory function in the aging rats that had been deprived of tactile stimu-lation as pups. Similarly, the more elaborate dendritic arborization noted in MRIs of the hippocampal region in massaged preterm neonates by Modi and Glover (1995) may be related to the superior memory perform-ance noted in the massaged newborns and their performance again at one year of age.

Pregnancy Massage

Preterm delivery may result from pregnancy anxiety, depression, and related obstetric complications. Because anxiety, depression, and related stress hormones can be decreased by massage therapy, as has been noted in many studies (see the section on alleviating stress, depression, and anxi-ety below), massage therapy was expected to have similar effects on preg-nant women. In many countries, pregnant women are massaged several times daily for relaxation and to reduce their anxiety levels (Older, 1982). In a recent study, pregnant women who were massaged, compared to pregnant women who experienced relaxation therapy, reported lower anxi-ety and depression and had lower stress hormone levels (cortisol and nor-epinephrine; Field et al., 1999). The massaged women experienced less sleep disturbance and less pregnancy pain (lower back and leg pains) and had fewer obstetric and postnatal complications, including lower prematu-rity rates.

PAIN REDUCTION DURING PAINFUL PROCEDURES

Childbirth Labor

In a study by Field, Hernandez-Reif, Taylor, Quintino, and Burman (1997), significant others of pregnant women were taught to massage the women during childbirth, while a control group received the standard breathing coaching throughout labor. The massaged women had lower anxiety and depression scores, decreased cortisol levels, less need for medication, shorter labor, fewer days in the hospital, and less postpartum depression. In current research, we are assessing the possibility that massage therapy stimulates oxytocin, which in turn could facilitate labor progression. Studies are needed to monitor the fetal response to the mother's reduced pain and decreased time in labor as well as the neonatal outcome.

Massage Therapy prior to Debridement for Burn Patients

Massage therapy has also been used to reduce anticipatory anxiety prior to debridement (skin brushing for severe burns) and to indirectly alleviate pain during that procedure (Field, Peck, et al., 1998). After a five-day course of thirty-minute massages prior to debridement, burn patients had lower anxiety levels and associated decreases in stress hormones (cortisol). Depression also decreased by day 5, probably because of the decrease in pain.

Postoperative Pain

An equivalent-groups design with a treatment group of nineteen patients and a control group of twenty patients was used to investigate the impact of massage therapy on patients' perceptions of postoperative pain (Nixon, Teschendorff, Finney, & Karnilowicz, 1997). Controlling for age, the results indicated that massage produced a significant reduction in patients' perception of pain over a twenty-four-hour period.

REDUCING PAIN IN CHRONIC PAIN CONDITIONS

Juvenile Rheumatoid Arthritis

Chronic pain is a problem for children with juvenile rheumatoid arthritis. Anti-inflammatory agents used for their pain have ceiling effects, and other drugs such as narcotics cannot be used due to their potentially addictive effects. Thus, massage therapy is being assessed for its usefulness for pain relief. In a study in which parents provided their children daily massages, several positive effects were noted (Field, Hernandez-Reif, Seligman, et al., 1997). The massaged children (compared to the control children who received progressive muscle relaxation) experienced (1) decreased anxiety and cortisol after the first and last sessions and (2) decreased pain and pain limitations on activities over the one-month period, as reported by the children, their parents, and their physicians.

Fibromyalgia

In a study on fibromyalgia syndrome (pain all over the body for no known etiology), patients were randomly assigned to one of three conditions: massage therapy, transcutaneous electrical stimulation (TENS, a steel roller the size of a pen that transmits a small, barely discernible current as it is rolled across the body), or transcutaneous electrical stimulation without current (SHAM TENS) for thirty-minute treatment sessions two times per week for five weeks (Sunshine et al., 1997). As compared with the TENS and SHAM TENS groups, the massage therapy patients reported lower anxiety and depression, and their cortisol levels were lower immediately after the therapy sessions on the first and last days of the study. The massage therapy group also showed greater improvement on a dolorimeter measure of pain and reported less pain, stiffness, and fatigue and fewer nights of difficult sleeping.

Lower Back Pain

Lower back pain is one of the most frequent causes of absenteeism and workers' compensation claims. Massage therapy appears to provide pain relief. In one study, twenty-four adults with chronic lower back pain were randomly assigned to a massage therapy or a progressive muscle relaxation group (Hernandez-Reif, Field, Krasnegor, & Theakston, 2001). Sessions were thirty minutes long and were conducted twice a week for five weeks. By the end of the study, the members of the massage therapy group showed significant improvement in range-of-motion tests, and they reported less pain and anxiety and improved mood. They also had lower depression scores and higher serotonin and dopamine levels by the end of the treatment. Taken together, these data suggest that massage therapy is an effective primary treatment for chronic lower back pain.

Another study on lower back pain involved massaging the hamstring muscle group of one randomly assigned lower extremity in a group of normal adults (Crosman, Chateauvert, & Weisberg, 1984). This treatment was considered relevant inasmuch as lower back pain is often exacerbated by tight hamstrings. The participants were given a nine- to twelve-minute massage treatment to the posterior aspect of one leg. Passive range of motion of both lower extremities was measured by taking the perpendicular distance from the floor to a table surface in a straight leg raise and by conventional goniometry for hip flexion and knee extension. Measurements were taken before and immediately after massage and seven days after the massage treatment. Immediate postmassage increases in range of motion were noted in the massaged legs and not in the nonmassaged legs.

Migraine Headaches

At least two studies have suggested that massage therapy is also effective for migraine headaches. In one study, twenty-six adults with migraines were assigned to either a massage therapy or a standard treatment control group (a group that received only medications for migraines; Hernandez-Reif, Dieter, Field, Swerdlow, & Diego, 1998). By the last day of the study, the massage therapy group showed fewer distress symptoms, reported less pain, had more headache-free days, was taking fewer analgesics, was having fewer sleep disturbances, and had higher serotonin (5HIAA in urine) levels.

In a second study (Puustjarvi, Airaksinen, & Pontinen, 1990), twenty-one female patients suffering from chronic tension headaches received ten sessions of upper-body massage consisting of deep-tissue techniques. When found, trigger points were carefully and forcefully massaged. The range of cervical movement, surface electroneuromyography (ENMG) on the frontalis and trapezius muscles, scores on Visual Analogue Scale (VAS), and the incidence of neck pain during a two-week period before and after the treatment, together with the Beck Depression Inventory (BDI), were taken for evaluation and follow-up. The range of movement in all directions increased, and the VAS and the number of days with neck pain decreased significantly. A significant change also occurred in ENMG on the frontalis muscle, and scores on the BDI showed significant improvement after the treatment.

Potential Models for Mechanisms of Touch and Pain Relief

Gate Theory

Pain alleviation has most frequently been attributed to the gate theory (Melzack & Wall, 1965). This theory suggests that pain can be alleviated by pressure or cold temperature because pain fibers are shorter and less myelinated than pressure and cold temperature receptors. Pressure or cold temperature stimuli are therefore received by the brain before the pain stimulus, the gate is closed, and the pain stimulus is not processed.

Serotonin

Another possibility is increased serotonin levels after massage therapy for both infants (Field, Grizzle, Scafidi, Abrams, et al., 1996) and adults (Hernandez-Reif et al., 2004); Ironson et al., 1996). Serotonin may inhibit the transmission of noxious nerve signals to the brain.

Sleep Deficits

Another potential theory for pain alleviation from massage therapy (Sunshine et al., 1997) relates to quiet or restorative sleep. During deep sleep, somatostatin is normally released. Without this substance, pain is experienced. Substance P is released when an individual is deprived of deep sleep, and it is notable for causing pain. Thus, when people are deprived of deep sleep, they may have less somatostatin and increased substance P, resulting in greater pain. One of the leading theories for the pain associated with fibromyalgia syndrome, for example, is the production of substance P due to deep sleep deprivation. One of the possible reasons the participants with fibromyalgia syndrome in the Sunshine et al. study experienced less pain following the massage therapy treatment period is that they were experiencing less sleep disturbance.

REDUCING NEUROMUSCULAR PROBLEMS

Multiple Sclerosis

Ambulation is a significant problem for patients with multiple sclerosis. Because massage therapy involves deep manipulation of muscles and can increase range of motion, it might be expected to improve ambulation. In a recent study, twenty-four adults (mean age = 48 years) diagnosed with multiple sclerosis and requiring unilateral support to walk were assigned to a massage therapy or a control group (Hernandez-Reif, Field, Field, & Theakston, 1998). The massage therapy group received thirty-minute massages twice a week for five weeks. The effects of the massage were assessed immediately after the massage using self-reports on stress levels and grip strength tests, and longer-term effects were assessed at the end of the study using self-reports on body image, self-esteem, depression, and functional activities, including ambulation. Although both groups reported being less anxious after the first and last day of the study, only the massage group reported less depressed moods. In addition, by the end of the study, the massage group's social lifestyle and functional activity status had improved significantly. However, grip strength was unaffected, and ambulation was only marginally improved.

Spinal Cord Injury

Two major problems for spinal cord injury patients are restricted range of motion and muscle atrophy in the unaffected areas. Massage therapy might be expected to alleviate at least the range-of-motion problem, as it did in the lower back pain study just reviewed. Twenty patients with spinal cord injury at the C5–C7 spinal cord levels were assigned to a massage therapy or a control group (Diego et al., 2002). The massage therapy group received thirty-minute massages twice a week for five weeks. The massages focused on participants' shoulders, arms, hands, and back muscles. The effects of the massage were assessed immediately after the session using self-reports on anxiety and mood, and the longer-term effects were assessed at the end of the study by physical therapists (unaware of group assignments), who evaluated activities of daily living, passive and active range of motion, and muscle activity. Participants in the massage group reported less anxiety and better mood following the five-week study. In addition, significant improvement occurred on functional living activities and in wrist and elbow range of motion.

A series of studies has addressed the effects of massage therapy on the Hoffmann reflex (H-reflex) amplitude in persons with a spinal cord injury. The studies, conducted by Morelli and colleagues (Morelli, Seaborne, & Sullivan, 1990, 1991; Sullivan, Williams, Seaborne, & Morelli, 1991), are considered among the best controlled massage therapy studies in the literature because of their reliance on the more objective neurophysiological measures. The purpose of this group of studies was to investigate the effects of massage therapy on neuromuscular excitability as measured by changes in the H-reflex. A reduction in the H-reflex amplitude is critical to the comfort of spinal cord injury patients for reducing cramps and spasms. In these studies, the H-reflex peak-to-peak amplitude was measured during and following a three-minute massage to the triceps muscle. Typically a 60 to 80 percent decrease in the H-reflex amplitude was observed during the massage, followed by a return to baseline levels immediately following the termination of the massage. In contrast to the activation of cutaneous receptors by light fingertip pressure, this stimulation of deep-tissue receptors by tendon-pressure muscle vibration inhibits activities along the reflex pathway as measured by the H-reflex. This suggests that deep-lying receptors override the influences exercised by superficial cutaneous receptors.

ENHANCING ATTENTIVENESS

Attention Deficits

Autism

One of the most salient problems of children with autism is their inattentiveness. Although they have also been anecdotally described as being extremely sensitive to touch and as typically disliking being touched, they showed surprisingly little resistance to being massaged in a recent study (Field, Lasko, et al., 1997). Massage may not have been aversive to them because it is predictable, unlike the social stimulation they frequently resist, and because it involves pressure. The children who were massaged, as opposed to the children who were held by their teachers and shown objects, showed a decrease in their off-task behavior in the classroom following a ten-day period of massage. Their "social relatedness" to their teachers also improved, and they showed fewer autistic behaviors (orienting to sounds and stereotypic behaviors).

Attention Deficit Hyperactivity Disorder (ADHD)

Children with ADHD have similar problems staying on task in the classroom. In a recent study, adolescents with ADHD were provided massage therapy or relaxation therapy for ten consecutive school days (Field, Quintino, Hernandez-Reif, & Koslovsky, 1998). The massage therapy group, compared with the relaxation therapy group, showed less fidgeting behavior following the sessions. In addition, after the two-week period, their scores on the Conners Scale (Conners, 1985) completed by their teachers (who were unaware of the group assignments) suggested that the children spent more time on task and were less hyperactive in the classroom.

Enhancing Alertness

In a job stress study, medical school faculty and staff received fifteen-minute chair massages during their lunch breaks (Field, Ironson, et al., 1996). These sessions involved deep pressure in the head, neck, shoulders, and back regions. Surprisingly, instead of becoming sleepier after their midday massage, the participants reported experiencing heightened alertness, much like a "runner's high." Electroencephalogram (EEG) recordings before, during, and after the massage sessions confirmed the participants' impressions. As compared with a group of relaxation therapy participants, their levels of alpha-wave activity significantly decreased during massage (in contrast to alpha levels typically increasing during sleep), suggesting a pattern of heightened alertness. A math computation task was added to determine whether this EEG pattern of heightened alertness translated into performance. Following the massage sessions, the computation time was significantly reduced, and computation accuracy increased.

ALLEVIATING STRESS, DEPRESSION, AND ANXIETY

Posttraumatic Stress Disorder

Posttraumatic stress disorder is characterized by depression and behavior problems in children. Many children in Florida showed posttraumatic stress symptoms following Hurricane Andrew in 1992, and several of the children's disciplinary problems in the classroom were exacerbated by the hurricane (Field, Seligman, Scafidi, & Schanberg, 1996). After a month of massage therapy (two times per week), their symptoms and their depression decreased in contrast to a control group (who watched a relaxing video). Anxiety also decreased, and self-image improved as reflected in their self-drawings. A girl's self-drawing, for example, on the first day was very small, had dark colors, and no facial features. By the last day, she drew a birthday party with balloons, sunshine and birds, and friends attending the party.

Child and Adolescent Psychiatric Patients

In a study on hospitalized depressed children and adolescents (Field et al., 1992), those who received back massages for a week were less depressed and anxious and had lower stress hormone levels (lower saliva cortisol levels as well as lower urinary cortisol and norepinephrine levels) than those in a control group who viewed relaxing videotapes, and time-lapse videotapes of their sleep–wake behavior revealed more organized sleep patterns. In addition, the nurses on the unit rated the massaged adolescents as being less anxious and more cooperative by the last day of the study. In a similar pilot study on adult patients with anxiety, massaged patients showed a decrease in stress response patterns, including decreased heart rate, electromyography (EMG), and skin resistance (McKechnie, Wilson, Watson, & Scott, 1983).

In a related study, thirty-two depressed adolescent mothers received ten thirty-minute sessions of massage therapy or relaxation therapy across a five-week period (Field, Grizzle, Scafidi, & Schanberg, 1996). Although both groups reported lower anxiety following their first and last therapy sessions, only the massage therapy group showed behavioral and stress hormone changes, including decreases in anxious behavior, pulse, and salivary cortisol levels. A decrease in urine cortisol and norepinephrine levels suggested lower stress following the five-week period for the massage therapy group.

Eating Disorders in Adolescent Women

Another group of people who experience severe depression are adolescents with eating disorders such as bulimia (overeating and vomiting) and anorexia. Adolescents with bulimia who received one month of twice-weekly massages along with their standard daily group therapy treatment (versus adolescents with bulimia who received only the standard group therapy) had fewer symptoms of depression, lower anxiety levels, and lower stress hormone (urinary cortisol) levels (Field, Schanberg, et al., 1998). Their eating habits also improved, and their body image was less distorted. In a similar study on adolescents with anorexia at the same hospital, the massaged women (relative to the standard group therapy control women) reported lower anxiety levels and had lower stress hormone (cortisol) levels (Hart et al., 2001). Over the one-month treatment period, they also reported less body dissatisfaction on the Eating Disorder Inventory (Garner, Olmstead, & Polivy, 1983) and had increased dopamine levels.

Chronic Fatigue

Depression is also a problem for adults with chronic fatigue syndrome. In a recent study with this population, participants were randomly assigned to a massage therapy or a SHAM TENS control group (Field, Sunshine, et al., 1997). Immediately after the sessions on the first and last days of the study, the massage therapy participants had lower depression and anxiety scores and lower stress hormone (salivary cortisol) levels than the SHAM TENS participants. Longer-term effects (last day vs. first day) indicated that the massage therapy group was experiencing fewer symptoms of depression as well as fewer somatic symptoms, more hours of sleep, lower urinary cortisol levels, and elevated urinary dopamine levels.

Depressed Elderly Volunteers Massaging Infants

For another study, a group of depressed elderly people was recruited to massage infants and to receive massage (Field, Hernandez-Reif, Quintino, Schanberg, & Kuhn, 1997). In a counterbalanced design, grandparent volunteers were giving a massage daily for one month, and then they were massaged themselves for one month. Their depression scores decreased following the one-month period of massaging the infants, and they experienced increased affect and self-esteem and decreased cortisol levels. The grandparent volunteers benefited more from giving than from receiving the massage, perhaps because, as they reported, they felt "awkward" receiving massages. Their lifestyle habits also improved more following the period of giving versus receiving massages (e.g., they reported drinking fewer cups of coffee per day, they made more social phone calls, and they made fewer trips to the doctor's office).

Models Underlying Touch Alleviating Depression

Depressed mood was decreased and anxiety levels and stress hormones (norepinephrine, epinephrine, cortisol) were reduced in all of the above studies. One potential mechanism is suggested by a recent study measuring frontal EEG activation following massage in depressed adolescents (Jones & Field, 1999). Shifts to a more positive mood were notably accompanied by shifts from right frontal EEG activation (normally associated with sad affect) to left frontal EEG activation (normally associated with happy affect), or at least to symmetry (midway between sad and happy affect), in both the mothers and their infants. Right frontal EEG activation (noted in chronically depressed adults and also observed in the depressed mothers and infants in our study) was shifted toward symmetry following a twenty-minute massage (Jones & Field, 1999). Chemical and electrophysiological changes from a negative to a positive balance may underlie the decrease in depression noted following massage therapy.

A related potential mechanism may be the increase noted in vagal activity following massage therapy (Field, 1995). The nucleus-ambiguous branch of the vagus (the "smart" vagus) stimulates facial expressions and vocalizations, which contribute to less depressed affect and, in turn, could feed back to effect less depressed feelings (Porges, 1997).

CARDIOVASCULAR SYMPTOMS OF STRESS

Fifteen-minute massages significantly lowered blood pressure in fifty-two participants monitored before and after massage sessions at work (Cady & Jones, 1997). Both systolic and diastolic blood pressures were decreased. In a group of participants with chronic high blood pressure, massage therapy reduced only the diastolic pressure (Hernandez-Reif et al., 2000). The mechanism for these decreases is not known and highlights the need for further study.

AUTOIMMUNE DISORDERS

Diabetic Children

In a study on the vagal activity and insulin levels following massage therapy, I had reported (as described earlier) that both vagal activity and insulin levels increased (Field, 1995). This led to the investigation of massage therapy effects on diabetic children's clinical course. In that study, we used parents as therapists, because the cost of daily massages was prohibitively expensive and because we knew that massaging children had helped the therapists (the volunteer grandparents) as well (Field, Hernandez-Reif, Quintino, et al., 1997). Involvement in the treatment of their children can be a particularly negative experience for parents of diabetic children, for example, monitoring dietary compliance, taking blood samples, and giving insulin shots. In this study, parents were given a more positive role in their children's treatment by massaging their children daily before bedtime. Immediately after the massage-therapy sessions, parents' anxiety and depressed mood levels were lower, as were their children's (Field, Hernandez-Reif, LaGreca, et al., 1997). At the end of the one-month period, the parents' assessment of their children's insulin and food regulation improved, and the children's blood glucose levels decreased from very high to normal-range values (from 158 to 118).

Asthmatic Children

Assuming that massage therapy might similarly benefit asthmatic children, we had parents give daily twenty-minute bedtime massages to their asthmatic children (Field, Henteleff, et al., 1998). Immediately after the massage, the parents' anxiety decreased, the children's self-reported anxiety levels decreased, the children's mood improved, and the children's cortisol levels decreased. Most important, over the one-month period, the children had significantly fewer asthma attacks and significantly improved pulmonary functions, including peak air flow, forced vital capacity, forced expiratory volume, average flow rate, and peak expiratory flow rate.

IMMUNE DISORDERS

HIV-Positive Adults

Immune disorders might be expected to benefit from massage therapy because of the decrease in cortisol levels noted in several previous studies. Elevated cortisol is known to dampen immune function. In a study we conducted on HIV-positive adults, natural killer (NK) cells and NK cell cytotoxicity (activity) increased following twenty days of massage therapy (Ironson et al., 1996). Twenty-nine gay men (twenty HIV-positive, nine HIV-negative) were massaged for one month and compared with a progressive muscle relaxation group. A subset of eleven of the HIV-positive men served as a within-subjects control group (one month with and one month without massages). Major immune findings included a significant increase in NK cell number, NK cell cytotoxicity, and subsets of CD8 cells. There were no changes in HIV disease progression markers (CD4, CD4/CD8 ratios), possibly because the HIV-positive men were already severely immune compromised. A significant decrease was also noted in urinary cortisol, and non-significant trends suggested decreased catecholamines. Decreased anxiety was significantly correlated with increased NK cell number.

Elevated stress hormones (catecholamines and cortisol) are noted to negatively affect immune function. The increase in cytotoxic capacity associated with massage therapy probably derives from the decrease in these stress hormones following massage therapy. Because NK cells are the front line of defense in the immune system, combating the growth and proliferation of viral cells, the HIV-positive patients who received the massage therapy might experience fewer opportunistic infections such as pneumonia and other viruses that often kill them. The increase in NK cells also suggests that cancer patients may benefit from massage therapy, inasmuch as NK cells are also noted to combat cancer cells.

Breast Cancer

Nineteen women (mean age = 53 years) with stage one or stage two breast cancer were assigned to a massage therapy or a control group (Hernandez-Reif, Field, Ironson, Weiss, & Fletcher, 1998). The massage therapy group received three forty-five-minute massages per week for five weeks. Lymphocyte markers (CD56+, CD3+, and CD11a+ cells) and NK cell numbers were significantly increased for the women in the massage group by the end of the study. Immediately after their first and last massage, the massage therapy group reported less anxiety, anger, and pain and improved mood. Longer-term changes for the massage therapy group included improved body image awareness and physical well-being, as well as decreased depression.

CONCLUSION

These, then, are the functions that have improved following massage therapy. In addition to each clinical condition being marked by unique changes such as the increased peak air flow noted in the asthma study and the decreased glucose levels noted in the children with diabetes, there was also a set of common findings. Across studies, decreases were noted in anxiety, depression, stress hormones (cortisol), and catecholamines. Increased parasympathetic activity may be the underlying mechanism for these changes. The pressure stimulation associated with touch may increase vagal activity, which in turn lowers physiological arousal and stress hormones (cortisol levels). The pressure is critical because light stroking is generally aversive (much like a tickle stimulus), and the above effects have not been noted for light stroking. Decreased cortisol in turn leads to enhanced immune function. Parasympathetic activity is also associated with increased alertness and better performance on cognitive tasks (Porges,

1997). Given that most diseases are exacerbated by stress and that massage therapy alleviates stress, this alternative treatment may help reduce stress-related disease.

Future directions for research may be discussed in the context of the most frequently raised questions about massage therapy. Those include the questions of whether massage therapy effects can be demonstrated in an equivalent way for healthy volunteer individuals in experimental conditions, in contrast to the typical demonstration on individuals with medical conditions. Additionally, can the massage therapy effects occur using mechanical massage stimulation, as opposed to human massage therapy? A third frequently raised question has to do with what the underlying mechanism for the effects of massage therapy is. Other questions occasionally brought up are whether massage therapy has lasting effects, whether there are contraindications for massage therapy, and whether any particular massage therapy techniques are more effective than others.

The literature has been equivocal about the question of massage therapy effects on healthy individuals. Most studies have focused on alleviating symptoms and combating disease, and no prevention studies appear in the literature at all. Probably the closest massage therapy studies that address the question are those focusing on sports and the effects of athletic massage. This, however, offers mixed results. Typically the studies have focused on the effects of athletic massage on delayed-onset muscle soreness and waste products. In such studies, it is hypothesized that athletic massage administered after extensive exercise (typically two hours after the exercise) would disrupt an initial crucial event in acute inflammation and the accumulation of neutrophils. This would result in a diminished inflammatory response and a concomitant reduction in delayed-onset muscle soreness and waste products. Generally, assessments are made before the exercise and at several intervals after the exercise. In many studies, the effects are positive, but in other studies negative results occurred. The conflicting results have stimulated at least three reviews of that literature. As for many of the questions, the assessment tools that we have may simply not yet be sufficiently developed. Measurement technology has, as already mentioned, been one of the most limiting problems in conducting massage therapy research.

The question of whether mechanical stimulation is as effective as stimulation provided by a massage therapist has never been addressed by directly comparing the two. However, an extensive literature on vibrator stimulation (most of which comes from Sweden) suggests significant therapeutic effects, at least for pain reduction (Lundeberg, 1984; Lundeberg, Abrahamsson, Bondesson, & Haker, 1987, 1988; Ottoson, Ekblom, & Hansson, 1981). In these studies, vibration (typically at 100 Hertz) is applied to various points in different locations—in one study, to the facial region affected by dental pain, and in another study, to different areas of the body in a patient suffering chronic musculoskeletal pain. Typically patients have reported a pain intensity reduction of 75 to 100 percent. The greatest pain reduction occurred in the area of pain, the affected muscle or tendon, the antagonistic muscle, or a trigger point outside the painful area. In most patients, the greatest pain-reduction effect occurred when the vibratory stimulation was applied with moderate pressure. To obtain a maximum duration of pain relief, the stimulation had to be applied for about twenty-five to forty-five minutes. After twelve months of treatment, most patients reported a greater than 50 percent reduction in analgesic drug intake, and in one study the vibratory stimulation was a more efficient pain suppressor than aspirin. Double-blind studies where the vibratory stimulator was compared with a "placebo unit" (the vibrator turned on to make the sound but not vibrating) also revealed significant vibrator effects. A more direct assessment of this question is needed, in which vibrator therapy is compared with manual therapy using the same participants with the same condition. Still another important question is whether self-massage can be as effective as being massaged by another individual.

The third question on underlying mechanisms has rarely been addressed. The most common theory—based on anecdotal data and a very mixed empirical literature—is that of massage increasing circulation or blood flow. Most of the sources suggesting that massage enhances circulation are from old literature that has been reviewed by Wakim (Wakim, Martin, Terrier, Elkins, & Krusen, 1949). As early as 1900, one author reported that, after massage, cutaneous temperature increased by three degrees. A subsequent study demonstrated an increase in the diameter and permeability of the capillaries following mechanical stimulation in frogs and mammals. In a later study, investigators measured skeletal muscle blood flow before, during, and after different forms of massage using a more sophisticated method for determination of blood flow called the Xenon washout method; during rigorous massage, blood flow increased comparable with exercise hyperemia (Hovind & Nielsen, 1974).

In contrast to the earlier studies, Shoemaker, Tiidus, and Mader (1997) reported a failure of manual massage to alter blood flow as measured by Doppler ultrasound. They noted that the mean blood velocity and blood flows for the brachial and femoral arteries, respectively, were not altered by any of the massage treatments, whether they were administered mild or deep treatments in either the forearm or the quadriceps muscle groups. Mild voluntary hand grip and knee extension contractions, in contrast, resulted in peak blood flow for brachial and femoral arteries, respectively, which were significantly elevated from rest. Shoemaker et al. concluded that light exercise was more beneficial than massage in increasing blood flow. Although the Doppler ultrasound methodology is currently the most sophisticated way to measure blood flow, the study suffered from several methodological problems, including the use of relatively little pressure (light Swedish massage was used) and a very small sample size (ten participants).

Another controversial body of literature involves sports massage. Several studies investigating the impact of massage on the reduction of delayed-onset muscle soreness have concluded that massage was ineffective. However, in these studies, massage was administered either immediately after exercise or twenty-four to forty-eight hours afterward. In contrast, data from the Netherlands suggest that massage should be administered between one and three hours after the termination of strenuous exercise.

Unlike the previous studies, Rodenburg, Steenbeek, Schiereck, and Bar (1994) found significant effects from administering the massage after exercise. They noted that the combination of a warm-up, stretching, and massage reduced some of the negative effects of exercise, including the delayed-onset muscle soreness and the creatine kinase activity in blood. However, some of their results were inconsistent, which may relate to their not having waited the full two hours to provide the massage. Rodenburg et al.'s study was also confounded by combining the three separate techniques of warm-up, stretching, and massage. Although suggesting that massage may be helpful for sports recovery and healthy individuals, the data also suggested the need for more tightly controlled studies that investigate the various parameters, such as the length of time after exercise that the massage is provided. Clearly, this variable alone contributed to significant inconsistency in the literature.

Other popularly posed questions, including the lasting effects of massage therapy following the termination of treatment, the contraindications for massage therapy, and the question of which techniques are the most effective, have not been addressed in the literature. Regarding the question of lasting effects, there is no reason to believe that massage effects would continue after the end of treatment, any more than drugs, diet, or exercise effects would be expected to persist. Contraindications such as varicose veins and cancer have been followed by massage therapists, although physician researchers in those areas refute the need for those contraindications. Again, more research is needed on these questions.

In summary, these questions highlight the need for further research. Some of these questions have not yet been addressed, and many conditions have not been studied in methodologically sound ways. Replications are needed for the methodologically sound studies, and more mechanism studies will hopefully be conducted as more sophisticated measurement technology is developed. In the interim, at least the existing literature that is well controlled suggests that massage therapy may be a promising treatment.

Aside from the need for additional research and replication studies, there will need to be a shift in the sociopolitical attitude toward touch. Increasing numbers of schools are mandating that teachers not touch children even as early as the preschool stage. The incidence of child abuse and litigations against teachers has increased even with these mandates, and the frequency of sexual harassment cases against adults has also increased despite the disappearing use of touch in social communication. This may be an American phenomenon, as social communication touch is still very present in European cultures like France and Italy, and touch therapies such as massage are one of the most popular forms of treatment in European countries to the extent that they are covered by insurance carriers. Similarly, physicians in Asian countries are heavily prescribing touch therapies, and, ironically, continuing to invite American "experts" to provide lectures and workshops in touch therapy techniques, such as infant massage. The physicians in Asia may be treating massage therapy as modern technology because they perhaps do not remember that the origins of touch therapies were in their own part of the world thousands of years ago.

Touch therapies may have a greater chance than touch as social communication in the current U.S. climate as part of the healthy body trend, along with diet and exercise. The increasing popular demand for alternative medicine may also help the return of massage therapy. In the interim, a larger body of methodologically sound research is needed to help inform this process.

REFERENCES

Brazelton, T. B. (1973). Neonatal Behavioral Assessment Scale. National Spastics Society Monograph #88. Philadelphia: J. B. Lippincott.

Cady, S. H., & Jones, G. E. (1997). Massage therapy as a workplace intervention for reduction of stress. *Perceptual & Motor Skills, 84,* 157–158.

Conners, C. K. (1985). The Conners Rating Scales: Instruments for the assessment of childhood psychopathology. Children's Hospital National Medical Center, Washington, DC.

Crosman, L. J., Chateauvert, S. R., & Weisberg, J. (1984). The effect of massage to the hamstring muscle group on range of motion. *Journal of Orthopaedic & Sports Physical Therapy, 6,* 168–172.

Diego, M. A., Field, T., Hernandez-Reif, M., Hart, S., Brucker, B., Field, T., et al. (2002). Spinal cord patients benefit from massage therapy. *International Journal of Neuroscience, 112*(2), 133–142.

Dieter, J., Field, T., & Hernandez-Reif, M. (1998). Weight gain can increase in preterm infants following only one week of massage. Paper presented at the 12th Annual International Conference on Infant Studies, Atlanta, April.

Field, T. (1995). Infant massage therapy. In T. Field (Ed.), *Touch in early development* (pp. 105–114). Hillsdale, NJ: Erlbaum.

Field, T. (1998). Touch therapies. In R. Hoffman, M. Sherrick, & J. Warm (Eds.), *Viewing psychology as a whole* (pp. 603–626). Washington, DC: American Psychological Association.

Field, T., Grizzle, N., Scafidi, F., Abrams, S., Richardson, S., Kuhn, C., et al. (1996). Massage therapy for infants of depressed mothers. *Infant Behavior & Development, 19,* 107–112.

Field, T., Grizzle, N., Scafidi, F., & Schanberg, S. (1996). Massage and relaxation therapies' effects on depressed adolescent mothers. *Adolescence, 31*(124), 903–911.

Field, T., Henteleff, T., Hernandez-Reif, M., Martinez, E., Mavunda, K., Kuhn, C., et al. (1998). Children with asthma have improved pulmonary functions after massage therapy. *Journal of Pediatrics, 132*(5), 854–858.

Field, T., Hernandez-Reif, M., Hart, S., Theakston, H., Schanberg, S., & Kuhn, C. (1999). Pregnant women benefit from massage therapy. *Journal of Psychosomatic Obstetrics and Gynaecology, 20,* 31–38.

Field, T., Hernandez-Reif, M., LaGreca, A., Shaw, K., Schanberg, S., & Kuhn, C. (1997). Massage therapy lowers blood glucose levels in children with diabetes. *Diabetes Spectrum, 10*(3), 237–239.

Field, T., Hernandez-Reif, M., Quintino, O., Schanberg, S., & Kuhn, C. (1997). Elder retired volunteers benefit from giving massage therapy to infants. *Journal of Applied Gerontology, 17*(2), 229–239.

Field, T., Hernandez-Reif, M., Seligman, S., Krasnegor, J., Sunshine, W., Rivas-Chacon, R., et al. (1997). Juvenile rheumatoid arthritis: Benefits from massage therapy. *Journal of Pediatric Psychology, 22*(5), 607–617.

Field, T., Hernandez-Reif, M., Taylor, S., Quintino, O., & Burman, I. (1997). Labor pain is reduced by massage therapy. *Journal of Psychosomatic Obstetrics and Gynecology, 18*(4), 286–291.

Field, T., Ignatoff, E., Stringer, S., Brennan, J., Greenberg, R., Widmayer, S., et al. (1982). Nonnutritive sucking during tube feedings: Effects on preterm neonates in an intensive care unit. *Pediatrics, 70*(3), 381–384.

Field, T., Ironson, G., Scafidi, F., Nawrocki, T., Goncalves, A., Burman, I., et al. (1996). Massage therapy reduces anxiety and enhances EEG pattern of alertness and math computations. *International Journal of Neuroscience, 86*, 197–205.

Field, T., Lasko, D., Mundy, P., Henteleff, T., Kabat, S., Talpins, S., et al. (1997). Brief report: Autistic children's attentiveness and responsivity improve after touch therapy. *Journal of Autism and Developmental Disorders, 27*(3), 333–338.

Field, T., Morrow, C., Valdeon, C., Larson, S., Kuhn, C., & Schanberg, S. (1992). Massage reduces anxiety in child and adolescent psychiatric patients. *Journal of the American Academy of Child and Adolescent Psychiatry, 31*, 125–131.

Field, T., Peck, M., Krugman, S., Tuchel, T., Schanberg, S., Kuhn, C., et al. (1998). Burn injuries benefit from massage therapy. *Journal of Burn Care and Rehabilitation, 19*, 241–244.

Field, T., Quintino, O., Hernandez-Reif, M., & Koslovsky, G. (1998). Adolescents with attention deficit hyperactivity disorder benefit from massage therapy. *Adolescence, 33*(129), 103–108.

Field, T., Scafidi, F., & Schanberg, S. (1987). Massage of preterm newborns to improve growth and development. *Pediatric Nursing, 13*(6), 385–387.

Field, T., Schanberg, S., Kuhn, C., Field, T., Fierro, K., Henteleff, T., et al. (1998). Bulimic adolescents benefit from massage therapy. *Adolescence, 33*(131), 555–563.

Field, T., Schanberg, S. M., Scafidi, F., Bauer, C. R., Vega-Lahr, N., Garcia, R., et al. (1986). Tactile/kinesthetic stimulation effects on preterm neonates. *Pediatrics, 77*(5), 654–658.

Field, T., Seligman, S., Scafidi, F., & Schanberg, S. (1996). Alleviating posttraumatic stress in children following Hurricane Andrew. *Journal of Applied Developmental Psychology, 17*, 37–50.

Field, T., Sunshine, W., Hernandez-Reif, M., Quintino, O., Schanberg, S., Kuhn, C., et al. (1997). Chronic fatigue syndrome: Massage therapy effects on depression and somatic symptoms in chronic fatigue. *Journal of Chronic Fatigue Syndrome, 3*, 43–51.

Garner, D. M., Olmsted, M. P., & Polivy, J. (1983). The Eating Disorders Inventory: A measure of cognitive-behavioral dimensions of anorexia nervosa and bulimia. In P. L. Darby, P. E. Garfinkel, D. M. Garner, & D. V. Coscina (Eds.), *Anorexia nervosa: Recent developments in research* (pp. 173–184). New York: Alan R. Liss.

Goldstein-Ferber, S. (1998). Massage in preterm infants. Paper presented at the 11th Annual International Conference on Infant Studies, Atlanta, April.

Hart, S., Field, T., Hernandez-Reif, M., Nearing, G., Shaw, S., Schanberg, S., et al. (2001). Anorexia nervosa symptoms are reduced by massage therapy. *Eating Disorders, 9*(4), 289–299.

Hernandez-Reif, M., Dieter, J., Field, T., Swerdlow, B., & Diego, M. (1998). Migraine headaches are reduced by massage therapy. *International Journal of Neuroscience, 96*, 1–11.

Hernandez-Reif, M., Field, T., Field, T., & Theakston, H. (1998). Multiple sclerosis patients benefit from massage therapy. *Journal of Bodywork & Movement Therapies, 2*, 168–174.

Hernandez-Reif, M., Field, T., Krasnegor, J., & Theakston, H. (2001). Lower back pain is reduced and range of motion increased after massage therapy. *International Journal of Neuroscience, 106*(3), 131–145.

Hernandez-Reif, M., Field, T., Krasnegor, J., Theakston, H., Hossain, Z., & Burman, I. (2000). High blood pressure and associated symptoms were reduced by massage. *Journal of Bodywork Movement Therapy, 4,* 31–38.

Hernandez-Reif, M., Ironson, G., Field, T., Hurley, J., Katz, G., Diego, M., Weiss, S., Fletcher, M., Schanberg, S., Kuhn, C., & Burman, I. (2004). Breast cancer patients have improved immune and neuroendocrine functions following massage therapy. *Journal of Psychosomatic Research 57* (1), 45–52.

Hovind, H., & Nielsen, S. L. (1974). Effect of massage on blood flow in skeletal muscle. *Scandinavian Journal of Rehabilitation Medicine, 6*(2), 74–77.

Ironson, G., Field, T., Scafidi, F., Hashimoto, M., Kumar, M., Kumar, A., et al. (1996). Massage therapy is associated with enhancement of the immune system's cytotoxic capacity. *International Journal of Neuroscience, 84,* 205–217.

Jinon, S. (1996). The effect of infant massage on growth of the preterm infant. In C. Yarbes-Almirante & M. De Luma (Eds.), *Increasing safe and successful pregnancy* (pp. 265–269). Amsterdam: Elsevier Science.

Jones, N. A., & Field, T. (1999). Massage and music therapies attenuate frontal EEG asymmetry in depressed adolescents. *Adolescence, 34*(135), 529–534.

Kuhn, C., Schanberg, S., Field, T., Symanski, R., Zimmerman, E., Scafidi, F., et al. (1991). Tactile kinesthetic stimulation effects on sympathetic and adrenocortical function in preterm infants. *Journal of Pediatrics, 119,* 434–440.

Lundeberg, T. (1984). Long-term results of vibratory stimulation as a pain relieving measure for chronic pain. *Pain, 20,* 13–23.

Lundeberg, T., Abrahamsson, P., Bondesson, L., & Haker, E. (1987). Vibratory stimulation compared to placebo in alleviation of pain. *Scandinavian Journal of Rehabilitation Medicine, 19*(4), 153–158.

Lundeberg, T., Abrahamsson, P., Bondesson, L., & Haker, E. (1988). Effect of vibratory stimulation on experimental and clinical pain. *Scandinavian Journal of Rehabilitation Medicine, 20*(4), 149–159.

McKechnie, A., Wilson, F., Watson, N., & Scott, D. (1983). Anxiety states: A preliminary report on the value of connective tissue massage. *Journal of Psychosomatic Research, 27*(2), 125–129.

Meaney, M. J., Aitken, D. H., Bhatnagar, M., Bodnoff, S. R., Mitchell, J. B., & Sarrieau, A. (1990). Neonatal handling and the development of the adrenocortical response to stress. In N. Gunzenhauser, T. B. Brazelton, & T. Field (Eds.), *Advances in touch: New implications in human development* (pp. 11–20). Skillman, NJ: Johnson & Johnson.

Melzack, R., & Wall, P. D. (1965). Pain mechanisms: A new theory. *Science, 150*(699), 971–979.

Modi, N., & Glover, J. (1995). Massage therapy for preterm infants. Paper presented at Touch Research Symposium, Providence, RI, April.

Morelli, M., Seaborne, D. E., & Sullivan, S. J. (1990). Changes in H-reflex amplitude during massage of triceps surae in healthy subjects. *Journal of Orthopaedic & Sports Physical Therapy, 12*(2), 55–59.

Morelli, M., Seaborne, D. E., & Sullivan, S. J. (1991). H-reflex modulation during manual muscle massage of human triceps surae. *Archives of Physical Medicine & Rehabilitation, 72*(11), 915–919.

Nixon, M., Teschendorff, J., Finney, J., & Karnilowicz, W. (1997). Expanding the nursing repertoire: The effect of massage on post-operative pain. *Australian Journal of Advanced Nursing, 14*(3), 21–26.

Older, J. (1982). *Touching is healing*. New York: Stein & Day.

Ottoson, D., Ekblom, A. T., & Hansson, P. (1981). Vibratory stimulation for the relief of pain of dental origin. *Pain, 10*, 37–45.

Porges, S. W. (1997). Emotion: An evolutionary by-product of the neural regulation of the autonomic nervous system. In C. S. Carter, I. I. Lederhendler, & B. Kirkpatrick (Eds.), *Annals of the New York Academy of Sciences*, vol. 807, *The integrative neurobiology of affiliation* (pp. 62–77). New York: New York Academy of Sciences.

Puustjarvi, K., Airaksinen, O., & Pontinen, P. J. (1990). The effects of massage in patients with chronic tension headache. *Acupuncture & Electro-therapeutics Research, 15*(2), 159–162.

Rodenburg, J. B., Steenbeek, D., Schiereck, P., & Bar, P. R. (1994). Warm-up, stretching and massage diminish harmful effects of eccentric exercise. *International Journal of Sports Medicine, 15*(7), 414–419.

Scafidi, F., & Field, T. (1996). Massage therapy improves behavior in neonates born to HIV-positive mothers. *Journal of Pediatric Psychology, 21*(6), 889–897.

Scafidi, F. A., Field, T. M., Schanberg, S. M., Bauer, C. R., Tucci, K., Roberts, J., et al. (1990). Massage stimulates growth in preterm infants: A replication. *Infant Behavior & Development, 13*(2), 167–188.

Scafidi, F. A., Field, T. M., Schanberg, S. M., Bauer, C. R., Vega-Lahr, N., Garcia, R., et al. (1986). Effects of tactile/kinesthetic stimulation on the clinical course and sleep/wake behavior of preterm neonates. *Infant Behavior & Development, 9*, 91–105.

Schanberg, S. (1995). The genetic basis for touch effects. In T. M. Field (Ed.), *Touch in early development* (pp. 67–80). Hillsdale, NJ: Erlbaum.

Shoemaker, J. K., Tiidus, P. M., & Mader, R. (1997). Failure of manual massage to alter limb blood flow: Measures by Doppler ultrasound. *Medicine and Science in Sports and Exercise, 29*(5), 610–614.

Sullivan, S. J., Williams, L. R., Seaborne, D. E., & Morelli, M. (1991). Effects of massage on alpha motoneuron excitability. *Physical Therapy, 71*(8), 555–560.

Sunshine, W., Field, T., Schanberg, S., Quintino, O., Kilmer, T., Fierro, K., et al. (1997). Massage therapy and transcutaneous electrical stimulation effects on fibromyalgia. *Journal of Clinical Rheumatology, 2*, 18–22.

Uvnas-Moberg, K., Widstrom, A. M., Marchini, G., & Winberg, J. (1987). Release of GI hormone in mother and infant by sensory stimulation. *Acta Paediatrica Scandinavica, 76*(6), 851–860.

Wakim, K. G., Martin, G. M., Terrier, J. C., Elkins, E. C., & Krusen, F. H. (1949). The effects of massage on the circulation in normal and paralyzed extremities. *Archives of Physical Medicine, 30*, 135–144.

Wheeden, A., Scafidi, F. A., Field, T., Ironson, G., Valdeon, C., & Bandstra, E. (1993). Massage effects on cocaine-exposed preterm neonates. *Journal of Developmental and Behavioral Pediatrics, 14*(5), 318–322.

CHAPTER 26

What We Really Know about Mindfulness-Based Stress Reduction

Scott R. Bishop

Mindfulness-Based Stress Reduction (MBSR) is a clinical program, originally developed to facilitate adaptation to medical illness, that provides systematic training in mindfulness meditation as a self-regulation approach to stress reduction and emotion management. Interest in MBSR has grown exponentially since its introduction approximately twenty years ago (Kabat-Zinn, 1982). There are an estimated 240 MBSR programs in North America and Europe, with new programs being established each year (Kabat-Zinn, Massion, Hebert, & Rosenbaum, 1998). With the introduction of a residential professional training program in MBSR now offered by the Center for Mindfulness in Medicine, Health Care, and Society at the University of Massachusetts Medical Center (Santorelli, 1999), the use of this approach will likely become even more widespread.

The primary goal of MBSR is to provide patients with training in meditation techniques to foster the quality of "mindfulness." *Mindfulness* has been broadly conceptualized as a state in which one is highly aware and focused on the reality of the present moment, accepting and acknowledging it, without getting caught up in thoughts that are about the situation or in emotional reactions to the situation (Kabat-Zinn, 1982, 1990). MBSR aims to teach people to approach stressful situations "mindfully" so they may respond to the situation instead of automatically reacting to it.

MBSR is now being used widely to teach patients to self-manage the stress and emotional distress commonly associated with a range of chronic illnesses and as a psychosocial treatment approach to some psychiatric disorders (Kabat-Zinn, 1990; Kabat-Zinn et al., 1998). However, the popularity of this approach has grown in the absence of rigorous scientific evaluation. Although there is some preliminary evidence that suggests that

MBSR may hold promise as an effective approach with applications in psychosomatic medicine and general psychiatry, there is a lot that we do not know about this treatment modality. This chapter will provide a comprehensive critical evaluation of MBSR as a relatively new treatment approach.

DESCRIPTION OF THE INTERVENTION

The primary focus of MBSR is on training participants in various meditation techniques that ostensibly result in the development of mindfulness. Although these various mindfulness training techniques differ somewhat in terms of procedures, they share the same goal of teaching participants to become more aware of thoughts and feelings and to change their relationship to them. The meditation techniques are used to develop a perspective on thoughts and feelings so that they are recognized as mental events rather than as aspects of the self or as necessarily accurate reflections of reality (Kabat-Zinn, 1982; Teasdale, Segal, & Williams, 1995). With repeated practice, mindfulness allows the participant to develop the ability to calmly step back from thoughts and feelings during stressful situations, rather than engaging in anxious worry or other negative-thinking patterns that might otherwise escalate a cycle of stress reactivity and contribute to heightened emotional distress.

A description of sitting meditation will illustrate the basic mindfulness training technique. The participant maintains an upright sitting posture, either in a chair or cross-legged on the floor, and attempts to sustain attention to the breath. Whenever attention wanders to inevitable thoughts and emotions as they arise, the participant simply acknowledges and accepts each thought and feeling, then lets go of them as attention is directed back to the breath. This process is repeated each time that attention wanders to thoughts and feelings. As sitting meditation is practiced, there is an emphasis on simply observing and accepting each thought or feeling without making judgments about it or elaborating on its implications, additional meanings, or need for action (Kabat-Zinn, 1982; Teasdale et al., 1995). Thus, sitting meditation aims to teach participants to passively observe thoughts and feelings simply as mental events with no inherent value of their own. Other techniques (e.g., body scan, yoga) are taught after the same basic procedure, although with a different object of focus to sustain attention.

MBSR typically consists of eight to ten weekly group sessions, with one session being a full day "retreat" (Santorelli, 1999). The format is largely skill-based and psychoeducational. There is considerable in-session experience and discussion of the various mindfulness-training techniques. Patients are educated about the psychophysiology of stress and emotions and provided with ways of approaching specific situations using the mindfulness skills. There is a program of homework exercises that largely involves practice of the mindfulness techniques, both formally as a daily meditation practice and informally as participants bring mindfulness to thoughts, emotions, and behaviors in their daily lives, particularly during times of stress. Participants are provided with audiocassettes that guide them through the mindfulness meditation exercises.

REVIEW OF OUTCOME STUDIES

There has been a paucity of controlled studies in clinical populations (Astin, 1997; Shapiro, Schwartz, & Bonner, 1998; Speca, Carlson, Goodey, & Angen, 2000; Teasdale et al., 2000) and only a few uncontrolled studies (Kabat-Zinn et al., 1992; Kabat-Zinn, Lipworth, & Burney, 1985; Kabat-Zinn, Lipworth, Burney, & Sellers, 1987; Kaplan, Goldenberg, & Galvin-Nadeau, 1993; Kristeller & Hallett, 1999; Miller, Fletcher, & Kabat-Zinn, 1995; Roth, 1997). Beyond obvious limitations of uncontrolled designs, the research has suffered from methodological problems that seriously limit the kinds of conclusions that can be drawn. These include inappropriate or inadequate use of statistics, the use of unvalidated measures, failure to control for concurrent treatments that might affect the outcome variables, and arbitrary determination of clinical response. A summary of all of the published studies to date relevant to the self-management of stress and mood symptoms associated with chronic illness, highlighting the main findings and the conclusions that can be drawn, follows. Because major depression and anxiety disorders commonly are associated with chronic illness and often warrant specific treatment as part of the overall psychosocial management of an illness, these studies are presented as well. The controlled studies are described first, followed by the uncontrolled studies.

Controlled Studies

Two studies in nonclinical samples, by Astin (1997) and Shapiro et al. (1998), have shown that MBSR may be effective in mitigating stress, anxiety, and dysphoria in the general population. The strength of these studies is in the use of randomization to groups, and in the case of Shapiro et al., matched randomization for important potential confounding variables (e.g., ethnicity). Also, the decision to attempt replication by having the control group participate in an MBSR program after the end of the randomized controlled trial in the latter study provides an additional test of efficacy. These studies are limited, however, in the use of an inactive control group. Since nonspecific factors, such as therapists' attention, social support, and positive expectancy can improve outcome (Grencavage, Bootzin, & Shoham, 1993; McCullough & Winston, 1991; Strupp, 1993), it is difficult to attribute the changes to the specifics of MBSR. A better design would include an additional active control group (i.e., with therapeutic attention, social support, and positive expectancy) in a three-arm trial. Any differences in postintervention scores in favor of MBSR could then be attributed to the specifics of the interventions. These studies also have questionable generalizability to clinical populations.

Only two randomized, controlled trials have been reported in clinical populations. Speca et al. (2000) provide the only rigorous test of MBSR in a medical population—a mixed sample of cancer patients. The results are impressive, with 65 percent and 35 percent reductions in total mood disturbance and stress symptoms, respectively. Also, time spent practicing meditation correlated with reductions in mood disturbance. This provides compelling evidence that the techniques had a therapeutic effect. However, it is not possible to rule out social desirability effects that may have been operative in patients' reports of mood and stress changes or their reports of treatment compliance. A measure of social desirability should be included in future controlled trials as a control variable. Also, posttreatment follow-up is needed to fully evaluate the long benefits of this approach.

Teasdale et al. (2000) provide the only other randomized controlled trial of an MBSR-based treatment in a clinical sample, with recently recovered depressed patients. This rigorously designed study also yielded impressive results. MBSR, combined with cognitive therapy, resulted in half the rate of relapse of depression over a sixty-week period for individuals who had had three or more previous episodes. If replicated, this combined approach would represent an important prophylactic treatment of recurrent depression. Unfortunately, because a combined treatment modality was used, it is not possible to make strong statements regarding the effectiveness of MBSR per se for the prevention of depressive relapse. Furthermore, its application for the treatment of major depression is yet unknown.

Uncontrolled Studies

The remaining studies are seriously limited by the reliance on uncontrolled repeated measures designs. Although the rigor of this design can be greatly improved with the inclusion of a nontreatment comparison group to control for regression toward the mean, only one study uses this approach (Kabat-Zinn et al., 1985). Unfortunately, that study did not match participants on potentially important variables that might have otherwise differentiated the groups in a way that would affect outcome. Although the available evidence does not currently support a strong endorsement of this intervention in any of the following clinical populations, some general statements can be made about the available evidence regarding the suggested efficacy of MBSR that awaits rigorous testing via randomized controlled trials.

In chronic pain, there is preliminary evidence that MBSR may assist patients with psychosocial adaptation as evidenced by reductions on self-report measures of emotional distress, psychiatric symptoms, and functional disability (Kabat-Zinn et al., 1985). More importantly, these gains may remain for up to four years after treatment (Kabat-Zinn et al., 1987). However, the impact of MBSR on psychosocial adaptation to pain may be more robust than lasting impact on pain symptoms. Although MBSR resulted in some mitigation of pain, it returned to preintervention levels within six months after treatment. It is possible that continued regular practice of mindfulness meditation may prove to be an effective long-term strategy for pain management, but this remains an empirical question. It is important to note that the majority of the patients who participated in the MBSR program had a long history of medical treatment with little or no improvement in either their pain status or emotional-behavioral status.

Despite the methodological limitations of the studies, the fact that these "treatment-resistant" patients improved at all is indeed impressive.

In terms of fibromyalgia, the one study published (Kaplan et al., 1993) has serious methodological limitations, including lack of a comparison group, failure to report descriptive and inferential statistics, and arbitrary determination of clinical response. In terms of the last, patients were identified as responsive to treatment if they showed at least a 25 percent improvement on at least half of the measures. There may be significant difficulties with giving each of the measures equal weights in defining clinical significance. Furthermore, using arbitrary criteria regarding clinical response is unnecessary. Clinical improvement can be determined objectively by using established cutoff scores on the measures included in the study. Also, the investigators combine illness symptoms with markers of adaptation when defining clinical response. Since psychosocial interventions frequently facilitate adaptation without impact on illness severity, it is important to consider these separately. While methodological limitations preclude strong statements regarding efficacy, it does seem that MBSR may have been associated with a significant reduction (39%) in severity of psychiatric symptoms.

In generalized anxiety and panic disorder, MBSR was associated with significant reductions in the severity of symptoms from pretreatment to posttreatment, with mean reductions to the nonclinical or subclinical range on all clinician ratings and self-report measures (Kabat-Zinn et al., 1992). The study used rigorous assessment procedures, including structured clinical interviewing (*DSM-III-R* criteria [American Psychiatric Association, 1987]) to select eligible patients and established psychometric instruments. Unfortunately, half of patients (55%) were also being treated pharmacologically during the MBSR program. It is unclear if the intervention had any significant therapeutic effect beyond the medication's. Patients apparently maintained their gains at a three-year follow-up, but half of the participants had received additional treatment for their anxiety disorder since ending the MBSR program (Miller et al., 1995).

In their study examining the efficacy of MBSR in binge eating disorder, Kristeller and Hallett (1999) excluded participants who were concurrently involved in a weight-loss program or psychotherapy, which obviously increases confidence in attributing change in symptoms to the MBSR. However, the lack of a comparison group is a major limitation. Although preliminary, the results suggest that MBSR may be a promising approach to both binge eating symptoms and the anxiety and depression that is frequently associated with binge eating disorder.

Although suffering similar methodological limitations as the other clinical investigations, the study by Roth (1997) is important in that it examines the efficacy of MBSR in a sample of patients within a low socioeconomic cohort and includes two samples from different ethnic backgrounds (i.e., English-speaking Americans and Spanish-speaking Latin Americans). Unfortunately, differences between the groups in terms of treatment response were not examined statistically. Observation of completion rates for the program suggested that they were much lower than previously reported (53% of the Anglo patients and 64% of the Latin Americans). Despite its limits, this study highlights the importance of examining the level of acceptability and compliance of this intervention approach in different populations.

In summary, there is some preliminary evidence that MBSR may be effective in various medical and psychiatric populations. The evidence is stronger for the efficacy of MBSR as a general stress reduction approach in nonclinical populations than clinical populations. Although replication is needed, MBSR seems to hold promise as a highly effective psychosocial approach for the management of stress and mood disturbance in cancer. The evidence in other medical and psychiatric conditions is less compelling, although preliminary evidence supports the argument that MBSR should be evaluated via randomized controlled trials.

OPERATIONAL DEFINITIONS, VALIDATION, AND MEASUREMENT

MBSR was adapted from traditional mindfulness meditation practices originating in Theravada and Mahayana Buddhism in India approximately 2,500 years ago (Goleman, 1977). The construct of "mindfulness," therefore, has its roots in Buddhism. The Abhidhamma (Kiyota, 1978) represents a compilation of the Buddhist psychology and philosophy and includes detailed descriptions of states of consciousness said to be attainable through meditative techniques. In the fifth century, the portion of the Abhidhamma that deals with meditation was summarized in a collection known as the *Visuddhimagga*, or "path of purification" (Buddhaghosa, 1976). Within these texts are descriptions of the qualities of mindfulness that are said to be attained through *vipassana*, or mindfulness meditation practice. For the most part, modern Western descriptions of the construct in the scientific literature have been consistent with the traditional Buddhist conceptualizations of mindfulness.

Unfortunately, the defining criteria for mindfulness have not been elaborated substantially beyond nonspecific descriptions of the construct. For example, mindfulness has been described as a state in which one is "fully present in the moment, focused on the reality of the situation," while "acknowledging and accepting it for what it is" (Kabat-Zinn, 1982, 1990; Teasdale et al., 1995). There have been no attempts to operationalize these qualities. However, each of the three dimensions emphasized in the literature seems to involve an aspect of attention regulation.

First, this seems to involve maintaining one's attention to a single point of awareness, while disengaging from thoughts or feelings about the object being observed or from irrelevant discursive thoughts. This ability is hypothesized to develop during meditation as the individual sustains attention to the breath to "anchor" it to the present moment and repeatedly disengages attention from thoughts and emotions as they inevitably arise. This is said to allow the individual to be "fully present in the moment." At a behavioral level, maintaining awareness to an object or situation over time would involve sustained attention (Parasuraman, 1998; Posner & Rothbart, 1992). To disengage from mental activity that might arise and focus back on the object or situation being observed would involve attention switching (Duncan, 1995).

Second, to "observe the reality of the present moment," the practitioner attends to the objective qualities of experience or a situation without immediately resorting to an active process of making judgments about it or elaborating on its implications, further meanings, or need for action. This is referred to as "bare attention" (Kabat-Zinn, 1982). During meditation, thoughts and emotions that spontaneously come into conscious awareness are observed as they are, although the practitioner attempts to inhibit the regular tendency to judge, interpret, or otherwise elaborate on them. This inhibition of elaborative secondary processing would require the ability to control attention to terminate thinking about, or otherwise elaborating on, the primary mental event so that it can be simply observed (Logan & Cowan, 1984; Logan, Schachar, & Tannock, 1997).

Third, the practitioner is said to remain open to experience, as all available information is intentionally observed without attachment to any particular point of view or outcome. This is thought to allow the person to "acknowledge and accept the situation for what it is." In meditation, thoughts and emotions that inevitably arise are simply accepted and observed; there are no attempts to change or escape from anything, nor are there attempts to hold onto or prolong anything. Instead, the practitioner remains open to observing the presence of each thought and emotion that arises, as well as its dissolution. In terms of implicated psychological processes, this seems to involve reliance less on preconceived ideas, beliefs, and biases and more on paying attention to all available information (Posner, 1975).

Mindfulness seems to reflect a kind of metacognitive ability (Marks, 1999) in which the participant has the capacity to observe his or her own mental processes. This process of "stepping back" and observing the flow of consciousness is thought to result in the recognition that each thought and feeling reflects a mental event with no more inherent value or importance than what the practitioner affords them. There seems to be a shift in perspective from automatically accepting the validity or relevance of each thought, to the suspension of commitment to any one thought or perspective. Thoughts are therefore treated as potentialities pending further evidence. Similarly, affect states are not inherently "pleasant" or "unpleasant" but are merely observed as mental events. This would be expected to improve affect tolerance and decrease reactivity in the presence of emotional states. Situations are approached with the same objective awareness; they consist of the unfolding of events with no inherent value other than what one affords them.

The shift in perspective on one's own experience seems to be further facilitated by a set of attitudes that are emphasized during MBSR. These attitudes involve a way of attending to experience and are practiced during the various mindfulness meditation techniques and applied more generally to real-life situations (Kabat-Zinn, 1990; Kabat-Zinn et al., 1998). Two of the more salient and related attitudes include "nonstriving," which has been described as a kind of surrendering to the moment, acknowledging and facing one's experience instead of fighting it or trying to make it something else, and "acceptance" of the situation. Also, the importance of dealing with the immediacy of the current situation, rather than possible futures or the past, is emphasized. The voluntary deployment of attention, in combination with these attitudes, is thought to result in a heightened state of awareness in which one is conscious of a particular situation and one's cognitive, emotional, and somatic experience in that situation in a way that fosters a greater sense of equanimity. Thus, in addition to attention regulation skills, mindfulness can be conceptualized in terms of a core set of attitudes and a general approach-orientation to experience.

At a conceptual level, mindfulness seems to share a number of features with other psychological constructs. It seems to be related to *absorption*, an individual's proclivity toward complete attentional involvement in one's perceptual, imaginative, and ideational experience (Tellegen & Atkinson, 1974). Both share a number of similar features, including an attentional focus on current experience and awareness of available stimuli. Unlike absorption, however, mindfulness does not involve a complete immersion in experience. In mindfulness, the person remains able to observe experience in a detached way, as if somewhat removed from the experience (Teasdale et al., 1995). Mindfulness may also be related to the personality trait of *openness* (Cattell, 1945; McCrae & Costa, 1985). Both constructs involve a reflective and contemplative approach to situations, open-mindedness, and a tendency toward curious introspection (McCrae & Costa, 1985; Teasdale et al., 1995). However, unlike openness to experience, mindfulness does not involve an effort to seek out novel experience or engage in active imagination. Instead, it involves directing attention to whatever happens to be within current experience. Mindfulness can also be differentiated from other attentional states such as *dissociation*, which involves an altered state of awareness that is typically characterized by restricted attention (Bernstein & Putnam, 1986). Unlike dissociative states, mindfulness involves an effort to direct attention to all available information.

MECHANISMS OF ACTION AND CLINICAL ISSUES

MBSR was developed to assist individuals in mastering meditation techniques and in becoming skillful in producing a state of mindfulness (Kabat-Zinn, 1982), the hypothesized primary active component (Kabat-Zinn, 1990; Santorelli, 1999). There is no evidence, however, that MBSR actually enhances one's ability to produce a state of mindfulness. In addition to the substantive significance of this gap in our knowledge, it also raises practical considerations. MBSR is a demanding clinical program, requiring participants to practice meditation for a minimum eight-week course of daily forty-five-minute sessions, ostensibly to develop the skill of cultivating mindfulness (Santorelli, 1999). MBSR may merely produce non-specific benefits, such as increased self-efficacy or social support, common mediators of many group interventions (Levenson, 1992; Newton & Doron,

2000; Williams & Williams, 1997). If MBSR does not induce mindfulness, or mindfulness is not the primary therapeutic component, then it becomes difficult to justify such a demanding program.

Even if mindfulness meditation proves to be a major therapeutic component, it may have nothing to do with "mindfulness"; it may simply produce deep relaxation (Alexander, Robinson, Schneider, Orme-Johnson, & Walton, 1994; Delmonte, 1984). Research needs to clarify whether mindfulness meditation produces some kind of altered awareness such as "mindfulness" or whether it simply reflects another relaxation technique. The next logical step for the field is thus to investigate the meditating role of mindfulness. However, "mindfulness" must first be conceptually defined; an appropriate measurement procedure must then be developed and its construct validity tested.

It is also important to evaluate the efficacy of this approach against other treatments developed or adapted to facilitate adjustment to illness. For example, cognitive therapy has been demonstrated as an effective treatment for many chronic illnesses, and it is generally accepted as the psychosocial treatment of choice for major depressive and anxiety disorders (Dobson, 1989; Gould, Otto, Pollack, & Yap, 1997; Morley, Eccleston, & Williams, 1999; Newton & Doron, 2000). If MBSR were to be adopted as a psychosocial approach, than it would be important that the efficacy of this approach meet or exceed that of other validated treatments. Furthermore, it cannot be assumed that because MBSR is effective for the management of stress and emotional distress associated with one type of chronic illness (e.g., cancer) that it will be effective for other illnesses (e.g., chronic pain).

There are also important questions concerning who might benefit from MBSR. Preexisting personality traits may influence recruitment and compliance. This issue is particularly relevant to this approach, considering the demands and somewhat unusual nature of the program. In addition, pretreatment personality traits or differences in attention control skills may also influence the ability to use meditation to develop mindfulness and mitigate stress and mood symptoms (de Ribaupierre, 2000). Indeed, it is entirely possible that the efficacy of this approach has more to do with the kinds of people who gravitate to the program than the approach itself. This needs to be investigated. Pretreatment levels of emotional distress and/or severity of psychiatric symptoms may influence efficacy as well. For example, severe stress or mood symptoms may impede the development or use of mindfulness to mitigate distress reactions. Furthermore, there needs to be some clarification regarding what types of mood states or psychopathology is responsive to this approach. These questions have important implications for the identification of potential patients who would be expected to benefit from this approach.

DISCUSSION

Group-based psychosocial interventions that facilitate adaptation and adjustment to chronic illness are effective, time-efficient, and cost-efficient. Consistent with the recognized goal of improving the quality of life of patients with chronic medical disorders, the integration of group-based psychosocial interventions into standard care is strongly recommended. A psychosocial treatment approach that can effectively assist patients to self-manage their stress and emotional distress and/or to treat mood and anxiety disorders commonly associated with chronic illness would be highly valued in most treatment settings.

Although MBSR has been presented as such an approach, there is insufficient evidence based on rigorous scientific methods to strongly recommend it at this time. However, there is some preliminary evidence that suggests that this approach should be evaluated. Certainly, with its current and growing popularity, among both the increasing number of health professionals who are using this approach and health consumers who are demanding it, this alone is enough of a reason to subject it to scientific scrutiny. In an era of increased accountability to demonstrate that our psychosocial interventions are indeed safe and effective, the issue regarding the paucity of empirical study is not a minor one.

Although preliminary evidence is promising, controlled studies are clearly needed. The efficacy of MBSR to self-manage stress and mood symptoms associated with cancer seems particularly promising, but it would be difficult based on a single randomized controlled trial to strongly recommend it at this time. The study is significant, however, as it represents the first rigorous test of the efficacy of this approach to foster adaptation to a medical illness. Replication is clearly needed to firmly establish its efficacy in this population. Clinicians are cautioned further against generalizing the efficacy of this approach based on this study to other chronic illnesses. The efficacy of MBSR should be investigated in each illness that it was adapted for until it has been shown that the treatment effects can generalize across illnesses. Finally, clinicians are cautioned against attempting to use this approach as a cure-all for any problematic mood-state or psychiatric disorder that presents with chronic illness. Substantial clarification regarding the specific markers of psychosocial distress or psychopathology associated with chronic illness that are amenable to this approach is needed.

The next logical step within future randomized controlled trials is to investigate questions concerning the meditating role of mindfulness. However, "mindfulness" needs to be operationalized and its construct validity tested, and a method of assessment needs to be developed, before researchers are able to investigate its mediating role. A systematic investigation of questions regarding the therapeutic mechanisms of MBSR raised in this chapter would then be possible.

It is time to subject this approach to serious scientific inquiry. MBSR seems to hold promise as a potentially effective treatment option that may assist some patients to self-manage stress and mood symptoms in the face of their illness. Scientist-practitioners who see value in the approach are urged to adopt rigorous methods of investigation so that its efficacy, indications, and limits of application within psychosomatic medicine can be clearly established. In the same vein, skeptics are cautioned that absence of evidence does not necessarily indicate absence of efficacy. It is hoped that this review will foster cautious optimism about the potential of this approach and direct investigators toward addressing relevant research questions that will result in an empirical base that can guide clinical practice.

REFERENCES

Alexander, C. N., Robinson, P., Schneider, R. H., Orme-Johnson, D. W., & Walton, K. G. (1994). The effects of transcendental meditation compared to other methods of relaxation and meditation in reducing risk factors, morbidity, and mortality. *Homeostasis in Health and Disease, 35*(4–5), 243–264.

American Psychiatric Association. (1987). *Diagnostic and statistical manual* of *mental disorders* (3rd ed., revised). Washington, DC: American Psychiatric Association.

Astin, J. A. (1997). Stress reduction through mindfulness meditation: Effects on psychological symptomatology, sense of control, and spiritual experiences. *Psychotherapy and Psychosomatics, 66*(2), 97–106.

Bernstein, E. M., & Putnam, F. W. (1986). Development, reliability, and validity of a dissociation scale. *Journal of Nervous and Mental Disease, 174*(12), 727–735.

Buddhaghosa, B. (1976). *Path of purification: Visuddhimagga* (B. Ñānamoli, trans.). Boulder, CO: Shambhala.

Cattell, R. B. (1945). The principal trait clusters for describing personality. *Psychological Bulletin, 42*, 129–161.

De Ribaupierre, A. (2000). Working memory and attentional control. In W. J. Perrig & A. Grob (Eds.), *Control of human behavior, mental processes, and consciousness: Essays in honor of the 60th birthday of August Flammer* (pp. 147–164). Mahwah, NJ: Erlbaum.

Delmonte, M. M. (1984). Physiological concomitants of meditation practice. *International Journal of Psychosomatics, 31*(4), 23–36.

Dobson, K. S. (1989). A meta-analysis of the efficacy of cognitive therapy for depression. *Journal of Consulting and Clinical Psychology, 57*(3), 414–419.

Duncan, J. (1995). Attention, intelligence, and frontal lobes. In M. S. Gazzaniga (Ed.), *The cognitive neurosciences* (pp. 721–733). Cambridge, MA: MIT Press.

Goleman, D. (1977). *The varieties of meditative experience.* New York: Dutton.

Gould, R. A., Otto, M. W., Pollack, M. H., & Yap, L. (1997). Cognitive behavioral and pharmacological treatment of generalized anxiety disorder: A preliminary meta-analysis. *Behavior Therapy, 28*, 285–305.

Grencavage, L., Bootzin, R. R., & Shoham, V. (1993). Specific and nonspecific effects in psychological treatments. In C. G. Costello (Ed.), *Basic issues in psychopathology* (pp. 359–376). New York: Guilford Press.

Kabat-Zinn, J. (1982). An outpatient program in behavioral medicine for chronic pain patients based on the practice of mindfulness meditation: Theoretical considerations and preliminary results. *General Hospital Psychiatry, 4*, 33–47.

Kabat-Zinn, J. (1990). *Full catastrophe living: Using the wisdom of your body and mind to face stress, pain, and illness.* New York: Bantam Doubleday Dell.

Kabat-Zinn, J., Lipworth, L., & Burney, R. (1985). The clinical use of mindfulness meditation for the self-regulation of chronic pain. *Journal of Behavioral Medicine, 8*(2), 163–190.

Kabat-Zinn, J., Lipworth, L., Burney, R., & Sellers, W. (1987). Four-year follow-up of a meditation-based program for the self-regulation of chronic pain: Treatment outcome and compliance. *Clinical Journal of Pain, 2*, 159–173.

Kabat-Zinn, J., Massion, A. O., Hebert, J. R., & Rosenbaum, E. (1998). Meditation. In J. C. Holland (Ed.), *Psycho-oncology* (pp. 767–779). New York:
Oxford University Press.

Kabat-Zinn, J., Massion, A. O., Kristeller, J., Peterson, L. G., Fletcher, K. E.,
Pbert, L., et al. (1992). Effectiveness of a meditation-based stress reduction
program in the treatment of anxiety disorders. *American Journal of Psychiatry,
149*(7), 936–943.

Kaplan, K. H., Goldenberg, D. L., & Galvin-Nadeau, M. (1993). The impact of a
meditation-based stress reduction program on fibromyalgia. *General Hospital
Psychiatry, 15*(5), 284–289.

Kiyota, M. (Ed.) (1978). *Mahayana Buddhist meditation: Theory and practice.*
Honolulu: University Press of Hawaii.

Kristeller, J. L., & Hallett, C. B. (1999). An exploratory study of a meditation-
based intervention for binge eating disorder. *Journal of Health Psychology,
4*(3), 357–363.

Levenson, J. L. (1992). Psychosocial interventions in chronic medical illness. An overview of outcome research. *General Hospital Psychiatry, 14*(Suppl. 6), 43S–49S.

Logan, G. D., & Cowan, W. B. (1984). On the ability to inhibit thought and
action: A theory of an act of control. *Psychological Review, 91*(3), 295–327.

Logan, G. D., Schachar, R. J., & Tannock, R. (1997). Impulsivity and inhibitory
control. *Psychological Science, 8,* 60–64.

Marks, D. F. (1999). Consciousness, mental imagery and action. *British Journal of
Psychology, 90*(4), 567–585.

McCrae, R. R., & Costa, P. T., Jr. (1985). Openness to experience. In R. Hogan
& W. H. Jones (Eds.), *Perspectives in Personality* (vol. 1, pp. 145–172).
Greenwich: JAI Press.

McCullough, L., & Winston, A. (1991). The Beth Israel Psychotherapy Research
Program. In L. E. Beutler & M. Crago (Eds.), *Psychotherapy research: An
international review of programmatic studies* (pp. 15–23). Washington, DC:
American Psychological Association.

Miller, J. J., Fletcher, K., & Kabat-Zinn, J. (1995). Three-year follow-up and clinical
implications of a mindfulness meditation-based stress reduction intervention in
the treatment of anxiety disorders. *General Hospital Psychiatry, 17*(3), 192–200.

Morley, S., Eccleston, C., & Williams, A. (1999). Systematic review and meta-
analysis of randomized controlled trials of cognitive behaviour therapy and behaviour therapy for chronic pain in adults, excluding headache. *Pain, 80*(1–2), 1–13.

Newton, T. L., & Doron, S.E. (2000). Cognitive-behavioral processes in managing
the stress and anxiety of medical illness. In D. I. Mostofsky & D. H. Barlow
(Eds.), *The management of stress and anxiety in medical disorders* (pp. 84–99).
Boston: Allyn & Bacon.

Parasuraman, R. (Ed.). (1998). *The attentive brain.* Cambridge, MA: MIT Press.

Posner, M. I. (1975). The psychobiology of attention. In M. S. Gazzaniga & C.
Blakemore (Eds.), *Handbook of psychobiology* (pp. 441–480). New York:
Academic Press.

Posner, M. I., & Rothbart, M. K. (1992). Attentional mechanisms and conscious
experience. In A. D. Milner & M. D. Rugg (Eds.), *The neuropsychology of consciousness* (pp. 91–112). London: Academic Press.

Roth, B. (1997). Mindfulness-based stress reduction in the inner city. *Advances,
13*(4), 50–58.

Santorelli, S. F. (1999). *Mindfulness-based stress reduction: Qualifications and recommended guidelines for providers.* Center for Mindfulness in Medicine, Health
Care, and Society. Worcester, MA: University of Massachusetts Medical Center.

Shapiro, S. L., Schwartz, G. E., & Bonner, G. (1998). Effects of mindfulness-based stress reduction on medical and premedical students. *Journal of Behavioral Medicine, 21*(6), 581–599.

Speca, M., Carlson, L. E., Goodey, E., & Angen, M. (2000). A randomized, wait-list controlled clinical trial: The effect of a mindfulness meditation-based stress reduction program on mood and symptoms of stress in cancer outpatients. *Psychosomatic Medicine, 62*(5), 613–622.

Strupp, H. H. (1993). The Vanderbilt Psychotherapy Studies: Synopsis. *Journal of Consulting and Clinical Psychology, 61*(3), 431–433.

Teasdale, J. D., Segal, Z., & Williams, J. (1995). How does cognitive therapy prevent depressive relapse and why should attentional control (mindfulness) training help? *Behaviour Research and Therapy, 33*, 25–39.

Teasdale, J. D., Segal, Z. V., Williams, J. M., Ridgeway, V. A., Soulsby, J. M., & Lau, M. A. (2000). Prevention of relapse/recurrence in major depression by mindfulness-based cognitive therapy. *Journal of Consulting and Clinical Psychology, 68*(4), 615–623.

Tellegen, A., & Atkinson, G. (1974). Openness to absorbing and self-altering experiences ("absorption"), a trait related to hypnotic susceptibility. *Journal of Abnormal Psychology, 83*(3), 268–277.

Williams, R. B., & Williams, V. P. (1997). Life skills training to ameliorate the impact of psychosocial factors on the development and course of medical illness. In N. A. Cummings, J. L. Cummings, & J. N. Johnson (Eds.), *Behavioral health in primary care: A guide for clinical integration* (pp. 205–218). Madison, CT: Psychological Press.

CHAPTER 27

Yoga for Stress Reduction and Injury Prevention at Work

Shira Taylor Gura

Every day, employees cope with various forms of stressors on the job. Increased risk for psychological and physical disorders may be due to emerging work-related trends such as working in repetitive and monotonous tasks, performing in a fast-paced environment, or fearing a layoff during an unstable period in the economy (Kasl, 1992). Psychological stress can be induced by extremely low or high demands on the individual and is a typical situation of many simple and repetitive work situations, in which health problems are common (Melin & Lundberg, 1997). Burnout is a growing problem in businesses everywhere. "Increasing numbers of executives are plain worn out, complaining of fatigue, anxiety, and ennui" (Dumaine, 1988, p. 88).

These factors have innumerable health and financial implications for both employees and employers. "Mental and emotional states can impinge upon and alter, for good or ill, any of the body's organs or systems" (Garfinkel et al., 1998, p. 139). Low job satisfaction and little variation in job task are significantly associated with back and shoulder pain (Bongers, de Winter, Kompier, & Hildebrandt, 1993). The majority of headaches that people experience are tension headaches resulting from chronic contraction of neck and shoulder muscles (Garfinkel et al., 1998). "With more and more people spending greater amounts of time at the computer, the number of people suffering from carpal tunnel syndrome, the most common type of repetitive strain injury, is on the rise" (Lasater, 2001). Job stress also may impact on an employee's mental health and cause depressive, anxiety, or paranoid symptoms (Dumaine, 1988). Costs to employers are considerable in terms of absentee rates, loss of productivity, and consumption of health care (van der Klink, Blonk, Schene, & van Dijk, 2001). Unfortunately, the stigma of "mental health disorders" or "stress-related disorders" thwarts many companies from becoming involved in occupational mental health and stress management (Quick, 1992). Yet, there has been increasing attention drawn to the legal responsibility of companies for health risks and disorders resulting from job stress (Heilbronn, 1992).

According to Jacobson (1988), forty-eight middle- to large-size Fortune 1,000 companies ranked "improving mental health" as one of the top three priorities for their companies. Yet, a health promotion and prevention report from the U.S. government illustrated that mental health initiatives were not even placed in its top six priorities (Office of Disease Prevention and Health Promotion, 1989). Although some companies have supported mental health promotion for their employees, there has not been a "focused national strategy in the United States to advance the mental and psychological health of individuals in the workplace" (Quick, 1992, p. 48).

FRAMEWORK FOR STRESS AT WORK

According to Ilgen (1990), the workplace is an appropriate and important setting in which to deal with these "crisis proportion" health issues. For many, the worksite is a "prime locus of activity" where employees spend the majority of their days, and the worksite is a vital setting to advance healthy lifestyles (Raymond, Wood, & Patrick, 1990). Quick (1992) employs a three-tiered prevention framework for dealing with stress-related health issues in the workplace:

- Primary intervention aims at "eliminating, reducing, or altering worksite demands" (e.g., task redesign programs).
- Secondary prevention aims at educating individuals on skills to manage stress (e.g., corporate fitness programs and relaxation training).
- Tertiary prevention aims at relieving suffering resulting from worksite demands (e.g., psychological counseling).

Although primary intervention may be the preferred initial starting point, circumstances do not always allow for this, due to individual traits and situational circumstances. Therefore, secondary prevention "seems to be the stage at which we most often begin" (Quick, 1992, p. 50).

Corporate health programs that do exist in the United States emphasize physical fitness and exercise (Gebhardt & Crump, 1990). Weiss, Fielding, and Baum (1990) report that lifestyle change is also a strong emphasis of corporate health programs. For example, Johnson & Johnson provides a worksite wellness program to its employees called Live for Life. This program enhances well-being through motivation and behavioral modifications. Lifestyle change is emphasized through weight reduction and control, nutrition education, and stress management.

Sarno (1991), a medical pioneer who has helped thousands of patients overcome their back conditions without drugs or surgery, states that the pain and tension felt in the neck, shoulder, and back are not mechanical problems and therefore cannot be cured by mechanical means. These symptoms are related to people's feelings and their personalities. Thus, the focus of treatment should be working with the mind. According to Sapolsky, "A critical shift in medicine has been the recognition that many of the damaging diseases of slow accumulation can be either caused or made far worse by stress" (1998, p. 3). Yet, Neal, Singer, Schwartz, and Schwartz (1983) claim that, overall, mental health education in corporate health programs is lacking. Therefore, an essential factor of the prevention strategy is education. One approach that teaches employees how to prevent or reduce risks of stress is Hatha yoga.

YOGA FOR STRESS REDUCTION AND INJURY PREVENTION

Hatha yoga, an ancient mind-body exercise that incorporates breathing and postures to unify and relax the mind and body, has recently been introduced to the American workplace (McDowell, 2001; Smith, 2001). Offering yoga to employees is a convenient and practical way to relieve tension from stresses on the job and educates employees to decrease risks of injury. The breathing and postural techniques can be used "as a means of quietly and unobtrusively coping with the crises that occur during the working day" (Heilbronn, 1992, p. 132). Yoga can be taught at group lunchtime workshops or after work hours in any space available at the worksite, such as a conference room. Once employees learn the techniques from a certified teacher, they can independently practice the techniques in their own workspaces.

Practicing yoga has been shown to reduce pain, relieve tension, reduce risks of injury, improve posture, improve communication, increase energy and attention span, and enhance feelings of overall wellness and well-being (Dworkis, 1997; Garfinkel et al., 1998; Lasater, 2001; Payne, 2000; Pirisi, 2000; Taylor, 2001). In an empirical research study, participants in a yoga-based regimen demonstrated improved grip strength and pain reduction in the carpal tunnel area of the wrists (Garfinkel et al., 1998). No other empirical research studies on the effects of yoga on musculoskeletal disorders (MSDs) exist.

Physiologically, yoga relaxes the body and mind (Sivananda Yoga Center, 2000). When employees are at work, focusing on productivity, deadlines, meetings, and phone calls, the sympathetic nervous system (otherwise known as the "fight-or-flight" system) kicks in. Heart rate, breathing, blood pressure, and adrenaline are increased. Also, in this focused state of work, employees may be unaware of their body positioning and motions and unconcerned about maintaining good postural alignment or taking rest breaks from repetitive movements.

Yet, when the individual is practicing the postures, deep breathing, and stretching movements of yoga while working, he or she increases awareness of his or her body positioning and motions and can elicit the relaxation response. In this case, the parasympathetic nervous system kicks in, where muscle tension is reduced, less oxygen in consumed, less carbon dioxide is eliminated, and there is a decrease in the activity of the sympathetic nervous system (Sivananda Yoga Center, 2000). Breathing is the only system bodily function that is involuntary as well as voluntary. "If you can learn to control your breath, you can learn to control, or at least influence, how you feel both emotionally and physically" (Dworkis, 1997, p. 17). In comparison to job stress, yoga has a dramatic and opposite effect on the body: decreased heart rate, breathing, and blood pressure. Being mindful of the body helps break the poor postural habits and encourages rest breaks from repetitive motions that may contribute to pain and risk for MSDs, thereby decreasing risks of injury. Yoga techniques are prevention skills for life.

Although yoga is based on exercises and poses, it is done "without the possibility of further stressing an already stressed-out body" (Dworkis, 1997, p. 15). Yoga classes begin with warm-ups such as head rolls or shoulder rolls. Classes continue with a series of standing, sitting, supine, and prone poses, most of which can be adapted to the sitting position. Finally, once the spine is completely warmed up, classes may end with a spinal twist and a deep relaxation.

A small independent study on the effects of yoga at the workplace showed that the participants who took the yoga classes had fewer absentee days due to illness or physical problems, experienced less tension and stress, and had a greater overall feeling of well-being than those who did not participate in the yoga classes. Employees also showed enhanced company morale and improved communication skills at work (Payne, 2000). In addition, employees who used a visual analog rating scale to measure levels of stress and musculoskeletal pain before and after a lunchtime yoga workshop at a telecommunications company in Pleasanton, California, and a law firm in Oakland, California, demonstrated a high drop in stress and musculoskeletal pain (see Tables 27.1 and 27.2).

As of 2002, yoga classes were being offered by In-Alignment, Inc., at four corporations in the San Francisco Bay area, including the Lawrence Livermore National Laboratory (a 10,000-person government agency), SBCLD (a 450-person telecommunications company), Navis (a 250-person software company), and Crosby, Heafey, Roach, and May (a 350-person law

Table 27.1. Yoga Workshop Statistics at a Telecommunications Company on July 23, 2001

Characteristic	Pre-Workshop	Post-Workshop	Improvement	% Reduction
Stress	171 (5.34)	91.5 (2.85)	79.5 (2.49)	46.6
Pain in the back, shoulders, neck, arms, wrists, or head	197 (6.35)	124 (4.00)	73 (2.35)	37.0

Notes: $n = 32$ employees. Numbers in parentheses represent averages. Participants rated themselves using a visual analog scale from 1–10; the higher the score, the greater the stress or pain.

Table 27.2. Yoga Workshop Statistics at a Law Firm on August 9, 2001

Characteristic	Pre-Workshop	Post-Workshop	Improvement	% Reduction
Stress	84 (6.46)	45 (3.46)	39 (3.00)	46.4
Pain in the back, shoulders, neck, arms, wrists, or head	72.5 (5.57)	38 (2.92)	34.5 (2.65)	47.6

Notes: n = 13 employees. Numbers in parentheses represent averages. Participants rated themselves using a visual analog scale from 1–10; the higher the score, the greater the stress or pain.

firm). Forty-five-minute classes were offered either during the lunch break (e.g., 12:00–12:45 P.M.) or after hours (e.g., 5:00–5:45 P.M.), and educational themes were incorporated into each session. Themes ranged from breathing techniques and body awareness to postural alignment and more. There were a minimum of six and maximum of ten persons per class, with between two and five classes offered at each company per week.

The Lawrence Livermore National Laboratory was the first organization to complete the eight-week In-Alignment series. Evaluations of the class suggest that employees have found significant benefits from participating in the classes. One computer programmer at the lab wrote:

> I find myself using what I learned in the yoga classes here at my workspace. The techniques help me release tension gained from working at the computer all day long. The breathing techniques were most beneficial in releasing emotional or physical stress from the workday.

Another employee, a physicist at the lab, wrote:

> I have certainly increased general awareness of my body and thoughts. The themes in each class provided a good way to remember to incorporate the techniques at work. I have improved my ability to concentrate and have also recognized I have the potential to be much more productive at work.

Besides the qualitative data that employees have offered as feedback, no quantitative data regarding longevity of the stress reduction throughout the day or improvements of work performance exist at this time. More research is needed in this area.

CONCLUSION

On a daily basis, employees face stressors while on the job. This stress may affect the employee's physical and psychological well-being as well as the employer's finances and company morale. "As corporate America rolls out the mats in the workplace, it has discovered the value-added benefits of yoga" (Smith, 2001, p. 69). Corliss claims that "Americans rush from their high-pressure jobs and tune into the authoritatively mellow voice of an instructor, gently urging them to solder a union between mind and body. These Type A strivers want to become Type B seekers ... to graduate from distress to de-stress" (2001, p. 54). With increased clarity and mental acuity, employees can return to their workdays with improved communication, enhanced teamwork, and increased productivity. "The resulting unification of body and mind ... can have powerful benefits for the rest of one's life, especially stress-related woes associated with professional's hectic lives" (Chanen, 1998, p. 79).

Hatha yoga has been shown to relax the body and mind, thereby promoting overall improvement in mental and physical health and well-being. Yoga at work is a convenient and practical needed outlet for work-related stressors. It teaches employees relaxation techniques to decrease tension and pain, as well as prevention strategies to reduce risks of injury on the job, thereby improving work performance.

REFERENCES

Bongers, P. M., de Winter, C. R., Kompier, M. A., & Hildebrandt, V. H. (1993). Psychological factors at work and musculoskeletal disease. *Scandinavian Journal of Work, Environment & Health, 19*(5), 297–312.

Chanen, J. S. (1998). Just say Om: Harried lawyers still their minds with yoga and meditation. *American Bar Association Journal, 84,* 78–79.

Corliss, R. (2001). The power of yoga. *Time, 157,* April 15, 2001, 54–63.

Dumaine, B. (1988). Cool cures for burnout. *Fortune, 117,* June 20, 1988, 88–91.

Dworkis, S. (1997). *Recovery yoga: A practical guide for chronically ill, injured, and postoperative people.* New York: Three Rivers Press.

Garfinkel, M. S., Singhal, A., Katz, W. A., Allan, D. A., Reshetar, R., & Schumacher, H. R., Jr. (1998). Yoga-based intervention for carpal tunnel syndrome: A randomized trial. *Journal of the American Medical Association, 280,* 1601–1603.

Gebhardt, D. L., & Crump, C. E. (1990). Employee fitness and wellness programs in the workplace. *American Psychologist, 45*(2), 262–272.

Heilbronn, F. S. (1992). The use of Hatha yoga as a strategy for coping with stress in management development. *Management Education & Development, 23,* 131–139.

Ilgen, D. R. (1990). Health issues at work: Opportunities for industrial/organizational psychology. *American Psychologist, 45*(2), 273–283.

Jacobson, M. (1988). Employers zero in on future health. *Business and Health, 5*(12), 36–39.

Kasl, S. V. (1992). Surveillance of psychological disorders in the workplace. In G. P. Keita and S. L. Sauter (Eds.), *Work and well-being: An agenda for the 1990s* (pp. 73–95). Washington, DC: American Psychological Association.

Lasater, J. (2001). Yoga for repetitive strain injury. OneBody, Inc. Retrieved August 7, 2001, from http://www.onebody.com/general/services/printjhtml7article=20003952&x=13&y=18.

McDowell, D. (2001). Harried Internet execs are finding relaxation and inner peace through yoga. *Yoga Journal,* January/February, 76–80.

Melin, B., & Lundberg, U. (1997). A biopsychosocial approach to work-stress and musculoskeletal disorders. *Journal of Psychophysiology, 11,* 238–247.

Neal, M. S., Singer, J. A., Schwartz, J. L., & Schwartz, G. E. (1983). *Yale-NIOSH occupational stress project.* New Haven: Yale University Press.

Office of Disease Prevention and Health Promotion (1989). Disease prevention and health promotion: The facts. *Prevention Report,* December 1–5. Washington, DC: GPO.

Payne, L. (2000). *The business of teaching yoga.* Los Angeles: Samata International Multi Media.

Pirisi, A. (2000). Carpal tunnel care: Take a break from your computer to prevent wrist injury. *Yoga Journal,* July/August, 35.

Quick, J. C. (1992). Health promotion, education, and treatment: Summary of panel comments. In G. P. Keita & S. L. Sauter (Eds.), *Work and well-being: An agenda for the 1990s* (pp. 63–64). Washington, DC: American Psychological Association.

Raymond, J. S., Wood, D. W., & Patrick, W. K. (1990). Psychology doctoral training in work and health. *American Psychologist, 45*(10), 1159–1161.

Sapolsky, R. M. (1998). *Why zebras don't get ulcers: An updated guide to stress, stress-related diseases, and coping.* New York: W. H. Freeman.

Sarno, J. E. (1991). *Healing back pain: The mind–body connection.* New York: Warner Books.

Sivananda Yoga Center (2000). *The Sivananda companion to yoga.* New York: Fireside.

Smith, W. (2001). Best Practices, Inc. *Yoga Journal,* July/August, 69–73.

Taylor, S. (2001). Introducing a yoga group in an acute inpatient psychiatric facility. *OT Practice, 6,* 22–23.

van der Klink, J. J., Blonk, R. W., Schene, A. H., & van Dijk, F. J. (2001). The benefits of interventions for work-related stress. *American Journal of Public Health, 91,* 270–276.

Weiss, S. M., Fielding, J. E., & Baum, A. (1990). *Health at work.* Perspectives in Behavioral Medicine series. Hillsdale, NJ: Erlbaum.

CHAPTER 28

Psychotherapy: A Cognitive Perspective

George S. Everly Jr. and Jeffrey M. Lating

I'm an old man and have known a great many troubles, but most of them never happened.

—Mark Twain

Like beauty, a stressor resides in the eye of the beholder. It should be clear by now that the patient's cognitive interpretation of the environment leads to the formation of a psychosocial stressor from an otherwise neutral stimulus. This concept has resulted in more eloquent phrasing such as "There are no things good or bad, but thinking makes them so" (Shakespeare); "It is not what happens to you that matters, but how you take it" (Hans Selye); "Men are disturbed not by things, but by the views which they take of them" (Epictetus); and "No one can make you feel inferior without your consent" (Eleanor Roosevelt).

If one accepts the concept that the primary determinant of any given psychosocial stressor is the cognitive interpretation or appraisal of that stimulus, then it seems reasonable to assume that a useful therapy in treating stress-related disorders might be a psychotherapeutic effort directed toward the cognitive-interpretational domain. Although clearly not the only psychotherapeutic technique of value in treating excessive stress, psychotherapy with cognitive restructuring or reinterpretation as a goal seems applicable, particularly in the treatment of pathogenic stress-response syndromes. The purpose of this chapter, therefore, is to review several cognitively based psychotherapeutic approaches that can be employed in the treatment of excessive stress arousal.

It is not our goal in this chapter to provide a "how-to" manual of cognitively based therapies. Excellent, practitioner-oriented guides are available elsewhere (see, e.g., Beck & Emery, 1985; Meichenbaum, 1985;

Meichenbaum & Jaremko, 1983). Rather, it is our hope that this chapter will sensitize the reader to the critical role that cognition plays in the initiation and prolongation of human stress and to the important role of cognitively based therapies in the treatment of stress-related problems.

COGNITIVE PRIMACY

The cognitive primacy postulation is the perspective accepted within this chapter. The individual's interpretation of the environment is the primary determinant in the elicitation of the stress response in reaction to a psychosocial stressor. A similar yet more extensive view is summarized by Roseman, who states, "A cognitive approach to the causation of emotion assumes that it is the interpretation of events rather than events per se that determine which emotion will be felt" (1984, p. 14).

Although Grinker and Spiegel (1945), when discussing the stress and emotions of flight crews dealing with the threat of war, were two of the first researchers to refer to the notion of appraisal, Arnold (1960) was the most explicit of the early theorists in support of cognitive primacy. She concluded that emotions are caused by the "appraisal" of the stimuli that one encounters. Given the perception of some environmental stimulus, subsequent emotions are a function not of the stimulus per se, but of the cognitive interpretation (appraisal) of that stimulus. Thus, Arnold was the first person to systematically state that there is a cognitive-mediational approach to the study of emotions, with appraisal as the core construct.

Lazarus first used the term *appraisal* in 1964, and by 1966 it became the essence of his theory of psychological stress (Lazarus, 1966). He and his colleagues extended Arnold's work to recognize the role of initial appraisal of a given environmental stimulus, but added the notion of *reappraisal*, which entails the cognitive interpretation of one's perceived ability to handle, cope with, or benefit from exposure to the stimulus. This work became known as the transactional model, and as described by Coyne and Holroyd:

> The Lazarus group applies the concept of appraisal to the person's continually reevaluated judgments about demands and constraints in transactions with the environment and options and resources for meeting them. A key assumption of the model is that these evaluations determine the person's stress reaction, the emotions experienced, and adaptational outcomes. (1982, p. 108)

Thus, the Lazarus group emphasized first a primary appraisal ("Is this situation a threat, challenge, or aversion?") and then a secondary one ("Can I cope or benefit from it?") in the origin of human adult emotions.

The basic position of the primacy of cognition in the cognitive-affective relationship is held by numerous theorists and researchers (Arnold, 1960, 1984; Chang, 1998; Dewe, 1992; Hemenover & Dienstbier, 1996; Lazarus, 1966, 1999; Levine, 1996; Peeters, Buunk, & Schaufeli, 1995; Terry, Tonge, & Callan, 1995). To reiterate, the cognitive primacy perspective argues "that cognitive activity is a 'necessary' as well as sufficient condition of emotion" (Lazarus, 1982, p. 1019). More specifically, cognitive activity here refers to "cognitive appraisal," the role of which is to mediate the relationships between people and their environments. In a recent monograph on stress and emotion, Lazarus succinctly notes: "Emotions are the product of reason in that they flow from how we appraise what is happening in our lives. In effect, the way we evaluate an event determines how we react emotionally. This is what it means to speak of cognitive mediation" (1999, p. 87). Commenting on the cognitive perspectives, Dobson and Shaw write that "they share an assumption that it is the perception of events, rather than events themselves, that mediates the response to different circumstances and ultimately determines the quality of adaptation of individuals" (1995, p. 159).

Although the preponderance of stress researchers supports the notion of cognitive primacy, not all writers have agreed. During the 1980s, Zajonc and Lazarus had vigorous literary disagreements regarding the merits of cognitive primacy. Zajonc (1984) argued that an affective reaction could occur independently or without cognitive participation under certain circumstances. While he provided specific reasons to support his contention for the independence of affect (e.g., phylogenetic and ontogenetic primacy, separation of neuroanatomical structures for affect and cognition, the periodic lack of correlation between appraisal and affect, the formation of new affective reactions established without apparent appraisal, and the consideration that affective states can be induced by noncognitive procedures), Lazarus provided effective rebuttals for each of the points.

Parkinson and Manstead (1992) presented a critique of appraisal theory; however, Lazarus's (1999) response to their criticism suggests that their points of disagreement are actually quite narrow. In fact, Lazarus suggests that they generally accept most of his theory on stress and emotion. He acknowledges that a definitive empirical separation of appraisal and emotion is arduous due to the obvious methodological limitations, but he contends that more empirical support is offered for cognitive primacy than for any other theories. Lazarus further argues that the theory of cognitive primacy should not be discarded unless one is prepared to offer a more encompassing and effective alternative explanation. Most researchers agree that a more effective alternative explanation to cognitive primacy is yet to come.

COGNITIVE-BASED PSYCHOTHERAPY

According to Bandura (1997, 1982a, 1982b), the primary factor in the determination of a stressful event is the individual's *perceived* inefficiency in coping with or controlling a potentially aversive situation. In this section, we review several models of cognitively based psychotherapeutic interventions that may be employed to alter the patient's perception (cognitive interpretation) of an environmental transaction that might be seen as potentially aversive. We then present a brief overview of the recently defined rubric of positive psychology.

Ellis's Model

Modern cognitive therapy is considered to have emerged in 1955 when Albert Ellis developed rational-emotive therapy, or RET (Arnkoff & Glass, 1992). Ellis (1971, 1973, 1984, 1991) has proposed that individuals often acquire irrational or illogical cognitive interpretations or beliefs about themselves or their environments. The extent to which these beliefs are irrational and important corresponds to the amount of emotional distress experienced by the individual. Ellis believes that the emotional disturbance experienced by the individual can be summarized using the following "ABC" model:

A		B		C
Activating	$\rightarrow$	Belief	$\rightarrow$	Emotional
experience				consequence

In Condition A, some environmental transaction involving the individual occurs, say, he or she is late for an appointment. In Condition B, the person generates some "irrational" belief about himself or herself based on the original experience—for example, "I'm stupid, worthless, and incompetent for being late." Condition C represents the emotional consequence—guilt, depression, shame, anxiety—that results *not* from the experience itself (A) but directly from the irrational belief (B).

Ellis employs his model of RET, which consists of adding a "D" to the ABC paradigm, representing a conscious effort to "dispute" the irrational cognitive belief that resulted in the emotional distress. The RET therapist may use techniques such as debating, role playing, social skills training, and bibliotherapy to challenge individuals' beliefs, often in a confrontational, forceful fashion. Therefore, regardless of the techniques used, the overall psychotherapeutic goal is to alter the individual's interpretation. Ellis has delineated a series of questions to assist in the disputation of irrational beliefs:

1. What irrational belief needs to be disputed?
2. Can this belief be rationally supported?
3. What evidence exists for the falseness of this belief?
4. Does any evidence exist for the truth of this belief?
5. What worse things could *actually* happen to me if my initial experience (activating experience) does not end favorably?
6. What good things can I make happen even if my initial experience does not end favorably?

Beck's Cognitive Therapy Model

The cognitive therapy process of Aaron T. Beck is considered the second major cognitive restructuring therapy (Arnkoff & Glass, 1992). Similar to RET, cognitive therapy assists the client in identifying maladaptive thinking and persuades him or her to develop a more adaptive view. However, whereas RET is more philosophically driven (Ellis, 1995), Beck's cognitive therapy is more empirically based and focuses on whether thoughts and beliefs are _realistic_, rather than whether they are _rational_ (Meichenbaum, 1995). As Beck notes:

> Based on my clinical observations and some systematic clinical studies and experiments, I theorized that there was a thinking disorder at the core of the psychiatric syndromes such as depression and anxiety. This disorder was reflected in a systematic bias in the way the patients interpreted particular experiences. (1995, p. vii)

Beck differentiates between three types of cognitions that may be involved in disrupted thinking: automatic thoughts, schemas, and cognitive distortions. _Automatic thoughts_ are considered a "surface-level" cognition that is brought to awareness quickly and readily and leads directly to the individual's emotional and behavioral responses. Cognitive _schemas_ are thought of as internal models of aspects of the self and the environment and are used to process information. They often lead individuals with emotional problems to develop perceptions of threat, loss, or danger. _Cognitive distortions_ serve, in essence, as a link between dysfunctional schemas and automatic thoughts. For example, when new information is processed cognitively, the material may be biased or skewed in order to make it consistent with a current schema.

Then, to challenge the patients' maladaptive thinking, Beck encourages the use of a Socratic dialogue, which relies on the ability of the treating therapist to ask questions in a probing manner that allows the patients to answer in a way to persuade _themselves_ to think differently. Beck and Emery describe in elaborate detail how cognitive restructuring principles can be used in the treatment of anxiety and stress-related disorders: "Anxious patients in the simplest terms believe, 'Something bad is going to happen that I won't be able to handle.' The cognitive therapist uses three basic strategies or questions to help the patient restructure this thinking" (1985, p. 200):

1. What is the evidence supporting the conclusion currently held by the patient?
2. What is another way of looking at the same situation but reaching some other conclusion?
3. What will happen if, indeed, the currently held conclusion/opinion is correct?

While examining each of these three strategic questions, it is important to keep in mind that individual differences may affect a patient's responses. It is also worth acknowledging that the therapist may need to employ all three strategies throughout therapy.

First, _what is the evidence?_ One goal of this strategy is to analyze the patient's cognitive patterns and search for "faulty logic." Therapists may help patients to correct faulty logic and ideas through questioning techniques that may allow them better to clarify the meaning (or meanings) and definitions of the problem. According to Beck (1993), individuals experiencing stress reactions tend to personalize events not relevant to them (egocentrism) and interpret situations in global and absolute terms. Therefore, the following are typical questions used to improve the patient's ability to process information and test reality:

- What is the evidence supporting this conclusion?
- What is the evidence against this conclusion?
- Are you oversimplifying causal relationships?
- Are you confusing habits or commonly held opinions with fact?
- Are your interpretations too far removed from your actual experiences?
- Are you thinking in "all-or-nothing" terms (i.e., black–white, either–or, on–off, or all-or-none types of decisions and outcome)?
- Are your conclusions in any way extreme or exaggerated?
- Are you taking selected examples out of context and basing your conclusion on such information?
- Is the source of information reliable?
- Is your thinking in terms of certainties rather than probabilities?
- Are you confusing low-probability with high-probability events?
- Are you basing your conclusions on feelings or values rather than facts?
- Are you focusing on irrelevant factors in forming your conclusions?

Through the use of such questions, patterns of faulty reasoning, such as projections, exaggerations, and negative attributions, may be discovered and corrected.

Second, *what is another way of looking at it?* The goal of this strategy is to help the patient generate alternative interpretations in lieu of the interpretation currently held. Strategies such as increasing both objectivity and perspective, or shifting or diverting cognitive set (Beck, 1993), may lead to reattribution, diminishing the significance of the environmental transaction or even restructuring the transaction to find something positive in the event.

Third, *so what if it happens?* The goal of this strategy is to help the patient "decatastrophize" the environmental transaction, as well as to develop coping strategies and problem-solving skills. It will be recalled from the multidimensional treatment model that *environmental engineering* (Girdano, Dusek, & Everly, 2005) and *problem solving* are merely terms that describe the therapeutic processes of this third strategic phase of therapy as described by Beck and Emery, who suggest that "therapist and patient collaboratively develop a variety of strategies that the person can use" (1985, p. 208).

Ultimately, the goal of therapy is to allow the patient to develop autonomous skills in each of these three strategic areas. The notions of "environmental engineering" and "problem solving" will be more formally integrated in the next model—Meichenbaum's stress inoculation training model.

Meichenbaum's Stress Inoculation Training

Using the principles contained in his classic text *Cognitive-Behavior Modification*, Meichenbaum (1977) developed a specialized, cognitively based therapy for the treatment of excessive stress in a therapeutic formula called "stress inoculation training" (SIT). Reflecting back on twenty years of SIT, Meichenbaum noted:

> In short, SIT helps clients acquire sufficient knowledge, self-understanding, and coping skills to facilitate better ways of handling expected stressful encounters. SIT combines elements of Socratic and didactic teaching, client self-monitoring, cognitive restructuring, problem solving, self-instructional and relaxation training, behavioral and imagined rehearsal, and environmental change. With regard to the notion of environmental change, SIT recognizes that stress is transactional in nature. (1993, p. 381)

The SIT paradigm consists of an overlapping, three-phase intervention. The first phase, the initial conceptualization phase, includes the development of a collaborative relationship between the client and trainer through the use of Socratic exchanges. The overall objectives of this phase include data collection and education to help clients reconceptualize their stressful experiences in a more hopeful and empowered manner.

In the second phase of SIT, coping and problem-solving skills are taught and rehearsed. Table 28.1 provides examples of self-statements that may be used as coping techniques. Skills acquisition in this phase encompasses more than self-statements; assertion training, anger control, study skills, parenting, and relaxation may be incorporated.

The third phase of SIT, application and follow-through, allows patients to apply the skills acquired in the preceding two phases across situations with increasing levels of actual stress. Therefore, techniques such as modeling, role playing, and *in vivo* exposure are used, as well as features of relapse prevention. The follow-up component allows for future extension of SIT uses.

These three phases of SIT are enumerated in greater detail in Table 28.2. (A valuable guide for practitioners on the use of SIT is also available; see Meichenbaum, 1985.)

Meichenbaum's SIT training is of special interest in this chapter because it manifests the belief that stress management is most effective when it is flexible and multidimensional. Similarly, SIT allows us to integrate the concept of "environmental engineering." The term *environmental engineering* is borrowed from the work of Girdano, Dusek, and Everly (2005), who first described it in 1979, and refers to any conscious attempts at manipulating environmental factors to reduce one's exposure to stressor events. Both proactive, environmental change and reactive problem solving must be included under this heading.

As implied earlier, one of the real strengths of SIT is its inherent flexibility, structured as it is around a cognitive foundation. SIT has been demonstrated to be of value in the control of anger, test anxiety, phobias, general stress, pain, surgical anxiety, essential hypertension, and posttraumatic stress disorder (see Meichenbaum, 1985, 1993).

Positive Psychology

The science of positive psychology is a recent designation predicated on fundamental issues such as happiness, well-being, excellence, and optimal

Table 28.1. Examples of Coping Self-Statements Rehearsed in Stress Inoculation Training

Preparing for a stressor

- What is it you have to do?
- You can develop a plan to deal with it.
- Just think about what you can do about it. That's better than getting anxious.
- No negative self-statements: Just think rationally.
- Don't worry: Worry won't help anything.
- Maybe what you think is anxiety is eagerness to confront the stressor.

Confronting and handling a stressor

- Just "psych" yourself up—you can meet this challenge.
- You can convince yourself to do it. You can reason your fear away.
- One step at a time: You can handle the situation.
- Don't think about fear; just think about what you have to do. Stay relevant.
- This anxiety is what the doctor said you would feel. It's a reminder to use your coping exercises.
- This tenseness can be an ally, a cue to cope.
- Relax; you're in control. Take a slow deep breath.
- Ah, good.

Coping with the feeling of being overwhelmed

- When fear comes, just pause.
- Keep the focus on the present; what is it you have to do?
- Label your fear from 0 to 10 and watch it change.
- You should expect your fear to rise.
- Don't try to eliminate fear totally; just keep it manageable.

Reinforcing self-statements

- It worked; you did it.
- Wait until you tell your therapist (or group) about this.
- It wasn't as bad as you expected.
- You made more out of your fear than it was worth.
- Your damn ideas—that's the problem. When you control them, you control your fear.
- It's getting better each time you use the procedures.
- You can be pleased with the progress you're making.
- You did it!

Source: Meichenbaum (1977). Copyright by Plenum Press. Reprinted by permission.

human functioning, among others (Seligman & Csikszentmihalyi, 2000). In essence, the focus of positive psychology is on what makes life worth living for individuals, families, and communities. We recognize and appreciate that positive psychology should not be construed as a subtype of cognitive therapy (Seligman, personal communication, June 2000); however, we believe that it is important to include the topic in this current chapter.

Table 28.2. Flowchart of Stress Inoculation Training

Phase One: Conceptualization

a. Data collection-integration

- Identify determinants of problem via interview, image-based reconstruction, self-monitoring, and behavioral observance.
- Distinguish between performance failure and skill deficit.
- Formulate treatment plan—task analysis.
- Introduce integrative conceptual model.

b. Assessment skills training

- Train clients to analyze problems independently (e.g., to conduct situational analyses and to seek disconfirmatory data).

Phase Two: Skills Acquisition and Rehearsal

a. Skills training

- Training instrumental coping skills (e.g., communication, assertion, problem-solving, parenting, study skills).
- Train palliative coping skills as indicated (e.g., perspective-taking, attention diversion, use of social supports, adaptive affect expression, relaxation).
- Aim to develop an extensive repertoire of coping responses to facilitate flexible responding.

b. Skills rehearsal

- Promote smooth integration and execution of coping responses via imagery and role play.
- Self-instructional training to develop mediators to regulate coping responses.

Phase Three: Application and Follow-through

a. Induce application of skills

- Prepare for application using coping imagery, using early stress cues as signals to cope.
- Role-play (1) anticipated stressful situations and (2) client coaching someone with a similar problem.
- "Role play" attitude may be adopted in real world.
- Exposure to in-session graded stressors.
- Use of graded exposure and other response induction aids to foster *in vivo* responding and build self-efficacy.

b. Maintenance and generalization

- Build sense of coping self-efficacy in relation to situations client sees as high risk.
- Develop strategies for recovering from failure and relapse.
- Arrange follow-up review.

General Guidelines for Training

- Attend to referral and intake process.
- Consider training peers of clients to conduct treatment. Develop collaborative relationship and project approachability.
- Establish realistic expectations regarding course and outcome of therapy.
- Foster optimism and confidence by structuring incremental success experiences.
- Respond to stalled progress with problem solving, versus labeling client "resistant."
- Include family members in treatment when this is indicated.

Source: "Stress Inoculation Training: Toward a Paradigm for Training Coping Skills," by D. Meichenbaum & R. Cameron (p. 121). In Meichenbaum & Jaremko, 1983. Copyright by Plenum Press. Reprinted by permission.

Seligman and Csikszentmihalyi (2000) acknowledge that positive psychology is not an original concept, and they give appropriate credit to many distinguished predecessors. What Seligman and Csikszentmihalyi note, however, is that since World War II, the emphasis of psychology as a science has been on assessing and treating mental illness. At the start of a new millennium, they suggest that we have reached a time in our history when we should formalize our research efforts to understand systematically what makes individuals and communities flourish. It will be interesting to observe the empirical and theoretical impact of positive psychology over the next several years, both within and outside of the social sciences.

SUMMARY

This chapter has focused on the role that psychotherapy can play in treating excessive stress. We have chosen to review cognitive-based psychotherapeutic interventions. The main points in this chapter are as follows:

1. Cognition plays the primary role in the initiation and propagation of a psychosocially induced stress response.
2. The genesis and features of "cognitive primacy" (the notion that affect is subsequent to cognition), as well as updates and critiques of the theory, are reviewed.
3. The rational-emotive therapy of Ellis (1971, 1973, 1984, 1991) is introduced as the first of modern, cognitive-based psychotherapeutic interventions to challenge and alter dysfunctional cognitions. Its core assumption is that individuals who suffer excessive stress may have a proclivity, albeit pathogenic, to accept irrational or otherwise inappropriate beliefs about environmental transactions. This propensity can be corrected by teaching the patient to "dispute" her or his irrational beliefs as they give rise to excessive stress arousal.
4. Beck's cognitive therapy is considered the second major cognitive restructuring therapy. It is viewed as a broader spectrum cognitive intervention that not only focuses on inappropriate cognitive patterns but also assists the patient in developing other coping and problem-solving activities. Three basic therapeutic strategies are employed to assist in cognitive restructuring: analyzing the nature of any evidence that affected the individual's cognitive interpretation; generating alternative interpretations via cognitive reattribution and searching for positive aspects inherent in the environmental transaction ("the silver lining"); and developing environmental engineering, adaptive coping strategies, and useful problem-solving techniques.
5. The broadest spectrum cognitive-based stress management intervention extends well beyond psychotherapy and is referred to as "stress inoculation training." In the paradigm developed by Meichenbaum (1977, 1985, 1993), the intervention consists of three basic stages: data collection and education; skills acquisition; and application and follow-through to a real-world setting. The multiple components of this approach are delineated in Table 28.2.

6. Cognitive-based interventions have demonstrated their utility in the treatment of a wide array of problems, including anger, pain, phobias, anxiety, general stress arousal, headaches, and posttraumatic stress disorder (see Meichenbaum, 1985).

7. Positive psychology is a recently developed designation predicated on the fundamental issues of happiness, well-being, and optimism. It is intended to promote an empirically based systematic study of these and other positive qualities.

REFERENCES

Arnkoff, D. B., & Glass, C. R. (1992). Cognitive therapy and psychotherapy integration. In D. Freedheim (Ed.), *History of psychotherapy: A century of change* (pp. 657–694). Washington, DC: American Psychological Association.

Arnold, M. (1960). *Emotion and personality* (2 vols.). New York: Columbia University Press.

Arnold, M. (1984). *Memory and the brain*. Hillsdale, NJ: Erlbaum.

Bandura, A. (1982a). The self and mechanisms of agency. In J. Suls (Ed.), *Psychological perspectives on the self* (pp. 3–39). Hillsdale, NJ: Erlbaum.

Bandura, A. (1982b). Self-efficacy mechanism in human agency. *American Psychologist, 37*(2), 122–147.

Bandura, A. (1997). *Self-efficacy: The exercise of control*. New York: Freeman.

Beck, A. (1993). Cognitive approaches to stress. In P. M. Lehrer & R. L. Woolfolk (Eds.), *Principles and practices of stress management* (2nd ed., pp. 333–372). New York: Guilford Press.

Beck, A. (1995). Foreword. In J. S. Beck, *Cognitive therapy: Basics and beyond* (p. vii). New York: Guilford Press.

Beck, A., & Emery, G. (1985). *Anxiety disorders and phobias: A cognitive perspective*. New York: Basic Books.

Chang, E. C. (1998). Dispositional optimism and primary and secondary appraisal of a stressor: Controlling for confounding influences and relations to coping and psychological and physical adjustment. *Journal of Personality and Social Psychology, 74*, 1109–1120.

Coyne, J. C., & Holroyd, K. (1982). Stress, coping, and illness. In T. Millon, C. Green, & R. Meagher (Eds.), *Handbook of clinical health psychology* (pp. 103–128). New York: Plenum Press.

Dewe, P. J. (1992). The appraisal process: Exploring the role of meaning, importance, control, and coping in work stress. *Anxiety, Stress, and Coping, 5*, 95–109.

Dobson, K. S., & Shaw, B. F. (1995). Cognitive therapies in practice. In B. Bongar & L. E. Bentler (Eds.), *Comprehensive textbook of psychotherapies: Theory and practice* (pp. 159–172). New York: Oxford University Press.

Ellis, A. (1971). Emotional disturbance and its treatment in a nutshell. *Canadian Counselor, 5*, 168–171.

Ellis, A. (1973). *Humanistic psychology: The rational-emotive approach*. New York: Julian.

Ellis, A. (1984). The use of hypnosis with rational-emotive therapy. *Journal of Integrative & Eclectic Psychotherapy, 2*, 15–22.

Ellis, A. (1991). The revised ABC's of rational-emotive therapy (RET). *Journal of Rational-Emotive and Cognitive-Behavior Therapy, 9*, 139–177.

Ellis, A. (1995). Reflections on rational-emotive therapy. In M. Mahoney (Ed.), *Cognitive and constructive psychotherapies: Theory, research, and practice* (pp. 69–86). New York: Springer.

Girdano, D. A., Dusek, D. E., & Everly, G. S., Jr. (2005). *Controlling stress and tension* (7th ed.). San Francisco: Pearson/Benjamin Cummings.

Grinker, R. R., & Spiegel, J. P. (1945). War neuroses in flying personnel overseas and after return to the U.S.A. *American Journal of Psychiatry, 101,* 619–624.

Hemenover, S. H., & Dienstbier, R. A. (1996). The effects of an appraisal manipulation: Affect, intrusive cognitions, and performance for two cognitive tasks. *Motivation and Emotion, 20,* 319–340.

Lazarus, R. S. (1966). *Psychological stress and the coping process.* New York: McGraw-Hill.

Lazarus, R. S. (1982). Thoughts on the relations between emotions and cognition. *American Psychologist, 37*(9), 1019–1024.

Lazarus, R. S. (1999). *Stress and emotion: A new synthesis.* New York: Springer.

Levine, L. J. (1996). The anatomy of disappointment: A natural test of appraisal models of sadness, anger, and hope. *Cognition and Emotion, 10,* 337–359.

Meichenbaum, D. (1977). *Cognitive-behavior modification.* New York: Plenum Press.

Meichenbaum, D. (1985). *Stress inoculation training.* New York: Plenum Press.

Meichenbaum, D. (1993). Stress inoculation training: A 20-year update. In P. M. Lehrer & R. L. Woolfolk (Eds.), *Principles and practice of stress management* (2nd ed., pp. 373–406). New York: Guilford Press.

Meichenbaum, D. (1995). Changing conceptions of cognitive behavior modification: Retrospect and prospect. In M. Mahoney (Ed.), *Cognitive and constructive psychotherapies: Theory, research, and practice* (pp. 20–26). New York: Springer.

Meichenbaum, D., & Jaremko, M. (1983). *Stress reduction and prevention.* New York: Plenum Press.

Parkinson, B., & Manstead, A. S. R. (1992). Appraisal as a cause of emotion. In M. Clark (Ed.), *Emotion* (pp. 122–149). Newbury Park, CA: Sage.

Peeters, M. C. W., Buunk, B. P., & Schaufeli, W. B. (1995). The role of attributions in the cognitive appraisal of work-related stressful events: An event-recording approach. *Work and Stress, 9,* 463–474.

Roseman, L. (1984). Cognitive determinants of emotion. In P. Shaver (Ed.), *Review of personality and social psychology* (pp. 11–36). Beverly Hills, CA: Sage.

Seligman, M. E. P., & Csikszentmihalyi, M. (2000). Positive psychology: An introduction. *American Psychologist, 55*(1), 5–14.

Terry, D. J., Tonge, L., & Callan, V. J. (1995). Employee adjustment to stress: The role of coping resources, situational factors, and coping resources. *Anxiety, Stress, and Coping, 8,* 1–24.

Zajonc, R. B. (1984). On the primacy of affect. *American Psychologist, 39*(2), 117–123.

CHAPTER 29

Stress and Diet

Elizabeth Somer

Have you ever:

- Caught a cold right after a big event?
- Craved candy bars when pressured to meet a deadline at work?
- Found yourself unable to think of a name, find the right word, or remember where you put your car keys when you're under stress?
- Lost your appetite when troubled or anxious?
- Gained or lost weight when a relationship ended?

If so, you've experienced firsthand what science is just beginning to understand: Stress, diet, mood, and immunity are interconnected.

For centuries, scientists believed the mind ruled, yet remained separate from, the body. Recently research on stress has changed the way we look at the human experience. What was first called the mind–body connection by questionable philosophers in the 1970s is now a respected science called psychoneuroimmunology, the study of how the mind, hormones, and the immune system communicate. In recent years more and more proof has pointed to the fact that the brain is not separate but is intricately intertwined with the body. What you eat, how well you cope with stress, how clearly you think today and in the future, your moods, and your risk for most major degenerative diseases are all interconnected. Let's first look at how stress affects the body, then investigate how diet can prevent the ravages of too much of the wrong kinds of stress.

PREHISTORIC STRESS

To be alive is to be under stress. Everything from the ring of a doorbell to the loss of a loved one can trigger the stress response. Some things are stressful in a positive way. A new job, falling in love, or taking an art class are potentially stressful events that prompt us to reach our goals, become better people, or stretch our creative limits. Some stress is even fun, such as the thrill of a hot air balloon ride or watching a suspenseful movie. However, stress also comes cloaked as worries, anger, jealousies, and fears, and these stressors—called *distress*—are the villains of health, although too much of any stress can be harmful.

Stress is your body's knee-jerk reaction to a threat. It is one of those survival-of-the-species basic instincts dating back to the beginning of life. To the cave dweller, stress meant physical danger. In those days a proper response to anything unusual or threatening was literally a matter of life and death. In Darwinian terms, those who responded quickly survived, while those who kicked back and ignored the threat didn't. The sight of a saber-toothed tiger triggered early people's nerves and glands to secrete numerous stress hormones such as cortisol. As a result, the cave dweller's pupils dilated, nostrils flared, and vision improved, all in an effort to better identify the nature of the attacking beast. Muscles tensed and prepared the body to run, jump, or face the enemy. Breathing, pulse rate, and blood pressure increased, while blood vessels constricted, speeding oxygen and blood to the muscles and away from the internal organs. The liver released large amounts of glucose (sugar) into the bloodstream, and fat fragments (called free fatty acids) were released from fat cells to provide the fuel to "fight or flee." Within a split second the body was transformed from a peaceful state to war mode.

Today we are essentially cave dweller bodies dressed in designer clothes. We have traded the threat of a saber-toothed tiger for rush-hour traffic, intense time schedules, overextended lifestyles, and overcrowding. Stress comes from within as anger, unrealistic expectations, fears, and self-doubts. Our hearts still race, our blood pressures climb, our blood vessels constrict, and the stress hormones flood our systems in response to these modern-day tigers. But instead of expending our rallied defenses, as our ancestors did by running for cover or standing up to fight, we stew in our own juices. Stress hormones linger in the bloodstream, blood cholesterol and sugar levels rise, and nerve chemicals release in record numbers. It is this stressful stew pot that is linked to the loss of brain power and suppressed ability to fend off infection and numerous diseases—from peptic ulcers, asthma, and colds to cardiovascular disease and possibly cancer. How well do you cut back on your day-to-day stress load? To find out, take the quiz in Box 29.1.

THE MIND–BODY CONNECTION

"The effects of stress on health and aging may be greater than we think," warns Robert Russell, M.D., professor of medicine and nutrition at Tufts University. In fact, stress is a major player in mood, food cravings, thinking, insomnia, and all aspects of emotional and physical health. The interactions between how you handle stress and your moods are far too complex to discuss in their entirety in this chapter. So here is a taste of how one stress hormone affects your mental and emotional well-being.

Box 29.1. Quiz: Tally Your Stress Points

Is your life balanced, with some peace and an occasional bout of frenzy, or is it always calm, or usually nuts? Rate each of the following statements as to whether it is *always true* (1), *never true* (5), or somewhere in between:

1. I eat at least three nutritious meals or snacks a day
2. I drink less than three cups of coffee, cola, or other caffeinated beverages daily.
3. I eat a minimal amount of sugary foods.
4. I get at least seven hours of sleep.
5. I give and receive affection and attention regularly.
6. I have a circle of close friends and relatives who live close by on whom I can rely. I feel comfortable disclosing my feelings and beliefs to them.
7. I believe most things will turn out all right and I am optimistic about the future.
8. I set aside at least thirty minutes a day for quiet time.
9. I do something fun at least three times a week.
10. I exercise at an intensity that causes me to perspire at least five times a week.
11. I avoid tobacco smoke.
12. I drink less than five alcoholic drinks a week.
13. I am able to pay my bills.
14. I only worry about things that really matter and I usually handle daily stresses successfully and quickly.
15. I am in good health.
16. I usually feel secure and relaxed and seldom feel nervous, jittery, or high strung.
17. I am happy with my home life.
18. I am happy with my work and/or community involvement.
19. I am able to quickly resolve conflicts at home and/or at work.
20. I am a good time manager.
21. I do not take street drugs, and I use prescription medications only when necessary and only with physician approval and monitoring.
22. I laugh or chuckle daily and belly laugh regularly. (The average person laughs 540,000 times in his or her life. That equates to a minimum of twenty-one laugh episodes each day!)

Scoring:

Under 36: Your stress level is relatively low.

37 to 46: You are moderately stressed and should take an inventory of your life to see what could be done to reduce your stress level.

47 to 57: Your life is very stressed and cannot support optimal health. Take action to reduce your stress load and increase your commitment to healthy habits and activities.

More than 57: Your life is extremely stressed. Don't waste another minute before making several changes to reduce the pressure. Choose a stress plan that will give you the greatest relaxation payoff for the least amount of effort.

Within a split second of experiencing something stressful, a center in the brain called the hypothalamus secretes a hormone called corticotropin-releasing factor (CRF). This stimulates another brain center called the pituitary to release adrenocorticotropic hormone (ACTH), which, in turn, triggers the adrenal glands to release stress hormones into the system, including cortisol. When cortisol reaches peak levels, this tells the hypothalamus to shut off CRF release. Long-term or repeated bouts of stress, however, clog this feedback loop. As a result, cortisol levels remain high for extended periods of time.

Short bursts of cortisol are helpful to the stress response, but long-term or chronic exposure to this hormone is toxic to the brain and body. Cortisol reduces the brain's ability to use glucose, especially the hippocampus, which is a relay station for short-term memory. Cortisol affects the functioning of many nerve chemicals, including serotonin, dopamine, and neuropeptide Y, thus affecting eating habits, mood, and brain function. Excessive exposure to cortisol also is toxic to brain cells, increasing free-radical damage and ultimately killing them. This results in loss of memory, inability to retain new information, and reduced capacity to learn. Elevated cortisol levels also amplify the stress response, increasing anxiety, irritability, insomnia, and eating disorders and interfering with our ability to relax. The harmful effects of stress are magnified when people feel overwhelmed or "out of control." In contrast, people who handle stress effectively, eat well, exercise regularly to burn off those stress hormones, and keep their cortisol levels low are healthier, live longer, and are most likely to maintain the brain power of a twenty-year-old!

Obviously, finding ways to both reduce unnecessary stress and effectively cope with the stress you can't avoid is critical to your health today and in the future. Dietary strategies for coping with stress are geared to:

1. Repairing any damage already done, as well as helping prevent future damage from cortisol and poor circulation that results from constricted blood vessels during stress.
2. Supplying the nutritional building blocks needed for optimal functioning of the brain, body, and immune system so these tissues can protect themselves against any harmful effects of the stress response.

HOW STRESS AFFECTS YOUR NUTRITION

Stress and nutrition are closely intertwined. A nutritional deficiency is a stress in itself, since suboptimal amounts of one or more nutrients place a strain on all of the body's metabolic processes dependent on that nutrient. For example, even a slight iron deficiency reduces the oxygen supply to the tissues and brain; oxygen-starved tissues then leave a person feeling tired, irritable, and unable to concentrate. Likewise an inadequate intake of the B vitamins places stress on the cells' ability to convert carbohydrates and fats into energy. Suboptimal amounts of antioxidants like vitamin C weaken the body's antioxidant defenses, exposing the tissues to damage and disease. In addition, how well your body is nourished prior to and during a stressful event will affect how well you handle the stress. In short, a well-nourished person will cope better than a poorly nourished one.

On the other hand, stress affects nutrient needs by reducing absorption, increasing excretion, altering how the body uses the nutrients, and even increasing the daily requirements for certain nutrients. Yet people's eating habits often are at their nutritional worst during high stress. People who frequently diet tend to overeat all the wrong foods when stressed, and even people who eat well during the best of times can lose their appetites during high-stress times. Consequently, a person is more vulnerable to nutritional deficiencies when stressed than during almost any other time in life, and these nutrient deficiencies amplify the stress.

Any type of stress—from the physical stress of disease or surgery to the emotional stress of losing a loved one or the mental stresses at work—upsets nutritional balance, which in turn makes the stress just that much worse. If the stress is short-lived, such as a temporary increase in workload or anticipation of an upcoming event, and you are already well-nourished, you will handle the situation with less anxiety, and the stress is not likely to significantly affect nutritional status. However, if you are marginally nourished prior to a stressful situation and/or the situation lasts for some time, such as a high-pressured job or years of juggling work and family responsibilities, you overtax your body's ability to handle this high-stress period, with nutritional status and overall health paying the price unless immediate action is taken to improve diet and coping skills.

WORRY AND THE COMMON COLD

Emotional and mental stress suppresses the immune system, thus reducing your ability to fight off colds, infections, and disease. Let's first take a brief look at what makes the immune system tick, then discuss how stress and nutrition affect it.

The War Zone

Your body is like a fortress under siege. Everything in the environment, from the food you eat to the people you greet, exposes you to viruses, bacteria, and other microorganisms (or "germs") that can cause infection and disease. Whether or not you succumb to the daily attacks depends greatly on the strength of your immune system.

The immune system is your body's main defense against both foreign invaders and abnormal cell growth such as cancer. The armed forces of this system include organs, tissues, millions of cells, and numerous chemicals. For example, specialized white blood cells, called B-cells, circulate in the blood and other body fluids, where they neutralize the toxins produced by bacteria. B-cells secrete chemicals called antibodies, which act like Patriot missiles specifically tailored to destroy foreign invaders. T-cells are the cornerstone of immunity within the cells. Among other things, T-cells produce chemicals called lymphokines, such as interferon, a protein that defends cells from viruses and is suspected to be a natural defense against cancer. Other specialized cells in the immune system include natural killer cells (free agents that act independently of other immune forces to locate and destroy germs); macrophages and monocytes, which surround and "neutralize" hostile substances; and other white blood cells.

This complex defense system provides constant feedback on the "state of the union." The result is a sensitive and intricate system of checks and balances that, in the presence of optimal nutrient intake and moderate to low stress, helps your body guarantee an armed defense that is efficient, quick, and specific against "germ warfare" and abnormal cell growth. On the other hand, a weakened immune system might fail to recognize an invader or to mount a strong attack. The results can be chronic or repeated infections, or more serious illnesses such as cancer.

Immunity, however, is not a black-and-white issue. "Whether the attacking organism or the immune system prevails depends on many factors, including a person's nutritional status, general health, stress level, and sleep patterns, as well as the force of the onslaught," says Darshan Kelley, Ph.D., research chemist at the Western Human Nutrition Research Center in Davis, California. It is the total picture that determines a person's resistance to disease.

The Stress Factor

As your heart starts racing and the perspiration appears on your brow, the stress response also is suppressing your immune system. As a result, antibody production decreases, T-lymphocytes retreat, and B-lymphocyte numbers decline. Even minor nuisances, such as loud noise and bright lights, can affect your body's natural defenses. Depression, loss of a loved one, and other major stresses suppress the immune system by as much as 50 percent in some people. Consequently, the more a person is stressed, the greater the need to support the defense system by:

- Eating breakfast
- Eating a nutrient-packed and low-fat diet
- Avoiding tobacco
- Limiting alcohol consumption
- Sleeping at least seven hours a night
- Working less than ten hours a day
- Exercising daily
- Using effective stress-management skills such as time management, deep breathing, meditation, progressive relaxation, yoga, music therapy, or aromatherapy
- Nurturing positive beliefs, attitudes, and expectations, including hope, trust, love, faith, and laughter, which enhance the immune system

STRESS-FIGHTING NUTRITION FACTORS

Diet, immunity, and stress are so intertwined that it is difficult to know where one stops and the next begins. One thing is clear: You can help lower cortisol levels, boost your natural defenses, calm yourself, and curb the negative effects of stress on your body and mind by fueling your body with the nutrients it needs to stay healthy. But it will take some focus and willpower to give your body what it needs rather than what it might be craving.

Why Do We Crave Sweets When We're Stressed?

The stress hormone cortisol scrambles our appetite-control chemicals, which affects food intake and mood. Cortisol turns on the production of neuropeptide Y (NPY), alters dopamine levels, and lowers serotonin. It's no wonder we make poor food choices when we're stressed, turning to sweets, salty snacks, and processed grains. Consequently, weight gain during stressful times might be a result of this altered chemistry, which prompts overeating, especially of sugary foods.

At a time when you need your mental, physical, and emotional reserves, sugar can leave you at wit's end, with plummeting blood-sugar levels and a host of brain chemicals in disarray. Sugar is an accomplice to many health problems, since it either replaces nutritious foods or adds unwanted calories. When sugar intake increases above 9 percent of total calories, your vitamin and mineral intake progressively decreases, which compromises your immune system and adds further stress to a body already under pressure. A high-sugar diet also increases urinary losses of calming minerals, including magnesium and chromium.

Larry Christensen, Ph.D., at the University of South Alabama reports that people suffering from emotional stress feel better if they eliminate sugar and coffee from their diets. In his studies, people were less stressed and

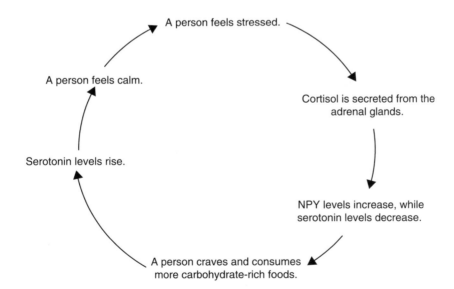

Figure 29.1. From Mood to Food and Back to Mood

showed improved emotional stability within two weeks of initiating low-sugar, low-caffeine diets. Dr. Christensen admits the relationship between specific dietary factors and psychological problems is poorly understood and might vary dramatically from one person to another. However, you have nothing to lose and everything to gain by adopting a nutrient-packed, low-sugar, and low-caffeine diet (see Box 29.2).

Box 29.2. Quick Fix Snacks

- 1 mango
- 4 cups of air-popped popcorn
- Drizzle 1 tablespoon of fat-free chocolate syrup over 2 cups of fresh strawberries
- 1 large pear
- Strawberry-kiwi pudding: Mix 1/2 cup fresh strawberries, two peeled and sliced kiwi, and one 6-ounce low-fat strawberry-kiwi yogurt. Place in a bowl and top with a sprig of fresh mint or one strawberry. Serve with two vanilla wafers.
- 1/2 cup fresh pineapple chunks with 1/2 cup 1 percent low-fat cottage cheese
- Candied-ginger fruit salad: In a bowl, mix one peeled and sectioned orange, half a peeled and sliced banana, half a peeled and diced mango or papaya, and one sliced plum. Toss fruit with 1 tablespoon orange juice concentrate, 1 teaspoon lemon peel, and 1 tablespoon crumbled candied ginger. Place in a parfait glass and serve with one ladyfinger cookie.
- Cranberry spritzer: Mix 8 ounces of cranberry juice with 8 ounces of sparkling water, ice cubes, and a twist of lemon.
- A large baked apple: Core an apple; fill its hollow with sugar-free cranberry soda pop and a dash of cinnamon and nutmeg. Bake at 350 degrees Fahrenheit for forty-five minutes.
- OJ ice cubes (a great alternative to munching on ice cubes!): Pour orange juice into ice cube trays and freeze.
- Large prawns, steamed and dipped in tomato-based cocktail sauce
- Low-fat tortilla chips with salsa
- Steamed pea pods with fat-free sour cream dip: Season with chili sauce, crushed garlic, lemon, grated orange peel, or curry
- Orange slices dipped in fat-free chocolate syrup
- Glacéed grapes: Rinse grapes in water, then roll lightly in granulated sugar
- Cherry tomatoes, cucumber slices, and hummus
- Cooked large white (fava) beans marinated in lemon juice, garlic, fresh sage, and wine
- Three fig bars and 1 cup of warmed nonfat milk flavored with almond extract and sprinkled with nutmeg
- Half a cantaloupe filled with 6 ounces of low-fat lemon yogurt and topped with 1 tablespoon of lemon zest
- Two slices of extra-lean ham lunch meat, twelve fat-free whole wheat crackers, and water
- Fruit parfait: In a parfait glass, mix the following with 1 tablespoon orange juice concentrate, layer, and top with 1 tablespoon light whipped cream: one orange, peeled and sectioned; 1/2 cup fresh strawberries; half a banana, sliced.

Stress and Fat Don't Mix

As if there wasn't enough wrong with high-fat diets, a study from the University of Maryland reports that high-fat diets, especially vegetable oils, raise stress hormone levels and interfere with the body's ability to calm itself even after the stress is over. Cutting back on fat and adopting a low-fat vegetarian diet lowers cortisol levels.

A low-fat diet also stimulates the immune system, while dietary fat—especially polyunsaturated fats found in vegetable oils, trans fatty acids (TFAs) in margarine and shortening, and saturated fats in meats and whole milk products—suppress the immune system. "Partially hydrogenated vegetable oils are a real problem," warns Mary Enig, Ph.D., former research associate at the University of Maryland and one of the first researchers to investigate TFAs in our food. What Dr. Enig began uncovering in the early 1980s has been confirmed by numerous studies since: TFAs, in amounts typically consumed by Americans, alter basic metabolic pathways, tamper with cell membranes, and generate free radicals that further suppress the immune response. The potential health risks of TFAs wouldn't be an issue except that we're eating a lot more than we think. Up until the turn of the century, the naturally occurring TFAs in meat and dairy products comprised a small portion of the diet (approximately 3 percent of total fat intake). But that changed dramatically when the food industry introduced hydrogenation into commercial food production, frying French fries and potato chips in hydrogenated vegetable oils. "People typically consume 10 to 15 grams of TFAs every day," warns Dr. Enig. Eliminating foods that contain these oils, including processed snack foods, fried fast foods, and margarine, would help maintain a strong immune system during times of stress.

Some fats boost immunity and reduce your risk for developing stress-related diseases, such as the oils in fish. Including two or three servings of fish in your weekly diet helps improve immune responses and reduce the risk for developing stress-induced colds, infections, and disease, including cancer. For example, in a study at the University of Marburg in Germany, fish oils lowered heart rates and blood pressure in a group of mentally stressed animals. Olive oil, on the other hand, appears neutral, neither raising nor suppressing immunity. Studies on animals support these findings and show that limiting total fat—by reducing saturated fats, corn and vegetable oils, and hydrogenated vegetable oils and holding constant or slightly increasing the intake of fish and olive oils—helps improve wound healing and immunity in stressed animals.

Fats, in the guise of sweet-and-creamy tastes like chocolate, desserts, ice cream, and even whole-milk yogurt, trigger the release of endorphins, the brain chemicals that calm and soothe. If these nerve chemicals are charting your course, then it is best to work with your chemicals, rather than against them. Plan nutrient-packed carbo snacks, such as raisin toast with all-fruit jam, or Cheerios and dried apricots, for your crave-prone times of the day. In addition, keep moving. Exercise helps use up the extra carbohydrates so they are not converted to fat. Until more is known about how fat affects the stress response and immunity, following a low-fat diet is the best bet.

CAFFEINE JITTERS, HIGH ANXIETY

Caffeine gives coffee and cola their punch. Virtually all of the caffeine in these beverages is absorbed and quickly distributed throughout the body. Within half an hour, caffeine's stimulating effects can be felt. Caffeine has a direct effect on the brain and central nervous system. Thought processes and regulatory processes, such as heart rate, respiration, and muscle coordination, are affected after drinking even one cup of coffee. Three or more cups can give you the "coffee jitters." In addition, coffee consumed with food can reduce mineral absorption, especially iron, by as much as 90 percent and can rob the body of other minerals, such as calcium and magnesium, needed during times of stress.

Caffeine lingers in the body for hours, escalating the stress response. In fact, caffeine alone can cause anxiety symptoms. As a consequence, coffee can add to the stress equation by aggravating the stress chemicals and interfering with sleep (coffee drinkers take longer to fall asleep, sleep less soundly, and wake up more often than nonusers). Substituting a cup of tea or a diet cola for an evening cup of coffee is not the solution, since both the tea and the cola contain the same amount of caffeine as a cup of instant coffee.

The Minerals

Researchers at the U.S. Department of Agriculture studied the effects of work-related stress on mineral status and found that despite adequate dietary intake, blood levels of several minerals dropped as much as 33 percent, and tissue stores for certain nutrients were depleted, during a five-day "Hell Week" at work where employees were given extra work and asked to meet difficult deadlines.

This loss of minerals jeopardizes the immune system and aggravates the stress response. For example, stress triggers the release of the stress hormones, which drains magnesium from the body and increases dietary requirements for the mineral. The stress-induced magnesium deficiency raises stress hormone levels, escalates the stress response, and causes stress-related depression and irritability. Studies on laboratory animals show that a magnesium deficiency increases sensitivity to noise and crowding and escalates stress-induced diseases such as ulcers, while animals whose diets are high in magnesium cope better and are at lower risk for disease.

The link between magnesium and stress is so strong that researchers at the American College of Nutrition recommend people supplement with magnesium during times of stress. According to Mildred Seelig, M.D., MPH, at the University of North Carolina, taking calcium supplements without also increasing magnesium intake upsets the ratio of these two minerals and intensifies a magnesium deficiency, which could further escalate the stress response. So it's prudent to also supplement with magnesium along with calcium. Your needs for chromium, copper, iron, selenium, and zinc also increase during stress.

The Antioxidants

Vitamins C and E and other antioxidant nutrients help regulate the immune system and are affected by stress as well. Both emotional and physical stress increase the amount of dietary vitamin C the body needs. The stress glands, including the adrenals and the pituitary, are major storage sites for vitamin C in the body. During times of stress, these stores are depleted, which could intensify the body's stress response by elevating stress hormone levels. This creates a Catch-22 situation, where stress-induced loss of vitamin C undermines the immune system's ability to defend against disease and escalates the stress response, which further depletes vitamin C levels and increases the likelihood of further stress. All it takes is an increase in vitamin C from fruits and vegetables or supplements to break this cycle. Vitamin E also is a key player in immunity; just supplementing with this vitamin can boost dwindling immune responses.

Typical American diets are low in vitamins C and E, and possibly other antioxidants, such as beta carotene. In addition, diet alone might not be enough during times of stress. "In our studies on seniors using 60 IU [International Units], 200 IU, and 800 IU of vitamin E, we found that the 200 IU daily dose was most effective in boosting immune function," says Simin Nikbin Meydani, DVM, Ph.D., professor of nutrition and immunology at Tufts University in Boston. It would take two and one-half cups of safflower oil or forty-six cups of spinach to reach this level of vitamin E. Consequently, supplements are necessary.

According to the latest national nutrition survey from the U.S. Food and Drug Administration, 99 percent of Americans are not eating antioxidant-rich diets that include at least five, and preferably nine, daily servings of fresh fruits and vegetables. If you're stressed and not consuming at least two fruits and vegetables at meals and snacks, then consider taking a supplement that contains at least 250 milligrams of vitamin C.

The B Vitamins

Our bodies' B vitamin requirements increase slightly during times of stress. Most of the B vitamins help develop or maintain the nervous system, which is in overdrive during stressful events. Your need for vitamins B_1, B_2, and other B vitamins increases as calorie intake increases, since these vitamins are essential in converting calories from food into energy in the body. Therefore, a deficiency results either from a vitamin-poor diet or from excessive intake of high-calorie, nutrient-poor foods, such as sweets and refined/highly processed foods. Even slight vitamin deficiencies further upset the nervous system and contribute to stress-related symptoms, such as irritability, lethargy, depression, and suppressed immunity.

Studies conducted at Loma Linda University and Oregon State University report that increasing vitamin B_6 intake raises blood levels of the vitamin and enhances the immune response. But large supplemental doses (250 milligrams or more) of vitamin B_6 can be toxic, so stick with a

ate-dose multiple that includes vitamin B_6 along with vitamin B_6–
oods, such as bananas, avocados, chicken (without the skin), fish,
d potatoes, and dark green leafy vegetables.

CHOLESTEROL AND HOSTILITY: IS THERE A CONNECTION?

For years people were told to lower their blood cholesterol levels and to take it easy, because aggressive and competitive personalities, called Type A's, are more prone to developing heart disease. Then researchers switched gears, reporting that people with very low blood cholesterol levels or who consumed low-fat diets might avoid heart disease, but were more depressed and aggressive and likely to commit suicide or die a violent death.

The obvious, but erroneous, assumption is to draw a direct link between low cholesterol levels and hostility. Some people even came to the conclusion that low-fat diets make people angry enough to kill themselves. Wrong. It is more likely that some other variable is linked to low cholesterol and hostility or that the link is nonexistent and only a fluke find in a few studies. For example, a study from the University of Edinburgh in the United Kingdom found no association between low cholesterol levels and anger. Some studies even reported that people's moods improved, showing less depression and aggressive hostility, when their blood cholesterol levels dropped. Even if low-fat diets did make people grumpy, a daily exercise program more than compensated by boosting mood, relieving depression and stress, and further lowering risk factors for heart disease such as elevated blood fats.

More recently, studies show that low intake of certain fats might aggravate an already stressed or angry disposition. Special fats found in fish oil, called the omega-3 fatty acids, help regulate mood by increasing serotonin levels, the nerve chemical that relieves depression. Low intake of fish oils lowers brain levels of serotonin in animals and increases aggressive and hostile behaviors. Similar effects have been noted in humans with lower fish oil consumption and serotonin levels, including increased rates of impulsive suicide attempts, according to researchers at the National Institute of Alcohol Abuse and Alcoholism in Bethesda, Maryland.

The lesson to be learned from this confusion is that one study does not a conclusion make. One study is like a thread in a tapestry of research that must be replicated over and over by other well-designed research studies before the results can be taken seriously enough to make general dietary and lifestyle recommendations. In the meantime, just make sure you add a few weekly servings of fish to the Feeling Good Diet!

CALM DOWN WITH EXERCISE

Our ancient ancestors knew what to do about stress: They ran away from it, or stood up and fought it. Exercise is still the best way to relieve stress, burn off those health-damaging stress hormones, boost your body's natural defenses against the ravages of stress, and prevent the wear and tear of the body that results in infection today and disease later in life. Exercise increases blood flow, encourages the growth of new cells in the brain and body, lowers cortisol levels, improves mood, and helps you see the bright side during stressful times. It acts as a natural tranquilizer and reduces fatigue, anger, and tension associated with stress. People who exercise regularly report less stress, are calmer, and handle stress better than sedentary folks.

Researchers disagree on whether strenuous or moderate exercise is the best, but they do agree that the more time you spend exercising, the better.

STRESS-PROOF BASICS

Obviously, too much stress isn't good for you, but sometimes it is unavoidable. So, when you can't beat stress, join it—but go into battle nutritionally well armed. When stressed, every bite counts. The Feeling Good Diet is the foundation of your defense strategies, with some modifications.

1. Cut back on colas. Granted, most people don't drink enough fluids when under stress and would benefit by hydrating their high anxiety; however, soda pop is not the best choice. Americans consume more than 450 servings per person per year of soft drinks; at five to nine teaspoons of sugar per serving, that equals 2,250 to 4,050 teaspoons of sugar from soft drinks alone, not counting the caffeine load. Limit your intake to no more than one 12-ounce serving of soda a day, preferably a decaffeinated, diet variety.
2. Savor a cup of coffee, but don't go back for seconds. Too much caffeine only increases anxiety. Switch to decaffeinated, grain-based beverages such as Postum, or mix regular coffee or tea with decaffeinated to cut back. For every cup of coffee or tea you have, drink two glasses of water.
3. Cut out sweets until the stress subsides. You don't have nutritional room for high-fat, high-sugar, or low-nutrient foods. Plus, sweets fuel the stress response. Instead, turn to naturally sweet fruits, whole grains, and other nutritious foods recommended in the Feeling Good Diet (see Box 29.3).
4. Keep fiber in mind. Often the digestive tract is hit hard by stress. To ensure normal bowel function, include at least five fiber-rich fresh fruits and vegetables, six servings of whole-grain breads and cereals, and one serving of cooked dried beans and peas in the daily diet. A variety of fibers is important, so don't depend on processed "bran" cereal for your daily fiber needs.
5. If you lose your appetite when you're under pressure, try to eat six to eight mini-meals throughout the day rather than force yourself to eat a few big meals. Listen to your body and eat foods that sound good, as long as they are wholesome choices. If you overeat when stressed, snack on low-fat goodies and eliminate high-fat temptations until your

Box 29.3. Calming Foods

The following snacks are low-fat, low-calorie, and packed with vitamins and minerals that help soothe a stressed body. Keep in mind that the total diet is what is important. No one food can transform an otherwise poor diet into a great eating plan.

Snack	Amount	Good source of
Sweet:		
Apricots, fresh	3 medium	Beta carotene, potassium, iron
Bananas	1 medium	Potassium, vitamin B_6, magnesium
Raspberries, fresh	2/3 cup	Beta carotene, vitamin C, potassium, iron, magnesium, manganese
Orange slices	1 cup	Vitamin C, folic acid, beta carotene, calcium, potassium
Papaya	1 medium	Beta carotene, vitamin C, potassium, calcium
Mango	1 medium	Beta carotene, niacin, vitamin B_6, folic acid, calcium, vitamin E, potassium
Strawberries, fresh	2 cups	Vitamin C, folic acid, potassium, iron, manganese
Frozen blueberries	$1^1/_4$ cups	Beta carotene, potassium, manganese
Peaches, canned in own juice, and nonfat yogurt	1 small, $^1/_2$ cup	Beta carotene, potassium; calcium, magnesium, vitamin B_2
Dried cranberries	2/3 cup	Vitamin B_6, potassium, calcium, iron, copper, manganese
Dried figs	2	Calcium, iron, magnesium, potassium, selenium
Raisin bread dipped in nonfat apple-spice yogurt	1 slice, $^1/_4$ cup	B vitamins, iron, calcium, magnesium, vitamin B_2
Crunchy:		
Fat-free refried beans, chips, and salsa	$^1/_4$ cup, 1 ounce, $^1/_4$ cup	B vitamins, iron, folic acid, vitamin C, magnesium, potassium, zinc

---

Box 29.3 (*Continued*)

Snack	Amount	Good source of
Celery sticks filled with nonfat ricotta cheese and unsweetened crushed pineapple	4 stalks, $^1/_3$ cup, $^1/_3$ cup	B vitamins, calcium, magnesium, potassium, zinc
Shredded carrots and raisins, with nonfat poppy seed dressing on whole wheat toast	1 cup, 1 tablespoon, 1 tablespoon, 1 slice	Beta carotene, B vitamins, calcium, iron, potassium, selenium, zinc
Red bell peppers with curried nonfat yogurt dip	2, $^1/_4$ cup	Vitamin B_6, folic acid, vitamin C, vitamin E, potassium
Baked tortilla chips	1 ounce	Iron, magnesium, zinc
Broccoli, raw, with nonfat sour cream dip	1 cup, $^1/_4$ cup	B vitamins, folic acid, vitamin C, vitamin E, calcium, iron, magnesium, potassium, selenium, zinc
Carrots with nonfat cream cheese and garlic dip	$1^1/_3$ cups, $^1/_4$ cup, 1 clove	Beta carotene, calcium, iron, potassium
Cantaloupe	$^1/_2$	Beta carotene, folic acid, vitamin C, calcium, magnesium, potassium
Tasty:		
Warm microwave whole-grain pretzel with mustard	1	Iron, zinc
Nonfat milk with almond extract	1 cup	Calcium, vitamin B_2, vitamin D
Wheat germ (sprinkled on anything)	$^1/_4$ cup	B vitamins, vitamin E, calcium, iron, magnesium, potassium, selenium, zinc

willpower returns. Stash nutritious foods in your glove compartment, desk drawer, briefcase, or purse or in the employee kitchen so you won't be caught off guard by a craving. Increase your exercise to compensate for the extra calories (see Box 29.4).

6. Eliminate alcohol or limit intake to five drinks a week or less. Alcohol adds further stress to the body and contains empty calories you can't afford to waste right now.

7. Take a moderate-dose multiple vitamin and mineral supplement that supplies a wide variety of vitamins and minerals, including the B vitamins, calcium, magnesium, chromium, copper, iron, manganese, molybdenum,

Box 29.4. Breakfast Quick Fixes

Are you burning the candle at both ends, with no time left for breakfast? The following meals can be prepared in five to ten minutes, so there is no excuse for not eating breakfast. Remember to allow yourself a few minutes to sit down, relax, and enjoy the meal!

Breakfast #1
1 cup oatmeal and 2 tablespoons toasted wheat germ, cooked in 1 cup nonfat milk, topped with 2 tablespoons raisins, 2 tablespoons chopped walnuts, and 1 tablespoon brown sugar. Serve with one sliced banana sprinkled with cinnamon powder. (Can be made in microwave to save even more time.)

Breakfast #2
One toasted whole wheat English muffin, topped with 2 tablespoons peanut butter. Serve with $1^1/_4$ cups fresh blueberries sprinkled with lemon zest and 1 cup nonfat milk flavored with vanilla, nutmeg, and/or NutraSweet.

Breakfast #3
1 cup shredded wheat minibiscuits, topped with 1 cup nonfat milk, 1 tablespoon chopped almonds, 2 tablespoons dried cranberries, and 1 tablespoon brown sugar. Serve with 1 cup fresh strawberries.

Breakfast #4
Two small or one large bran muffin with 2 tablespoons cashew butter. Serve with $^3/_4$ cup hot cocoa made with nonfat milk and sugar-free mix and a half cantaloupe or honeydew melon, drizzled with lime juice.

Breakfast #5
Two slices low-fat French toast (made with nonfat milk), sprinkled with powdered sugar. Serve with $^1/_2$ cup stewed prunes and 1 cup fresh-squeezed orange juice.

Breakfast #6
Two pancakes, made with low-fat Bisquik, nonfat milk, eggs, and 1 tablespoon wheat germ per pancake, topped with 2 tablespoons nonfat sour cream, $^1/_4$ cup apricots canned in their own juice, and one banana, peeled and sliced. Serve with 1 cup nonfat milk or vanilla-flavored soy milk.

Breakfast #7
Vegetable omelette: Whip one whole egg and two egg whites and pour into nonstick, 10-inch frying pan coated with vegetable spray. Cover and cook over medium heat until cooked through and firm. Remove in one piece, place on plate, fill with steamed vegetables (onions, garlic, zucchini, mushrooms, red peppers, etc.) and fresh herbs. Fold egg mixture over vegetables/herbs to form an omelette. Serve with one slice whole wheat bread, toasted, topped with 1 tablespoon apricot preserves, and 6 ounces grapefruit juice.

Breakfast #8
Breakfast burrito: Sauté chopped onion, garlic, and green pepper in 1 tablespoon water until tender. Add $^1/_2$ cup egg substitute, salt and pepper to taste, and scramble. Heat a 10-inch flour tortilla and fill with egg mixture, $^1/_2$ ounce grated sharp cheddar cheese, and 1 tablespoon fresh salsa. Serve with 1 cup fresh orange juice and a decaffeinated latte made with skim milk.

Breakfast #9
Two whole-grain frozen waffles, toasted and topped with 2 tablespoons fat-free sour cream and 1 cup fresh blueberries. Serve with 1 cup orange juice.

selenium, and zinc. Vitamin E is safe in adult doses up to 400 IU, and vitamin C is safe up to 1,000 milligrams for most adults.

Avoid supplements labeled as "stress" or "therapeutic" formulations. At best, these products are a waste of money. At worst, their imbalanced formulations could aggravate a preexisting nutrient deficiency, which would

---

Box 29.5. Herbs and Supplements to Fight Stress: What Works, What Doesn't, and Why

- *Chicken soup:* Chicken soup contains cysteine, a compound that thins the mucus in the lungs, making it easier to expel.
- *Echinacea:* This herb appears to naturally stimulate your immune system by turning on blood chemicals that regulate the duration and intensity of the immune response. Thus, either the capsules or the drops taken several times during the day might curb cold and flu symptoms. Make sure the product states on the label that it is standardized, or you're likely to see little or no results. Don't take echinacea for more than two to three weeks at a time, however, since its protective effects might wear off with prolonged use.
- *Garlic:* Garlic contains potent antibacterial and antiviral compounds that might help fend off stress-induced colds and infections.
- *Ginseng:* This root might enhance immunity and act as a tonic in animals; there are no well-designed scientific studies to show a similar effect in humans. Many products on the market contain little or none of the active ingredients in ginseng, the ginsenosides. So look for products that contain the root or a standardized ginsenoside content.
- *Herbs and spices:* Licorice soothes an irritated throat, fenugreek lubricates and soothes coughs, and capsaicin in red and cayenne peppers relieves nasal stuffiness. The herb horehound is an effective expectorant, and hyssop helps treat upper respiratory infections. Teas made from chamomile also might soothe a stressed body.
- *Kava:* This South Pacific plant has antianxiety effects, might reduce pain, and improves mental clarity. Kavalactones in kava act on the part of the brain where emotions and moods are processed. Optimal doses are unknown, although 100 milligrams of kava extract taken three times daily has proven effective in some studies. Look for products standardized to contain at least 70 percent kavalactones (60 to 75 milligrams/capsule). Do not take with prescription drugs, when driving or operating heavy equipment, with alcohol, if you are under 18, or if you're pregnant or nursing.
- *Valerian:* This root might act as a mild tranquilizer, depressing the central nervous system and relieving muscle spasms. The herb is typically taken an hour before bedtime in a dose of 50 to 100 drops of the tincture or tea prepared from 1 teaspoon of dried root. Might cause stomach upsets.
- *Zinc lozenges:* This form of zinc might not prevent the common cold, but a handful of studies show that it might shorten the duration and severity of some symptoms, such as coughing, headaches, hoarseness, congestion, and sore throat. Taking one or two of these daily is worth a try, but watch out for overdoses. More than 35 to 50 milligrams of zinc taken daily over time actually suppresses the immune system and could interfere with your body's efforts to get well.

further compromise your immune defenses and ability to cope with stress. "Balance is the key with the minerals," says Adria Sherman, Ph.D., professor of nutritional sciences at Rutgers University. "These nutrients interact, and it is their unified effect on immunity that is important." Dr. Sherman also emphasizes that this balance is best found in nutritious foods, not supplements (see Box 29.5).

SUGGESTED READING

Ascherio, A., & Willett, W. C. (1997). Health effects of trans fatty acids. *American Journal of Clinical Nutrition, 66*(Suppl. 4), 1006S–1010S.

Askew, E. W. (1995). Environmental and physical stress and nutrient requirements. *American Journal of Clinical Nutrition, 61*(Suppl. 3), 631S–637S.

Bánhegyi, G., Braun, L., Csala, M., Puskás, F., Somogyi, A., Kardon, T., et al. (1998). Ascorbate and environmental stress. *Annals of the New York Academy of Sciences, 851*, 292–303.

Dantzer, R. (1997). Stress and immunity: What have we learned from psychoneuroimmunology? *Acta Physiologica Scandinavica. Supplementum, 640*, 43–46.

Durlach, J., Bac, P., Durlach, V., Rayssiquier, Y., Bara, M., & Guiet-Bara, A. (1998). Magnesium status and ageing: An update. *Magnesium Research, 11*, 25–42.

Enig, M. (1996). Trans fatty acids in diets and databases. *Cereal Foods World, 41*, 58–63.

Hakim, A. A., Ross, G. W., Curb, J. D., Rodriquez, B. L., Burchfiel, C. M., Sharp, D. S., et al. (1998). Coffee consumption in hypertensive men in older middle-age and the risk of stroke: The Honolulu Heart Program. *Journal of Clinical Epidemiology, 51*, 487–494.

Henrotte, J., Aymard, N., Allix, M., & Boulu, R. G. (1995). Effect of pyridoxine and magnesium on stress-induced gastric ulcers in mice selected for low or high blood magnesium levels. *Annals of Nutrition & Metabolism, 39*, 285–290.

Kamara, K., Eskay, R., & Castonguay, T. (1998). High-fat diets and stress responsivity. *Physiology & Behavior, 64*, 1–6.

Kelley, D. S., Taylor, P. C., Nelson, G. J., & Mackey, B. E. (1998). Dietary docosahexaenoic acid and immunocompetence in young healthy men. *Lipids, 33*, 559–566.

Lehmann, E., Kinzler, E., & Friedemann, J. (1996). Efficacy of a special kava extract (*Piper methysticum*) in patients with states of anxiety, tension and excitedness of non-mental origin: A double blind placebo-controlled study of four weeks treatment. *Phytomedicine, 3*, 113–119.

McEwen, B. S., Conrad, C. D., Kuroda, Y., Frankfurt, M., Magarinos, A. M., & McKittrick, C. (1997). Prevention of stress-induced morphological and cognitive consequences. *European Neuropsychopharmacology, 7*(Suppl. 3), S323–S328.

Melchart, D., Linde, K., Worku, F., Bauer, R., & Wagner, H. (1994). Immunomodulation with echinacea: A systematic review of controlled clinical trials. *Phytomedicine, 1*, 245–254.

Mossad, S. B., Macknin, M. L., Medendorp, S. V., & Mason, P. (1996). Zinc gluconate lozenges for treating the common cold: A randomized, double-blind, placebo-controlled study. *Annals of Internal Medicine, 125*, 81–88.

Rosch, P. J. (1995). The stress–food–mood connection: Are there stress-reducing foods and diets? *Stress Medicine, 11*, 1–6.

Rousseau, D., Moreau, D., Raederstorff, D., Sergiel, J. P., Rupp, H., Muggli, R., et al. (1998). Is a dietary n-3 fatty acid supplement able to influence the cardiac effect of the psychological stress? *Molecular and Cellular Biochemistry, 178*, 353–366.

Rudolph, D. L., & McAuley, E. (1998). Cortisol and affective responses to exercise. *Journal of Sports Sciences, 16*, 121–128.

Scully, D., Kremer, J., Meade, M. M., Graham, R., & Dudgeon, K. (1998). Physical exercise and psychological well being: A critical review. *British Journal of Sports Medicine, 32*, 111–120.

Seelig, M. (1989). Cardiovascular consequences of magnesium deficiency and loss: Pathogenesis, prevalence, and manifestations—Magnesium and chloride loss in refractory potassium repletion. *American Journal of Cardiology, 63*, 4G–21G.

Wells, A. S., Read, N. W., Laugharne, J. D., & Ahluwalia, N. S. (1998). Alterations in mood after changing to a low-fat diet. *British Journal of Nutrition, 79*, 23–30.

CHAPTER 30

Exercise Treatment for Major Depression: Maintenance of Therapeutic Benefit

Michael Babyak, James A. Blumenthal, Steve Herman, Parinda Khatri, Murali Doraiswamy, Kathleen Moore, W. Edward Craighead, Teri T. Baldewicz, and K. Ranga Krishnan

Aerobic exercise has been prescribed for the treatment of a wide range of medical disorders, including cardiovascular disease (O'Connor et al., 1989; Oldridge, Guyatt, Fischer, & Rimm, 1988), hyperlipidemia (Tran, Weltman, Glass, & Mood, 1983), osteoarthritis (Keefe et al., 1996), fibromyalgia (Wigers, Stiles, & Vogel, 1996), and diabetes (Soman, Koivisto, Deibert, Felig, & DeFronzo, 1979). In addition, exercise may have a number of psychological benefits (Folkins & Sime, 1981; Plante & Rodin, 1990), and it has been suggested as a potential treatment for a variety of psychiatric conditions, especially depression (Gullette & Blumenthal, 1996; North, McCullagh, & Tran, 1990). Epidemiological studies have shown an inverse relation between physical activity and mental health (Farmer et al., 1988; Stephens, 1988). It has been shown, for example, that physical activity is inversely related to depressive symptoms (Lobstein, Mosbacher, & Ismail, 1983; Stephens, 1988) and that individuals who increased their activity over time were at no greater risk for depression than individuals who had been physically active all along (Camacho, Roberts, Lazarus, Kaplan, & Cohen, 1991). Moreover, individuals who had been physically active in the past but who became inactive were 1.5 times more likely to become depressed than those who consistently maintained a high level of physical activity.

Interventional studies also have provided evidence of the value of aerobic exercise in reducing depression (Blumenthal, Williams, Needels, & Wallace, 1982; Greist et al., 1979; Martinsen, Hoffart, & Solberg, 1989;

Martinsen, Medhus, & Sandvik, 1985; McNeil, LeBlanc, & Joyner, 1991).
Martinsen et al. (Martinsen et al., 1985; Martinsen et al., 1989), for
example, found that depressed patients who underwent exercise training
reported significant reductions in depressive symptoms compared with
patients receiving occupational therapy. However, these findings are not
conclusive, because patients also were receiving concomitant psychotherapy
and more than half were taking antidepressant medication.

Recently we demonstrated that the efficacy of sixteen weeks of aerobic
exercise training was comparable to that of standard pharmacotherapy
(Blumenthal et al., 1999). In that study (the Standard Medical Intervention and Long-term Exercise, or SMILE, study), 156 patients with major
depressive disorder (MDD) were randomly assigned to exercise training,
pharmacotherapy (sertraline), or a combination of exercise and medication.
After sixteen weeks of treatment, patients in all three groups exhibited significant reductions in depressive symptoms. Although patients tended to
respond more quickly in the medication group, there were no clinically or
statistically significant group differences after sixteen weeks. Questions
remained, however, about whether patients would continue to exercise on
their own after termination of the treatment period and what impact exercise therapy would have on depression over an extended follow-up period.
This is an important issue, because current treatment guidelines recommend continuous therapy for six months or longer to reduce the risk of
recurrence or relapse (Agency for Health Care Policy and Research,
1993). The present study reports six-month follow-up data on participants
previously enrolled in SMILE.

METHODS

Participants

Participants were volunteers age 50 and older who met *DSM-IV* criteria
for MDD (American Psychiatric Association, 1994) and scored at least 13
on the Hamilton Rating Scale for Depression (HRSD; Williams, 1988) at
study entry. In addition, participants also met the following criteria:

1. Not currently taking antidepressant medication
2. Not currently using other medications that would preclude their being
   randomly assigned to either medication or exercise conditions (e.g.,
   quinidine or metoprolol)
3. No current problem with alcohol or substance dependence
4. No medical contraindications to exercise (e.g., significant orthopedic
   problems or cardiopulmonary disease that would prevent regular aerobic exercise)
5. No primary axis I psychiatric diagnosis other than major depression
   (e.g., bipolar disorder or psychosis)
6. Not imminently suicidal
7. Not currently in psychotherapy that was initiated within the past year
8. Not already participating in regular aerobic exercise

Additional details of recruitment and selection criteria were reported by Blumenthal et al. (1999).

Depression Measures

Three measures of depression were used to evaluate subjects: the Diagnostic Interview Schedule (DIS), HRSD, and Beck Depression Inventory (BDI).

Diagnostic Interview Schedule

Patients were interviewed by a clinical psychologist using the depression-relevant sections of the DIS (Robins, Helzer, Croughan, & Ratcliff, 1981). Subjects were considered to meet *DSM-IV* criteria for MDD if they exhibited either persistent depressed mood or loss of interest or pleasure plus the following additional symptoms, for a total of at least five symptoms: sleep disturbance, weight loss or change in appetite, psychomotor retardation or agitation, fatigue or loss of energy, feelings of worthlessness or excessive guilt, impaired cognition or concentration, or recurrent thoughts of death.

Hamilton Rating Scale for Depression

The HRSD (Williams, 1988) is a seventeen-item clinical rating scale that was used to evaluate eligibility for the study, as well as treatment outcome. To evaluate inter-rater reliability, ten randomly selected interviews were independently rated by two clinicians. The intraclass correlation for the two raters was 0.96.

Beck Depression Inventory

The BDI (Beck, Ward, Mendelson, Mock, & Erbaugh, 1961) is a twenty-one-item self-report questionnaire consisting of symptoms and attitudes relating to depression. The items are summed in a total score; higher numbers indicate greater depression, with a range of 0 to 63.

Interventions

On completion of the baseline assessment, participants were randomly assigned to one of three treatments: exercise, medication, or combined exercise and medication.

Exercise

Subjects in the exercise group attended three supervised exercise sessions per week for sixteen consecutive weeks. Participants were assigned training ranges equivalent to 70 to 85 percent of heart rate reserve

(Karvonen, Kentala, & Mustala, 1957), which was calculated from the maximum heart rate achieved during a treadmill test. Each aerobic session began with a ten-minute warm-up period, followed by thirty minutes of continuous cycle ergometry or brisk walking/jogging at an intensity that would maintain heart rate within the assigned training range. The exercise session concluded with five minutes of cooldown exercises. Heart rate (radial pulse) and perceived exertion were monitored and recorded three times during each exercise session by a trained exercise physiologist.

Medication

Subjects in the medication group received sertraline (Zoloft), a selective serotonin-reuptake inhibitor. This medication was selected because of its documented efficacy and favorable side effect profile for the elderly (Cohn et al., 1990). Medication management was provided by a staff psychiatrist, who met with each patient at the beginning of the study and during weeks 2, 6, 10, 14, and 16. At these meetings, the psychiatrist evaluated treatment response and side effects and titrated the dosage accordingly. Treatment was initiated with 50 mg and titrated until a well-tolerated therapeutic dosage was achieved up to 200 mg. An effort was made to follow standard "usual care" guidelines for medication management, with the exception that a change to a different antidepressant was not permitted during the course of the study.

Combined Exercise and Medication

Subjects in the combination group received concurrently the same medication and exercise regimens described above.

Follow-up Assessments

Depression evaluations using the DIS, HRSD, and BDI were conducted at baseline, immediately after the four-month treatment period, and six months after treatment ended (i.e., ten months after study entry). All evaluations were conducted in the hospital clinic, with the exception of that for one participant who could not return to the laboratory for the six-month evaluation and was instead interviewed by telephone.

Criteria developed by the MacArthur Foundation Research Network were used to classify therapeutic response (Frank et al., 1991). Subjects were classified as being in *full remission* if they no longer met criteria for MDD and had an HRSD score less than 8 after four months of treatment. Subjects were considered *recovered* if they continued to remain in full remission for more than six months (i.e., at the six-month follow-up visit). A classification of *partial recovery* was used to designate subjects who did not meet criteria for MDD but still exhibited significant depressive symptoms as reflected by an HRSD score between 8 and 14. Subjects were considered to have *relapsed* if they were initially considered in remission after four months of treatment but were found at the six-month follow-up visit to meet *DSM-IV* criteria for MDD or to have an HRSD score of 15 or higher.

At the outset of the six-month follow-up evaluation, and before the current level of depression was assessed, participants were asked about the nature and extent of any therapeutic activity engaged in during the follow-up period, including use of antidepressants or any form of psychotherapy. Subjects were then questioned about the extent of their participation in regular exercise activity during the six months since the treatment phase ended. Inquiry was directed at three forms of exercise: aerobic exercise, weight training, and vigorous leisure-time activity. In each instance, subjects were asked how many times per week, if at all, they engaged in that particular type of exercise and the usual duration (in minutes) of sessions.

RESULTS

Summary of Findings after Four Months of Treatment

Outcomes immediately after four months of treatment are reported in detail in Blumenthal et al. (1999). Briefly, intention-to-treat analyses showed that the groups had similar remission rates with respect to presence or absence of current MDD ($p = .67$): 60.4 percent of patients in the exercise group, 65.5 percent in the medication group, and 68.8 percent in the combined group no longer met *DSM-IV* criteria for MDD. When the additional criterion of an HRSD score below 8 was added to the classification scheme, the rates of remission were again comparable for the three groups ($p = .58$). Finally, after adjustments for initial levels of depression were made, the groups still did not differ on HRSD ($p = .39$) or BDI ($p = .40$) scores immediately after completion of treatment.

Findings after Ten Months (Six-Month Follow-up Visit)

Follow-up assessments were available on 133 (85.6%) of the original 156 enrolled patients. Twenty of the twenty-three patients who dropped out of treatment before completion of the treatment program were not available for follow-up. Three additional patients who completed the four-month assessment (one in each group) declined to participate in the six-month follow-up. There were no group differences in the lost-to-follow-up rate for each treatment group (exercise: $n = 9$, 17 percent; medication: $n = 6$, 13 percent; combination: $n = 8$, 15 percent; $p = .89$).

Depression at Ten Months

When all participants available at follow-up were considered and adjustments were made for corresponding BDI scores at four months, self-reported depressive symptoms (i.e., BDI scores) did not vary among persons initially assigned to the exercise (mean $\pm$ SE $= 8.9 \pm 0.77$), medication

(11.0 ± 0.81), or combined exercise and medication (10.6 ± 0.75) groups ($p = .13$). However, when interviewer ratings in which the presence of MDD was defined as either *DSM-IV* diagnosis or an HRSD score above 7 were used, it was found that participants in the exercise group exhibited lower rates of depression (30%) than participants in the medication (52%) and combined groups (55%) ($p = .028$).

Status of Remitted Subjects

A more detailed analysis of depression rates at the six-month follow-up visit was conducted among the eighty-three patients who had been assessed as being in remission at the end of the four-month treatment period. At the six-month follow-up, participants were categorized as recovered (no *DSM-IV* diagnosis of MDD and an HRSD score below 8 for more than six months), partially recovered (no *DSM-IV* diagnosis of MDD and an HRSD score between 8 and 14), or relapsed (*presence of DSM-IV* diagnosis of MDD regardless of HRSD score or an HRSD score 15 or higher) (Frank, et al., 1991). To assess the relation between treatment and outcome classification, we used a proportional odds regression model, in which the three-level outcome (full recovery, partial recovery, or relapse) served as the dependent variable, with baseline HRSD score specified as a covariate. Two dummy variables carrying treatment effects, with medication as the reference group, served as predictors in the model. This analysis revealed a significant overall treatment effect ($\chi^2(2) = 8.30$, $p = .016$).

Specifically, participants in the exercise group were more likely than those in the medication group to be partially or fully recovered at the six-month visit (OR [odds ratio] = 6.10, $p = .01$). In contrast, patients receiving combination therapy were no more likely to be categorized as partially or fully recovered than were patients in the medication group (OR = 1.32, $p = .57$). In addition, only 8 percent of remitted patients in the exercise group had relapsed, compared with 38 percent in the medication group and 31 percent in the combination group (see Figure 30.1).

Exercise Participation and Other Interventions during the Follow-up Period

At the end of the four-month intervention, all patients were educated about MDD and were encouraged to continue with some form of treatment on their own, including exercise or medication. Although 64 percent of subjects in the exercise group and 66 percent of those in the combination group reported that they continued to exercise, 48 percent of participants in the medication group initiated an exercise program during the six-month follow-up period ($p = .17$). The groups differed significantly in the number of subjects using antidepressant medication, with 40 percent of subjects in the combination group, 26 percent in the medication group, and 7 percent in the exercise group reporting antidepressant use during

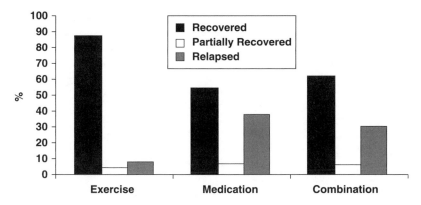

Figure 30.1 Clinical Status at Ten Months
The chart shows the clinical status at ten months (six months after treatment) among patients who were remitted ($n = 83$) after four months of treatment in the Exercise ($n = 25$), Medication ($n = 29$), and Combination ($n = 29$) groups. Compared with participants in the other conditions, those in the Exercise condition were more likely to be partially or fully recovered and were less likely to have relapsed.

the six months ($p = .001$). Twenty-two (16%) of the participants entered psychotherapy at the end of the four-month intervention (medication: $n = 7$; combination: $n = 8$; exercise: $n = 7$; $p = .99$).

Multiple logistic regression analysis was used to assess the relation of exercise and medication to MDD diagnosis at six months. Medication use was coded as 0 (no) or 1 (yes), and exercise was quantified as the number of minutes per week of aerobic exercise, scaled to increments of 1 standard deviation (about fifty minutes). Age, gender, and baseline HRSD scores were included in the model as control variables. These analyses revealed that patients who reported that they engaged in regular aerobic exercise during the six-month follow-up period were less likely to be classified as depressed at the end of that period (see Table 30.1), adjusting for depression level at study entry, age, gender, and antidepressant medication use

Table 30.1. Logistic Regression Predicting MDD Defined by *DSM-IV* and HRSD Criteria at Six Months

Variable	Standardized OR	95% Confidence Interval	p
Age	1.21	0.83–1.74	.321
Female	1.05	0.73–1.54	.768
Baseline HRSD score	1.41	0.95–2.09	.093
Antidepressant (no/yes)	1.31	0.91–1.89	.152
Exercise (~50 min/wk)	0.49	0.32–.74	.0009

during the follow-up period ($p < .0009$). HRSD scores at four months also were inversely related to minutes of exercise per week (-0.33, $p < .001$).

A further analysis was conducted using HSRD scores at four months as a covariate to rule out the possibility that the relationship between exercise and ten-month depressive status was confounded by the severity of depression present at the end of treatment. HRSD scores at four months were significant predictors of HRSD scores at ten months (standardized $OR = 2.23$, $p = .002$); however, minutes of exercise per week remained a significant predictor of depressive status, with little change in the effect size (standardized $OR = 0.550$, $p = .010$).

DISCUSSION

Results of this relatively large, single-center clinical trial indicate that exercise is a feasible therapy for patients suffering from MDD and may be at least as effective as standard pharmacotherapy. As reported previously (Blumenthal et al., 1999), the majority of patients in all three treatment groups exhibited a clinically significant reduction in depressive symptoms at the end of four months of treatment. The analyses presented in this report indicate that in most instances these improvements persisted for at least six months after the termination of treatment. Among patients who had been assessed as being in full remission at the end of the four-month treatment period, participants in the exercise group were less likely to relapse than participants in the two groups receiving medication.

Interestingly, combining exercise with medication conferred no additional advantage over either treatment alone. In fact, the opposite was the case, at least with respect to relapse rates for patients who initially responded well to treatment. This was an unexpected finding because it was assumed that combining exercise with medication would have, if anything, an additive effect. The reasons for this are open to speculation. It was apparent that there may have been some "antimedication" sentiment among some study participants, as evidenced by expressions of disappointment when notified of their assignment to a group in which they would receive medication in addition to exercise. During treatment, several in the combined group mentioned spontaneously that the medication seemed to interfere with the beneficial effects of the exercise program. It is unclear how this would occur physiologically, and the explanation might have more to do with psychological factors. One of the positive psychological benefits of systematic exercise is the development of a sense of personal mastery and positive self-regard, which we believe is likely to play some role in the depression-reducing effects of exercise. It is conceivable that the concurrent use of medication may undermine this benefit by prioritizing an alternative, less self-confirming attribution for one's improved condition. Instead of incorporating the belief "I was dedicated and worked hard with the exercise program; it wasn't easy, but I beat this depression," patients might incorporate the belief that "I took an antidepressant and got better." The possibilities here are interesting, and future research might well focus on attitudinal and attributional factors associated with patient response to exercise therapy.

Self-reported participation in exercise during the follow-up period was inversely related to the incidence of depression at ten months. Each fifty-minute increment in exercise per week was associated with a 50 percent decrease in the odds of being classified as depressed. Limitations of the study design prevent us from concluding that exercise *caused* depressive symptoms to be reduced at the six-month follow-up, because it is possible that patients who continued to exercise after the intervention did so because they already were less depressed at the end of the treatment period. Indeed, the significant inverse correlation we observed between post-treatment HRSD scores and weekly minutes of aerobic exercise during the follow-up period could be interpreted as showing that patients exercise if they are less depressed. We note, however, that after controlling for post-treatment depression level, the number of minutes of exercise per week still predicted depressive status six months after treatment. Together these results suggest a potential reciprocal relationship between exercise and depression: Feeling less depressed may make it more likely that patients will continue to exercise, and continuing to exercise may make it less likely that the patient will suffer a return of depressive symptoms. Another possibility, which we introduced in our original report (Blumenthal et al., 1999), is that the benefits of the exercise program may be attributed, at least in part, to the social support aspects of the exercise group setting. Such an explanation would be less likely to apply to the present findings, however, because continuation of exercise during the follow-up period generally took place in an individual, rather than a group, setting.

There are several additional limitations of the present study, the most significant of which concerns the special nature of our study population. The sample consisted of patient-volunteers who responded to advertisements seeking participants for a study of exercise therapy for depression. We presume that these participants believed exercise to be a credible treatment modality for depression and were favorably inclined toward participation. That this is the case is supported by the number of patients (48%) in the medication group who initiated an exercise program on their own after the formal treatment phase ended. In contrast, only 26 percent of patients in the medication group chose to continue pharmacotherapy, and only 6 percent of patients in the exercise group initiated pharmacotherapy. The question remains whether the impressive results of the SMILE study will be applicable to the general population of middle-aged and older patients with MDD and whether exercise "prescribed" by a clinician will be accepted and complied with to the same extent as when it is sought out and adopted on one's own.

Another issue concerns the substantial degree of "crossover" in treatment modality after completion of the four-month period of formal therapy. The fact that almost half of the participants in the medication group switched on their own to an exercise program renders meaningful intergroup comparisons at the six-month follow-up problematic. However, the finding that self-reported exercise, independent of the original treatment group, was associated with reduced depression provides potential support for the value of exercise as a treatment for MDD. In addition, although we used the intention-to-treat principle in conducting our analyses, 15 percent of the original cohort were unavailable for follow-up. It is unknown how these missing data may have influenced the results, although it should be noted that most of the subjects who were not followed up at ten months dropped out of the treatment program prematurely and virtually all were not improved at the time of their dropping out.

A final limitation concerns the lack of independent verification of post-treatment therapeutic activity (medication, psychotherapy, and exercise). During the follow-up period, participants were assessed solely by self-report, which raises the possibility of inaccuracies in these data. To have arranged for independent verification, however, would itself potentially compromise the intended naturalistic conditions for the follow-up period. For example, the use of diaries or pill counts would have conveyed expectations that could have influenced subject's behavior over the period. It is also notable that ratings of depression and of posttreatment exercise participation were made by the same interviewer (albeit blinded to initial treatment group assignment), which raises the possibility of potential bias in the data obtained. It is recommended that future studies incorporate separate, blind ratings of exercise participation to avoid this potential confounding factor.

Despite these limitations, the present findings suggest that a modest exercise program (e.g., three times per week with thirty minutes at 70 percent of maximum heart rate reserve each time) is an effective, robust treatment for patients with major depression who are positively inclined to participate in it and that clinical benefits are particularly likely to endure among patients who adopt exercise as a regular, ongoing life activity.

REFERENCES

Agency for Health Care Policy and Research (1993). Depression Guideline Panel. Vol. 1, *Depression in primary care*. Vol. 2, *Treatment of major depression*. Clinical practice guideline No. 5, AHCPR Publication No. 93-0551. Washington, DC: U.S. Department of Health and Human Services.

American Psychiatric Association (1994). *Diagnostic and statistical manual of mental disorders* (4th ed.). Washington, DC: American Psychiatric Association.

Beck, A. T., Ward, C. H., Mendelson, M., Mock, J., & Erbaugh, J. (1961). An inventory for measuring depression. *Archives of General Psychiatry, 4,* 561–571.

Blumenthal, J. A., Babyak, M. A., Moore, K. A., Craighead, W. E., Herman, S., Khatri, P., et al. (1999). Effects of exercise training on older patients with major depression. *Archives of Internal Medicine, 159*(19), 2349–2356.

Blumenthal, J. A., Williams, R. S., Needels, T. L., & Wallace, A. G. (1982). Psychological changes accompany aerobic exercise in healthy middle-aged adults. *Psychosomatic Medicine, 44*(6), 529–536.

Camacho, T. C., Roberts, R. E., Lazarus, N. B., Kaplan, G. A., & Cohen, R. D. (1991). Physical activity and depression: Evidence from the Alameda County Study. *American Journal of Epidemiology, 134*(2), 220–231.

Cohn, C. K., Shrivastava, R., Mendels, J., Cohn, J. B., Fabre, L. F., Claghorn, J. L., et al. (1990). Double-blind, multicenter comparison of sertraline and amitriptyline in elderly depressed patients. *Journal of Clinical Psychiatry, 51*(Suppl. B), 28–33.

Farmer, M. E., Locke, B. Z., Moscicki, E. K., Dannenberg, A. L., Larson, D. B., & Radloff, L. S. (1988). Physical activity and depressive symptoms: The NHANES I Epidemiologic Follow-up Study. *American Journal of Epidemiology, 128*(6), 1340–1351.

Folkins, C. H., & Sime, W. E. (1981). Physical fitness training and mental health. *American Psychologist, 36*(4), 373–389.

Frank, E., Prien, R. F., Jarrett, R. B., Keller, M. B., Kupfer, D. J., Lavori, P. W., et al. (1991). Conceptualization and rationale for consensus definitions of terms in major depressive disorder: Remission, recovery, relapse, and recurrence. *Archives of General Psychiatry, 48*(9), 851–855.

Greist, J. H., Klein, M. H., Eischens, R. R., Faris, J., Gurman, A. S., & Morgan, W. P. (1979). Running as treatment for depression. *Comprehensive Psychiatry, 20*, 41–54.

Gullette, E. C. D., & Blumenthal, J. A. (1996). Exercise therapy for the prevention and treatment of depression. *Journal of Practical Psychiatry and Behavioral Health, 5*, 263–271.

Karvonen, M. J., Kentala, E., & Mustala, O. (1957). The effects of training on heart rate: A longitudinal study. *Annales Medicinae Experimentalis et Biologiae Fenniae, 35*(3), 307–315.

Keefe, F. J., Kashikar-Zuck, S., Opiteck, J., Hage, E., Dalrymple, L., & Blumenthal, J. A. (1996). Pain in arthritis and musculoskeletal disorders: The role of coping skills training and exercise interventions. *Journal of Orthopaedic and Sports Physical Therapy, 24*(4), 279–290.

Lobstein, D. D., Mosbacher, B. J., & Ismail, A. H. (1983). Depression as a powerful discriminator between physically active and sedentary middle-aged men. *Journal of Psychosomatic Research, 27*, 69–76.

Martinsen, E. W., Hoffart, A., & Solberg, O. (1989). Comparing aerobic with nonaerobic forms of exercise in the treatment of clinical depression: A randomized trial. *Comprehensive Psychiatry, 30*(4), 324–331.

Martinsen, E. W., Medhus, A., & Sandvik, L. (1985). Effects of aerobic exercise on depression: A controlled study. *British Medical Journal (Clinical Research Ed.), 291*(6488), 109.

McNeil, J. K., LeBlanc, E. M., & Joyner, M. (1991). The effect of exercise on depressive symptoms in the moderately depressed elderly. *Psychology and Aging, 6*(3), 487–488.

North, T. C., McCullagh, P., & Tran, Z. V. (1990). Effect of exercise on depression. *Exercise and Sport Sciences Reviews, 18*, 379–415.

O'Connor, G. T., Buring, J. E., Yusuf, S., Goldhaber, S. Z., Olmstead, E. M., Paffenbarger, R. S., Jr., et al. (1989). An overview of randomized trials of rehabilitation with exercise after myocardial infarction. *Circulation, 80*(2), 234–244.

Oldridge, N. B., Guyatt, G. H., Fischer, M. E., & Rimm, A. A. (1988). Cardiac rehabilitation after myocardial infarction: Combined experience of randomized clinical trials. *Journal of the American Medical Association, 260*(7), 945–950.

Plante, T. G., & Rodin, J. (1990). Physical fitness and enhanced psychological health. *Current Psychology: Research & Reviews, 9*(1), 3–24.

Robins, L. N., Helzer, J. E., Croughan, J., & Ratcliff, K. S. (1981). National Institute of Mental Health Diagnostic Interview Schedule: Its history, characteristics, and validity. *Archives of General Psychiatry, 38*(4), 381–389.

Soman, V. R., Koivisto, V. A., Deibert, D., Felig, P., & DeFronzo, R. A. (1979). Increased insulin sensitivity and insulin binding to monocytes after physical training. *New England Journal of Medicine, 301*(22), 1200–1204.

Stephens, T. (1988). Physical activity and mental health in the United States and Canada: Evidence from four population surveys. *Preventive Medicine, 17*, 35–47.

Tran, Z. V., Weltman, A., Glass, G. V., & Mood, D. P. (1983). The effects of exercise on blood lipids and lipoproteins: A meta-analysis of studies. *Medicine and Science in Sports and Exercise, 15*(5), 393–402.

Wigers, S. H., Stiles, T. C., & Vogel, P. A. (1996). Effects of aerobic exercise versus stress management treatment in fibromyalgia: A 4.5 year prospective study. *Scandinavian Journal of Rheumatology, 25*(2), 77–86.

Williams, J. B. (1988). A structured interview guide for the Hamilton Depression Rating Scale. *Archives of General Psychiatry, 45*(8), 742–747.

CHAPTER 31

Attitudes and Beliefs about 12-Step Groups among Addiction Treatment Clients and Clinicians: Identifying Obstacles to Participation

Alexandre B. Laudet

Participation in 12-step groups such as Alcoholics Anonymous, both during and after formal treatment, is associated with better outcomes among substance users. Twelve-step programs (12SG) are a form of mutual help or mutual aid based on the premise that individuals who share a common behavior that they identify as undesirable can collectively support each other and eliminate that behavior.[1]

One of the essential aspects of mutual-help groups, in contrast to other, more traditional forms of treatment, is the absence of professional involvement. Alcoholics Anonymous, the first and largest 12-step organization, was started by a group of individuals dependent on alcohol at a time when little or no assistance was available to such persons. Subsequently, the organization contributed to the establishment of formal substance-user treatment in the first part of the twentieth century; over time, the medicalization of treatment services placed mutual-help organizations at the periphery of service delivery so that such organizations were sometimes viewed as competing with formal treatment and criticized for their lack of professionalism. In the last two decades, 12-step organizations have become largely integrated with most formal treatment models, thus becoming somewhat homogenized and mainstreamed (see next section; for a detailed discussion of the historical relationship between mutual-help organizations and treatment services addressing substance use, see White, 1998). While attending 12-step meetings is an important part of participating in these organizations, 12SG members are also encouraged to "work the program" and to embrace the 12-step ideology (described below).

The effectiveness of 12SGs may be somewhat limited by a high attrition rate. Moreover, a large minority of substance users never attend 12-step meetings. Little is known about reasons for dropping out or for nonattendance. Treatment professionals can play a critical role in fostering 12-step participation among their clients, yet we know very little about professionals' attitudes and beliefs about 12-step fellowships. Several aspects of the 12-step program have been identified as potential stumbling blocks for both clinicians and substance users. Little is known about the prevalence of these beliefs or about whether they constitute obstacles to participation. In this study, treatment professionals and clients were surveyed about their attitudes and beliefs concerning 12-step fellowships toward identifying potential obstacles to participation.

According to the prevalent Western view of substance-use disorders, addiction is a chronic relapse-prone disorder (American Psychiatric Association, 1994; Leshner, 1997).[2] For many substance users, maintaining abstinence requires ongoing support. Twelve-step groups constitute such a support: meetings are widely available and free of charge. Participation in 12SGs during and after formal treatment has been associated with positive outcomes; while the majority of studies limit their investigation to substance use outcomes (Fiorentine & Hillhouse, 2000a; Kaskutas, Bond, & Humphreys, 2002; Project MATCH Research Group, 1997), the few that have assessed the influence of 12SG participation on a broader set of domains, such as psychological adjustment, have also reported positive findings (Timko, Moos, Finney, Moos, & Kaplowitz, 1999; Vaillant et al., 1983). Several researchers have noted that, as the duration and intensity of treatment services are decreasing, one of the most important tasks for clinicians is to foster stable engagement in 12SG so that clients have a support network available once they are no longer engaged in formal clinical services (Mankowski, Humphreys, & Moos 2001).

ROLE OF TREATMENT IN FOSTERING 12-STEP PARTICIPATION

Clinicians can contribute to the Institute of Medicine's (1990) goal of broadening the base of treatment for substance use–related problems within the community in which they work (Caldwell, 1999). The importance of collaboration between service providers and 12SGs has been acknowledged by several professional organizations. For example, the American Psychiatric Association has noted that "referral [to 12-step groups] is appropriate at all stages in the treatment process, even for patients who may still be substance users" (American Psychiatric Association, 1995). Further, 12SGs and 12-step tenets are increasingly being integrated into formal services. According to the national study by Roman, Blum, and Johnson (1998) on a representative sample of 450 private substance-user treatment centers, 90 percent of the facilities based their treatment on 12-step principles and variations of this model, with nearly half of the remaining 10 percent incorporating 12-step principles in combination with other approaches, including encouraged attendance at 12SG meetings. The prevalence of the latter was demonstrated by results from a survey on 12-step referral practices conducted among substance-user treatment program directors in the Department of Veterans Affairs health care system: 79 percent of patients were referred to Alcoholics Anonymous and 45 percent to Narcotics Anonymous (Humphreys, 1997).

Results from two studies conducted by Humphreys, Huebsch, Finney, and Moos speak to the important role that treatment and treatment professionals play in facilitating clients' engagement in 12SGs. The first study investigated how treatment programs' theoretical orientation influences clients' participation in, and benefits derived from, 12SGs (Humphreys et al., 1999). Findings indicated that clients in 12-step and eclectic treatment programs (combining 12-step and cognitive-behavioral approaches) had higher rates of subsequent 12SG attendance than did clients in the cognitive-behavioral (CB) treatment programs. Moreover, program orientation moderated the effectiveness of 12SG participation: as the degree of programs' "12-stepness" increased, the positive relationship between 12SG participation and outcome (substance use and psychosocial) became stronger.

The second study extended the investigation to cost-effectiveness and reported that, compared to patients treated in CB programs, those treated in 12-step–oriented programs had significantly greater involvement in 12SGs at follow-up, fewer outpatient continuing care visits after discharge, and fewer days of inpatient care, resulting in 64 percent higher annual costs for the CB programs (Humphreys & Moos, 2001). Psychiatric and "substance abuse" outcomes were comparable across treatments, except that 12-step patients manifested higher rates of abstinence at follow-up. The authors concluded that professional treatment programs that emphasize 12-step approaches increase their patients' reliance on cost-free, mutual-help groups and thereby lower subsequent health care costs without compromising outcomes.

Further evidence for the important role that treatment professionals play in fostering engagement in 12SGs comes from an AA membership survey where one-half of respondents reported being introduced to the fellowship by a treatment professional (Alcoholics Anonymous, 1998). Finally, the importance of treatment professionals' role in fostering clients' 12-step participation is also underlined by a recent study where the authors reported that treatment clients' attendance at 12SGs was consistent over a six-month treatment episode, suggesting that the pattern of attendance established early in treatment is critical (Weiss et al., 2000).

In spite of the crucial role clinicians can play in drug users' treatment, there has been very little research on their beliefs and practices (Forman, Bovasso, & Woody, 2001; Kasarabada et al., 2001). In particular, although referrals to 12SGs are increasing (Weiss et al., 2000), little is known about addiction professionals' beliefs concerning these organizations or about their experience in referring clients. Available findings suggest that addiction professionals are favorable toward 12SGs (Freimuth, 1996). For example, results from a recent survey assessing staff members' beliefs about addiction treatment was conducted in Delaware prior to implementing the National Institute on Drug Abuse's Clinical Trials Network; 82 percent of staff surveyed agreed with the statement "12-step groups should be used more" and 84 percent with "spirituality should be emphasized more"

(Forman et al., 2001). Although informative, such findings are limited, and additional research is needed. It is important to gain a greater understanding of what treatment professionals think and believe about 12-step organizations, as these cognitions may influence referral practices and bear on client outcomes (Humphreys, Noke, & Moos, 1996; Noordsy, Schwab, Fox, & Drake, 1994; Salzer, Rappaport, & Segre, 2001).

ATTRITION TO 12-STEP GROUPS AND NONATTENDANCE

Although the majority of substance users report some lifetime attendance at a 12SG (Humphreys, Kaskutas, & Weisner, 1998), few maintain stable affiliation over time. Attrition tends to be high. The few available studies report declines in participation beginning three to six months after initiation of attendance (Kissin & Ginexi, 2000; Timko, Finney, Moos, Moos, & Steinbaum, 1993; Tonigan, Miller, & Connors, 2000). Alcoholics Anonymous has noted that results from successive Triennial Membership Surveys show "a slow attrition of newcomers during the first year" and acknowledged this phenomenon as "a challenge to AA" (Alcoholics Anonymous, 1990; McIntire, 2000).

In addition to the large number of substance users who may stop attending 12SGs, a significant minority never attend at all. For instance, in his twenty-four-month study conducted among cocaine users, Fiorentine (1999) reported that 26 percent of participants never attended 12-step meetings following formal treatment. To date, little is known about obstacles to participation in 12SGs (McCrady, 1998). Elucidating this issue has important clinical implications, because empirical evidence suggests that abstinence rates decline significantly following treatment among substance users who never attend or who stop attending 12-step meetings (Fiorentine, 1999).

We note that in the Western context where substance use and its treatment have become medicalized, "retention" in services and in other forms of help is viewed as a desirable and positive outcome. However, much social stigma is attached to substance use and, by extension, to participation in substance-use services. Thus, one should consider that if help-seeking and the desire to resolve substance-use related problems are viewed as an effort at personal growth, retention in substance-user services may be inconsistent with these goals because of the labeling attached to being "in drug treatment" or "in AA (or a similar 12SG)."

ATTITUDES AND BELIEFS ABOUT 12-STEP GROUPS

Participation in 12-step meetings is typically voluntary, especially after treatment. Behavior is based on attitudes that rest on personal beliefs (Fishbein, 1980), and it is reasonable to suggest that substance users' attitudes and beliefs about 12SGs play a critical role in whether they choose to participate. However, substance users' attitudes about 12-step have received scant empirical attention. Tonigan et al. recently wrote: "Conspicuously absent [from the literature] has been the measurement of the subjective reactions of individuals to AA related practices and beliefs" (2000); in particular, they pointed to the need to examine substance users' perception of the helpfulness of AA toward sobriety. In an investigation of predictors of engagement in formal treatment, Fiorentine, Nakashima, and Anglin (1999) reported findings suggesting that perceived utility or helpfulness of services is critical to participation.

Three studies have examined the association between perceived helpfulness of 12SGs and meeting attendance among samples of illicit drug users, alcohol-dependent clients, and dually diagnosed persons; they have shown a significant association between positive attitudes towards 12-step's helpfulness and attendance (Bogenschutz and Akin, 2000; Brown, O'Grady, Farrell, Flechner, & Nurco, 2001; Tonigan et al., 2000). Two large prospective studies have broadened the investigative scope beyond perceived helpfulness to embracement of 12-step ideology or the disease-model view of addiction (e.g., total abstinence goal, need for lifelong 12-step attendance, and importance of relying on external support or a "higher power"). Both research teams reported a significant association between beliefs consistent with the 12-step program and greater subsequent levels of 12-step participation (Fiorentine & Hillhouse, 2000b; Mankowski et al., 2001). These studies greatly contribute to broadening our understanding of predictors of 12-step participation. However, they do not address directly an equally important question: What may constitute obstacles to participation in 12SGs? Several aspects of the 12-step program have been identified as potential stumbling blocks.

POTENTIAL OBSTACLES TO PARTICIPATION IN 12-STEP GROUPS

In spite of being the most frequently used resource for substance use–related problems in the United States (Kurtz, 1990; Room & Greenfield, 1993; Weisner, Greenfield, & Room, 1995), 12-step fellowships have been and remain the subject of controversy, and several aspects of the recovery program have been identified as potential stumbling blocks for both substance users and clinicians (Chappel & DuPont, 1999; Laudet, 2000b). This is due to a multiplicity of factors.

The 12-step program's views of addiction and recovery are derived from a blend of tenets from the Oxford Group practicing first-century Christianity, the advice of Carl Jung to an early AA member, and the observations of Dr. Silkworth; as such, they are neither scientific nor rational (Marron, 1993). The program's emphasis on spirituality, surrender, and powerlessness contradicts contemporary dominant Western cultural norms of self-reliance and widespread secularism (Davis & Jansen, 1998) and constitutes a stumbling block for many (Connors & Dermen, 1996; Ellis & Schoenfeld, 1990). Clearly, the social premium placed on self-reliance may be more an idealized principle than an adaptive strategy, particularly in light of overwhelming empirical evidence for the critical role of social support in promoting physical and mental health and in coping with stress (Taylor, 1995). Nonetheless, the reliance on external support, and particularly on spiritual support, that is one of the cornerstones of the 12-step program has been identified as a potential cultural point of resistance to these organizations (Peteet, 1993; Smith, Buxton, Bilal, & Seymour, 1993). That this and related aspects of the 12-step philosophy play a part in individuals' decisions not to participate in 12SGs was suggested recently by a small study conducted among nineteen (white, highly educated, and employed) members of Moderation Management (Klaw and Humphreys, 2000). Participants consistently attributed their decision to drop out of AA after attending only a few meetings to an aversion to the spiritual focus of the program and to conflicts with AA's concepts of surrender and powerlessness.[3]

The spiritual aspect of the 12-step program is perhaps the strongest point of resistance, but it is not the only one. Substance users often have questions or express concerns when 12SGs are introduced—for example, their problem is "not that bad," they know of someone who relapsed while involved in a 12SG, or they associate 12SGs with "skid-row drunks" (McCrady, 1998). Some treatment professionals may also be concerned about the "dangers" and limitations of 12SGs (Chesler, 1990; Galinsky and Schopler, 1994; Kurtz, 1997). Common concerns about these groups include their lack of professionalism, lack of empirical support for their effectiveness, the risk that members will become overly dependent on the group or get bad advice from other group members, and that the usefulness of these groups is limited in time (i.e., only needed in early recovery) or in scope (i.e., deal with only one substance while clients have multiple issues (for a review, see Chappel and DuPont, 1999).

Overall, many widely held beliefs about the 12-step program—whether or not these beliefs are "accurate"—may constitute obstacles to participation. While much has been written about potentially limiting or controversial aspects of the 12-step program, little research has been conducted to determine what substance users and referring clinicians think about these organizations. In particular, there has been virtually no research to determine whether controversial aspects of the 12-step program constitute obstacles to participation or on what other factors may play a role in substance users' decisions to not attend 12SGs. In this regard, it is important to include frontline clinicians in the research process as "they develop insights that might not occur to researchers" (Forman et al., 2001).

This study seeks to identify potential obstacles to participation in 12SGs by surveying substance users and referring clinicians. The research questions addressed in the present study are:

1. What are substance users' and clinicians' attitudes concerning the helpfulness and usefulness of 12SGs as a recovery resource?
2. What do substance users and clinicians perceive to be major positive and negative aspects of 12SGs?
3. What do substance users and referring clinicians perceive to be obstacles to 12-step participation?

METHOD

Samples

One hundred and one clients and 102 staff members were interviewed at five separate outpatient substance-user treatment programs in New York City (all programs contacted agreed to participate). The client sample was selected from the client base of the collaborating agencies using a random number table. All staff members who have clinical contact with clients were recruited to participate in the study. Participation in the study was voluntary and based on informed consent. The study was approved by the Institutional Review Board of the National Development and Research Institutes, Inc. (NDRI), and by the review process of the agencies where participants were recruited. Data were collected using personal interviews that were conducted at the programs and lasted approximately forty minutes for both clinicians and clients; participants received twenty dollars for their time. Data collection was conducted between May 2001 and January 2002.[4] Refusal rate was estimated at less than 5 percent for clients and 12 percent for staff.

Measures

The study used a questionnaire consisting of structured items and inventories (adapted from previous studies as noted in each individual section below) and open-ended questions developed from qualitative interviews conducted during the preliminary phase of the study and presented elsewhere (Laudet, 2000a). Parallel versions of the instruments were developed for clients and clinicians so that the wording of the items was similar for both groups of participants. Both versions of the instrument began with a series of questions about sociodemographic and background information (substance use, treatment, and 12-step attendance history for clients; education, training, and professional experience for staff members). The instrument was pretested for feasibility and length; minor adjustments were made for clarity in the phrasing of several items. The final client instrument consisted of 290 items; the clinicians version, of 267 items (Flesch-Kincaid Grade Level score = 7.0 for both). Following this introductory section, the domains and measures used for this study were:

- **Attitudes about 12-step.** (1) Helpfulness of 12SGs: "In your experience, how helpful or harmful are 12-step groups?" This item was previously used by Salzer, McFadden, and Rappaport (1994) in a study assessing mental health professionals' views on mutual-help groups (scale ranges from 0 = very harmful to 10 = very helpful; 5 = neither harmful nor helpful). (2) Importance of 12SGs: "How important a role do you believe 12SG can play in a comprehensive treatment system?" and "How important a role do you believe 12SG can play in the recovery process?" Rating scale ranged from 0 = not at all important to 10 = extremely important. (3) Role of 12SGs in the recovery process: "Which of the following best describes the role 12SG should play in the recovery process?" The answer categories, reflecting the three positions identified by Farquharson (1995) in his work with community mental health professionals were that 12SGs have minimal usefulness, are a useful addition to formal treatment, or are crucial to the recovery process. (4) Level of interest in obtaining further information about 12SGs: "How interested would you be in obtaining further training or information about 12-step groups?" Possible responses: Extremely, very much, moderate, a little, not at all.

- **Beliefs about 12-step groups.** Three open-ended questions were used to collect information about perceived benefits, limitations, and potential dangers of 12SGs: (1) "What can 12-step groups do for people (what are the benefits)?" (2) "What can 12-step groups not do for people (what are the limitations)?" and (3) "What are the potential dangers of 12-step groups?" Codes for the open-ended items used in the study were developed on the first thirty completed interviews; based on a subsample of twenty-five instruments coded by two independent researchers, inter-rater reliability was $r = 0.90$.

- **Obstacles to participation.** Information about potential obstacles to 12-step participation was collected using both open-ended and structured items. First, clients and clinicians were asked a series of open-ended questions designed to elicit information about why substance users may choose not to attend 12SGs. Clients who were not currently attending 12SGs were asked their reason(s) for not attending, and all clients, regardless of current attendance status, were asked about obstacles to 12-step attendance using items phrased in general terms (e.g., "What are some of the obstacles to people becoming engaged in 12-step?"). It was felt using this phrasing would elicit information that clients may be reluctant to reveal directly, such as personal reasons for nonattendance (e.g., ongoing drug use, ambivalence about quitting) and aspects of 12-step meetings or of the recovery program with which clients may be uncomfortable (e.g., sharing personal information with other members, the concept of a higher power). Answers to these items were coded as described in the beliefs section.

Next, participants completed a scale consisting of items describing potential obstacles to participation. After determining through social science database searches that there was no existing instrument available to assess clients' and staff members' beliefs about 12SGs, an instrument was developed. The instrument consists of items describing positive and negative aspects of 12SGs; the current study uses only the negative aspect subscale. A pool of items was generated from reviews of the extant literature (summarized above), as well as from pilot interviews with both clients and staff members (Laudet 2000a) and from statements previously used by Meissen, Mason, and Gleason (1991) in a study of future clinicians' attitudes and intentions toward mutual-help groups (e.g., "12SGs can be dangerous because the leaders are not professionally trained"). After deleting redundant items, the final list consisted of twelve items presented in the Results section (Cronbach's alpha = 0.74 for the client sample and 0.67 for the clinician sample). Respondents were asked, "Please indicate the extent to which you agree or disagree with each statement." The response categories were 1 = strongly disagree, 2 = disagree, 3 = agree, 4 = strongly agree. In an effort to maximize the richness of the information collected on potential obstacles to 12-step participation, the open-ended items were asked first to ensure that answers would not be influenced by the content of the structured items.

RESULTS

Description of Samples

Clients

Sample characteristics are summarized in Table 31.1. Study participants were mostly members of ethnic minority groups. Among the 26 percent of respondents describing themselves as Hispanic, most were Puerto Ricans, with two from the Dominican Republic and one from Costa Rica.

Table 31.1. Selected Description of Samples

Clients ($n=101$)		Clinicians ($n=102$)	
Male	50%	Male	29%
African American	59%	African American	61%
Hispanic	26%	Hispanic (all Puerto Rico)	23%
Puerto Rico	(23%)		
Dominican Republic	(2%)	Education	
Costa Rica	(1%)	Graduate degree	34%
		Bachelor's degree	40%
Primary substance		High school/some college	26%
Crack cocaine	31%		
Marijuana	28%	Professional experience, mean years (SD)	
Powder cocaine	17%	In current job	5.3 (5.3)
Alcohol	15%	In treatment field	7.6 (6.2)
Heroin	8%		
		Referral to 12-step (estimated mean %)	
Substance use		Clients referred to 12-step	75%
Past year	82%	Referred clients who become affiliated	44%
Past month	32%		
12-step attendance			
Lifetime	66%		
Current	43%		

Participants ranged in age from 18 to 59 (mean = 36, SD = 10). Over half (53%) did not complete high school, 27 percent held a high school diploma or GED, and 20 percent had some college or vocation training beyond high school.

The most frequently cited primary substance abuse problem was crack cocaine (31%). Mean age of first substance use was 16. Eight out of ten (82%) reported using drugs or alcohol in the year preceding the interview, one-third (32%) in the past month. Over half of the participants (59%) reported that this was their first enrollment in treatment services for substance-abuse problems. Two-thirds of participants (62%) reported some regular lifetime 12-step attendance (defined as "for one month or longer"); 43% reported current attendance. Alcoholics and Narcotics Anonymous were the fellowships most often mentioned among participants with lifetime attendance.

Clinicians

Participants were mostly female and African American or Hispanic (see Table 31.1). One-third held a graduate degree, 40 percent a bachelors' degree, 21 percent some college credits, and 6 percent a high school diploma. Job titles were: counselor (44%), social worker (20%), case manager (17%), clinical supervisor (13%), and paraprofessional social worker (e.g., case aide—6%). On average, participants had 5.3 years of experience in their current position (mean; SD = 5.3) and a total of 7.6 years of experience in the treatment field (mean; SD = 6.2). All clinicians reported referring clients to 12SGs; on average, they reported referring three-quarters of their clients and estimated that 44 percent of clients referred participated in 12SGs.

Attitudes about 12-Step Groups

Findings (summarized in Table 31.2) indicate that both clients and clinicians generally held highly positive views of 12SGs. Clinicians consistently gave significantly more positive ratings than did clients and expressed higher levels of interest in obtaining further information about the groups.

Beliefs about 12-Step Groups

First, participants were asked about the *benefits* of 12SGs (see Table 31.3). Twenty-three percent of the clients did not know or did not provide an answer. The most frequent answers provided by both clients and clinicians were: the opportunity to help improve yourself and your life, help with sobriety and recovery, and fellowship with recovering peers.

Next, participants were asked what are the *limitations* of 12SGs. Fully one-half of clients did not know or provided no answer. Substance users' lack of motivation or willingness to change was cited most frequently by

Table 31.2. Ratings of 12-Step Groups among Outpatient Drug User Treatment Clients and Clinicians

	Clients (n = 101)	Clinicians (n = 102)
Ratings of 12SGs, mean (SD)		
Helpfulness of groups[a]	8.02 (2.14)	9.57 (1.17)[c]
Importance of groups in comprehensive treatment system[b]	7.86 (2.30)	9.27 (1.40)[c]
Importance of groups in the recovery process[b]	8.70 (1.84)	9.52 (1.06)[c]
Role 12SGs should play in the recovery process[c]		
12SGs are of minimal usefulness	5%	0%
12SGs are a useful addition to formal treatment	62%	46%
12SGs are crucial to the recovery process	33%	54%
Interested in obtaining further training or information about 12SGs?[c]		
Not at all/a little	29%	7%
Moderately	21%	7%
Very much/extremely	50%	86%

Notes: Independent sample *t*-tests were used to compare continuous variables; Mantel-Haenszel tests for linear association were used for ordinal categorical variables.
[a] 0 = very harmful to 10 = very helpful
[b] 0 = not at all to 10 = extremely
[c] $p < 0.01$

clients and was the second most frequent answer among clinicians ("no limitations" was the most frequent answer provided by clinicians).

With respect to *potential dangers* of 12SGs, the most frequent answer among both clinicians and clients was "nothing," followed by "it does not address denial" (e.g., not listening to what other members say, not doing the right thing).

Obstacles to Participation in 12-Step Groups

We first examined reasons for nonattendance at 12SGs among clients who had reported no lifetime attendance and among those who reported past but not current attendance. Among never-attendees (n = 38), reasons for nonattendance were: do not feel I need it (47%), treatment program is enough (21%), do not like or believe in groups (12%), still using or picked up (6%), unable to attend (e.g., time, health; 6%), not required to attend (6%), and did not know about 12SGs (2%). Among substance users who reported prior but no current attendance (n = 19), reasons for nonattendance were: do not like or believe in groups (22%), still using or picked up (22%), unable to attend (e.g., time, health; 22%), I got the message (22%), and it did not help (12%).

Second, we asked all client participants: "What are some of the reasons why people do not attend 12SG?" The most frequent answer was "People

Table 31.3. Perceived Benefits, Limitations, and Dangers of 12-Step Groups among Outpatient Drug User Treatment Clients and Clinicians

	Clients ($n=101$)	Clinicians ($n=102$)
Benefits of 12-step groups		
Opportunity to improve yourself and your life	24%	25%
Support, fellowship with peers	18	37
Help with sobriety and recovery	20	30
Emotional well-being	8	0
Role models/positive environment for a drug-free life	0	8
Remembering where you came from	5	0
Misc. other	2	0
Don't know, not sure	23	0
Limitations of 12-step groups		
No limitations	7%	29%
Denial/You have to want it/need motivation	31	25
Cannot change everything in your life	7	0
Cannot provide concrete services	4	0
Negative mentions (e.g., triggers relapse, chaotic)	10	14
It is not for everyone (e.g., on medications)	0	10
Negative comparisons to formal treatment	0	10
Convenience	0	3
Religious aspect	0	2
Confidentiality issues	0	2
Clients limitations (insecure, anxious)	0	5
Don't know, not sure	51	0
Potential dangers of 12-step groups		
Nothing	33%	44%
Not hearing what is said, does not address denial	13	19
Expecting too much/Not recognizing need for other kinds of help	6	0
Risk of confronting sensitive issues without professional help	2	9
Can trigger relapse	5	4
Breach confidentiality/Lack of anonymity	3	2
Getting bad feedback/listening to wrong person	3	3
Members can become overly dependent on the group	0	4
No professional supervision/Groups not monitored	0	3
Attend groups for social aspects only, e.g., meet male/female	0	3
Availability/instability of groups	0	2
Being mandated to go	0	1
Not being able to identify with other members	0	1
Misc. Other	5	5
Don't know	30	0

Table 31.4. Obstacles to Participation in 12-Step Groups: Clinicians' and Clients' Perspectives

	Clients ($n=101$)	Clinicians ($n=102$)
Denial, lack of motivation	14%	25%
Using, not ready to stop	21	8
People, places, and things	16	0
Getting there (no child care, transportation, convenience of meetings)	0	27
Time constraints/responsibilities	7	10
Negative view, ignorance of 12SGs	5	8
Confidentiality, visibility	5	1
Clients' limitations and problems (e.g., anxious, low self-esteem)	0	8
Nothing	5	3
Having to go alone	0	5
Misc.	0	5
Don't know, not sure	27	0

don't want to or are not ready to stop using" (9%), followed by "People can do it on their own" (21%) and negative view or ignorance about 12SGs (15%). The other answers were: still using (8%) and being embarrassed or not wanting to be seen at 12SGs (7%). Ten percent were not sure.

Third, we asked both clients and clinicians: "What are some of the obstacles to people/clients becoming engaged in 12-step groups" Results are presented in Table 31.4. Denial, lack of readiness to stop, and "People, places and things," a 12-step expression referring to people and situations that are associated with or trigger substance use, were the most frequent obstacles cited by clients. Denial was also a frequent answer among clinicians. Over one-third of clinicians' answers centered on practical issues of scheduling and convenience: getting there (no child care, lack of transportation, inconvenient meeting time or place; 27%), and time constraints/responsibilities (10%).

Turning to the "negative aspects of 12-step groups" scale, principal components factor analysis with Varimax rotation produced four interpretable factors accounting for a total of 60 percent of the variance in the item responses. The four factors, consistent with prior literature identifying possible points of resistance to 12SGs were labeled "Negative consequences of participation," "Recovery stage limitation," "Religion and powerlessness," and "Lack of professionally trained leadership." The individual items and factor loadings are presented in Table 31.5.

The items forming the four factors generally had moderate levels on internal reliability as measures by Cronbach's alpha (Negative consequences of participation, alpha $= 0.62$; Recovery stage limitation, alpha $= 0.65$; Religion and powerlessness, alpha $= 0.63$; and Lack of professionally trained

Table 31.5. Negative Aspects of 12-Step Groups Scale: Clients and Clinicians Percent Agree/Strongly Agree and Factor Structure

	Clients ($n = 101$)	Clinicians ($n = 102$)	Factor loading
Negative consequences of participation			
Can get retraumatized or triggered in a 12SG	35%	64%*	0.86
12SGs can lead to pick-up or relapse	34	38	0.75
Can become dependent on 12SGs	55	67	0.61
Recovery stage limitation			
Can't benefit from 12SG early in recovery	18%	3%*	0.78
12SGs only helpful early in the recovery process	17	4*	0.66
Need to achieve sobriety before starting 12SGs	23	7*	0.66
Religion and powerlessness			
12SGs can be too intense for some people	68%	56%*	0.79
Religious aspect of 12SGs is an obstacle for many	61	30*	0.63
Emphasis on "powerlessness" can be dangerous	48	29*	0.63
Lack of professionally trained leadership			
12SG meeting leaders dominate the rest of the group	21%	16%**	0.74
12SG should seek professional guidance	56	36*	0.62
12SGs can be dangerous because the leaders are not professionally trained	26	14*	0.64

Note: Mantel-Haenszel test for linear association $*p < .01$, $**p < .05$.

leadership, alpha $= 0.57$). Independent t-tests conducted to compare substance users' and staff members' four factors scores were all significant ($p < 0.01$). For ease of interpretation, significance tests between the two groups' ratings are presented for the individual items rather than for the factor scores. Data show that generally, clients are significantly more likely than are clinicians to agree with statements on the negative aspects of 12SGs. This is true for the items concerning the recovery stage limitation of the groups, emphasis on religion and powerlessness, and lack of professionally trained leadership. The only dimension in which clinicians were equal or more likely than clients to express agreement with the statements was that concerning risks of 12-step participation, particularly the risk of becoming retraumatized or triggered.

DISCUSSION

The first research question was "What are substance users' and clinicians' attitudes concerning the helpfulness and usefulness of 12-step groups as a recovery resource?" Treatment clients and clinicians surveyed held positive views of 12SGs' helpfulness, importance in the recovery process as well as in a comprehensive treatment system. These findings replicate earlier reports summarized earlier (Brown et al., 2001; Forman et al., 2001).

The second research question was: "What do substance users and clinicians perceive to be positive and negative aspects of 12-step groups?" Both groups of participants cited peer support, help with recovery, and the opportunity to improve one's life as the major benefits of 12SGs. The major limitation of 12SGs cited by both groups of participants can be succinctly expressed by the 12-step saying, "It works if you work it." That is, 12SGs cannot help persons who are not ready or willing to seek help (this is further discussed below). Indeed, nearly half of the clients who were not attending a 12SG said they did not feel they needed it and another 20 percent felt the treatment program was sufficient. While some substance users may be able to recover without the support of 12-step fellowships (Timko, Moos, Finney, & Lesar, 2000; Toneatto, Sobell, Sobell, & Rubel, 1999), most are not; 12SGs are often cited as an important source of support among individuals who have achieved stable recovery (Laudet, Savage, & Mahmood, 2002). Yet in the present study, less than one-half of clients were attending a 12SG, and clinicians estimated that less than half of the clients they refer to 12SGs become affiliated. This underlines the importance of addressing the third research question: "What do substance users and referring clinicians perceive to be obstacles to 12-step participation?"

In answers to the open-ended items, lack of readiness or motivation for change was cited as a major obstacle to 12-step participation by both substance users and by clinicians. Motivation has previously been identified as a critical factor in both engagement in and outcome of formal substance user treatment interventions, as well (Simpson & Joe, 1993). Over one-third of clinicians also cited practical issues of convenience (e.g., lack of transportation or child care) and scheduling as potential barriers to 12SG participation; relatively few clients cited these concerns. In the United States, 12-step meetings are generally thought to be widely available to all who wish to attend, because the 12-step fellowships hold numerous meetings, especially in large cities such as New York City, where this study was conducted. However, it may be that practical matters such as not having access to child care or to transportation constitute obstacles that tend to be overlooked by researchers. We note recent findings by Mankowski et al. (2001) reporting a significant association between "geographical density" of 12-step meetings and greater levels of participation. Present findings on this issue emphasize the importance of including frontline clinicians in the research process, as they can contribute valuable insights that may otherwise remain unexplored.

Few study participants mentioned any of the "controversial" aspects of the 12-step program reviewed earlier in their spontaneous answers concerning limitations of 12SGs or obstacles to participation. When participants were asked to indicate their level of agreement with statements describing these aspects of the 12-step program, findings varied across broad dimensions. Over half of both substance users and clinicians agreed that "the religious aspect of 12-step groups is an obstacle for many," and nearly half of clients agreed that "the emphasis on powerlessness can be dangerous." Consistent with recommendations of the American Psychiatric Association (1995) that referral to 12SGs is appropriate at all stages in the treatment process, few participants from either group endorsed the belief that the usefulness of 12SGs is limited to a specific stage of recovery. Items concerning the lack of professionally trained leadership received moderate levels of agreement. Of note is the finding that significantly more substance users than clinicians agreed with the statement "12SG should seek professional guidance." This is consistent with the pattern reported earlier where substance users consistently expressed less favorable—and here, more negative—views of 12SGs than did clinicians.

The only exception to this pattern emerged in findings concerning potential risks of participation in 12SGs; in particular, nearly twice as many clinicians as clients expressed agreement with the statement that "clients can get retraumatized or triggered in 12-step groups." This difference between the two groups of participants may be due in part to the fact that clinicians based their answers on years of professional experience with large numbers of clients and were therefore more likely to have observed instances where clients were triggered as a result of attending a 12SG. Clients' answers, on the other hand, are likely to have been based on their personal experience or that of a few members of their social network and thus to be more limited. This difference in perspectives may also partially explain the consistent pattern of findings indicating that clinicians are significantly more positive about 12-step than are clients.

The present results have important clinical implications. First, a sizable proportion of clients had little experiential knowledge of 12SGs. Nearly four out of ten reported no prior attendance, and a large minority were unable to mention benefits or limitations of 12SGs. This suggests that there is a strong need for clinicians to inform and educate clients about the groups. In the present sample, 50 percent of substance users expressed relatively little interest in obtaining further information about 12SGs. It is not possible in this study to determine whether that is because they do not feel the need for such groups (and thus need no information, see below) or because they feel they "know all about it." Because 12-step concepts are ubiquitous in the treatment context and common lore among substance users, it is important that clinicians open the dialogue with clients about prior experience with 12SGs, as well as about what they know and believe about these groups and where these cognitions come from (e.g., personal experience or hearsay). Substance users are often ambivalent about recovery, especially early on, and may be quick to form an opinion about 12-step programs based on limited experience or friends' accounts.[5]

Clinicians should elucidate such questions and emphasize the importance of keeping an open mind and of attending different types of meetings (e.g., round robin meetings, meetings for beginners, and open and closed meetings, as well as the many specialized meetings such as for women, gays and lesbians, veterans, and so forth, as appropriate), because some formats are likely to be a better fit than others. In that respect, we note that although 12SG meetings share a general structure, philosophy, and format, they also may be sufficiently flexible to reflect the local ecology and the different needs and interests of participating community members (Humphreys & Woods, 1993). Consequently, 12SGs may be equally utilized and effective because they attend to the needs and interests of the gender and ethnic populations they serve (Hillhouse & Fiorentine, 2001). Thus, processes of engagement, participation, retention, attrition, and effectiveness are likely to be influenced not only by the general tenets and format of the 12-step program (e.g., working the twelve steps, peer support, emphasis on honesty and introspection) but also by the specific 12-step meetings clients attend. This suggests that in addition to familiarizing themselves with the 12-step model, clinicians would be well advised to be informed about the individual group meetings that are held in the communities (e.g., membership characteristics, group norms).

When discussing 12-step participation, specific clients' concerns and misconceptions should also be identified and addressed on a case-by-case basis. Overall, is it paramount that clinicians work in collaboration with clients to find a good fit between the clients' needs and inclinations on the one hand and the tools and support available within 12SGs on the other (Caldwell, 1999; Caldwell & Cutter, 1998). I acknowledge that such "matching" of individual needs and circumstances to specific types of help, while highly desirable, is difficult to implement in practice and rarely is an integral part of treatment planning, implementation, or evaluation. Services that are most often delivered in group sessions do not allow for individualization of treatment orientation or consideration of individual life and recovery stages. When feasible, individual sessions between client and clinician should include a discussion of prior participation in, and beliefs about, 12SGs to maximize the likelihood that clients will consider such organizations as a resource in their change process. Finally, in discussing attendance at 12SGs, it is important for treatment professionals to look beyond clinical issues (e.g., readiness for change, see below) and to address clients' socioenvironmental context on a case-by-case basis, as some obstacles to 12-step attendance may be overlooked (e.g., availability of child care or money for transportation).

The second point of clinical relevance follows from the finding that aspects of the 12-step program previously identified as potential points of resistance, such as the spiritual emphasis, were rarely mentioned spontaneously by either substance users or by clinicians. Instead, lack of motivation to enter recovery or reluctance to recognize that recovery requires external support ("I don't need it") appears to be a major barrier to affiliation with 12SGs. Caldwell (1999) has discussed lack of change readiness as a possible obstacle to 12SG participation. The change process involves a fairly long initial stage, in which denial about addiction needs to be broken down (Marron, 1993). Individuals who do not believe they have a problem or who believe that that their problem is not severe enough to require help are not likely to seek help. Asked about reasons why people may not attend 12SGs, 20 percent of substance users said that "people can do it on their own," and only one-third of clients (versus one-half of clinicians) viewed 12SGs as crucial to the recovery process. Denial of a problem or of a problem's severity is a major barrier to seeking and obtaining help. Decrease in denial during treatment is a significant predictor of 12SG attendance after treatment (McKay, Alterman, McLellan, & Snider, 1994). Commenting on high rates of early attrition, AA has suggested that it may be that "some individuals are not convinced of their addiction" (Alcoholics Anonymous, 1990).

The only requirement for 12-step membership is "the honest desire to stop" substance use (Alcoholics Anonymous, 1976). Given that desire, the 12-step program of recovery suggests that admitting powerlessness over drugs and alcohol (that is, admitting that one cannot recover by willpower alone) is the first step toward recovery. Current data suggest that low levels of motivation to change (desire to stop) and the belief that one may not need external help to recover (i.e., not being powerless over a substance or substance use) represent significant reasons why substance users may elect not to participate in 12SGs. Because findings also indicate that substance users view 12SGs as a helpful recovery resource, interventions designed to enhance motivation for change (Miller & Rollnick, 1991) and recognition of the need for external support are suggested as means of fostering 12-step participation.

Further, a number of factors have been identified as predictors of help-seeking among substance users; while most studies have investigated predictors of help-seeking in formal treatment services, findings may also help focus clinical strategies designed to enhance participation in 12SGs during and after treatment services. Predictors of help-seeking include greater severity of dependence; greater substance-related health and psychosocial problems; use of illicit drugs (versus alcohol), especially heroin and cocaine; greater network encouragement to seek help and social pressure to cut down; belief that one is unable to quit on one's own; and belief in the efficacy of services or other forms of help (Delaney, Grube, & Ames, 1998; George & Tucker, 1996; Hajema, Knibbe, & Drop, 1999; Hasin & Grant, 1995; Kaskutas, Weisner, & Caetano, 1997; Kessler et al., 2001; Tucker, 1995).

It is important to note that 12SGs may not be suited to all substance users (Brown et al., 2001), so nonattendance or disengagement should not necessarily be interpreted as a lack of commitment to the recovery process. A number of addiction recovery mutual-help groups have emerged in an effort to provide support to individuals who find 12SGs' goals or ideology unsuitable. These groups include Secular Organization for Sobriety (SOS), Rational Recovery, Women for Sobriety (WFS), and Moderation Management (Horvath, 1997; Klaw & Humphreys, 2000). However, because of the limited availability of meetings held by these organizations and the wide availability of

12-step meetings, it is important to gain a greater understanding of why some substance users do not participate. We note that because findings from the current study suggest that the main obstacles to participation in 12SGs are not 12-step specific but rather center on clinical issues (e.g., motivation for change), present results may apply to participation in other mutual-aid groups as well. Additional research is greatly needed in this area.

This study has several limitations that should be considered in interpreting the results. In addition to the use of relatively small samples of convenience, clients' prior and current rates of 12-step attendance were lower than reported elsewhere (Humphreys et al., 1998). The relatively low attendance rates may be explained in part to the high percentage of participants who were receiving addiction services for the first time.

In addition to these sample limitations, other study limitations point to directions that future research might take in that area. This study focused on identifying obstacles to participation in 12SGs. It did not examine the association among clients' stage of recovery, 12-step–related attitudes, and 12-step attendance, nor did it consider staff's recovery status in relationship to attitudes about 12SGs. One study examining the role of staff's recovery status on beliefs about addiction reported a positive but nonsignificant association between being in recovery and endorsing the disease-model view of addiction (Humphreys et al., 1996). Another important question that this study did not examine is that of the association between staff's attitudes about 12SGs and referral practices.

In spite of these limitations, this early study constitutes an important step toward identifying and addressing obstacles to participation in 12-step groups. It is my hope that findings reported here will contribute to focusing additional research on this important topic. Of particular interest would be cross-cultural comparisons of clinicians' and substance users' views of 12SGs and of other mutual-help recovery organizations, as well as comparisons between urban and rural geographical regions where the availability of services and views on substance use may vary significantly.

NOTES

1. Twelve-step groups such as AA (for alcoholics), NA (narcotics users), GA (gamblers), and OA (overeaters) are traditionally categorized as "self-help" groups, which is misleading. A useful and more accurate treatment paradigm taxonomy, in a field deluged with many stereotypes and myths, would be professional-based treatment, mutual help/aid, and self-help or "natural recovery."

2. The author recognizes that terms such as *addiction, treatment*, and *recovery* can be viewed in other cultures and from other perspectives on substance use as labels that may carry stigmatizing connotations. Such terms are used here because they are widely accepted as convention and understood in the field, particularly in the United States and where the English language is used in scientific literature—and should not be interpreted as an endorsement of the negative labels they sometimes convey.

3. The two other areas of conflict cited in the study were (1) feeling out of place among AA members because one's drinking problem was less severe and (2) being unable to relate to unemployed, homeless, or otherwise "down and out" members. Klaw and Humphreys note that the Moderation Management members

surveyed were predominantly an "elite" of highly educated, employed, Caucasian persons.

4. Analyses conducted to detect any differences in the variables under study between data collected before and after September 11, 2001, yielded no significant findings.

5. The term *recovery* as used in the literature most often refers broadly to positive outcome among substance users but is rarely defined. While a detailed discussion of the concept of recovery is beyond the scope of this study, we note that recovery is not a finite event, but rather a process that often begins with multiple attempts to change and may ultimately include total abstinence from substance use. More importantly, recovery entails a lifelong complex, dynamic, and multidimensional effort toward self-change. Further, the term is also bound in Western culture and especially in the ideology of 12-step programs, as members typically identify as being "in recovery," whereas persons who resolved substance use–related problems through other means such as unassisted (natural) resolution may not readily identify with that term.

REFERENCES

Alcoholics Anonymous (1976). *Alcoholics Anonymous: The story of how many thousands of men and women have recovered from alcoholism* (3rd ed.). New York: Alcoholics Anonymous World Services.

Alcoholics Anonymous (1990). *Alcoholics Anonymous 1989 membership survey.* New York: Alcoholics Anonymous World Services.

Alcoholics Anonymous (1998). *Comments on A.A.'s triennial surveys.* New York: Alcoholics Anonymous World Services.

American Psychiatric Association. (1994). *Diagnostic and statistical manual of mental disorders* (4th ed.). Washington, DC: American Psychiatric Association.

American Psychiatric Association (1995). Practice guideline for the treatment of patients with substance use disorders: Alcohol, cocaine, opioids. *American Journal of Psychiatry, 152*(Suppl. 11), 1–59.

Bogenschutz, M. P., & Akin, S. J. (2000). Twelve-step participation and attitudes toward 12-step meetings in dual diagnosis patients. *Alcoholism Treatment Quarterly, 18*(4), 31–45.

Brown, B. S., O'Grady, K. E., Farrell, E. V., Flechner, I. S., & Nurco, D. N. (2001). Factors associated with frequency of 12-step attendance by drug abuse clients. *American Journal of Drug and Alcohol Abuse, 27*(1), 147–160.

Caldwell, P. E. (1999). Fostering client connections with Alcoholics Anonymous: A framework for social workers in various practice settings. *Social Work in Health Care, 28*(4), 45–61.

Caldwell, P. E., & Cutter, H. S. (1998). Alcoholics Anonymous affiliation during early recovery. *Journal of Substance Abuse Treatment, 15*(3), 221–228.

Chappel, J. N., & DuPont, R. L. (1999). Twelve-step and mutual-help programs for addictive disorders. *Psychiatric Clinics of North America, 22*(2), 425–446.

Chesler, M. A. (1990). The "dangers" of self-help groups: Understanding and challenging professionals' views. In T. J. Powell (Ed.), *Working with self-help* (pp. 301–323). Silver Spring, MD: National Association of Social Workers Press.

Connors, G. J., & Dermen, K. H. (1996). Characteristics of participants in Secular Organizations for Sobriety (SOS). *American Journal of Drug and Alcohol Abuse, 22*(2), 281–295.

Davis, D. R., & Jansen, G. G. (1998). Making meaning of Alcoholics Anonymous for social workers: Myths, metaphors, metaphors, and realities. *Social Work, 43*(2),169–182.

Delaney, W., Grube, J. W., & Ames, G. M. (1998). Predicting likelihood of seeking help through the employee assistance program among salaried and union hourly employees. *Addiction, 93*(3), 399–410.

Ellis, A., & Schoenfeld, E. (1990). Divine intervention and the treatment of chemical dependency. *Journal of Substance Abuse, 2*(4), 459–468.

Farquharson, A. (1995). Developing a self-help perspective: Conversations with professionals. *Canadian Journal of Community Mental Health, 14*(2), 81–89.

Fiorentine, R. (1999). After drug treatment: Are 12-step programs effective in maintaining abstinence? *American Journal of Drug and Alcohol Abuse, 25*(1), 93–116.

Fiorentine, R., & Hillhouse, M. P. (2000a). Drug treatment and 12-step program participation: The additive effects of integrated recovery activities. *Journal of Substance Abuse Treatment, 18*(1), 65–74.

Fiorentine, R., & Hillhouse, M. P. (2000b). Exploring the additive effects of drug misuse treatment and Twelve-Step involvement: Does Twelve-Step ideology matter? *Substance Use & Misuse, 35*(3), 367–397.

Fiorentine, R., Nakashima, J., & Anglin, M. D. (1999). Client engagement in drug treatment. *Journal of Substance Abuse Treatment, 17*(3), 199–206.

Fishbein, M. (1980). A theory of reasoned action: Some applications and implications. In H. E. Howe Jr. & M. M. Page. (Eds.), *1979 Nebraska Symposium on Motivation* (pp. 65–116). Lincoln: University of Nebraska Press.

Forman, R. F., Bovasso, G., & Woody, G. (2001). Staff beliefs about addiction treatment. *Journal of Substance Abuse Treatment, 21*(1), 1–9.

Freimuth, M. (1996). Psychotherapists' beliefs about the benefits of 12-step groups. *Alcoholism Treatment Quarterly, 14*(3), 95–102.

Galinsky, M. J., & Schopler, J. H. (1994). Negative experiences in support groups. *Social Work in Health Care, 20*(1), 77–95.

George, A. A., & Tucker, J. A. (1996). Help-seeking for alcohol-related problems: Social contexts surrounding entry into alcoholism treatment or Alcoholics Anonymous. *Journal of Studies on Alcohol, 57*(4), 449–457.

Hajema, K. J., Knibbe, R. A., & Drop, M. J. (1999). Social resources and alcohol-related losses as predictors of help seeking among male problem drinkers. *Journal of Studies on Alcohol, 60*(1), 120–129.

Hasin, D. S., & Grant, B. F. (1995). AA and other helpseeking for alcohol problems: Former drinkers in the U.S. general population. *Journal of Substance Abuse, 7*(3), 281–292.

Hillhouse, M. P., & Fiorentine, R. (2001). Twelve-step program participation and effectiveness: Do gender and ethnic differences exist? *Journal of Drug Issues, 31*(3), 767–780.

Horvath, A. T. (1997). Alternative support groups. In J. H. Lowinson, P. Ruiz, R. B. Millman, & J. G. Langrod (Eds.), *Substance abuse: A comprehensive textbook* (3rd ed., pp. 390–396). Baltimore, MD: Williams & Wilkins.

Humphreys, K. (1997). Clinicians' referral and matching of substance abuse patients to self-help groups after treatment. *Psychiatric Services, 48*(11), 1445–1449.

Humphreys, K., Huebsch, P. D., Finney, J. W., & Moos, R. H. (1999). A comparative evaluation of substance abuse treatment. V. Substance abuse treatment can enhance the effectiveness of self-help groups. *Alcoholism, Clinical and Experimental Research, 23*(3), 558–563.

Humphreys, K., Kaskutas, L. A., & Weisner, C. (1998). The relationship of pre-treatment Alcoholics Anonymous affiliation with problem severity, social resources and treatment history. *Drug and Alcohol Dependence, 49*(2), 123–131.

Humphreys, K., & Moos, R. (2001). Can encouraging substance abuse patients to participate in self-help groups reduce demand for health care? A quasi-experimental study. *Alcoholism, Clinical and Experimental Research, 25*(5), 711–716.

Humpreys, K., Noke, J. M., & Moos, R. H. (1996). Recovering substance abuse staff members' beliefs about addiction. *Journal of Substance Abuse Treatment, 13*(1), 75–78.

Humphreys, K., & Woods, M. D. (1993). Researching mutual help group participation in a segregated society. *Journal of Applied Behavioral Science, 29*(2), 181–201.

Institute of Medicine (1990). *Broadening the base of treatment for alcohol problems: Report of a study by a committee of the Institute of Medicine, Division of Mental Health and Behavioral Medicine.* Washington, DC: National Academy Press.

Kasarabada, N. D., Hser, Y. I., Parker, L., Hall, E., Anglin, M. D., & Chang, E. (2001). A self-administered instrument for assessing therapeutic approaches of drug-user treatment counselors. *Substance Use & Misuse, 36*(3), 273–299.

Kaskutas, L., Bond, J., & Humphreys, K. (2002). Social networks as mediators of the effect of Alcoholics Anonymous. *Addiction, 97*(7), 891–900.

Kaskutas, L. A., Weisner, C., & Caetano, R. (1997). Predictors of help seeking among a longitudinal sample of the general population, 1984–1992. *Journal of Studies on Alcohol, 58*(2), 155–161.

Kessler, R. C., Aguilar-Gaxiola, S., Berglund, P. A., Caraveo-Anduaga, J. J., DeWit, D. J., Greenfield, S. F., et al. (2001). Patterns and predictors of treatment seeking after onset of a substance use disorder. *Archives of General Psychiatry, 58*(11), 1065–1071.

Kissin, W., & Ginexi, E. M. (2000). The impact of self-help involvement on recovery course. Presented at the 62nd Annual Scientific Meeting of the College on Problems of Drug Dependence, San Juan, PR.

Klaw, E., & Humphreys, K. (2000). Life stories of Moderation Management mutual help group members. *Contemporary Drug Problems, 27*(4), 779–803.

Kurtz, L. F. (1990). The self-help movement: Review of the past decade of research. *Social Work with Groups, 13*(3), 101–115.

Kurtz, L. F. (1997). *Self-help and support groups: A handbook for practitioners.* Thousand Oaks, CA: Sage.

Laudet, A. (2000a). Clinicians' role in enhancing affiliation with self-help recovery groups. Presented at the 128th Annual Meeting of the American Public Health Association, Boston.

Laudet, A. (2000b). Substance abuse treatment providers' referral to self-help: Review and future empirical directions. *International Journal of Self-Help and Self-Care, 1*(3), 195–207.

Laudet, A. B., Savage, R., & Mahmood, D. (2002). Pathways to long-term recovery: A preliminary investigation. *Journal of Psychoactive Drugs, 34*(3), 305–311.

Leshner, A. I. (1997). Addiction is a brain disease, and it matters. *Science, 278*(5335), 45–47.

Mankowski, E. S., Humphreys, K., & Moos, R. H. (2001). Individual and contextual predictors of involvement in twelve-step self-help groups after substance abuse treatment. *American Journal of Community Psychology, 29*(4), 537–563.

Marron, J. T. (1993). The twelve steps: A pathway to recovery. *Primary Care,* *20*(1), 107–119.

McCrady, B. (1998). Recent research in twelve-step programs. In A. W. Graham & T. K. Schultz (Eds.), *Principles of addiction medicine* (2nd ed., pp. 707–718). Chevy Chase, MD: American Society of Addiction Medicine.

McIntire, D. (2000). How well does A.A. work? An analysis of published A.A. surveys (1968–1996) and related analyses/comments. *Alcoholism Treatment Quarterly, 18*(4), 1–18.

McKay, J. R., Alterman, A. I., McLellan, A. T., & Snider, E. C. (1994). Treatment goals, continuity of care, and outcome in a day hospital substance abuse rehabilitation program. *American Journal of Psychiatry, 151*(2), 254–259.

Meissen, G. J., Mason, W. C., & Gleason, D. F. (1991). Understanding the attitudes and intentions of future professionals toward self-help. *American Journal of Community Psychology, 19*(5), 699–714.

Miller, W. R., Rollnick, S. (1991). *Motivational interviewing: Preparing people to change addictive behavior.* New York: Guilford Press.

Noordsy, D. L., Schwab, B., Fox, L., & Drake, R. E. (1994). The role of self-help programs in the rehabilitation of persons with severe mental illness and substance abuse disorders. In T. J. Powell (Ed.), *Understanding the self-help organization: Frameworks and findings* (pp. 314–330). Thousand Oaks, CA: Sage.

Peteet, J. R. (1993). A closer look at the role of a spiritual approach in addictions treatment. *Journal of Substance Abuse Treatment, 10*(3), 263–267.

Project MATCH Research Group (1997). Matching alcoholism treatments to client heterogeneity: Project MATCH posttreatment drinking outcomes. *Journal of Studies on Alcohol, 58*, 7–29.

Roman, P. M., Blum, T. C., & Johnson, J. A. (1998). National Treatment Center Study, summary report (no. 3): Second wave on-site results. University of Georgia.

Room, R., & Greenfield, T. (1993). Alcoholics Anonymous, other 12-step movements and psychotherapy in the US population, 1990. *Addiction, 88*(4), 555–562.

Salzer, M. S., McFadden, L., & Rappaport, J. (1994). Professional views of self-help groups. *Administration and Policy in Mental Health, 22*(2), 85–95.

Salzer, M. S., Rappaport, J., & Segre, L. (2001). Mental health professionals support of self-help groups. *Journal of Community & Applied Social Psychology, 11*(1), 1–10.

Simpson, D. D., & Joe, G. W. (1993). Motivation as a predictor of early dropout from drug abuse treatment. *Psychotherapy: Theory, Research, Practice, Training, 30*(2), 357–368.

Smith, D. E., Buxton, M. E., Bilal, R., & Seymour, R. B. (1993). Cultural points of resistance to the 12-Step recovery process. *Journal of Psychoactive Drugs, 25*(1), 97–108.

Taylor, S. E. (1995). *Health psychology* (3rd ed.). New York: McGraw-Hill.

Timko, C., Finney, J. W., Moos, R. H., Moos, B. S., & Steinbaum, D. P. (1993). The process of treatment selection among previously untreated help-seeking problem drinkers. *Journal of Substance Abuse, 5*(3), 203–220.

Timko, C., Moos, R. H., Finney, J. W., & Lesar, M. D. (2000). Long-term outcomes of alcohol use disorders: Comparing untreated individuals with those in Alcoholics Anonymous and formal treatment. *Journal of Studies on Alcohol, 61*(4), 529–540.

Timko, C., Moos, R. H., Finney, J. W., Moos, B. S., & Kaplowitz, M. S. (1999). Long-term treatment careers and outcomes of previously untreated alcoholics. *Journal of Studies on Alcohol, 60*(4), 437–447.

Toneatto, T., Sobell, L. C., Sobell, M. B., & Rubel, E. (1999). Natural recovery from cocaine dependence. *Psychology of Addictive Behaviors, 13*(4), 259–268.

Tonigan, J. S., Miller, W. R., & Connors, G. J. (2000). Project MATCH client impressions about Alcoholics Anonymous: Measurement issues and relationship to treatment outcome. *Alcoholism Treatment Quarterly, 18*(1), 25–41.

Tucker, J. A. (1995). Predictors of help-seeking and the temporal relationship of help to recovery among treated and untreated recovered problem drinkers. *Addiction, 90*(6), 805–809.

Vaillant, G. E., Clark, W., Cyrus, C., Milofsky, E. S., Kopp, J., Wulsin, V. W., et al. (1983). Prospective study of alcoholism treatment: Eight-year follow-up. *American Journal of Medicine, 75*(3), 455–463.

Weisner, C., Greenfield, T., & Room, R. (1995). Trends in the treatment of alcohol problems in the US general population, 1979–1990. *American Journal of Public Health, 85*, 55–60.

Weiss, R. D., Griffin, M. L., Gallop, R., Luborsky, L., Siqueland, L., Frank, A., et al. (2000). Predictors of self-help group attendance in cocaine dependent patients. *Journal of Studies on Alcohol, 61*(5), 714–719.

White, W. L. (1998). *Slaying the dragon: The history of addiction treatment and recovery in America*. Bloomington, IL: Chestnut Health Systems.

Glossary

ABC Model of Emotional Reaction (Albert Ellis) A model that describes the relationship between an experience (termed "A" for "activating experience") and an emotional reaction (termed "C" for "consequence"). According to this model, experiences cause emotional reactions to occur through meditating (intermediary) causes (termed "B" for beliefs). For example, if an individual experiences extreme emotional upset (C) after being cut off in traffic (A), a mediating cause of the emotional upset was a belief (B). Perhaps the individual believed that the person who cut her off in traffic did so with the express purpose of making her angry.

Absorption The state of being extremely immersed or involved in an experience.

Adrenal glands There are two adrenal glands, one located above each kidney. The adrenal glands release stress hormones into the body, including adrenaline (epinephrine) and cortisol. The hormones released by the adrenal glands produce many of the aspects of stress arousal, including increased heart rate.

Adrenaline (epinephrine) A hormone released by the adrenal glands. Its primary stress effects are on the cardiovascular system.

Adreno-corticotropic hormone (ACTH) A hormone released by the pituitary gland. ACTH travels from the pituitary gland to the adrenal glands, causing the release of particular stress hormones, including cortisol and aldosterone.

Affect (noun) Feeling or emotion. Sometimes used to refer to the outward expression of emotion, for example, in body language or facial expression.

Alcoholics Anonymous (AA) A mutual-help group for the treatment of alcohol addiction.

Allostasis The attempts by the body to maintain homeostasis during the fight-or-flight (stress) response. This process is energy-consuming. Over time, allostasis has the potential to cause damage to the body.

Allostatic load Damage caused to the body by the allostatic response. *See* Allostasis.

Alzheimer's disease A type of dementia primarily involving a specific form of memory deficit—an inability to form new memories.

Ambulation Walking.

Amino acid An organic compound that is a "building block" for proteins in the body.

Amygdala Part of the limbic system, located in the temporal lobe of the brain, the amygdala plays a role in emotion. It is especially associated with fear and pleasure.

Anterograde amnesia An inability to form new memories, associated with damage in one or more regions of the brain.

Aphasia An inability to produce speech; caused by brain damage.

Appraisal Also called "cognitive appraisal." An assessment or evaluation that affects one's reaction to potentially stressful events. A *primary appraisal* is one's appraisal (evaluation) of the degree to which an event is stressful. A *secondary appraisal* is one's evaluation of the degree to which one can cope with an event, and how one will cope with an event. Both types of appraisal—evaluation of the event itself and evaluation of one's ability to cope—affect the perceived assessment of the stressfulness of the entire circumstance.

Arcus senilis The existence of a cloudy ring around the cornea of the eye, associated with the decomposition of fatty deposits in the bloodstream.

Atherosclerosis Also known as "hardening of the arteries," atherosclerosis is a disease that causes scarring of the arterial blood vessels.

Attribution The meaning people attribute to life events. For example, if someone spills coffee, one person might attribute it to clumsiness, another to bad luck, and a third to the situation (maybe there was an earthquake).

Autonomic nervous system (ANS) One of two primary divisions of the central nervous system. The ANS is responsible for the maintenance of largely involuntary functions, such as blood pressure, heart rate, respiration, and body temperature.

Axis I disorder A disorder that falls on Axis I of the five axes in the *Diagnostic and Statistical Manual of Mental Disorders*. An Axis I disorder refers to a clinical mental disorder, other than a personality or developmental disorder or general medical condition.

Beck's cognitive therapy model A psychotherapy model that emphasizes that the client restructure his cognitions as a means to attain better mental health.

Behavioral disengagement A coping mechanism that involves giving up on solving a problem.

Behaviorism A paradigm in psychology that emphasizes the study of observable events ("behaviors") and holds that internal mental events (such as emotions and thoughts) cannot be studied scientifically because they are unobservable (only the person who is experiencing them can report on them—no one else can verify the existence of mental events).

Bipolar disorder A psychiatric condition, formerly referred to as "manic–depression," in which episodes of depression alternate with episodes of "mania" (a syndrome characterized by extremely high energy, impulsivity, elevated or irritable mood, and other symptoms).

Cardiovascular disease A class of diseases involving the heart, arteries, and veins. Used especially to refer to diseases related to atherosclerosis.

Catecholamine A class of hormones that includes adrenaline (epinephrine) and noradrenaline (norepinephrine).

Ceiling effect In pharmacology, a ceiling effect means that administering higher doses of a medication produces smaller incremental treatment effects.

Cognition Mental processes of an individual; the internal thought states such as beliefs, desires, and intentions.

Cognitive-behavioral therapy (CBT) A form of therapy that focuses on changing one's cognitions (beliefs, thoughts, assumptions, etc.) and behaviors. For example, when used to treat depression, the therapist would examine and attempt to change the client's negative belief system (i.e., low self-esteem and general pessimism) and encourage the client to engage in behaviors that could elevate mood.

Cognitive mediation The idea that beliefs "mediate" (or intervene between) external events and one's reaction (which may be emotional, behavioral, or both). For example, the event might be that your boss emailed you, saying that he wants to speak to you, and your immediate reaction is anxiety. In order to have this reaction to this ambiguous situation, you must have had a belief such as "I did something wrong and my boss discovered it."

Cognitive primacy perspective In the stress arena, this is the idea that the individual's appraisal or interpretation of the environment is the primary cause of the stress reaction to an event or stimulus.

Cognitive therapy A form of therapy which focuses on changing one's cognitions (beliefs, thoughts, assumptions, etc.). For example, when used to treat depression, the therapist would examine and attempt to change the client's negative belief system (i.e., low self-esteem and pessimism).

Confound (verb) In research, to produce a situation that makes the results difficult to interpret. *See* Confounding factor.

Confounding factor Also called "confounding variable" or "confound." In research, this is a factor or variable that affects one's results in a way that makes the results difficult to interpret. More specifically, in an experiment, if some variable varies systematically with the manipulated independent variable, this first variable is called a confound. It can ruin an experiment.

Construct validity A property of a psychological test. The psychological test possesses construct validity if it indeed measures what it intends to measure.

Contraction band necrosis A condition in which contraction of the heart muscle may lead to heart damage.

Control group In an experiment, this is a group of people that does NOT receive the treatment of interest. This group serves as a comparison group to the experimental group. *See* Experimental group.

Coping An individual's attempts to master demands that he or she appraises as threatening or challenging. Coping does not imply a successful outcome.

Coronary heart disease (CHD) Also known as coronary artery disease (CAD), heart disease, and ischemic heart disease. CHD occurs when the arteries that supply blood to the heart harden and become narrow due to an accumulation of plaque in the artery walls (atherosclerosis). This narrowing means less blood can flow through the arteries to the heart, and less blood flow means less oxygen to the heart, which damages the heart muscle. CHD can result in angina (chest pain), heart attack, heart failure, or arrhythmia.

Correlation A numeric measure of the strength of the association between two variables.

Correlation coefficient A measure of the strength of the association between two variables. The coefficient can be positive or negative, indicating the direction of the relationship. Correlations range from −1.0 to +1.0. A correlation coefficient of zero means that there is no linear association between two variables.

Correlational research design A type of research design in which the researcher investigates variables or factors as they exist, without attempting to manipulate any factors. For example, if one were to measure heart disease and diet utilizing a correlational research design, one would measure both the dietary habits and heart disease indicators of research participants, then obtain a *correlation coefficient* (q.v.) for these two factors (diet and heart disease). Contrast this with the description for *experimental research design*.

Corticotropin-releasing factor (CRF) A substance released by the hypothalamus (a brain structure). CRF activates the pituitary gland to release ACTH, which in turn activates the adrenal glands to release stress hormones.

Cortisol A type of hormone (corticosteroid) that is involved in the response to stress. Cortisol suppresses the immune system and increases blood pressure and blood sugar levels.

Covariate In statistics, a covariate is a variable that may be predictive of the outcome of interest in the study. A covariate may be of interest on its own, or it may be a confounding variable.

C-reactive protein (CRP) A protein produced by the liver. CRP levels rise when there is inflammation in the body. Some studies show an association between elevated CRP levels and heart disease.

Cross-sectional study A form of research that involves looking at some subset of a population all at the same time (as opposed to a longitudinal study).

Declarative (explicit) memory Memory for information, such as one's knowledge of history or of a foreign language. Compare with *episodic, procedural*, and *semantic* memories.

Dendrite Part of a nerve cell. A dendrite conducts a nerve signal to the cell body of the neuron.

Dendritic arborization The growing, or branching, of dendrites on a neuron.

Dependent variable The response measure in an experiment.

Diagnostic and Statistical Manual of Mental Disorders A book published by the American Psychiatric Association that lists, describes, and categorizes various mental disorders. This book, also known as the *DSM*, utilizes a system of five axes to give a profile of an individual along several dimensions (for example, two axes specify psychiatric diagnoses and one axis specifies medical conditions). *DSM* codes are a standard used in the mental health field and provide a means by which health practitioners can communicate with each other and with insurance companies using a common language.

Diathesis A predisposition, or susceptibility, to develop a disease or disorder. For example, someone may have a family history of heart disease.

Diathesis-stress model Also called "diathesis-stress approach." A theory which claims that both constitutional (usually genetic) predisposition (diathesis) and life experiences (stress) contribute to an individual's developing a disease or mental health disorder. For example, in an individual who is genetically predisposed to schizophrenia (diathesis), some triggering life event (stress) could combine with the diathesis, resulting in schizophrenia.

Dissociative state A psychological state involving an altered state of consciousness. Most commonly, one has little or no awareness of aspects of mind that are dissociated.

Dissociative symptoms Symptoms that indicate an altered consciousness or awareness. Most commonly, one has little or no awareness of aspects of mind that are dissociated.

Dopamine A neurotransmitter, or chemical messenger in the brain, that appears to be involved in a number of psychological states, including experiencing pleasure and experiencing psychotic symptoms.

Double-blind study A study in which both the participants and researchers are unaware of significant aspects of the study if awareness of
these aspects could influence the results. For example, in a study of
medication treatment for depression, the study would be double-
blind if both the researchers and the participants were unaware of
which participants received the medication treatment and which participants received an inert substance ("placebo").

Dummy variable A variable for which there are only two possible values:
"0" or "1." These values could represent any binary variable, for
example "yes" or "no," or "Democrat" or "Republican."

Dysthymia A psychiatric condition involving a low to moderate level of
depression that persists for at least two years.

Electroencephalogram (EEG) A record of brain activity as measured by a
device called an electroencephalograph.

Emotion-focused coping A category of coping mechanisms that involves
managing the emotional responses to a stressor. Some examples
include emotional distancing, denial, reappraisal, and drug or alcohol
use. Contrast with *problem-focused coping.*

Enacted support (received support) Supportive acts that one receives.
Enacted support may be emotional, tangible, or informational.

Endocrine system A system of glands that secrete hormones. These hormones help regulate mood, growth and development, metabolism,
and sexual function.

Epinephrine *See* Adrenaline.

Episodic memory Also known as "autobiographical memory," episodic
memory is the explicit memory of events (including times, places,
and emotions associated with these events). Compare with *declarative, procedural,* and *semantic* memories.

Existential psychology A paradigm in psychology which emphasizes that
the main motive for humans is a search for meaning. Humans may
create meaning in their lives in many ways, for example, through
spiritual or religious beliefs, through relationships with others, or
through producing a creative product.

Explained variance (or variance explained) Variation exists in a sample
of scores. For example, if one has a list of people's scores on a stress
questionnaire, these scores will vary from one another. Likewise, levels of illness will vary among individuals. If one is interested in predicting levels of illness from stress scores, she will be able to do so to
some degree if illness and stress are correlated. The degree to which
stress predicts illness can be described by the *variance* (variations) in
illness scores that is *explained* by the variance (variation) in stress
scores.

Explanatory style An individual's general tendency or style regarding the
explanation of events. For example, some people tend to have an

optimistic explanatory style while others tend to have a pessimistic explanatory style.

Experimental research design A type of research design in which the researcher *manipulates* a variable (called the independent variable) and observes the effect of this manipulation on another variable (called the dependent variable). For example, if a researcher studied the relationship between heart disease and diet using the experimental research design, she would manipulate diet—meaning that she would assign different types of diets to different groups of participants—then observe the effect of diet on heart disease. In this type of design, if done well, the researcher can determine whether a cause–effect relationship exists between the independent and dependent variables (in this case, whether diet is causally related to heart disease).

External locus of control The idea that external circumstances and the environment are more important than internal factors in predicting future successes or failures. People with an external locus of control might think that luck is more important than personal effort for future success. These people would also be more likely to see themselves as victims of circumstance.

Factor analysis A statistical procedure that is used to summarize overlapping (redundant) information. The procedure is based in the correlation coefficient. For example, if the personality traits sociability, sense of humor, and dominance are highly correlated, it may make sense to speak of these traits as one *factor* rather than to identify them as independent traits. Factor analysis is a relatively objective method for determining whether information can or should be summarized in this way.

Fibromyalgia A chronic syndrome characterized by fatigue, pain in fibrous tissues, possible sleep disturbances and anxiety, and other symptoms.

Fight-or-flight reaction Also called "fight-or-flight response." This is the "stress response," and it (presumably) prepares an individual to fight or flee from a threat. It involves all body systems; the prime themes are mobilization of energy for the emergency that is occurring and conservation of energy from "vegetative functions." For example, characteristics include increased heart rate and blood pressure, a utilization of energy stores (for example, sugar in the liver), and decreased digestion.

Free fatty acid A by-product of broken-down triglycerides (fat stored in body tissues) that can adhere to blood vessels and contribute to atherosclerosis (q.v.).

Gender role theory The theory that cultural expectations for women and men are associated with women and men adopting specific roles in society.

General Adaptation Syndrome (GAS) Identified by Hans Selye, this is a general stress reaction. It involves three phases: the *alarm phase* (the fight-or-flight response, q.v.), the *resistance phase* (a partial stress reaction in which, with continued stress, arousal continues to occur in only one or several body systems rather than all body systems), and the *exhaustion phase* (during which disease or malfunction of one or more organ systems occurs, and possibly, death).

Glial cell A type of brain cell that functions primarily as "supportive" to neurons. For example, glial cells "mop up" excess chemicals surrounding neurons.

Glucocorticoid A type of steroid (a hormone) that is able to bind with cortisol receptors. Cortisol is a glucocorticoid that supports various metabolic, immune, cardiovascular, and homeostatic functions.

Glucose Blood sugar. It circulates in the blood and serves as "food" to body tissues.

Glycerol A component of fat. It may circulate in the blood vessels and may be utilized by the body when energy is needed.

Glycogen The form of glucose (blood sugar) when it is stored in body tissues.

Hardiness (including commitment, control, and challenge) A cluster of personality traits that plays a role in enabling an individual to cope with stress. Commitment is characterized by possessing a clear value system, feeling committed to life and specific goals, and experiencing life as worthwhile. Control is the belief that one is in control of his outcomes. Challenge is a positive attitude toward change—a view that changes are challenges rather than threats.

Hassles Also called "daily hassles" or "minor hassles." Everyday events— such as losing one's keys, being stuck in traffic, or having a small disagreement with a person—which may produce the stress response.

Hatha yoga A major branch of yoga which emphasizes postures, physical control, and breathing.

Hippocampus A brain structure, located in the temporal lobe, that is part of the limbic system. The hippocampus is important in memory and navigation.

Hoffman reflex A spinal cord reflex.

Hypothalamic-pituitary-adrenal (HPA) axis Part of the neuroendocrine system, the HPA axis controls reactions to stress. The HPA axis also plays a role in regulating digestion, the immune system, and energy storage.

Hypothalamus A small structure at the base of the brain that regulates body functions, including appetite and body temperature. The hypothalamus also controls the release of hormones from the pituitary gland. It is often referred to as initiating the stress response.

Independent variable In an experiment, an independent variable is a variable that is manipulated by the researcher. *See* Dependent variable.

Informed consent In research, informed consent is a procedure involving informing the research participants about the nature of a study and obtaining consent from the participants prior to conducting the study. In many cases, researchers are allowed to limit their disclosure about the nature of the study and possibly to deceive participants in some way, if doing so is necessary for the success of the study and is unlikely to harm the participants.

Insulin A hormone that is secreted by the pancreas, insulin regulates carbohydrate metabolism. Disturbances in the body's insulin balance can cause diabetes, reactive hypoglycemia, or prediabetes (Metabolic syndrome).

Internal locus of control People with an internal locus of control see themselves as responsible for the outcomes of their own actions. They often believe they control their own destinies. They are less likely to feel like a victim of circumstance than someone who has an external locus of control.

Internal reliability (also called "internal consistency reliability") On a questionnaire, internal reliability is the degree to which the test items on a scale measure the variable of interest (for example, extraversion, stress, or alcoholism) consistently. To possess high internal consistency reliability, all items on a particular scale should measure the same concept.

Ischemia A restriction of the blood supply to body tissue. This causes oxygen deprivation, resulting in tissue damage.

Karasek's demand-control model Also known as "Karasek's job strain model." An organizational stress model that categorizes jobs on two dimensions: demand and control (degree of freedom of decision in the job). According to the model, these two dimensions are related to degree of job stress.

Life Events and Difficulties Schedule (LEDS) Developed in 1978 by Brown and Harris, the LEDS lists forty events that are believed to produce strong emotion. Each event is rated on twenty-eight rating scales in terms of prior experience, plans and preparation, immediate reactions, and consequences and implications, among other things.

Limbic system A collection of structures within the brain responsible for processing emotion, emotional memory, and motivation.

Longitudinal study A form of research that involves following the same participants over a long period of time (as opposed to a cross-sectional study).

Lymphocyte A type of white blood cell involved in the immune system.

Major life events stress A way of viewing stress. In this view, "major life events" (significant events, such as death of a loved one, a jail term, promotion, or marriage) are viewed as stressors (causes of the stress reaction). According to this perspective, any significant life change, even if it is perceived as positive, has the potential to produce the stress response.

Matched randomization A type of "control" used in an experimental study.

Mediation (statistical) When a variable explains the relationship between an independent variable (IV) and a dependent variable (DV), it is said to *mediate* that relationship. The mediator is the mechanism through which an IV influences a DV; it explains *how* or *why* one variable affects another. For example, if we're looking at the relationship between age and the number of pounds a person can lift, we might find that people who practice lifting weights three times a week for a month can lift more weight, on average, than people who never practice lifting weights. The weight-lifting practice *mediates* the relationship between people's ages and the number of pounds they can lift. Contrast statistical mediation (explains *how* or *why*) with statistical *moderation* (explains *when* or *for whom*).

Mental disengagement A type of coping technique that involves mentally distancing oneself from a stressor. People who engage in mental disengagement choose not to think about the stressor.

Meta-analysis A statistical technique to compare and integrate the results of many different studies.

Mindfulness The state of being aware of what is happening in the present moment.

Minnesota Multiphasic Personality Inventory (MMPI) A self-report inventory used to measure psychopathology.

Mitogen A substance that induces mitosis (cell division).

Moderation (statistical) A moderator is a variable that explains *when* or *for whom* an independent variable (IV) has a stronger relationship to a dependent variable (DV). For example, if we were looking at the relationship between age and number of pounds a person can lift, we might find that the relationship is moderated by sex: that men can lift more pounds of weight than women of the same age. Sex would be said to moderate the relationship between age and number of pounds people can lift. Contrast statistical moderation (explains *when* or *for whom*) with statistical *mediation* (explains *how* or *why*).

Multiple regression A statistical technique that finds the relationship between one dependent variable and many independent variables.

Myocardial infarction A heart attack. A myocardial infarction occurs when lack of oxygen causes damage to part of the heart muscle.

Neurohormone A hormone produced by nerve cells that circulates in the bloodstream.

Neuropeptide A messenger hormone that is produced in the brain and other organs of the body. It fits into the receptor sites of lymphocytes (a type of white blood cell) and thus can "communicate" with lymphocytes.

Neuropeptide Y A neurotransmitter found in the brain and autonomic nervous system. Neuropeptide Y is involved in a wide variety of functions, including stress and anxiety responses, sexual functioning, and food intake.

Neurotransmitter A chemical used to relay electrical signals between a neuron and another cell (often another neuron). It is often called a "chemical messenger" and is responsible for "communication" between neurons and other cells, including affecting the firing rate of the cell that receives the message. Some examples of neurotransmitters are serotonin, dopamine, and noradrenaline.

Noradrenaline (norepinephrine) A chemical that functions as both a hormone and a neurotransmitter. As a hormone, it works in conjunction with adrenaline (epinephrine) during the stress response (for example, to increase heart rate and blood pressure). As a neurotransmitter, it has many functions. For instance, noradrenaline appears to malfunction in some cases of depression.

Norepinephrine *See* Noradrenaline.

Omega-3 fatty acid A type of fatty acid found in a variety of foods, including fish and some nuts. Omega-3s have been found to protect against depression, memory loss, behavioral problems in children, and other types of psychological dysfunction.

Openness to experience A personality trait characterized by openness to experiences. An individual who is high in this trait describes himself as intellectual, cultured, curious, and possessing artistic interests.

Operationalization In research, the process of defining a concept by specifying the operations that will measure the concept.

Oxytocin A hormone produced by the pituitary gland that causes contractions during childbirth and that stimulates the production of milk.

Parasympathetic nervous system Part of the autonomic nervous system, the parasympathetic nervous system increases digestion and aids in rest (by decreasing blood pressure and heart rate). It is often active when an organism is not under stress.

Path analysis A statistical technique used to understand the relationships among a number of variables that were studied using a non-experimental method. A primary goal of path analysis is to shed light on causal relationships among variables that cannot be studied experimentally or for which experimental study is very difficult.

Perceived support One's perception of the amount and types of support that she receives from others. Perceived support can be emotional, tangible, or informational.

Pituitary gland A tiny gland located at the base of the brain, the pituitary gland controls the functions of other endocrine glands. Because of this control function, it is often called the "master gland."

Placebo effect A treatment effect produced by a "sham" or inert substance. The placebo effect is due to the experience of receiving any type of treatment at all, even a treatment that should not produce any effect. For example, in studies of the effects of medication, place-bos (inert substances such as sugar pills) are given to some research participants in order to test that the treatment of interest (the medication) has a treatment effect above and beyond the effect of the placebo.

Polyunsaturated fat A type of vegetable fat that helps to reduce blood cholesterol levels if eaten in place of saturated fat.

Positive expectancy An expectation that something positive will occur. A positive expectancy can operate in a particular context or it may exist as a more generalized personality trait in some people.

Positive psychology A paradigm in psychology in which the focus is on mental health and on the more positive, self-actualizing, and benevolent attributes of humans.

Posttraumatic stress disorder (PTSD) A psychiatric syndrome which arises in the aftermath of exposure to a traumatic stressor. Symptoms include anxiety, reliving of the traumatic experience (through nightmares or flashbacks), and a dulling of everyday, ordinary emotions, such as happiness and sadness.

Power analysis (statistical) In the analysis of data, a power analysis is a procedure that determines whether certain aspects of the study, including the sample size, are sufficient for producing an effect that may be measurable, if an effect truly exists.

Primary appraisal An evaluation or assessment of the stressfulness of an event.

Priming effect A cognitive or perceptual effect. If an individual has prior experience with an event, he may be "primed" to respond in a certain way to that event or similar events. For example, one group of participants is shown a series of drawings of animals and a second group is shown a series of drawings of people. Next, when shown an ambiguous drawing that could be either a rat or a man, those who just saw animals tend to identify the drawing as a rat and those who just saw people tend to identify it as a man.

Problem-focused coping A category of coping mechanisms that involves attempts to change the stressor. Some examples include planning, confrontive coping, active coping, and restraint coping. Contrast with *emotion-focused coping*.

Procedural memory Also known as "implicit memory." Skills acquired through learning. It does not involve the conscious recall of information. Compare with *declarative, episodic,* and *semantic* memories.

Progressive muscle relaxation A stress management technique that involves progressively relaxing the muscle groups through first tensing then relaxing each muscle. Progressive muscle relaxation generally begins with the distal muscles (hands, feet), and progresses to proximal muscles such as those of the torso and the head.

Prospective study A study that looks at future behavior. Specifically, participants are measured on some factor prior to the event of interest. For example, when studying whether diet causes cancer, people's dietary habits are studied prior to any cancer diagnosis; then, after some time, the researchers note those participants who developed cancer during the study and see if the cancer diagnosis is related to diet. This controls for a "hindsight" bias that people sometimes have—if people were studied only after developing cancer, for example, those who developed cancer may incorrectly remember that they had a poor diet. Contrast with *retrospective study*.

Psychoanalysis A paradigm in psychology, originally associated with Sigmund Freud, in which the emphasis is on unconscious causes of behavior.

Psychoanalytic theory A general psychological theory, most closely associated with Sigmund Freud, that emphasizes unconscious factors as causes of normal and abnormal behavior.

Psychogenic amnesia A form of amnesia involving the loss of personal information. Also known as "functional amnesia," psychogenic amnesia is not the result of brain injury. The presumed cause is often psychological in nature.

Psychometric Of or relating to psychological measurement.

Psychoneuroimmunology Professional field concerned with the relationship between psychological factors, such as stress and personality, and the immune system.

Psychosomatic disorders Chronic physical disorders of unknown cause, presumably with psychological causes.

Random assignment (also called "randomization to groups" or "random assignment to control group and experimental group") The assignment of each participant to either a control group or an experimental group is random—that is, each participant is equally likely to be assigned to either group. Random assignment is one of the controls used in an experiment, meaning that it is one of the ways used to ensure that the control group and the experimental group differ in only one way—members of the control group are not exposed to the independent variable whereas members of the experimental group are exposed to the independent variable

Rational-emotive therapy A form of cognitive therapy developed by Albert Ellis. In this form of therapy, clients are encouraged to dispute their irrational assumptions or appraisals and replace the irrational assumptions with rational assumptions.

Regression analysis (statistical regression) A statistical procedure in which an individual's standing on one variable (for example, stress), is used to predict his standing on another variable (for example, health). Statistical regression can be conducted if the two (or more)

variables (in this case, stress and health) are correlated with one another.

Regression toward the mean The tendency for extreme scores to test as more moderate scores upon repeated measurements. For example if an individual scored 150 on an IQ test (an extremely high score), upon repeated measurement, she would be more likely to score lower than 150 (closer to the mean) rather than higher than 150.

Repeated measures design (also called "within subjects design") A research design in which one or more of the independent variables is a "within subjects variable." A within subjects variable is one in which the same participants receive different "levels" of the independent variable. For example, if a researcher studied the effects of different levels of social rejection (low and high) on self-esteem, and social rejection was studied as a within-subjects variable, then the same participants would experience low social rejection during part of the study and high social rejection during another part of the study.

Repressive coping style A coping style that involves keeping oneself unaware of stressors.

Retrospective study A study that looks at past behavior. This type of research design can be subject to bias. If, for example, a researcher studied the relationship between diet and cancer by asking cancer patients to recall their diets over the prior twenty years, the patients may incorrectly remember that they had poor diets. Contrast with *prospective study.*

Saturated fat A type of fat found in high amounts in many foods, including red meats, eggs, full-fat dairy products, and some vegetable products such as coconut oil and palm oil. Ingestion of high amounts of saturated fat is associated with increased risk for heart disease and some cancers.

Secondary appraisal A self-evaluation or assessment about whether one is capable of coping with an event (stressor), and how one will cope with the event.

Self-derogation A tendency to belittle oneself.

Self-disputing The practice of countering one's irrational or negative thoughts.

Self-efficacy The belief that one is effective in an area. For example, if an individual has high self-efficacy for academics, then she believes that she does well at academic work.

Self-report measure A type of measure or assessment in which an individual reports on his or her behaviors, thoughts, emotions, and other psychological characteristics. The most common form of self-report is the questionnaire.

Semantic memory The memory of meanings, understandings, and facts. Compare with *declarative, episodic, and procedural* memories.

Serotonin A neurotransmitter that plays a role in mood, sleep, sexuality, and appetite.

Sertraline (Zoloft) An antidepressant medication that operates primarily by modifying the activity of the neurotransmitter serotonin.

Social desirability effect In research, an effect that is primarily of concern in self-report research. Some responses of some participants may be affected by social expectations regarding what is desirable. For example, people may be more likely to describe themselves positively than negatively, and may tend to describe themselves in relation to gender expectations (i.e., men may describe themselves as dominant and women may describe themselves as nurturing).

Social Readjustment Rating Scale (SRRS) A checklist of forty-three good and bad life events that can increase stress levels. Points are assigned to each event, and total scores suggest the degree of susceptibility to illness and mental health problems.

Social support Types of support people receive from other people. These can include emotional support, informational support, and tangible support.

Somatostatin A hormone that inhibits the secretion of other hormones, including growth hormone.

Spontaneous recovery In conditioning, spontaneous recovery is when a learned behavior reappears "spontaneously" after a period of time during which the learned behavior was not exhibited.

Standard deviation (SD) A statistical measure of variability of a list of scores. It indicates how "spread out" the data are. SD is computed by taking the difference between each value and the mean of the data set, squaring each difference, taking the average of these squares, and then taking the square root of that result.

Standardized procedures In research, standardized procedures involve treating all participants in the same way (except that, in the case of the experiment, some participants receive the independent variable and some do not). Standardized procedures reduce potential error in a study. In an experiment specifically, standardized procedures operate as a "control"—an attempt to ensure that the experimental and control groups differ only by the presence or absence of the independent variable.

State anxiety A temporary experience, or "state" of anxiety. Contrast with *trait anxiety*.

Stress inoculation training A type of stress management technique that involves mental preparation (inoculation) for a stressor that will occur in the future. In stress inoculation training, an individual will imagine and rehearse a potentially stressful event and talk himself through the challenges that he anticipates will arise.

Stress prevention model The theory that social support operates to prevent the occurrence and negative impact of stressors.

Substance P A protein substance that increases pain messages by stimulating nerve endings.

Support deterioration model The theory that the occurrence of stress serves to deteriorate one's level of social support.

Sympathetic nervous system Part of the autonomic nervous system, the sympathetic nervous system is activated during the "fight-or-flight" response. It increases heart rate and blood pressure and decreases digestive activity.

Trait anxiety Anxiety that appears to exist as a trait in an individual. That is, the anxiety is present in the individual with some consistency and regularity. Contrast with *state anxiety*.

Transactional model A model for understanding stress that emphasizes that the environmental event (potential stressor) and the cognitive faculties of the individual are constantly in transaction, through the process of appraisal.

Trans fatty acid (TFA) A fatty acid that has been produced by hydrogenating vegetable oils. TFAs increase the risk of heart disease and are found in margarine, many processed foods, fried foods, and other foods.

Triglyceride The form in which fat is stored in body tissues.

t-Test A statistical technique that is used to test whether mean values of variables are reliably different. For example, a researcher may use a t-test to test the mean level of stress experienced by women against the mean level of stress experienced by men in a particular research sample to determine if these mean values are different, and if the difference is large enough that we can conclude that the difference is not due to chance.

12-step group One of a number of mutual-help groups, such as Alcoholics Anonymous and Narcotics Anonymous, devoted to the treatment of addictions.

Type A behavior pattern A cluster of traits that increases one's risk for heart disease. These traits include achievement motivation, hostility, and an overconcern with time.

Unipolar (major) depression A psychiatric syndrome that includes a variety of symptoms, including sad or blank mood, negative thinking, appetite change, change in sleeping pattern (insomnia or hypersomnia), and others.

Ventricular fibrillation Potentially dangerous irregular heartbeats caused by the reduction of blood flow to the heart.

Within-subjects research design *See* Repeated measures design.

Index

About the Editors
and Contributors

ALAN MONAT received his Ph.D. in Psychology from the University of California, Berkeley, in 1972 under the guidance of Richard S. Lazarus; and subsequently, they collaborated on several articles and books. Since 1972, Alan Monat has taught in the Department of Psychology and, more recently, has served as Associate Dean of the College of Science at the California State University, East Bay (formerly, California State University, Hayward). He taught stress and coping and personality courses for about thirty years and consults in and conducts workshops on stress and coping. In addition to his professional interests, Monat enjoys music, listening to books, and playing tennis.

The late RICHARD LAZARUS was an eminent, internationally known figure in psychology, one of the field's foremost authorities on emotion and stress. He was a graduate of the City College of New York and earned his doctorate from the University of Pittsburgh. He won numerous awards, including a Guggenheim Fellowship, the American Psychological Association's Distinguished Scientific Contribution to Psychology Award, and honorary doctorates from the University of Haifa and the Johannes Gutenberg University. He was a professor of psychology for forty-five years at the University of California, Berkeley, and authored fourteen earlier books, including the classic, *Stress, Appraisal, and Coping*, co-authored with Susan Folkman, and two books co-authored with his wife of fifty-seven years, Bernice.

GRETCHEN REEVY received her Ph.D. in Psychology from the University of California, Berkeley, in 1994. Since 1994, she has taught in the Department of Psychology at California State University, East Bay, specializing in personality and stress and coping courses. Her research interests are in stress and coping, personality, social support, and gender differences. Reevy enjoys running, swimming, and reading and has a love for animals.

LANCE ARMSTRONG is a professional athlete, cancer survivor, and seven-time winner of the Tour de France.

MICHAEL BABYAK, Ph.D. is Associate Clinical Professor of Medical Psychology, Duke University Medical Center, Durham, North Carolina.

TERI T. BALDEWICZ (KARCHER) Ph.D. is the Director of Global Client Services, Kendle International, Cary, North Carolina.

SCOTT R. BISHOP, Ph.D. works at Princess Margaret Hospital and is Assistant Professor, Department of Psychiatry, University of Toronto, Ontario, Canada.

JAMES A. BLUMENTHAL, Ph.D. is Professor of Medical Psychology and Assistant Professor of Medicine, Duke University Medical Center, Durham, North Carolina.

NAOMI BRESLAU, Ph.D. is Professor, Department of Psychiatry, Case Western Reserve University School of Medicine, Cleveland, Ohio, and Clinical Professor, Department of Psychiatry, University of Michigan School of Medicine, Ann Arbor, Michigan.

JIM BRIGHT, Ph.D. is the Senior Lecturer in Psychology, University of New South Wales.

ROBERT CHRISMAN, Ph.D. is the founding publisher and editor-in-chief of *The Black Scholar*.

CARY L. COOPER, CBE is Professor of Organizational Psychology and Health at Lancaster University Management School, Lancaster University.

W. EDWARD CRAIGHEAD, Ph.D. is a Professor in the Department of Psychology, University of Colorado, Boulder.

PHILIP DEWE, Ph.D. is Professor of Organizational Behavior and Head of the Organizational Psychology Department, Birkbeck College.

MURALI DORAISWAMY, M.D. is the Division Head, Department of Psychiatry and Behavioral Science, Duke University Medical Center, Durham, North Carolina.

DAVID F. DUNCAN, Ph.D. is a Clinical Associate Professor of Medical Science, Brown University School of Medicine.

GEORGE S. EVERLY JR., Ph.D. is with the Affiliate Faculty, Loyola College in Maryland and Associate, Bloomberg School of Public Health, The Johns Hopkins University, Baltimore, Maryland.

TIFFANY M. FIELD, Ph.D. is Director, Touch Research Institute, Faculty, School of Psychology, Fielding Graduate University, Santa Barbara, California.

JANE GILLHAM, Ph.D. is visiting Assistant Professor at Swarthmore College and Codirector of the Penn Resilience Project.

JULIA GOLIER, M.D. is Associate Professor of Psychiatry, Bronx VA Medical Center, New York.

SHIRA TAYLOR GURA is a Yoga instructor for a wide variety of populations in health centers throughout southern New Jersey.

STEVE HERMAN, Ph.D. is Assistant Clinical Professor of Medical Psychology, Duke University Medical Center, Durham, North Carolina.

MARIE T. HERNANDEZ, Ph.D. is Department of Anthropology and Social Work, University of Houston.

ROGER R. HOCK, Ph.D. is Professor and Program Director, Psychology Program, Mendocino College, Mendocino, California.

MOHAN ISAAC, M.D. is Associate Professor, School of Psychiatry and Clinical Neuroscience, University of Western Australia, Perth, Western Australia.

ALEKSANDAR JANCA, M.D. is Professor of Psychiatry and Head of School, School of Psychiatry and Clinical Neuroscience, University of Western Australia, Perth, Western Australia.

SALLY JENKINS is an award-winning columnist for the *Washington Post*. She has co-written many best-selling sports books.

FIONA JONES, Ph.D. is Principal Lecturer, Department of Psychology, University of Hertfordshire.

SUSAN KENNEDY, Ph.D. is Associate Professor of Psychology, Denison University.

PARINDA KHATRI, Ph.D. is a Licensed Clinical Psychologist and Director of Integrated Care with Cherokee Health Systems.

CHRIS L. KLEINKE, Ph.D., (late) Professor, University of Alaska, Anchorage.

K. RANGA KRISHNAN, M.D. is Professor and Chair, Department of Psychiatry and Behavioral Science, Duke University Medical Center, Durham, North Carolina.

ELIZABETH NORTON LASLEY is a science writer with a specialization in neuroscience.

JEFFREY M. LATING, Ph.D. is Professor of Psychology, Loyola College, Baltimore, Maryland.

ALEXANDRE B. LAUDET, Ph.D. is NIH-funded Principal Investigator at the National Development and Research Institutes, Inc. (NDRI) in New York City.

ALYSSA LEE, B.A., B.Sc. is Senior Research Officer, School of Psychiatry and Clinical Neurosciences, University of Western Australia, Perth, Western Australia.

EMILY LEES, Ph.D. is Assistant Professor, Nursing, Houston Baptist University, Houston, Texas.

SALVATORE R. MADDI, Ph.D. is Professor, Department of Psychology and Social Behavior, University of California, Irvine.

COLLEEN R. MacQUARRIE, Ph.D. is Assistant Professor, Department of Psychology, University of Prince Edward Island, Canada.

BRUCE McEWEN, Ph.D. is Professor and Head of the Harold and Margaret Milliken Hatch Laboratory of Neuroendocrinology, Rockefeller University, New York.

KATHLEEN MOORE, Ph.D. is Research Assistant Professor, Department of Mental Health Law and Policy, Florida Mental Health Institute, University of South Florida, Tampa.

DEAN ORNISH, M.D. is Clinical Professor of Medicine, University of California, San Francisco and Founder of Preventive Medicine Research Institute in Sausalito, California.

CANDACE B. PERT, Ph.D. is Research Professor, Department of Physiology and Biophysics, Georgetown University School of Medicine, Washington, D.C.

LAURA A. PETERSEN, M.D., MPH is Associate Professor of Medicine, Baylor College of Medicine and Associate Director and Chief, Division of Health Policy and Quality, Houston Center for Quality of Care and Utilization Studies, Houston, Texas.

KAREN REIVICH, Ph.D. is Research Associate and Lecturer in the Department of Psychology at the University of Pennsylvania, Philadelphia, Pennsylvania, and Codirector of the Penn Resiliency Project.

ROBERT M. SAPOLSKY, Ph.D. is Professor of Biology and Neurology, Stanford University, Palo Alto, California.

CARLLA SMITH, Ph.D., (late) Professor of Psychology, Bowling Green University.

ANDREW SOLOMON is an author and a winner of the National Book Award for *The Noonday Demon*, and a professional lecturer.

ELIZABETH SOMER, M.A., R.D. is Nutrition correspondent for NBC's *Today Show*, and author, editor, and nationally recognized nutrition expert.

LORNE SULSKY, Ph.D. is Associate Professor, Department of Psychology, University of Calgary.

LeCHAUNCY D. WOODARD, M.D., MPH. is Assistant Professor, Baylor College of Medicine and Houston Center for Quality of Care and Utilization Studies, Houston, Texas.

RACHEL YEHUDA, Ph.D. is Professor of Psychiatry, the Mount Sinai School of Medicine, New York, New York.

MOSHE ZEIDNER, Ph.D. is Professor of Education and Social Psychology, University of Haifa, Mount Carmel, Israel.